Angela Kim Harkins

Reading with an "I" to the Heavens

Ekstasis

Religious Experience
from Antiquity to the Middle Ages

General Editor
John R. Levison

Volume 3

De Gruyter

Angela Kim Harkins

Reading with an "I" to the Heavens

Looking at the Qumran Hodayot
through the Lens of Visionary Traditions

De Gruyter

ISBN 978-3-11-061085-7
e-ISBN 978-3-11-025181-4
ISSN 1865-8792

Library of Congress Cataloging-in-Publication Data

A CIP catalog record for this book has been applied for at the Library of Congress.

Bibliographic information published by the Deutsche Nationalbibliothek

The Deutsche Nationalbibliothek lists this publication in the Deutsche Nationalbibliografie;
detailed bibliographic data are available in the Internet at http://dnb.dnb.de.

This volume is text- and page-identical with the hardback published in 2012.
Printing and binding: Hubert & Co. GmbH & Co. KG, Göttingen

∞ Printed on acid-free paper
Printed in Germany
www.degruyter.com

For my husband, Franklin

Acknowledgments

There are many people to thank who helped bring this book to print. The first of these is the outstanding Interlibrary Loan staff, especially John Cayer, at Fairfield University who labored to make available many texts that were not in our library's holdings. I wish to acknowledge the generous support of my Senior Vice President for Academic Affairs, Rev. Paul Fitzgerald, S.J., who supported this work by funding a pre-tenure leave in spring 2010 during which time much of the research for this book began. I am also grateful to the *Wabash Center for Teaching and Learning in Theology and Religion* which funded a summer of writing during which a draft of this manuscript was written. I offer thanks to my dean Robbin Crabtree, my chair Nancy Dallavalle, and my colleague Paul Lakeland for their generous research support of my conference travels where I presented many of the ideas in this book. Many people have saved me from countless errors– any that remain are mine. Special thanks to my colleagues at Fairfield for their generous friendship, conversations about the academic life, and for discussing many of the ideas that appear in this book during various stages of its development: Dennis King Keenan, John Thiel, Ron Davidson, Marti LoMonaco, Lynne Porter, Linda Henkel, Shannon Harding, Dave Crawford, Mike Andreychik, and members of my writing circle: especially Elizabeth Petrino and Bob Epstein. I apologize if I have forgotten anyone.

Many colleagues and friends outside of my home institution have played an instrumental role in the development of ideas that appear in this book and who have been willing conversation partners: Christopher Frechette, S.J., Martha Reinecke, Richard Ascough, Max Grossman, Joe Angel, Seth Sanders, Greg Goering, Kevin Sullivan, Francoise Mirguet, Liz King Keenan, and Jeremy Corley. I wish to thank in a special way Eileen Schuller for her important work on the Qumran hodayot manuscripts, without which this work would not have been possible. Special thanks to the series editor Jack Levison, the anonymous reviewers of the proposal, and to the members of the editorial board at de Gruyter press, especially Albrecht Doehnert.

The ideas that appear in this book were presented in earlier form at various meetings: the SBL Religious Experience in Early Judaism and Christianity group (2011), the ISBL Non-biblical Scrolls group (2010), the ISBL Apocrypha and Pseudepigrapha group (2010, 2011), and the MAR-SBL (2011), all of which have been excellent venues to discuss the research that appears in this work. Preliminary forms of the ideas presented in this book have been published in earlier works which are fully detailed in the bibliography: *Henoch* (2010), *Journal for the Study of the Pseudepigrapha* (2011), and an essay in the recent festschrift for James C. VanderKam (Brill, 2012). All of the ideas that have previously appeared in these publications have been significantly developed and improved in this monograph.

I wish to thank in a special way my generous teachers at Notre Dame, Jim VanderKam, Joe Blenkinsopp, and Gene Ulrich, who taught me much about texts and the second temple period; and Joe Amar, my Syriac and Arabic teacher, with whom I had many conversations about prayer and the power of prayer.

I especially want to thank Frances Flannery, Rod Werline, and Colleen Shantz for their stimulating scholarship on Religious Experience. I have truly benefited in numerous ways from my conversations with this group. I want to acknowledge Kelley Coblentz Bautch for her excellent work on the Book of the Watchers and its geography and especially for her encouragement during the early stages of this project. I have learned so much from her, not just academically through her writings, but also from her exemplary model of generosity and kindness.

Finally I wish to thank in a special way my family: my mother Sophia Kim, who has always been a beautiful model of faith, humility, and hard work. She has been my first and best teacher. I also thank my sister Stellar and her family for their graciousness. In closing, I cannot enumerate the countless ways that my husband has contributed to this work and to my life. I wish to dedicate this book to Franklin for his tireless example of the love of God and the love of learning.

Contents

Introduction

*All the foundations of my frame
crumble, my bones are disarticulated, and
my bowels heave like a ship in a raging
storm. My heart pounds noisily to the
destruction, and a whirling wind overwhelms
me from the destructiveness of their rebellion!*
(1QH XV, 5–8)

Vivid language about the body and first person speech make for compelling reading. The *New York Times* best-selling work by Dave Pelzer, *A Child Called "It,"* is the first in a series of controversial memoirs that retells in excruciating detail both the physical and psychological horrors of child abuse.[1] Pelzer's work not only describes the dark depths of child abuse but also the powerful transformations that were experienced later in life. From a rhetorical perspective, the first person voice and vivid details about the body and its experiences in Pelzer's writing are so vividly described that a modern reader assumes it is a memoir of historical events, yet Pelzer's writings have been critiqued as fabricating fanciful narratives that have little or no grounding in lived experience.[2] This is not the first time that the historical truth-telling of autobiographical writing has been challenged. Since the 1950s, the genre of autobiography has been critically understood as a highly fictionalized account that does not chronicle how a person existed historically, but rather how a

---

1   Dave Pelzer, *A Child Called "It": One Child's Courage to Survive* (Omaha: Omaha Press, 1993; repr. Health Communications, 1995); idem, *The Lost Boy: A Foster Child's Search for the Love of a Family* (Health Communications, 1997); idem, *A Man named Dave: A Story of Triumph and Forgiveness* (Dutton, 1999); idem, *Help Yourself: Celebrating the Daily Rewards of Resilience and Gratitude* (Dutton, 2000); idem, *The Privilege of Youth: A Teenager's Story of Longing for Acceptance and Friendship* (Dutton, 2004); idem, *Moving forward: Taking the Lead in Your Life* (Center Street, 2008).

2   See the article by Pat Jordan, "Dysfunction For Dollars," *New York Times,* July 28, 2002, which raises serious doubts about Pelzer's credibility by noting that his family members deny that the enormity of the abuse he recounts, detailing Pelzer's incredibly lucrative career as a motivational speaker, and reporting on his glib mannerisms.

person would like to be remembered as being.[3] Northrop Frye describes the creative impulses that drive the writing of autobiography as the same ones that motivate the writing of fiction.[4] Even though serious critiques of the genre were proposed during the mid-twentieth century, Ann Jefferson states, "the conjunction of autobiography and fiction in actual writing practice is still apt to be felt as something of a scandal."[5] More recently, Carolyn Barros has characterized autobiography's classic literary form not as history but as a rhetorical fictionalized narrative, which follows the predictable form of culminating in the transformation of the individual who is described.[6]

Ironically, just as Gusdorf and Frye were questioning the historical truth-telling of autobiography, Eliezer Sukenik, the first scholar to work on the Qumran hodayot, attached this genre-label to these texts along with the presumption that they could be used for historical reconstruction. In the *editio princeps* of 1QH^a, Sukenik writes, "Most of the hymns strike a distinctive personal note. Of particular interest from this viewpoint is the long chapter in column 4 in which the author refers to himself as a man who hoped for special revelations from the godhead and who, despite his opponents, had many followers flocking to him to listen to his teaching. A possible inference is that the author was the Teacher of Righteousness often mentioned in these scrolls, as

---

3   Georges Gusdorf, "Conditions and Limits of Autobiography," *Autobiography: Essays Theoretical and Critical* (trans. James Olney; Princeton: Princeton University Press, 1980), 28–48, here 45; trans from "Conditions et limites de l'autobiographie," in *Formen der Selbstdarstellung: Analekten zu einer Geschichte des literarischen Selbstportraits* (ed. Günther Reichenkron and Erick Hass; Berlin: Duncker & Humblot, 1956). See too the excellent survey of the critical discussion of autobiography by Olney in *Autobiography*, 3–27. A fuller discussion of the anachronistic application of the genre of autobiography to the Qumran hodayot is available in Angela Kim Harkins, "Who is the Teacher of the Teacher Hymns?" 449–67.

4   Herman Northrop Frye, *Anatomy of Criticism: Four Essays* (Princeton: Princeton University Press, 1957), 307.

5   Ann Jefferson, "Autobiography as Intertext: Barthes, Sarraute, Robbe-Grillet," in *Intertextuality* (ed. Michael Worton and Judith Still; New York: Manchester University Press, 1990), 108–29, here 108.

6   Carolyn Barros, *Autobiography: Narrative of Transformation* (Ann Arbor: University of Michigan, 1998). Her study analyzes autobiography from a rhetorical approach, identifying three key elements: *persona*, *figura*, and *dynamis* (19–49). Notably, the literary theme of transformation is the element that is present in all of Dave Pelzer's writings.

well as in the 'Zadokite Document' of the Damascus Covenanters."[7] Sukenik's first impressions quickly became a standard way of thinking about the Qumran hodayot and can be said to be the very beginnings of what is known popularly as the Teacher Hymns Hypothesis, a problematic theory that seeks to recover historical details from the Qumran hodayot.[8] During a critical period in the study of the hodayot, Qumran scholars in the 1960s with interest in historical reconstruction sought to identify the ancient speaker of the hodayot as the Teacher of Righteousness on the basis of historical and literary analysis.[9] Such an approach favors the goals and methodology of historical Jesus research.

This book is a study of the rhetorical use of the "I" and the vivid language of embodiment in the Qumran hodayot, and it proposes that both function instrumentally to generate within an ancient reader a religious experience of transformation and ascent. This practice of reading is one in which the reader seeks to reenact the affective experiences described in the text, creating the subjectivity of the lyrical subject in himself. This opening passage illustrates the remarkable ways that vivid language about the body and its parts in the Qumran hodayot evoke affective experiences. As Carol Newsom has noted about such a text as this: "The language throughout is highly personal and highly emotional. A heightened, dramatic, highly figured quality characterizes the experience."[10] Embodiment language is rhetorically powerful, and writings that make detailed and dramatic references to the body make compelling reading for both ancient and modern readers alike, especially so when presented in first person speech.

Recent scholars have critically questioned the historicity of the events reported in autobiographical genres. The text examined in this

---

7   Eleazar Sukenik (*Dead Sea Scrolls of the Hebrew University,* 39) had earlier expressed that the hodayot were autobiographical meditations in his first writings on the scroll from the late 1940s.

8   See Angela Kim Harkins, "Who is the Teacher of the Teacher Hymns? Re-examining the Teacher Hymns Hypothesis Fifty Years Later," in *A Teacher for All Generations: Essays in Honor of James C. VanderKam* (ed. Eric F. Mason et al; SJSJ 153/I; Leiden: Brill, 2012), 449–67.

9   Perhaps the biggest problem with applying historical Jesus methods to the study of the hodayot is that, unlike the NT writings and Jesus sayings, the Qumran texts do not enjoy any ancient attributions to any historical figure. The key scholars here are the three Heidelberg School scholars, Jeremias, Becker, and Kuhn.

10 Carol A. Newsom, *The Self as Symbolic Space: Constructing Identity and Community at Qumran* (STDJ 52; Leiden: Brill, 2004), 296.

study is the specific Qumran hodayot collection that has been recon-structed as 4Q428 to include only those compositions known tradition-ally as the "Teacher Hymns" (hereafter TH) and the second group of "Community Hymns" (hereafter CH II), corresponding to 1QH IX-XXVIII. This specific Cave 4 collection, 4Q428 is recognized as the oldest form of the hodayot and shows a general orientation toward a progressive ascent into the heavens. Such aspects of how the Qumran hodayot may have been used for religious experiences have been gen-erally neglected in the scholarship on these texts in favor of textual, lit-erary, and historical studies, although recent years have shown a grow-ing interest in these topics.[11]

I. The Proposal

In chapter one I discuss the major theoretical foundations for this book: post-structuralist understandings of embodied subjectivity and its influ-ence on ritual and performance studies. Reiterated ritual practices gen-erate a subjectivity that is sentient, that has phenomenal and affective ex-periences. Reenacting ritual experiences can create the predisposition

---

11   Consider the recent summary of scholarship by Eileen M. Schuller, "Recent Scholarship on the Hodayot 1993–2010," *CBR* 10 (2011): 119–62; there the author mentions the growing interest in themes concerning the heavenly and celestial aspects of the hodayot in the work of Devorah Dimant, "Men as Angels: The Self-Image of the Qumran Community," in *Religion and Politics in the Ancient Near East* (Bethesda: University Press of Maryland, 1996), 93–103; Björn Frennesson, *'In a Common Rejoicing.' Liturgical Communion with Angels in Qumran* (Uppsala: Uppsala University Library, 1999); Esther Chazon, "Human and Angelic Prayer in Light of the Dead Sea Scrolls," in *Liturgical Per-spectives: Prayer and Poetry in Light of the Dead Sea Scrolls. Proceedings of the Fifth International Symposium of the Orion Center for the Study of the Dead Sea Scrolls and Associated Literature, 19–23 January 2000* (STDJ 48; Leiden: Brill, 2003), 35–48; eadem, "Liturgical Function in the Cave 1 Hodayot Collection," in *Qum-ran Cave 1 Revisited: Texts from Cave 1 Sixty Years after Their Discovery: Proceed-ings of the Sixth Meeting of the IOQS in Ljubljana* (STDJ 91; Leiden: Brill, 2010), 135–49; Peter Schäfer, *The Origins of Jewish Mysticism* (Tübingen: Mohr Sie-beck, 2009); Philip S. Alexander, *The Mystical Texts: Songs of the Sabbath Sacrifice and Related Manuscripts* (London: T & T Clark, 2006); idem, "Qumran and the Genealogy of Western Mysticism," in *New Perspectives on Old Texts: Proceedings of the Tenth International Symposium of the Orion Center for the Study of the Dead Sea Scrolls and Associated Literature, 9–11 January, 2005* (ed. Esther G. Chazon and Betsy Halpern-Amaru; STDJ 88; Leiden: Brill, 2010), 215–35.

for religious experience, but they do not guarantee that one will take place.

Chapter two proposes that the rhetorical "I" and the vivid language about the body and its experiences function together to construct a highly imitable affective script for transformation. The experiences of the speaker of the hodayot are not reports of any one historical person. Instead they are constructed from popular experiences of well-known visionaries. It is through the experiences of the imaginal body and the rhetorical "I" that a subsequent reader is granted access to the events of transformation that are described. The reader's own sensory functions and affective responses are shaped and formed by imitating the affective experiences of the imaginal body in the Qumran hodayot. Moshe Idel's groundbreaking proposal that the arousal of fear and the expression of tears is an instrumental practice for inducing visionary experiences informs the discussion of affect in this chapter. This chapter introduces the scholarship of emotions and performance theory. I propose that the Method Theory approach to acting, associated with Constantin Stanislavsky, can be a useful way of imaging how ancient visionaries disciplined their affective memories so as to recall them as needed in order to intensify their ritualized reenactments.

Chapter three uses critical spatial theory to illuminate a progressive order to the compositions in the hodayot, and to outline two different models of religious experience. Here I propose that the critical spatial theory, associated with Michel Foucault, Henri Lefebvre and Edward Soja, can be profitably applied to the Qumran hodayot.[12] These theories make a distinction between Firstspace, space as it is *perceived* empirically (*l'espace perçu*), and Secondspace, the space that is *conceived* (*l'espace conçu*) or constructed by religious texts and traditions. Religious experiences in Secondspace, I propose, can be understood as scripted reenactments of transformation which differ from experiences in Thirdspace, the space

---

12 The major theoretical works on critical spatial theory are Michel Foucault (trans. Jay Miskowiec), "Of Other Spaces," *Diacritics* 16 (1986): 22–27; Henri Lefebvre, *The Production of Space* (trans. Donald Nicholson-Smith; Oxford: Blackwell, 1991 [1974]); Edward W. Soja, *Thirdspace: Journeys to Los Angeles and Other Real-and-Imagined Places* (Malden: Blackwell, 1996. An excellent example of the application of critical spatial theory to the understanding of religious and mystical texts is Carmel Bendon Davis, *Mysticism & Space: Space and Spatiality in the Works of Richard Rolle, The Cloud of Unknowing Author, and Julian of Norwich* (Washington, D. C.: Catholic University of America Press, 2008).

of *lived experience* (*l'espace vécu*).[13] Thirdspace offers the possibility of new
religious experiences and differs from Secondspatial reenactments by the
intensity of the individual's lived experience of the event.[14] Examples of
Thirdspatial experiences are described in chapters four and five. Chapter
three proposes that the experiences described in TH and CH II can be
conceptualized as a series of events marked by a progressive spatialization that moves from places of imprisonment, to paradise, to heaven.
Reading through the rhetorical "I" in the text allowed the one who
prayed the hodayot to enter into the textual environs and to re-experience the scripted events that are described. Here, using the language of
critical spatial theory, I present the spatial descriptions of the hodayot as
highly contoured phenomenal descriptions of religious geography (Secondspace). The reading and reenactment of Secondspace descriptions
can be understood within the framework of habitus theory as seeking
to generate a predisposition for religious experiences.[15] When the reader
successfully reenacts the affective script that is offered by the rhetorical
"I," he is able to experience moments of transformation through these
choreographed moments of illumination and ascent into the heavens.
The collection known as 4Q428 which is formed by the TH and CH
II groups is shaped by a progressive movement out from places of punishment, through Paradise, and brings the reader into the heavens.

Chapter four is a diachronic look at the hodayot. I propose that certain compositions show signs that an individual has gone beyond the reenactment of texts and achieved a qualitatively different type of religious
experience in which he has been transformed from being a viewer of a
religious vision into a full participant in a scene and an author of a new
experience altogether. I propose understanding this type of religious experience as a Thirdspace experience of the text. Chapter four proposes
that the composition known as 1QH XIII, 22-XV, 8 was generated as a
result of meditating upon the apocalyptic imagery in column XI. How

---

13   Lefebvre, *The Production of Space*, 39–45.
14   These distinctions are discussed in further detail in chapter three.
15   The association between Secondspace construction of realities and habitus
     theory is made by Davis, *Mysticism & Space*, 59–99. While Davis relies upon
     Pierre Bourdieu's understanding of habitus (*The Logic of Practice* [trans. Richard
     Nice; Cambridge: Polity Press, 1990], 53), I prefer to return to Aristotle's un-
     derstanding of habitus for reasons I discuss in chapter one (Aristotle's ἕξις which
     refers to a certain state produced by practices and ἔθος which refers to a general
     custom; discussed in *Nicomachean Ethics*, [trans. W. D. Ross; Oxford: Claren-
     don Press, 1925], 1103a14–1103a26).

the new experience was generated is described as a process that involves the body's experience of emotion and memory recall. This chapter presents various neuropsychological ways of understanding how the arousal of fear caused by meditating upon the apocalyptic imagery in columns XI could have generated the kinds of experiences reported in the lengthy hodayah in 1QH XIII, 22-XV, 8.

Chapter five discusses another lengthy composition, 1QH XVI, 5-XVII, 36, and proposes that this vision of the well-watered garden, like the composition discussed in chapter four (1QH XIII, 22-XV, 8), can be understood as another instance of a text that has been generated by the arousal of affect. The resulting *lived experience* of space (*l'espace vécu*) is the detailed report of being in an otherworldly garden space. The heightened sensory stimuli of descriptions of paradise commonly found in texts from this time period may explain how the vision of the well-watered garden that appears here can be imaged as a reader's further glimpse of what the otherworldly paradise is like. According to this model of religious experience, such a report is the product of performative reading practices. The faculties of sense perception are heightened as the reader seeks to reenact the emotions of being in paradise, which is only a stop on a further journey into the heavens. Like the places of punishment, garden spaces are associated with fear since they are the places where the deity pronounces judgment. The chapter concludes with a discussion of the space of the heavens, what I understand to be the goal and orientation of the hodayot scroll. Signs in the manuscript mark the liminal points of transition between paradise and the celestial realm. The rhetorical elements in these compositions that follow the blank line in 1QH XVII, 37 reflect a fully lived participatory experience of the heavens.

The rhetorical "I" of the hodayot, the vivid language of the body and its phenomenal sensations, and the richly contoured spatial descriptions help the ancient reader of the hodayot to read with an "I" to the heavens. The rhetorical and compositional aspects of these Qumran prayers reflect a practice of performative reading and reenactment that has a religious and theological purpose. Readers familiar with the Qumran hodayot will see that this study is concerned to understand how these anonymous texts, associated with the *maskil* were used and experienced by the Qumran community. In this respect, I start with the same questions posed by Carol Newsom in her study, *The Self as Symbolic*

Space—what do the hodayot do?[16] —but the conclusions that this book offers are very different from hers. The performative reading of the hodayot as I propose in this study was not only to create a common subjectivity for all members of the sect, including the newly initiated. Instead, the kind of religious experiences that the hodayot report are remarkable experiences that should be recognized as being had by an elite member of the community-the *maskil*.[17] The display of the right performative emotions in ritual reenactments was a status-securing event that functioned to establish and reinforce the *maskil* as a religious virtuoso.

II. Basic Orientation to the Qumran Hodayot

The Qumran hodayot scroll from Cave 1 was first examined by Eliezer Sukenik in 1947.[18] The scroll known as 1QH^a has been long thought to contain at least two different groupings of prayers that scholars have come to know as the Teacher Hymns, hereafter TH, and the Community Hymns, hereafter CH. According to the reconstructions of the scroll conducted independently by Hartmut Stegemann and Émile Puech, the two groups of CH are positioned around the TH collection.[19] One

---

16 Newsom, *The Self as Symbolic Space,* 2.

17 Here I follow the view of Philip Alexander that the person who experiences the events described in the hodayot known as the SGH is one who ascends into the heavens. Such an individual stands in the tradition of rare and remarkable figures like Enoch and Levi; "Qumran and the Genealogy of Western Mysticism," 221.

18 The hodayot scroll from Cave 1 was one of the first Dead Sea Scroll manuscripts to be seen by Eliezer L. Sukenik. For the early publications of these texts, see Eliezer L. Sukenik, מגילות גנוזות: מתוך גניזה קדומה שנמצאה במדבר יהודה. סקירה שנייה (Jerusalem: Bialik Foundation 1950), ★32-★50; and idem, אוצר המגילות הגנוזות (prepared for the press by Nahman Avigad; Jerusalem: Magnes, 1954; Eng. *The Dead Sea Scrolls of the Hebrew University* [Jerusalem: Magnes, 1955]). Two of the hodayot compositions, what are today commonly known as 1QH X, 22–32 and XI, 20–37 were published even earlier in idem, מגילות גנוזות: מתוך גניזה קדומה שנמצאה במדבר יהודה. סקירה ראשונה (Jerusalem: Bialik Foundation, 1948), ★29- ★33. Sukenik's early publications on the hodayot are valuable for his descriptions of how the scroll was found and its physical condition.

19 Hartmut Stegemann's dissertation on the material reconstruction of the hodayot scroll "Rekonstruktion der Hodajot: Ursprüngliche Gestalt und kritisch bearbeiteter Text der Hymnenrolle aus Höhle 1 von Qumran" (Ph.D. diss; University of Heidelberg, 1963) was never published, although there were plans to

group of CH precedes the TH in 1QH[a] and constitutes columns I–IX of that scroll known as CH I, and another group follows the TH and constitutes part of column XVII to the end of that scroll known as CH II. Remarkably, the scroll known as 1QH[a], a key text for many early scholarly understandings of the Qumran community, was not made available as a reconstructed scroll in its entirety until 2009 in DJD 40. While Sukenik's *editio princeps* was widely available early on, it did not present a reconstructed glimpse of the scroll, but only a picture of the scroll as it was discovered with the largest and most intact sections presented first with the fragmentary sections following.[20] This delay in publication, I think, has resulted in some overlooked aspects of this collection that are worthy of consideration.

The hodayot are attested in as many as eight different manuscripts from Caves 1 and 4, scrolls that demonstrate that varying orders and arrangements of these prayers were in circulation with a majority of them from Cave 4. There are also copies of manuscripts that resemble the hodayot prayers, but for various formal reasons were judged to be 'hodayot-like' and not copies of the hodayot known principally from

---

publish it in the Göttingen series SUNT in the 1960s. His notes were used in the preparation of the critical edition that appeared recently as *Qumran Cave 1. III. 1QHodayot[a] with Incorporation of 1QHodayot[b] and 4QHodayot [a-f]* (ed. Hartmut Stegemann with Eileen Schuller; trans. Carol Newsom; DJD 40; Oxford: Clarendon Press, 2009); for a full discussion of the publication and reconstruction of 1QH see Schuller's discussion there at 1–53. The scroll 1QH was also reconstructed independently by Émile Puech, "Quelques aspects de la restauration du Rouleau des Hymns (1QH)," *JJS* 39 (1988): 38–55. Stegemann's unpublished dissertation was summarized briefly by Heinz-Wolfgang Kuhn, *Enderwartung und gegenwärtiges Heil: Untersuchungen zu den Gemeindeliedern von Qumran* (SUNT 4; Göttingen: Vandenhoeck & Ruprecht, 1966), 16–17 and by Hans Bardtke, "Literaturbericht über Qumran IX. Teil: Die Loblieder (Hodajot) von Qumrân," *TRu* 40 (1975): 213–14; see the discussion by Schuller, DJD 40.4 n.16. Many years later, Stegemann gave his own account of his reconstruction in "The Material Reconstruction of 1QHodayot," in *The Dead Sea Scrolls: Fifty Years after Their Discovery: Proceedings of the Jerusalem Congress, July 20–25, 1997* (ed. Lawrence H. Schiffman, Emanuel Tov, and James C. VanderKam, executive editor Galen Marquis; Jerusalem: IES in cooperation with the Shrine of the Book, Israel Museum, 2000), 272–84.

20 E. Sukenik, *Dead Sea Scrolls of Hebrew University,* 38; idem, אוצר, 32–33; it is also narrated well by H. Stegemann in "The Material Reconstruction of 1QHodayot," 272–79.

1QH[a].[21] The Cave 4 hodayot scrolls, published by Eileen Schuller in
DJD 29 (1999), had been used to reconstruct badly damaged or otherwise unreadable areas in 1QH[a].[22] Of the Cave 4 copies, the one known
as 4Q428 (4QH[b]) is the oldest copy of the hodayot, dating to the middle
Hasmonean period.[23] It is also the one most similar in order and arrangement to 1QH[a] which, in contrast, is one of the youngest hodayot manuscripts with a date of the early Herodian period.[24] I have chosen this
manuscript, 4Q428, as the form of the hodayot to examine in this
study because of its early dating and its general similarities in order
and arrangement to 1QH[a]. Elsewhere I have argued that 4Q428 was
not an exact replica of 1QH[a] but rather began with the composition
known today as 1QH IX, 1-X, 4, a text that has been described as an
introductory composition.[25] In my essay from 2010, I proposed that
4Q428 was an earlier form of 1QH[a] but, contrary to DJD 29, it was
not an exact replica of the cave 1 scroll. My examination of the textual
development of 1QH[a] sought to consider questions that many scholars
had not asked, namely why is the TH collection sandwiched oddly between two units of CH.[26] I argued there that 4Q428 contained only the
text from 1QH IX to the end of the scroll, basically the TH and the CH

---

21   Eileen M. Schuller, "Hodayot," *Qumran Cave 4: XX. Poetical and Liturgical
     Texts, Part 2* (DJD 29; ed. Esther Chazon et al; Oxford: Clarendon Press,
     1999), 233–54. In the case of 4Q433, Schuller reports that "there is no over-
     lapping text [with 1QH]. Formally this text is *Hodayot*-like, with a first-person
     speaker and second-person address to God (אתה, frg.1 4) (233–34); see too John
     Strugnell and E. M. Schuller, "Further Hodayot Manuscripts from Qumran?"
     in *Antikes Judentum und frühes Christentum. Festschrift für Hartmut Stegemann zum
     65 Geburtstag* (ed. B. Hollmann, W. Reinbold, A. Steudel; BZNW 97; Berlin,
     New York: de Gruyter, 1998), 51–72. These texts are certainly worthy of fur-
     ther attention.
22   Schuller, DJD 29.69–232.
23   Schuller, DJD 29.146 for discussions of the dating.
24   Jean Starcky, "Les quatre étapes du messianism à Qumrân," *RB* 70 (1963):
     481–505, at 483 n. 7 he observes that the scribal hands of 1QH are from
     the Herodian period.
25   See Angela Kim Harkins, "A New Proposal for Thinking about 1QH[A] Sixty
     Years after its Discovery," in *Texts from Cave 1 Sixty Years after Their Discovery*,
     101–34. Much of the discussion of 4Q428 can be found there at 125–32.
26   I proposed in that essay that the CH I collection was added at a later date, and
     placed in the beginning of the pre-existing TH + CH II collection so as to not
     disturb the literary and theological progression in the scroll which culminated
     with the SGH, "A New Proposal for Thinking about 1QH[A] Sixty Years
     after its Discovery," 134 n. 63.

II collections (TH + CH II), based on the literary and orthographic characteristics and the sparse evidence of overlapping texts from CH I. The relationship between the TH and CH II was closer than the relationship both between the TH and CH I and between CH I and CH II. It is also the case that the reconstructed length and height of the columns of 4Q428 indicates a collection of many fewer compositions than the large scroll known as 1QH^a.[27] In that essay, I proposed that the scroll 4Q428 was organized purposefully around the literary theme of human communion with angels. The scroll known as 4Q428, a text that contains overlapping evidence for the TH and CH II but not for CH I, became for me a point of interest in the development of the hodayot collection. When read in a series, 4Q428 moves in a thematic progression that culminates with the extraordinary composition known popularly as the 'self-glorification hymn,' hereafter known as SGH. I concluded in that essay that the unit known as CH I was added at a later time, at the beginning of TH + CH II, so as not to disturb this progressive crescendo to the SGH.

The proposal that is offered here about these Qumran prayers is one that adopts a holistic view of the collection. Based on the organization of these prayers in a series, what can be said about how these texts were experienced by the ancient Qumran reader? I mentioned earlier that the full publication of the reconstructed scroll known as 1QH^a was only recently made available to scholars. This massive delay in publication indicates to me that many scholars were not curious about and had not considered seriously the larger redactional features of the hodayot collection. In fact, the majority of studies of the Qumran hodayot tends to atomize or isolate specific compositions or particular sub-collections. A notable example of this practice of approaching the hodayot in a piecemeal fashion is the over-studied collection known as TH, the centrally located group of hymns that literally takes center stage in the

---

27 The column height of 4Q428 has been reconstructed as having approximately twenty-two to twenty-four lines, in contrast to 1QH which has as many as forty to forty-one lines. Given the much shorter height of 4Q428's columns, the scroll, if it had been an exact replica of 1QH would have to be about nine and a half meters—an exceedingly short and fat scroll. Such an instrument would have been difficult to handle; see Harkins, "Thinking about 1QH^A Sixty Years After its Discovery," 126–27; also Schuller, DJD 29. See Emanuel Tov ("The Copying of a Biblical Scroll," *JRH* 26 (202): 189–209) who observes that there is a positive correlation between the height of the column and the length of the scroll (193).

scholarly view of the hodayot.[28] The great attention shown to the TH compositions apart from the CH material, in the history of scholarship on this scroll is due in part to their excellent preservation in 1QH. Both CH units are far more fragmentary than the beautifully preserved sheets of the TH (cols. X-XVII). The traditional scholarly understanding of this group of hodayot, known popularly as the TH Hypothesis, has had a lasting influence on the hodayot and so I discuss it in chapter two of this monograph. The TH texts may be regarded as the first no-table example of the scholarly practice to isolate specific parts of the ho-dayot scroll without regard for the whole. The second notable example is the composition known as the SGH. The SGH composition has gen-erated much interest,[29] but since its textual reconstruction depended

---

28 For further discussion of the disproportionate attention given to the TH in the scholarship on the hodayot, see Angela Kim Harkins, "The Community Hymns Classification: A Proposal for Further Differentiation," *DSD* 15 (2008): 121–54.

29 Early on, Maurice Baillet proposed that the speaker of this text was the Arch-angel Michael; Maurice Baillet entitled this composition the "cantique de Mi-chel et cantique des justes," ("Canticle of Michael and the canticle of the right-eous"); Baillet, *Qumrân grotte 4.III (4Q482–4Q520)* (DJD 7; Oxford: Claren-don, 1982), 26–29, pl. VI; also idem, "'Le volume VII de 'Discoveries in the Judaean Desert.' Présentation," in *Qumrân. Sa piété, sa théologie et son milieu* (ed. M. Delcor; BETL 46; Paris-Gembloux: Duculot/Leuven: University of Leuv-en, 1978), 75–78. Morton Smith, "Ascent to the Heavens and Deification in 4QMᵃ'" in *Archaeology and History in the Dead Sea Scrolls: The New York University Conference in Memory of Yigael Yadin* (ed. Lawrence H. Schiffman; JSPSup 8; JSOT/ASOR 2; Sheffield: JSOT, 1990), 181–88; John J. Collins, *The Scepter and the Star: The Messiahs of the Dead Sea Scrolls and Other Ancient Literature* (ABRL; New York: Doubleday, 1995), 136–53; idem, "A Throne in the Heavens: Apotheosis in pre-Christian Judaism," *Death, Ecstasy, and Other Worldly Journeys* (ed. John J. Collins and Michael A. Fishbane; Albany: State University of New York Press, 1995), 41–58; Eileen Schuller, "4QHodayotᵃ," DJD 29. 95–108; eadem, "A Hymn from a Cave Four *Hodayot* Manuscript: 4Q427 7 i + ii," *JBL* 112 (1993): 605–28; eadem, "The Cave 4 Hodayot Manuscripts: A Preliminary Description," *JQR* 85 (1994): 137–50; repr. as "The Cave 4 Hôdāyôt Manuscripts: A Preliminary Description," in *Qumranstu-dien: Vorträge und Beiträge der Teilnehmer des Qumranseminars auf dem internationa-len Treffen der Society of Biblical Literature, Münster, 25.–26. Juli 1993* (ed. Heinz-Josef Fabry, Armin Lange und Hermann Lichtenberger; Göttingen: Vanden-hoeck & Ruprecht, 1996), 87–100; Devorah Dimant, "A Synoptic Compar-ison of Parallel Sections in 4Q 427 7, 4Q491 11 and 4Q471B," *JQR* 85 (1994): 157–61; and John J. Collins and Devorah Dimant, "A Thrice-Told Hymn: A Response to Eileen Schuller," *JQR* 85 (1994): 151–55; Esther Eshel, "Self-Glorification Hymn," in DJD 29.421–32; eadem, "The Identification of the

upon certain Cave 4 manuscripts that were not published until the 1990s, the mystical elements found in this composition have not really influenced how scrolls scholars think about the Qumran hodayot generally. Even to this day, scholars who view the SGH from a mystical perspective frequently offer very little substantial discussion of how the religious experiences described herein fit within the larger material and literary context of the Qumran hodayot.[30] In the case of the SGH, it

'Speaker' of the Self-Glorification Hymn," *The Provo International Conference on the Dead Sea Scrolls: Technological Innovations, New Texts, and Reformulated Issues* (ed. Donald W. Parry and Eugene Ulrich; STDJ 30; Leiden: Brill, 1999), 617–35; Elliot Wolfson, "Mysticism and the Poetic-Liturgical Compositions from Qumran: A Response to Bilhah Nitzan," *JQR* 85 (1994): 185–202, esp. 200–201; James R. Davila, "Heavenly Ascents in the Dead Sea Scrolls," in *The Dead Sea Scrolls after Fifty Years: A Comprehensive Assessment* (ed. Peter W. Flint and James C. VanderKam with the assistance of Andrea E. Alvarez; Vol. 2; Leiden: Brill, 1999), 461–85, esp. 473–76; Seth Sanders, "Writing, Ritual, and Apocalypse: Studies in the Theme of Ascent to the Heaven in Ancient Mesopotamia and Second Temple Judaism," (Ph.D. diss.; Baltimore: Johns Hopkins University, 1999), 273–81; Michael O. Wise, "מי כמוני באלים: A Study of 4Q491c, 4Q471b, 4Q427 7 and 1QH^A 25:35–26:10," *DSD* 7 (2000): 173–219; John J. Collins, "Amazing Grace: The Transformation of the Thanksgiving Hymn at Qumran," *Psalms in Community: Jewish and Christian Textual, Liturgical, and Artistic Traditions* (ed. Harold W. Attridge and Margot E. Fassler; SBLSS 25; Atlanta: Society of Biblical Literature, 2003), 75–86; Paolo Augusto de Souza Nogueira, "Ecstatic Worship in the Self-Glorification Hymn (4Q471B, 4Q427, 4Q491C). Implications for the Understanding of an Ancient Jewish and Early Christian Phenomenon," *Wisdom and Apocalypticism in the Dead Sea Scrolls and in the Biblical Tradition* (ed. F. García Martínez; BETL 168; Leuven: Leuven University Press, 2003), 385–93; Florentino García Martínez, "Old Texts and Modern Mirages: The 'I' of Two Qumran Hymns," in *Qumranica Minora I: Qumran Origins and Apocalypticism* (ed. E. Tigchelaar; STDJ 63; Leiden: Brill, 2007), 105–25; Seth L. Sanders, "Performative Exegesis," *Paradise Now: Essays on Early Jewish and Christian Mysticism* (ed. April D. DeConick; SBLSS 11; Atlanta: Scholars, 2006), 57–79; and Joseph Angel, *Otherworldly and Eschatological Priesthood in the Dead Sea Scrolls* (STDJ 86; Leiden: Brill, 2010), 132–46; idem, "The Liturgical-Eschatological Priest of the *Self-Glorification Hymn*," *RevQ* 96 (2010): 585–605. An alternative view about the SGH has been offered by Eric Miller who has proposed that the speaker of the "Self-Glorification Hymn" is Enoch himself; Eric Miller, "The Self-Glorification Hymn Reexamined," *Henoch* 31 (2009): 307–24.

30   The notable exception to this is the study by Philip Alexander which engages well the question of the continuity of the themes of ascent into the heavens and communion with angels throughout the hodayot collection; *The Mystical Texts*. Especially well taken is his insistence that prayer texts like the hodayot were used for religious and not literary purposes; "it is perfectly conceivable that

is not uncommon to find its mystical elements discussed with other Dead Sea Scroll compositions, with surprisingly very little engagement of what these mystical elements might mean within the larger literary and material context of the hodayot. In fact, critical scrolls scholarship displays a disturbing habit of severing the mystical SGH from its material and literary context of the hodayot altogether.[31] While recognizing that the majority of studies of the hodayot and religious experience have been focused largely on the SGH, the present study seeks to expand the frame of reference to consider how the larger context of the hodayot in which the mystical composition known as the SGH was discovered can be understood as contributing to a religious experience in the reader.

Because a majority of scholars have become accustomed to discussing the hodayot as distinct units instead of as a literary corpus, this monograph seeks to look at the collection holistically by addressing some unanswered questions surrounding how the shape of the earliest collection in 4Q428 (TH + CH II) may give insights into how these prayers were experienced religiously. Of special interest here is how the collection's rhetorical and literary elements together with its purposeful redaction may have guided the one who prayed to a religious experience. This study seeks to fill a gap in hodayot studies caused by inattention to the larger questions of redaction and rhetorical shaping of the Qumran hodayot. It proposes that the oldest form of 1QH, known as 4Q428, is

---

the community would have performed liturgies which they did not invent, and the presumption must surely be that if a prayer-text was found in their library it was at some time used" (98).

31 Some classic examples of this can be seen in the major critical editions in DJD 29 where the fragments of the same manuscript text are published twice (!) by two different scholars: E. Eshel in "471b. 4QSelf-Glorification Hymn (=4QH^e frg. 1?)," DJD 29:421–35 and E. Schuller in "431. 4QHodayot^e," DJD 29:199–208. Schuller writes that the case can be made that the four fragments that came to be known as 4Q471 "could have been part of the same scroll as the single fragment that had previously designated as 4QH^e" (199). Schuller goes on to state that all of the fragments appear to have been produced by the same scribal hand and can be reconciled within a single reconstructed scroll (199–200, also see foldout plate III). Also see the forthcoming and long awaited edition of *Outside the Bible* (New York: JPS, 2012) in which the editors have chosen to publish the text of SGH independently from 1QH. Oftentimes, discussion of the SGH takes place in comparison with non-hodayot texts but without engagement of the hodayot themselves; e. g., Angel, *Otherworldly and Eschatological Priesthood in the Dead Sea Scrolls;* idem, "The Liturgical-Eschatological Priest," and Sanders, "Performative Exegesis," 74–76.

organized purposefully toward a heavenly experience. The performative reading of the texts in the TH and CH II in series functioned to simulate a journey for the one who prayed: this journey begins in places of punishment, moves to paradise, and culminates in the heavens. In this scenario, the ancient reader sought to reenact the affective script that the hodayot offer. At times a reader could even hope to have a religious experience of his own, one in which he no longer imitated scripted roles but became transformed into a full participant in a new event.

This book has three theoretical foundations: (1) post-structuralist understandings of embodied subjectivity, which are discussed in chapter one; (2) developments in neuropsychology that have shed new light on the embodied mind and emotions, which are discussed in chapter two and four; and (3) models of critical spatiality, which are engaged in chapters three and five. Neuropsychological understandings of the interconnectedness between the mind, body, and subjectivity have been brought to bear on the phenomenal study of religious experience with useful results.[32] Armin Geertz refers to these types of approaches

---

32 The successful application of interdisciplinary and phenomenological approaches to religious experience in early Judaism and Christianity include the following key studies that have greatly influenced the work in this book: Alan F. Segal, "Religious Experience and the Construction of the Transcendent Self," in *Paradise Now*, 27–40; idem, "Religiously Interpreted States of Consciousness: Prophecy, Self-Consciousness, and Life After Death," in *Life After Death: A History of the Afterlife in the Religions of the West* (New York: Doubleday, 2004), 322–50; Moshe Idel, "Mystical Techniques," in *Essential Papers on Kabbalah* (ed. Lawrence Fine; New York: New York University Press, 1995), 438–94; Daniel Merkur, "The Visionary Practices of Jewish Apocalyptists," *Psychoanalytic Study of Society* (ed. L. Bryce Boyer and Simon A. Grolnik; vol. 14; Hillsdale, N. J.: Analytic Press, 1989), 119–48; and also April D. DeConick (ed.), *Paradise Now*; Frances Flannery, Colleen Shantz, and Rodney A. Werline (eds), *Experientia, Volume 1: Inquiry into Religious Experience in Early Judaism and Early Christianity* (SBLSS 40; Atlanta: Scholars, 2008); Colleen Shantz, *Paul in Ecstasy* (Cambridge: Cambridge University Press, 2009).

Examples of the broader interest in neuropsychological understandings of the embodied mind in the field of religious studies include Eugene G. D'Aquili and Andrew B. Newberg, *The Mystical Mind: Probing the Biology of Religious Experience* (Minneapolis: Fortress, 1999); Ann Taves, *Religious Experience Reconsidered: A Building-Block Approach to the Study of Religion and Other Special Things* (Princeton: Princeton University Press, 2009); Armin W. Geertz, "Brain, Body and Culture: A Biocultural Theory of Religion," *Method and Theory in the Study of Religion* 22 (2010): 304–321; Andrew Newberg, *Principles of Neurotheology* (Burlington: Ashgate, 2010); William Grassie, *The New Sciences of Re-*

as a "biocultural theory of religion."[33] This book applies these theoretical insights about the embodied subjectivity to performance and ritual
studies and proposes a model of reading and praying wherein a reader
sought to reenact scripted events of affect in order to create the subjectivity of the textualized speaker within himself. A reader's emotions
were aroused by vivid reports of phenomenal sensations of being in places of punishment, paradise, and the heavens. These textualized experiences simulated actual bodily responses of emotion that then displayed
themselves in the form of heart palpitations or endocrine changes. In addition to reenacting these scripted religious experiences, a reader could
also hope to achieve a new phenomenal experience of his own—one in
which he was not imitating scripted events but participating in new experiences altogether. Theoretical understandings of space and phenomenal sensations are joined to the rhetorical construction of subjectivity
that result from the use of the first person voice. Together these elements could have succeeded, I propose, in creating different types of religious experiences from the reading of texts.

Many hodayot studies are necessarily related to the complex material
aspects of the text and its reconstruction, some of which have already
been mentioned. This body of research is the most technical and speci-
alized. A broader group of hodayot scholarship engages traditional historical-critical questions that are of interest to Qumran scholars who are
concerned to reconstruct the origins of the community from texts. An
even broader literature on hodayot scholarship deals with the images and
allusions to scripture that they contain. But few studies of the hodayot
have asked the question, how did members of the Qumran community
experience the hodayot as prayer texts?[34] One notable exception is
Carol Newsom's study, *Self as Symbolic Space,* which proposes that the
hodayot functioned to indoctrinate members into a sectarian worldview. The current study differs from Newsom's insofar as it focuses
on religious experience, not sociological identities, and it examines
the experience of reading the TH + CH II compositions in a series,
a topic that is not discussed at length in her book.

---

ligion: *Exploring Spirituality from the Outside In and Bottom Up* (New York: Palgrave Macmillan, 2010), esp. 93–110; Manuel A. Vásquez, *More than Belief: A
Materialist Theory of Religion* (New York: Oxford University Press, 2011).

33 Geertz, "Brain, Body and Culture."
34 Newsom, *The Self as Symbolic Space.*

Understanding the hodayot from the perspective of religious experience entails a reconstruction of prayer practices. In doing so, I hope to expand the scholarly discourse on these Qumran texts to researchers who are interested in the larger phenomena related to religious experience—visionary experiences and ascent into the heavens. Because my interest is religious and not sociological, specifically visionary aspects of the hodayot are given careful consideration. I have sought to address how these texts imitate or presume knowledge associated with early Jewish visionary traditions such as those attached to the figure of Enoch. Here it is worth noting that the Qumran Cave in which the hodayot collection that this study examines, 4Q428, was found, alongside a majority of hodayot copies, is the same Cave that yielded as many as eleven copies of Enochic manuscripts. The hodayot's relationship to these early Jewish non-canonical traditions is an understudied aspect of these texts that has been overlooked in favor of tracing scriptural and canonical sources. I hope that this book will begin a conversation about the hodayot among scholars who are non-Qumran specialists and that all researchers who come to examine the hodayot will do so without the pre-conceived expectations that the long-standing Teacher Hymns Hypothesis has placed on these interesting texts. It is my view that the hodayot offer much that has not yet been fully examined that is of interest to a broader discussion of phenomenal religious experiences.

III. Traditional Scholarly Ways of Reading and Interpreting the Hodayot

This book proposes a new way of understanding the Qumran hodayot from the perspective of religious experience that is in tension with traditional understandings of the Teacher Hymns, a collection so called because it has long been thought to express the reports of an actual historical person's experiences, the Teacher of Righteousness or some other historical figure. Here it is necessary to discuss briefly the scholarship associated with this historical understanding of the TH because it has become such a popular way of understanding these hodayot. The view known widely as the Teacher Hymns Hypothesis is associated most closely with three German scholars from the 1960s known as the Heidelberg School[35] whose historical work relied upon the literary study published by Günther Morawe in 1961.[36] Morawe identified two major literary groups in the scroll, which he called *Die Danklieder* and *Die hymnischen Bekenntnislieder*.[37] Morawe's study appeared one year after Svend Holm-Nielsen's publication, which can be understood as an alternative way of understanding the hodayot scroll. Holm-Nielsen understood the scroll as a composite collection, not unlike the biblical Psalter, and proposed that these prayers were written by different unknown authors.[38] Holm-Nielsen identified two literary groups, which he called "psalms of thanksgiving" and "hymns." He writes that "the more one busies oneself with the Hodayot, the more their apparent uniformity disappears."[39]

At least two scholarly trajectories emerged from the independent work on the hodayot by Morawe and Holm-Nielsen, both of which recognized two distinct literary groups in the large scroll known as 1QH. Building upon Morawe's study, the group that Schuller calls the Heidelberg School went on to draw historical and authorial conclusions about the literary patterns that they observed in the scroll, and as-

---

35 Eileen M. Schuller refers to this core of scholarship as the 'Heidelberg School' in DJD 29.74. The three scholars are Gert Jeremias, *Der Lehrer der Gerechtigkeit* (SUNT 2; Göttingen: Vandenhoeck & Ruprecht, 1963); Jürgen Becker, *Das Heil Gottes: Heils-und Sündenbegriffe in den Qumrantexten und im Neuen Testament* (SUNT 3; Göttingen: Vandenhoeck & Ruprecht, 1964); and H.-W. Kuhn, *Enderwartung und gegenwärtiges Heil*.

36 Scholars of the Heidelberg School differed in small details from Morawe, but generally followed his literary analysis of the scroll; Günter Morawe, *Aufbau und Abrenzung der Loblieder von Qumran: Studien zur gattungsgeschichtlichen Einordnung der Hodajoth* (Berlin: Evangelische Verlagsanstalt, 1961). For example, Kuhn wanted to identify a third category for what is now known as 1QH XI, 20–37 because there was no 'mediator of revelation' but scholars did not consider this to warrant a different category; *Enderwartung und gegenwärtiges Heil*, 23–25.

37 Morawe, *Aufbau und Abrenzung*, 31–33.

38 Svend Holm-Nielsen, *Hodayot: Psalms from Qumran* (ATDan 2; Aarhus: Universitetsforlaget, 1960). Later studies by Bonnie Pedrotti Kittel, *The Hymns of Qumran* (SBLDS 50; Atlanta: Scholars, 1981); D. Dombkowski Hopkins, "The Qumran Community and 1Q Hodayot: A Reassessment," *RevQ* 10 (1981): 323–64; and Julie A. Hughes, *Scriptural Allusions and Exegesis in the Hodayot* (STDJ 59; Leiden: Brill, 2006) adopt Holm-Nielsen's basic understanding of the hodayot that it was not possible to draw authorial conclusions from these texts.

39 Holm-Nielsen, *Hodayot*, 320.

signed an authorial identity to the texts known as *Die Danklieder* by re-naming them the Teacher Hymns.[40] This label attached these composi-tions to the putative figure known as the Teacher of Righteousness who is mentioned in the Qumran texts known as 1QpHab and CD. This move made explicit what had become a general scholarly assumption that there was a relationship between the hodayot and the Teacher of Righteousness. Such a view had been proposed very early on by Suke-nik and reiterated in the earliest publications about 1QH.[41] The second trajectory, represented by Holm-Nielsen, denied the presence of a uni-form and consistent author throughout the scroll, but ceded that there are two large literary groups which generally correspond to what is now popularly known as the Teacher Hymns and the Community Hymns, attributing the coherence of each of these groups to formal lit-erary conventions. Even though the scholars associated with the Heidel-berg School and Holm-Nielsen went on to draw very different conclu-sions about the authorship and history of the two literary groups in the scroll, they independently agreed that there were at least two major lit-erary divisions in this scroll. Summarizing these findings, Gert Jeremias maintained that the distinct quality of the Teacher Hymns resided in their "lebendigen Sprache," which contrasted with the "erstarrte Wen-dungen und monotone Wiederholungen" of the rest of the scroll.[42] These lively qualities of the TH are the vivid and detailed descriptions of what will be described in chapter two as the language of the body and its phenomenal experiences.

---

40 The labels 'Teacher Hymns' and 'Community Hymns' were assigned by Heinz-Wolfgang Kuhn, *Enderwartung und gegenwärtiges Heil*, 24–25. According to the traditional TH Hypothesis, the TH correspond roughly to 1QH cols. X–XVII with many scholars omitting col. XI from this classification; there are two small groups of CH (from the beginning of the scroll to col. IX; col. XVIII to the end of the scroll).

41 See Sukenik, *The Dead Sea Scrolls of Hebrew University*, 39; while Morawe also associated the hodayot with the Teacher of Righteousness, he never identifies him explicitly as the author; *Aufbau und Abgrenzung*. See J. Philip Hyatt, "The View of Man in the Qumran 'Hodayot,'" *NTS* 2 (1956): 276–84, here 277; Hans Bardtke, "Considérations sur les Cantiques de Qumrân," *RB* 63 (1956): 220–33, here 227–28; Jean Carmignac, "Les elements historiques des 'hymns' de Qumran," *RevQ* 2 (1959/1960): 205–22; Menahem Mansoor, *The Thanksgiving Hymns: Translated and Annotated with an Introduction* (STDJ 3; Leiden: Brill, 1961); M. Delcor, *Les Hymnes de Qumran (Hodayot): texte hébreu, introduction, traduction, commentaire* (Paris: Letouzey et Ané, 1962), 22.

42 See Jeremias, *Der Lehrer der Gerechtigkeit*, 171.

Of the two perspectives from the 1960s scholarship, the conclusions of the Heidelberg School have had the strongest impact on how scholars perceive the hodayot. Scholars who were impressed by the strong and distinctive literary style, which I will refer to as the strong 'I' of the TH, went on to draw conclusions that, in my view, the texts do not warrant by claiming that the hodayot in X–XVII give evidence of an actual historical person's experiences of distress and deliverance.[43] Historical studies of the TH have not only sought to identify the figure as the Teacher of Righteousness, but have even made claims that implicate specific historical individuals.[44]

In previous studies, I have proposed that the longstanding scholarly view that there are two major groups in the scroll, the TH and the surrounding CH material, in fact obscured: (1) the heterogeneity of the CH material; and (2) the common traits found in the TH and CH II.[45] While I continue to use the labels 'Teacher Hymns' and 'Community Hymns' for the sake of convenience, I find that they confuse more than clarify the issues. Because these labels stem from the Heidelberg School's historical understanding of the hodayot, they perpetuate the

---

43 Morawe, *Aufbau und Abgrenzung der Loblieder*, 37. Like Morawe, Jeremias notes a qualitative difference in the 'I' of the TH group and the rest of the scroll; *Der Lehrer der Gerechtigkeit*, 171. So too, see Paul Schulz's study of the literary style of the TH in *Der Autoritätsanspruch des Lehrers der Gerechtigkeit in Qumran* (Meisenheim am Glan: Verlag Anton Hain, 1974). N.B., there is some slight variation among the compositions identified as belonging to this TH category; a chart of these differences is available in Michael C. Douglas, "The Teacher Hymn Hypothesis Revisited: New Data for an Old Crux," *DSD* 6 (1999): 239–66.

44 Perhaps two of the most famous studies that emerge from the historical study of the hodayot are that by Michael O. Wise, *The First Messiah: Investigating the Savior before Jesus* (New York: HarperCollins, 1999), who identifies the speaker of the hodayot as a historical first century BCE figure named Judah; and Israel Knohl, *The Messiah before Jesus: The Suffering Servant of the Dead Sea Scrolls* (trans. David Maisel; Berkeley: University of California Press, 2000), who identified the speaker of the hodayot as Menahem, the son of Hezekiah.

45 For a discussion of the similarities between the Teacher Hymns and the second group of Community Hymns and the dissimilarities of both to the first group of Community Hymns, see Angela Kim Harkins, "A New Proposal for Thinking about 1QH^a," 101–134. Especial notable are the orthographic trends that show some alignment between the TH and the CH II. In an earlier study, I critiqued the traditional label of 'Community Hymns' as obscuring significant literary differences throughout these compositions, see eadem, "The Community Hymns Classification," 127–31; see too Sarah Tanzer, "The Sages at Qumran: Wisdom in the Hodayot," (Ph.D. diss., Harvard University, 1987).

popular notion that a historical identification of some of the hodayot with the figure known as the Teacher of Righteousness is possible. In an extensive defense of the Teacher Hymns Hypothesis, Michael C. Douglas shows a troubling reliance on modern historical Jesus methodology.[46] While such a methodological approach may be suitable for modern historical studies of ancient Christian texts, it is problematic when applied to the anonymous hodayot, which have no ancient attributions that associate them in any way with the alleged figure known as the Teacher of Righteousness. The earliest attribution of the hodayot to any ancient figure dates to the late 1940s to the modern scholar Eliezar Sukenik, who was the first to propose that these compositions were the autobiographical meditations of the Teacher of Righteousness known from other Qumran texts.[47] The strong and distinctive language in the TH, assumed to be a sign of originality and authenticity, has been mistakenly identified as belonging to a single historical figure. Given what is known about the writing of second temple prayers and their preference for stereotypical language, Douglas's operative assumption that original or distinctive speech is more authentic than traditional language is anachronistic for the texts of this time period.

Nevertheless, the provocative Teacher Hymn Hypothesis continues to be widely cited in the scholarship on the hodayot. Drawing such conclusions about the strong and dramatic language in these texts reflects anachronistic assumptions about authorship—assumptions that I discuss in chapter two as originating in Romantic Period understandings of the author.[48] Such expectations assume the creative genius of the poet to be mirrored in the dramatic and lively qualities found in the art. In the case

---

46   Michael C. Douglas, "Power and Praise in the Hodayot: A Literary Critical Study of 1QH 9:1–18:14," (Ph.D. diss., University of Chicago, 1998); the core of which was published as "The Teacher Hymn Hypothesis Revisited."

47   Sukenik, מגילות גנוזות : סקירה שנייה, 22; and *The Dead Sea Scrolls of the Hebrew University,* 39.

48   See my essay, "Who is the Teacher of the Teacher Hymns? Re-Examining the Teacher Hymns Hypothesis Fifty Years Later," in Vol. 1 of *A Teacher for All Generations: Essays in Honor of James C. VanderKam* (ed. Eric F. Mason et al; SJSJ; Leiden: Brill, 2012), 449–67. There I discuss in greater detail the 'Heidelberg School' and Romantic assumptions about authorship. I also critique the common identification of the TH as autobiographical writings of a person who existed historically; autobiography is more commonly a modern genre that does not appear prior to the Renaissance. Furthermore, as a genre, it is best understood as a literary construct of a person as he or she desires to be remembered and should not be understood as an historical account of how a person was.

of the Qumran hodayot, the genius of the author, the purported Teacher of Righteousness, was presumably demonstrated by the vibrant literary qualities expressed in the TH. Such a view that more vivid and dramatic texts possess greater authenticity than writings that rely on more stereotypical language prizes literary originality over traditional formulations. These expectations fit modern understandings of authorship but do not comport with recent studies. Research by Judith Newman and Esther Chazon has demonstrated that the composition of prayer texts from this time period reflects the desire to present innovative prayer compositions in language that was recognizable and familiar from established and authoritative scriptural traditions.[49] Notable here is the important study by Esther Chazon that demonstrates that second temple prayer texts employ compositional techniques that consciously imitate established scriptural phraseology, highlighting the inappropriate judgments of modern scholars about imitative styles.[50] The cumulative effect of these studies on second temple prayer literature is to emphasize that ancient authors sought to associate their work with older established traditions and a conscious desire to erase signs of a distinctive literary style. The frequent use of stereotypical language and traditional formulations helped to secure the authority of newly composed prayer texts during the second temple period.

Reservations about the usefulness of the Teacher Hymn Hypothesis have been expressed by other scholars of the hodayot, most recently by Carol Newsom: "[b]ut what about the other widespread assumption that these compositions are to be understood as representing the persona of the Teacher of Righteousness? That is a much trickier question than I think it is generally taken to be."[51] While Newsom correctly expresses concerns about the Heidelberg School's Teacher of Righteousness identification, she substitutes it with an early theory of Jacob Licht that as-

---

49 Judith H. Newman, *Praying by the Book: The Scripturalization of Prayer in Second Temple Judaism* (SBLEJL 14; Atlanta: Scholars, 1999) and Esther G. Chazon, "Scripture and Prayer in 'The Words of the Luminaries'," and other essays in *Prayers that cite Scripture* (ed. James L. Kugel; Cambridge: Harvard University, 2006), 25–41.

50 Chazon, "Scripture and Prayer," 25–41.

51 Newsom, *Self as Symbolic Space*, 288. Other scholars who expressed doubt about the early identification of the "I" in the Hodayot as the Teacher of Righteousness include Jacob Licht, מגילת ההודיות: ממגילות מדבר יהודה (Jerusalem: Bialik, 1957), 22–26; Holm-Nielsen, *Hodayot*, 316–31; and Dombkowski Hopkins, "The Qumran Community and 1Q Hodayot," 323–64.

signed the authorial voice to the office of the *mebaqqer* or to the *maskil.* In doing so she does not move beyond conceptualizing these texts as belonging to a specific (albeit unidentified) figure in ancient Judaism.[52]

Instead of the historical approach, the proposal that is advanced here shares a similar perspective with exegetical studies that have sought to analyze and identify the strong and distinctive literary style of the 'I' in the Teacher Hymns with prophetic figures known from scripture. Such studies can be situated with the foundational work of Holm-Nielsen, who sought to identify the many scriptural allusions in the hodayot. Scholarly approaches in this vein seek to analyze passages in the Teacher Hymns as allusions to one or another scriptural passage, and in so doing identify the 'I' of the hodayot with celebrated biblical personalities, often prophets. Notable in this regard is Julie A. Hughes, who concludes that scholars have overlooked the significance of the allusions to Ezekiel and to Jeremiah.[53] Many of the exegetical studies of the Teacher Hymns have also sought to align them with the Suffering Servant texts from Deutero-Isaiah, although this is an identification that has been vigorously debated.[54]

This study assumes that the Teacher Hymns exhibit typical compositional techniques for this time period and reuse familiar scriptural texts and images from early Jewish literature, but that they do not intend to rewrite any one specific text. Like the biblical Psalter and other prayers from the second temple period, the hodayot use stereotypical formulae

---

52 Ultimately, I think that my study could be compatible with such theories.

53 Hughes, *Scriptural Allusions and Exegesis in the Hodayot*; notice however that her conclusions confuse more than clarifies when she writes: "I have, not altogether fancifully, suggested that these are neither Teacher nor Community Hymns but representative examples of a sectarian 'class exercise' in poetic interpretation" (233); and goes on to write that "the lowliest member of the community could have written such a poem as a tribute to his teacher" (234). Hughes' proposal that the compositions come from a classroom literary exercise is puzzling and reflects the unfortunate influence that the "*Teacher* Hymns Hypothesis" exerts upon her thinking.

54 The identification of the speaker of the Teacher Hymns as the suffering Servant from Isaiah (Isa 42:1–4; 49:1–7; 50:4–9; and 52:13–53:12) appeared early on and was vigorously debated; André Dupont-Sommer, "Le rouleau des Hôdâyôt," *Semitica* 7 (1957): 5–23; Jean Carmignac, "Les citations de l'Ancien Testament, et specialement des poems du Serviteur, dans les hymnes de Qumran," *RevQ* 2 (1960): 357–94; also Wise, *The First Messiah*, 290; John J. Collins, "Teacher and Servant," *Revue d'histoire et de philosophie religieuses* 80 (2000): 37–50.

and allude to known images and traditions that are also attested in other texts which reappear in the hodayot due to their memorable qualities. In the case of the images of strongly valenced negative events, reports of bodily agonies, imprisonment, or other terror-inducing experiences make lasting impressions on the mind and are easily recalled during subsequent meditations on similar topics. A reconstruction of this process is described in chapter four. The arousal of strong emotions during memory construction and recall may be the mechanism by which certain visionary images come to be reused over and over. Because of these compositional techniques, prayer texts like the hodayot have a limited usefulness for historical reconstruction. Additionally, I differ from the majority of exegetical studies insofar as I do not wish to limit the discussion of scriptural personalities to one or another figure. Although I am interested in examining how traditions, specifically those associated with Enoch and Daniel appear in the hodayot, it is largely because these connections with visionary literature have been overlooked in the scholarship; I do not claim that either one bears an exclusive influence.

Chapter 1
Creating an Embodied Subjectivity for Religious Experience

This chapter begins a larger inquiry into how the Qumran hodayot may have been experienced phenomenally by an ancient reader. As prayers written in the first person voice, the hodayot are texts that describe a variety of religious experiences, but those of special interest for our study are the ones that report illumination, vertical ascent, and communion with celestial beings. It is worthwhile to begin by acknowledging that scholars differ regarding the extent to which religious experience may be recovered from the literary texts that describe them. Scholarly views on mystical literature range from minimalist approaches, which prefer to see such texts as strictly literary sources for historical or literary analysis,[1] to maximalist ones, which seek to construct the religious experience behind these texts in antiquity.[2] This study is more like the lat-

---

1   See Peter Schäfer, whose scholarship is summarized in his recent, *The Origins of Jewish Mysticism* (Tübingen: Mohr Siebeck, 2009), see esp. the outline of his historical-critical approach to mystical literature, 1–26, esp. 24–26; Martha Himmelfarb, *Ascent to Heaven in Jewish and Christian Apocalypses* (New York: Oxford University Press, 1993); eadem, "From Prophecy to Apocalypse: The Book of the Watchers and Tours of Heaven," *Jewish Spirituality: From the Bible through the Middle Ages* (ed. Arthur Green; New York: Crossroad, 1986): 145–65; esp. 154; also the especially helpful analysis by Ra'anan Boustan, "The Study of Heikhalot Literature: Between Mystical Experience and Textual Artifact," *Currents in Biblical Research* 6 (2007): 130–60; Annette Yoshiko Reed, *Fallen Angels and the History of Judaism and Christianity: The Reception of Enochic Literature* (New York: Cambridge University Press, 2005); David Halperin, *The Merkabah in Rabbinic Literature* (New Haven: American Oriental Society, 1980).

2   Philip Alexander, *The Mystical Texts*; Andrei Orlov, *The Enoch-Metatron Tradition* (Tübingen: Mohr Siebeck, 2005), esp. 3–5 where he situates his own work in the pseudepigraphic literature in relationship to scholars like Schäfer and Halperin; James R. Davila, *Descenders to the Chariot: The People behind the Hekhalot Literature* (SJSJ 70; Leiden: Brill, 2001); Christopher Rowland, *The Open Heaven: A Study of Apocalyptic in Judaism and Early Christianity* (London: SPCK, 1992), 240–47; also Christopher Morray-Jones, "Transformational Mysticism

ter than the former insofar as it is concerned with reconstructing a model for how texts can be related to practices of religious experience.[3] This study takes seriously Michael Stone's view that literary accounts of visionary experience have some origin in a religious experience of *ekstasis*: "while in many cases the extant books may preserve mere literary formulations about these matters, behind them there probably does live a genuine practice of ecstasies."[4] In a later essay Stone goes on to write there that "[i]n the end, it should not strike us as very surprising that religious men and women in antiquity had a spiritual life, that religious experience formed a part of their world. They talked of it in conventional, traditional terms, using the language of their culture and perhaps of their particular school or group. That raises challenges for scholars. . . . If we are even partly right, however, then a considerable rethinking of our approach to the literature is demanded."[5] Elliot R. Wolfson offers a fuller account of the relationship between the literary text and religious experience:

> Study should not be reduced to mere exegesis devoid of any experiential component; on the contrary, one must assume that the visions and revelatory experiences recorded in the apocalypses are not simply literary forms but reflect actual experiences deriving from divine inspiration. It can be assumed, therefore, that at least some of the apocalyptic visions arose from reflection on scripture: exegesis of recorded visions leads to revelation of God.[6]

---

in the Apocalyptic-Merkabah Tradition," *JJS* 43 (1992): 1–31; James D. Tabor, *Things Unutterable: Paul's Ascent to Paradise in its Greco-Roman, Judaic, and Early Christian Contexts* (Studies in Judaism; Lanham, MD: University Press of America, 1986); Ithamar Gruenwald, *Apocalyptic and Merkavah Mysticism* (AGJU 14; Leiden: Brill, 1980); Gershom Scholem, *Major Trends in Jewish Mysticism* (3d ed.; New York: Schocken Books, 1954).

3   See studies such as those represented by the recent collections, April D. DeConick (ed.), *Paradise Now*; and the important collection edited by Flannery, Shantz, and Werline, *Experientia, Volume 1: Inquiry into Religious Experience*.

4   Michael E. Stone, "Apocalyptic—Vision or Hallucination?" in *Selected Studies in Pseudepigrapha &Apocrypha: With Special Reference to the Armenian Tradition* (SVTP 9; Leiden: Brill, 1991), 428. Also idem, *Ancient Judaism: New Visions and Views* (Grand Rapids: Eerdmans, 2011), 90–121

5   Michael E. Stone, "A Reconsideration of Apocalyptic Visions," *HTR* 96 (2003): 167–180, here 180.

6   Elliot R. Wolfson, *Through a Speculum That Shines: Visions and Imagination in Medieval Jewish Mysticism* (Princeton: Princeton University Press, 1994), 124.

This perspective that visionary texts reflect some aspect of actual religious experience also informs the work of Alan F. Segal, Daniel Merkur, and the groundbreaking proposal by Moshe Idel.[7] So too, this study holds that it is possible for a text to reflect actual religious experience and also show signs of complex literary development that reflect the cultural and historical circumstances of their composition.

The concerns that often surround the study of religious experience seek to authenticate real from false reports of religious experience or highlight its subjective aspects. These concerns reflect post-enlightenment suspicions of bodily experiences, often understood to be emotional and spiritual experiences, and favor disembodied rational objective accounts. Yet recent research into cognitive processes has emphasized the embodied mind and has understood cognitive processes to be richly informed by sensory experiences.[8] Past studies sought to avoid the charge that religious experience was subjective and interior by focusing upon the historical and literary aspects of visionary traditions which were perceived to be more certain and objective. Michael E. Stone described this strategy in the following way:

> Scholars studying these writings deal with their composition, date, and coherence by basing themselves on the 'more objective' criteria of literary form and tradition criticism; on historical grammar (if applicable); on translation characteristics; on the extent of the *vaticinium ex eventu* in historical overviews; on insights yielded by other, more recent methodologies; and so forth. In these studies, the religious life and experience ascribed to the pseudepigraphic authors are rarely taken into account.[9]

Interdisciplinary methods such as those represented in the volume *Experientia* seek to circumvent the criticism that religious experience is too subjective to yield significant findings by anchoring their discussions in objective neuropsychological and biological processes.[10] Armin W. Geertz argues strongly in favor of a "biocultural theory of religion," an interdisciplinary model of religion that seeks to balance biological

---

7 Alan F. Segal, "Religious Experience and the Construction of the Transcendent Self," 27–40; Moshe Idel, "Mystical Techniques," 438–94; Daniel Merkur, "The Visionary Practices of Jewish Apocalyptists," 119–48.

8 More detailed discussion of this may be found in chapter two and four.

9 Stone, "A Reconsideration of Apocalyptic Visions," 168.

10 Flannery, Shantz, and Werline (eds.), *Experientia, Volume 1*. C. Shantz, *Paul in Ecstasy* is an excellent example of interdisciplinary ways of studying religious experience.

and cultural contexts of religious experience.[11] While biological models alone cannot fully explain the reports of religious experience found in apocalyptic texts, these material descriptions of religious experience can be useful in supplementing and enriching the usual historical-critical examination of these ancient texts. An especially fruitful line of research is the study of the role that emotions and their strategic arousal play in the inducement of religious experiences.[12] An excellent example of this is the recent work by Steven Weitzman on the role of emotion in the Qumran War Scroll.[13] Weitzman offers the compelling proposal that the highly ritualized language in the War Scroll seeks to induce a religious experience by arousing key emotions needed for battle: "the War Scroll can be plausibly read as offering a perfectly rational plan of action at least by the standards of rationality adhered to by the foes against whom Jews were fighting in this period, whether Greeks in the Tradition of Xenophon and Onasander or Romans in the tradition of Julius Caesar and Frontinus, who acknowledged that an army's emotional state could be the most decisive factor in a battle."[14] Weitzman uses comparative material to examine questions that textual and literary studies of the War Scroll have not been able to address in order to construct a phenomenal understanding of the text in its time period. This study of the Qumran hodayot also seeks to bring relevant theoretical understandings of subjectivity and emotion from neuropsychological and social psychological perspectives to answer questions about religion and prayer in the hodayot that are not adequately addressed by strictly textual, historical, and literary studies.

Previous hodayot scholarship has devoted much attention to understanding the historical and literary aspects of these writings from Qum-

---

11   Armin W. Geertz, "Brain, Body and Culture," 304–21.

12   See for example the argument in Daniel I. Block, "Text and Emotion: A Study in the 'Corruptions' in Ezekiel's Inaugural Vision (Ezekiel 1:4–28)," *CBQ* 50 (1988):418–442; that the problems in the textual tradition of Ezekiel's vision can be explained as a consequence of the prophet having an actual religious experience: "the reason why the account of the inaugural vision appears so garbled and contains so many obscurities lies in the emotional state of the recipient, who by internal data is purported to have been the narrator of the experience as well" (433). The author unfortunately does not discuss exactly how he understands 'emotion' or the process by which this type of religious experience would have occurred.

13   Steven Weitzman, "Warring against Terror: The *War Scroll* and the Mobilization of Emotion," *JSJ* 40 (2009): 213–41.

14   Weitzman, "Warring against Terror," 239.

ran.[15] While those topics are not exhausted, few scholars have considered how these texts may have been read and experienced at Qumran from the phenomenological perspective of religious experience.[16] This chapter seeks to describe what is meant by "religious experience" in the context of the Qumran hodayot, the theoretical post-structural framework that informs performance and ritual theory, and the role of bodily practices in the creation of subjectivity.

I. Religious Experience as Bodily Experience

Religious experience can refer to a number of altered states of consciousness, including ecstasy, out of body experience, and mystical ascent. In the case of the hodayot, religious experience is described through language of the body and understood as an extraordinary phenomenal and transformative encounter with the divine. The transforma-

---

15 A number of historically-oriented studies were conducted on the hodayot in the 1960 s which Eileen Schuller refers to as the Heidelberg School in DJD 29.74: Gert Jeremias, *Der Lehrer der Gerechtigkeit*; Jürgen Becker, *Das Heil Gottes*; and Heinz-Wolfgang Kuhn, *Enderwartung und gegenwärtiges Heil*. These three scholars of the Heidelberg School relied much on the literary divisions identified in the earlier work of Günter Morawe, *Aufbau und Abgrenzung*. Their historical conclusions about the TH are known as the Teacher Hymn Hypothesis; (notice that M. C. Douglas refers to them as the 'Göttingen School' in "Power and Praise in the Hodayot." Douglas' major conclusions appear in "The Teacher Hymn Hypothesis Revisited," 239–66. See also M. O. Wise, *The First Messiah* and I. Knohl, *The Messiah Before Jesus,* each of whom have offered identifications for the historical figure standing behind some of the hodayot. A critical discussion of the popular TH Hypothesis is offered in chapter two.

   Major literary studies on the hodayot include S. Holm-Nielsen, *Hodayot*; B. P. Kittel, *The Hymns of Qumran*; J. A. Hughes, *Scriptural Allusions and Exegesis in the Hodayot.*

16 C. A. Newsom, *The Self as Symbolic Space* and eadem, "Constructing 'We, You, and the Others' through Non-Polemical Discourse," *Defining Identities: We, You, and the Other in the Dead Sea Scrolls* (ed. Florentino García Martínez and Mladen Popović; STDJ 70; Leiden: Brill, 2008), 13–21, esp. 18–20. Newsom follows Bo Reike's proposal that the hodayot were read in a manner similar to Philo's description of the Therapeutae who are said to read after meals first the leader and then a community; see B. Reike, "Remarques sur l'histoire de la form (Formgeschichte) des texts de Qumran," in *Les manuscrits de la mer Morte: Colloque de Strasbourg 25–27 Mai 1955* (ed. J. Daniélou et al.; Paris: Presses universitaires de France, 1957), 38–44.

tive experience appears as a number of different kinds: from danger to safety (rescue);[17] from weakness to strength (empowering);[18] from impurity to purity (cleansing);[19] from ordinary knowing to revealed knowing (illumination);[20] from a lowly state to an exalted one (eleva-

17 See 1QH X, 25–26; X, 36–37; XI, 6–7; XII, 22–23; XIII, 8–9; XIII, 15; XIII, 20; XV, 15; "In You I take refuge from all the pain … You save me for an eternal escape" XVII, 28–29; "(You) are like a guardian with his embrace You provide for all your creatures" XVII, 36; "with Your right hand of Your power to save all of them, by the strength of Your might" XXIII, 8–9.

18 1QH IX, 34a; X, 9–11; XI, 38; XII, 9; XII, 24a; XII, 29; XII, 37; XIII, 17; XIII, 27; XV, 9–13; XV, 17; XV, 22; "making them stand before You" XV, 34; "You establish my foot" XV, 41; a soothing from suffering and restoration to health XVII, 10–13 and XVII, 24–25); on God's incomparable strength XVIII, 12–14; XVIII, 25; XVIII, 34; XIX, 6; on God's strength XIX, 11; "You have opened up my shattering pains and you have comforted me in my grief" XIX, 35; XXI, 8; "How can I stand before the storm[y] wind? [As for me, He shall establish me]" XXI, 26; "You restore him" XXI, 16; "he is magnified by [Your] glory. Do not withdraw Your hand []so that he may become one who holds fast to Your covenant, and stands before You" XXIII, 9–11; "who makes known the strength of His hand" XXVI, 14; "restoring the steps of those who wait for knowledge" XXVI, 15.

19 1QH IX, 34b; XI, 22; XIII, 11; XV, 33; "You expel a perverted spirit from within me" XVI, 1–2; XIX, 13–14; "cleanse me with Your righteousness" XIX, 33–34; "And You opened a foun[tain] to correct the way of the creature of clay, and the guilt of one born of a woman according to his deeds" XXIII, 13–14.

20 1QH X, 20; XII, 6–7; XII, 24b; XII, 28; XIII, 13–14; XIII, 18; XIII, 28; "opening my ears" XIV, 7; "sevenfold light" XV, 27–28; "You have given me insight..made known mysteries" XV, 29–30; "You open my ears … so that my heart understands your truth" XV, 41; "You have placed (words) in my mouth" XVI, 17; "by my hand You open their font" XVI, 22; "my light shines forth by means of Your glory" XVII, 26–27; "You have shined the insight of Your judgment on me" XVII, 31); "You have made [th]e[se things] known to me" (XVIII, 16); "my heart is opened to the eternal font" XVIII, 32–33; "You have [enlighten]ed me in the counsel of Your truth, and You have given me insight into Your wonderful deeds" XIX, 7; on God's knowledge see XIX, 11; XIX, 12–13; XIX, 19–20; "You have given to your servant the insight of knowledge to understand Your wonders" XIX, 30–31; XX, 14–16, 18; "You have [properly prepar]ed an ear of dust, and You have engraved the things that will be eternally onto the heart [of stone]" XXI, 13–14; "in an eternal abode for the light of the most perfect light, an eternal splendor" XXI, 15; "I know by means of the spirit which You put inside me" XXI, 34; "You shall]make me [kno]w O my God!" XXI, 11; "You Yourself revealed to my ear" XXI, 26; "You have opened my heart to Your understanding, and You revealed [my] ears" XXI, 31;

tion);[21] and from human to angelic company (union with angels).[22] These categories of transformation are not mutually exclusive ones, and reports of rescue and empowerment can be conflated. Of these types of transformations, the most significant ones for our discussion are illumination, elevation, and union with angels. Philip Alexander remarks that "there was an active practice of ascent within the Qumran community,"[23] and argues in favor of situating Qumran within later traditions of mysticism.[24] It is important, however, to state here that the

---

"You open the ear of dust. . . You establish it in the ea[rs of] Your servant forever . . .[] the [re]ports of Your wonder shine forth before the eyes of all who hear [You]" XXIII, 5–8; "You have opened [a foun]tain in the mouth of Your servant; and on his tongue You have engraved the measuring line [to a] nnounce these things to the creature according to his understanding, and to an interpreter, to dust like myself" XXIII, 11–13; "You have make known [at the appointed t]ime the judgment of Your truth. And You have opened the ear of the flesh and [you gave] to humanity [insight] into the plan of Your mind, and You caused fles[h] to understand the appointed time" XXV, 11–13; "sealing up] mysteries and revealing hidden things," XXVI, 14–15.

21 1QH XI, 20–21; XIII, 24; XIII, 11; "raise up a shoot" XIV, 18; "raise up the standard... lift a banner..." XIV, 37; "exalted my ray over" XV, 26–27; XIX, 15; on God's truth shining forth XIX, 29; "You have made me stand up in (my) station" XXI, 15; "and in Your land and among the sons of gods he shall be glorified" XXIII, 23; "rai[sing up those who stumble and those among them who fall" XXVI, 15; "He lif[ts up the poor one from the dust to the eternal height, and to the clouds] He makes him tall in stature, and (he is) with [the divine beings in the congregation of the community" XXVI, 27–28.

22 1QH XIV, 16; "in order to unite wi[th] the sons of Your truth; in the lot with Your holy ones.... In order to position himself in place before You with the eternal hosts and spirits [of eternity] and in order to be renewed with all that i[s] and will be and with those who know in a single joyous song" XIX, 14–15, 16–17; "for according to their insight You have brought them near, and according to their dominion they serve You in [their] rank[s]" XX, 25–26; "You have brought [] into a covenant with you; and You have revealed (to) a heart of dust to be careful" XXI, 10; "the so]ns of gods, to unite with the sons of heaven" 23:30; "as for me, my station is with the divine beings" XXVI, 7; "Exalt [together with the eternal host!" XXVI, 11; "worship in a common [assembly!" XXVI, 14.

23 Alexander, *The Mystical Texts*, 90.

24 Alexander, "Qumran and the Genealogy of Western Mysticism," 218. He defines mysticism as having three elements: (1) "the first is that mysticism arises from religious *experience*, the experience of a transcendent divine presence which stands behind the visible, material world;" (2) "the mystic, having become award of a transcendent presence, is filled with a desire for a closer relationship with it;" (3) "mysticism always demands a *via mystica*, a way by which the mystic sets out to attempt union/communion with the divine," 219, 220.

Qumran hodayot were found in many fragmentary copies from Cave 4, providing evidence that no single standard form of the collection was yet in place.[25] This study of the hodayot and how they may have been used for religious experience has in mind the specific form of the collection known from 1QH[a] and also the reconstructed hodayot scroll known as 4Q428 (one of the oldest hodayot manuscripts dating to the middle Hasmonean period), which I have proposed elsewhere was an early form of 1QH[a] that included only the TH and CH II groups of hodayot.[26] References to these three different types of transformation are given in the following table.

According to the table, a majority of the references to illumination, vertical ascent, and communion with heavenly beings takes place in the areas known traditionally as the Teacher Hymns (TH) and the second group of Community Hymns (CH II), with a heavy concentration of elements in the text that Esti Eshel first called the 'self-glorification hymn' (SGH).[27] Many scholars hold the view that the SGH reflects an extraordinary religious experience of some sort of ascent into the heavens,[28] yet there is has been little scholarly engagement of how the SGH relates to the larger literary and material context of the hodayot.[29]

Table 1 on the previous pages shows references to the speaker's physical movement into the company of angels throughout the TH and the second group of CH. Similar to other reports of mystical experience, the speaker of the hodayot describes a unitive aspect to his experiences of communion with angels. These reports differ in important ways, however, from the experience of *unio mystica* that frequently ap-

---

25 One could say, however, that during the early Herodian period the arrangement of the collection known to us as 1QHodayot[a] was beginning to be preserved as a recognizable arrangement.

26 See A. K. Harkins, "Thinking about 1QH[A] Sixty Years after its Discovery," 101–34.

27 Esther Eshel, "4Q471b: A Self-Glorification Hymn," *RevQ* 17 (1996): 189–91.

28 The SGH is usually described as having two distinct recensions: in his discussion of them P. Alexander (*The Mystical Texts*) writes that the speaker's positioning in the heavens and ascent into the heavens is striking (86–90). Alexander is right to describe the recensional variations among the two different copies of the SGH as evidence that "the hymn was in active use within the community, and that someone felt he had the authority and the experience to vary it" (89).

29 The notable exception is P. Alexander, *The Mystical Texts*, which seeks to identify points of continuity between the SGH and other hodayot in the collection.

Table 1
Religious Experience in the Hodayot (1QH^a)

Sheet	Col. #	Divisions per Stegemann (2003)	Type	References to Religious Experience: illumination, vertical ascent, communion with heavenly beings
i	I		CH I	No text
	II		CH I	No text
	III		CH I	No text
	IV			
		IV, 21–27	CH I	
		IV, 28		Full blank line
		IV, 29–37	CH I	
		IV, 38–??	CH I	
ii	V	V, 1–12?	CH I	No text
		V, 12–VI, 33	CH	
	VI			
		VI, 34–VII, 11	CH I	
	VII			
		VII, 12–20	CH	
		VII, 21–VIII, 41	CH I	
	VIII			
iii	IX	IX, 1–X, 4	Intro to TH	
	X			
		X, 5–21	TH	
		X, 22–32	TH	
		X, 33–XI, 5	TH	Illumination: אתה]אלי האירותה פני לבריותכה (11:4) "[You] are my God, You have illuminated my face before Your covenant"
	XI			
		XI, 6–19	TH	
		XI, 20–37	TH	Vertical Ascent: אודכה אדוני כי פדיתה נפשי משחת ומשאול אבדון העליתני לרום עולם ואתהלכה במישור לאין חקר (XI, 20–21) "I give thanks to You, my Lord, because You have redeemed my life from the Pit, and from Sheol Abaddon You have lifted me up to an eternal height, so that I may walk around on an endless plain." — Communion with Angels (cf. XIX, 16): להתיצב במעמד עם צבא קדושים ולבוא ביחד עם עדת בני שמים ותפלי לאיש גורל עולם עם רוחות דעת להלל שמכה ביחד רנה (XI, 22–24) speaker is the 'perverted spirit', the following is in 3rd person: "in order to position him in place with the host of holy ones and to bring (him) together with the congregation of the sons of heaven. And for man, You cast an eternal lot with spirits of knowledge, so that (they) might praise Your name in a single joyous song…!"
		XI, 38–XII, 5	TH	

Table 1 Religious Experience in the Hodayot (1QH^a) *(Continued)*

Sheet	Col. #	Divisions per Stegemann (2003)	Type	References to Religious Experience: illumination, vertical ascent, communion with heavenly beings
	XII			
		XII, 6–XIII, 6	TH	Illumination:
iv	XIII			אודכה אדוני כיא האירותה פני לבריתכה ומ[ ]] °[ ]אדורשכה וכשחר נכון לאור[תי]ם הופעתה לי (XII, 6–7; cf. XII, 24) "I thank you O Lord, because You have illuminated my face for Your covenant; [ ]and as certain as the dawn, You have shown me lights." — Communion with heavenly beings וישומעוני ההולכים בדרך לבכה ויערוכו לכה בסוד קדושים (XII, 25–26) "And those who walk in the path of Your heart shall heed me, and they shall arrange themselves before You in the council of the holy ones." — Illumination: ובי האירותה פני רבים (XII, 28) "Through me, You have illuminated the Many"
		XIII, 7–21	TH	Being refined to a sevenfold purity (cf. XV, 27): ולמען הגבירכה בי לנגד בני אדם הפלתה באביון ותביאהו במצר[ף]כזהב במעשי אש וככסף מזוקק בכור נופחים לטהר שבעתים (XIII, 17–18) "In order to make manifest Your power in me before the sons of Adam, You have acted wonderfully with the poor-one; You have brought him into the furna[ce] like gold in the workings of fire, and like silver being refined in the crucible of the blacksmiths, to a sevenfold purity."
		XIII, 22–XV, 8	TH	Vertical movement
	XIV			עם ענוים בטאטאיי רגליכ[ה יחד] עם נמהרי צדק
	XV			להעלות משאון יחד כול {נמה}אביוני חסד (XIII, 23–24) "And with the poor people in the sweepings of Your feet, together with those who are eager for righteousness, to lift (them) up from the mire together with all the faithful poor." — Communion with heavenly beings הביאותה °[ ] סודכה לכול אנשי עצתכה ובגורל יחד עם מלאכי פנים (XIV, 15–16) "You have brought [ ] Your council, for all the men of your assembly, and in the lot together with the angels of the presence."
		XV, 9–28	TH	Walking about in the presence of God להתהלך לפניך בגבול [ ]ים לשבולי כבוד וחיים ושלום לאין ה[סר ו]ל[ו]א להשבת לנצח (XV, 17–18) "In order to walk back and forth in your presence in the realm of [ ] for trails/paths of glory and life and peace, without turning and without ceasing forever" — Exaltation of the speaker's ray ותרם קרני על כול מנאצי (XV, 25) "And You have raised my ray over all who insult me." — Exaltation and sevenfold illumination (cf. XIII, 17–18) ותרם קרני למעלה והופעתי באור שבעתים

Table 1 Religious Experience in the Hodayot (1QHª) *(Continued)*

Sheet	Col. #	Divisions per Stegemann (2003)	Type	References to Religious Experience: illumination, vertical ascent, communion with heavenly beings
				(XV, 26–27) "And You have raised my ray ever upward, and I shine forth in a sevenfold light"
		XV, 29–36	CH ?	Standing in the presence of God בהמון רחמיכה להעמידם לפניכה לעולמי עד (XV, 32–34) "In the abundance of your mercies, to make them stand before You forever and ever"
	XVI	XV, 37–XVI, 4	TH	Being brought before the presence of God וכול בני אמתכה ^{תביא} בסליחות לפניכה לטהרם מפשעיהם ברוב טובכה ובהמון רחמיכה להעמידם לפניכה לעולמי עד (XV, 33–34) "And all the sons of Your truth you bring in pardons before You, in order to purify them from their transgressions with the plentitude of Your goodness and with the abundance of Your mercies, to make them stand before You forever and ever."
v	XVII	XVI, 5–XVII, 36	TH	Glorification of speaker and illumination ובוז צרי לי לכליל כבוד וכשלוני לגבורת עולם כי בשכלֿלֿ ה הודעתני]ובכבודכה הופיע אורי כי מאור מחושך האירותה (XVII, 25–27) "And the contempt of my foes becomes an eternal crown and my stumbling becomes an eternal power, because by Yo[ur] insight [You have made known to me] and by Your glory, my light shone forth because you make light shine from darkness."
		XVII, 37		Full blank line
	XVIII	XVII, 38–XIX, 5	DH+	*Transition? Possible conclusion to TH?*
	XIX			
	XX	XIX, 6–XX, 6	CH II	Communion with heavenly beings and vertical elevation להוחד עם בני אמתך ובגורל עם קדושים להרים מעפר תולעת מתים לסוד א[מתכה] ומרוח נעוה לבינתכֿהֿ ולהתיצב במעמד לפניכה עם צבא עד ורוחו[ת עולם] ולהתחדש עם כול ה[יוה] ונהיה ועם ידעים ביחד רנה (XIX, 14–17) "so that he might be united with the sons of Your truth, and in the lot with the holy ones, to lift (him) up from the dust of the worms of dead ones, to the counsel of [Your trut]h; and from a perverted spirit to Your understanding; and to position him in place before You, with the (heavenly) host and spiri[ts of eternity]; and in order to renew (him) with all th[at is] and that will be, and with the ones who know, in a single joyous song."
vi	XXI	XX, 7–XXII, 42	CH II	Liturgical language in XX, 7–13 Possible reference to being elevated (cf. XIX, 14)
	XXII			לה]תקומם לפני נגע (XXII, 10) "[to r]ise up in the face of affliction" — Possible reference to being positioned in a heavenly assembly (cf. XIX, 16) במעמד העמדתני כי (XXII, 15) "You have made me stand in position"
	XXIII	XXIII, 1–XXV, 33	CH II	Glorification of the "servant" among the sons of God

Table 1 Religious Experience in the Hodayot (1QH^a) *(Continued)*

Sheet	Col. #	Divisions per Stegemann (2003)	Type	References to Religious Experience: illumination, vertical ascent, communion with heavenly beings
	XXIV			וֹבאַרצכה ובבני אלים יכבד
vii	XXV			(XXIII, 23) "In Your land, and he shall be glorified among the sons of gods (=angels)"
				—
				Communion with heavenly beings
				להתיד עם בני שמים
				(XXIII, 30) "to unite with the sons of heaven"
		XXV, 34–XXVII, 3	CH II	"Self Glorification Hymn" =SGH (reconstructed from 4Q427 7 i)
	XXVI			Comparison of speaker with heavenly beings
	XXVII			מי כמוני באלים
				(XXVI, 4–5) "who is like me among the angels?"
				—
				Communion with heavenly beings
				כיא אני עם אלים מעמדי
				(XXVI, 7) "as for me, my station is with angels,"
				—
				Rejoice in the holy dwelling, together with heavenly beings
				הללו במעון קודש [יחד בצבא עולם] רוממו
				(XXVI, 10–11) "[Rejoice in the abode of the Holy One], Raise up (your voice) [together in the eternal heavenly host]"
				—
				Vertical ascent into the heavenly realm; communion with heavenly beings
				וירֹ[ם מעפר אביון לרום עולם ועד שחקים] יגביה בקומה ועם [אלים בעדת יחד
				(XXVI, 27–28) "and He ra[ises up] a poor one from the dust, to an eternal height; [and until] the height of [the clouds] in stature, and with [angels in a single congregation"
				—
				In the presence of God and communion with heavenly beings
				ולהתיצב במעמד] לפניכה ולבוא ביחד עם בני שמים ואין מליץ
				(XXVI, 36) "In order to position in place [in Your presence; and to bring (him) together with the sons of heaven, without a mediator"
		XXVII, 4– XXVIII?	CH II	Very fragmentary
	XXVIII			

pears in the mystical traditions of western and eastern religions. According to Elliott Wolfson, most traditions of mystical union fit within a "tendency rooted in Neoplatonic ontology and epistemology: contemplation of God results in a form of union whereby the soul separates from the body and returns to its ontological source in the One. Insofar as the One is beyond intellect and being, the return to the One is depicted in figurative terms as a mystical merging of the soul in the Godhead."[30] Formulated as such, Wolfson's description of *unio mystica* does not appear in the hodayot. Philip Alexander observes that Wolfson's essay has made Qumran scholars reluctant to think of the scrolls in mystical categories.[31] Qumran texts, along with other apocalyptic Jewish and some Christian writings, exemplify a phenomenal model that differs from *unio mystica* which emerges from ancient Near Eastern and Mesopotamian mythology wherein the "human being crosses the boundary of space and time and becomes part of the heavenly realm."[32] In this model, a clear spatial and phenomenal aspect persists in the religious experience that takes place, a topic that will be given further treatment in chapter three. In other words, the kind of religious experience in the hodayot is *not* conceptualized as a purely spiritual one whereupon the visionary's soul dissolves and is lost in the Godhead. On the contrary, the body and phenomenal bodily experiences play a key role in how the religious experience is conceptualized here, as is true for other texts of this time period. This study agrees with Alexander's perspective that mystical experiences were present at Qumran, however the divide that separates the transcendent creator from the creature is always maintained. At Qumran, the desire for union is with the highest order of created beings, the angels, who enjoy the closest relationship to God.[33] Even so, the union desired with angelic beings does not result in the "obliteration of the ontological distinction between angels and humanity."[34]

II. Affective Experience as Bodily Experience

The body and the body's phenomenal experiences figure prominently in the hodayot's articulation of religious experiences. Transformation, ascent, and communion with angels are physically described through the body's faculties of sensory perception. The intensity of these experiences enjoyed by the lyrical subject simulate and stimulate the bodily

---

30 Elliot R. Wolfson, "Mysticism and the Poetic-Liturgical Compositions from Qumran: A Response to Bilhah Nitzan," *JQR* 85 (1994): 185–202, here 186.
31 Alexander, "Qumran and the Genealogy of Western Mysticism," 217.
32 Wolfson, "Mysticism and the Poetic-Liturgical Compositions from Qumran," 186; see the comments by Alexander, "Qumran and the Genealogy of Western Mysticism," 217–218.
33 Alexander, "Qumran and the Genealogy of Western Mysticism," 222.
34 Alexander, "Qumran and the Genealogy of Western Mysticism," 225.

sensations of the reader and engage aspects of affect that are worth considering. This section discusses the wide-ranging scholarship on the emotions, an enterprise that engages the humanities, social sciences, and biological sciences. This research has been steadily growing and is characterized by a number of theoretical insights, including critiques of established understandings of emotion that bear the influence of an enlightenment worldview.[35] Various tensions in the scholarship on emotions exist; a primary one being that between biological and the cultural understandings of emotion. In the context of religion, emotions offer an excellent example of an embodied experience that can be examined from "a combination of theories from neurobiology, social psychology, anthropology, cognitive science, archaeology and comparative religion."[36] This type of interdisciplinary approach to the study of religious experience, as proposed by Armin W. Geertz, presumes that cognition is embodied and profoundly enculturated within religious systems.[37]

The scholarship on emotion resembles that on religious experience insofar as both emotion and religious experience are viewed typically as subjective phenomena that are immeasurable. Similar to the cultural bias against mysticism, emotions have long been viewed with suspicion.[38] David Franks even goes so far as to describe the scholarly perceptions and expectations about emotions as a common bias against emotions in the western world:[39] "Much of our bias toward emotion in general stems from a particular notion of rationality that grew out of the enlightenment and fueled the Industrial Revolution . . . . Ideally, ration-

---

35 A good clear discussion of the major theoretical issues surrounding emotion may be found in Catherine Lutz and Geoffrey M. White, "The Anthropology of Emotions," *Annual Review of Anthropology* 15 (1986): 405–36. The biological understanding of emotion is referred to as "material." Lutz and White refer to this particular tension as "materialism and idealism." Other tensions that they identify in the scholarship from the natural and social sciences include: "positivism and interpretivism," "universalism and relativism," "individual and social," and "romanticism and rationalism" (406–9).

36 Geertz, "Brain, Body and Culture," 313.

37 Geertz, "Brain, Body and Culture," 304–21.

38 For an excellent recent discussion of the scholarly prejudice against mystical experiences and the study of them, see C. Shantz, *Paul in Ecstasy*, 20–66.

39 David D. Franks, "The Bias Against Emotions in Western Civilization," in *Sociology of Emotions* (ed. Catherine G. Valentine, Steve Derné, and Beverley Cuthbertson Johnson (New York: 1999), 29–34.

al-efficient thought set out to purge itself of all considerations of value, and thus emotion."[40]

Gary Ebersole's work on the social history of emotions offers an important starting point for any discussion of the emotions within religious contexts. He critiques modern assumptions and expectations about the emotions as being unduly influenced by enlightenment conceptualizations and preoccupied with distinguishing 'real' from 'fake' experiences.[41] Enlightenment thinking exerts the false expectation that emotions, as they are experienced and perceived today, are unchanging and have been experienced uniformly in all cultures and in all time periods. The concern to distinguish between authentic and inauthentic experiences of emotion can be considered an extension of this enlightenment impulse to systematize affect into a polarity of experiences in order to ultimately dismiss them altogether from the concerns that really matter—pure rationality and objectivity. Biologically based approaches to the study of emotion, also known as "material" approaches, can also be conceptualized within a larger enlightenment desire to validate these experiences in an objective manner, but they can be profitably merged with social and cultural understandings.[42] The resulting biocultural models of affective experiences seek a non-reductive consideration of the body in the study of phenomenal religious experiences.

The physical study of the human brain was necessarily limited to the number of patients who sustained unique injuries that allowed for the study of localized regions. A famous example is Phineas Gage, a nineteenth century man who suffered a tragic head injury that resulted in irreparable damage to the orbitofrontal and ventromedial cortex of his brain.[43] The severe changes in Gage's personality that resulted led scien-

---

40   Franks, "The Bias Against Emotions in Western Civilization," 34.

41   Gary Ebersole, "The Function of Ritual Weeping Revisited: Affective Expression and Moral Discourse," *History of Religions* 39 (2000): 211–46; reprinted in *Religion and Emotion: Approaches and Interpretations* (ed. John Corrigan; Oxford: Oxford University Press, 2004), 185–222.

42   Natural and social science approaches can be in tension with each other because the former generally seeks to isolate biological processes within a context of universalizable norms while the latter seeks to isolate phenomena within specific cultural contexts.

43   John T. Cacioppo, Gary G. Berntson, Tyler S. Loring, Catherine J. Norris, Edith Rickett, and Howard Nusbaum, "Just Because You're Imaging the Brain Doesn't Mean You Can Stop Using Your Head: A Primer and Set of First Principles," *Journal of Personality and Social Psychology* 85 (2003): 650–61. Phineas Gage is discussed on 652.

tists to associate certain regions of the brain with various aspects of social behaviors and affect. Obviously, individuals such as Gage are rare and rely upon random and tragic accidents. Technology has made possible the study of cognitive processes without physical injury to the brain. Even so, the role that such empirical data plays in the understanding of complex social processes must be weighed carefully. The isolation of specific sensory and motor functions is a valuable starting point but it should not be used to oversimplify complex social processes which can lead to a biological determinism.[44] The growing sophistication of brain imaging technology has allowed for the greater incorporation of neuroscientific data to the study of complex social processes like affect, resulting in the rise of interdisciplinary approaches.[45] This type of integrative study can be called "social neuroscience."[46] This blended model of natural and social science approaches seeks to refine how the embodied brain is involved with social cognition, emotion and other behaviors.

While scholars have long been aware of the role that emotions play within the context of religion, the discussion has been seriously underdeveloped and plagued by the same general problems that affect interdisciplinary emotion studies across disciplines. The concerns over emotion found in the natural and social science disciplines find similar expression within the context of religious studies. According to John Corrigan:

> Scholarly expositions of religions have tended to appeal to emotion as if it were a universal, rich in explanatory power, a common denominator of experience bridging the widely varying contexts of lived traditions. From such a starting point, historical researchers have distinguished among religious groups by remarking that one was 'more emotional' than the other. Philosophers and theologians have arranged analyses of religious ideas around poles of 'emotion' and 'reason.'[47]

44 Cacioppo et al, "Just Because Your Imaging the Brain Doesn't Mean You Can Stop Using Your Head," 653.

45 John T. Cacioppo, Gary G. Berntson and John F. Sheridan, Martha K. McClintock, "Multilevel Integrative Analyses of Human Behavior: Social Neuroscience and the Complementing Nature of Social and Biological Approaches," *Psychological Bulletin* 126 (2000): 829–43.

46 Cacioppo, Berntson, Loring, Norris, Rickett, and Nusbaum, "Just Because You're Imaging the Brain Doesn't Mean You Can Stop Using Your Head," 650–661.

47 John Corrigan (ed), *Religion and Emotion: Approaches and Interpretations* (New York: Oxford University Press, 2004), 6.

Research on the emotions tends to be peripheral in the field of religious studies, with a significant number of affect studies concentrated on women mystics from the medieval period, although there is growing interest in emotions in other areas.[48] Important in these studies of medieval mystics is the spiritual practice of reenacting the text, what Sarah McNamer refers to as "iterative affective performances."[49]

The popular publications of the neuropsychologist Antonio Damasio pose serious challenges to the implicit assumption that emotions and cognitive processes are independent from one another. Damasio's influence on emotion research is remarkably wide-ranging due to the fact that his publications are strategically positioned to be widely accessible across disciplines. Emotions are indeed a powerful way of knowing. For scholars in the Humanities, Damasio's articulation of the biological basis of emotion and the embodied mind has highlighted the artificial and oversimplified Cartesian understanding of opposition between emotion and reason in the western world in the Humanities.[50] He attributes the neglect that emotions have suffered in scientific scholarship

---

48   Some examples of studies on the role of the emotion of desolation in medieval Christian women mystics include the excellent study by Sarah McNamer, *Affective Meditation and the Invention of Medieval Compassion* (Philadelphia: University of Pennsylvania Press, 2010); Ellen Ross, "'She Wept and Cried Right Loud for Sorrow and for Pain.' Suffering, the Spiritual Journey, and Women's Experience in Late Medieval Mysticism," in *Maps of Flesh and Light: The Religious Experience of Medieval Women Mystics* (ed. Ulrike Wiethaus; Syracuse: Syracuse University Press, 1993), 45–59. Ross writes of the importance of extended meditation upon visual and literary depictions of the suffering Christ in the process of imitating Christ (Ross, "'She Wept and Cried,'" 46–47).

Examples of emotion studies in other non-medieval areas include Matthew A. Elliott, *Faithful Feelings: Rethinking Emotion in the New Testament* (Grand Rapids: Kregel, 2006); David A. DeSilva, "The Strategic Arousal of Emotions in the Apocalypse of John: A Rhetorical-Critical Investigation of the Oracles to the Seven Churches," *NTS* 54 (2008): 90–114; Stephen C. Barton, "Eschatology and the Emotions in Early Christianity," *JBL* 130 (2011): 571–91. See too recent collection of essays examining the role of emotion in the deuterocanonical literature; Renate Egger-Wenzel and Jeremy Corley (ed.), *Emotions from Ben Sira to Paul* (DCLY; Berlin: de Gruyter, 2011). I am grateful to Jeremy Corley and Renate Egger-Wenzel for bringing this to my attention, but these essays were largely unavailable to me during the writing of my manuscript. The collection reflects a growing scholarly interest in the role of emotion in the humanities.

49   McNamer, *Affective Meditation*, 2.

50   Antonio R. Damasio, "A Second Chance for Emotion," in *Cognitive Neuroscience of Emotion* (ed. Richard D. Lane and Lynn Nadel; New York: Oxford University, 2000), 12–23.

of the twentieth century to the "lack of an evolutionary perspective in the study of brain and mind," "the disregard for the notion of homeostatic regulation," and a "noticeable absence" of a holistic understanding of the human organism in the modern disciplines of cognitive science and neuroscience.[51]

Neuropsychologists describe the biological basis for emotions as a series of physical responses that take place in the body and brain. Humans are predisposed to certain automatic biological responses to given situations. Certain neuropsychological processes can be said to occur naturally and generally stand outside the conscious control of the individual. Stimuli are detected by the "emotionally-competent" receptors in the brain, which are then processed somatically by the body prior to intellectual awareness through various autonomic and endocrine responses.[52] In this study, emotions are strictly understood as bodily expressions and differ from what are commonly referred to as feelings. As bodily processes, it is useful to understand emotions as visible and measurable changes in heart palpitation and endocrine levels that physical display of trembling, perspiration, blushing, pupil dilation, etc.[53] The various regions of the brain responsible for the processing of emotion, sensory perception, and higher order thinking are connected in complex two way networks. The close interrelationship between these various processes is important to recognize. Emotions constitute an important way of embodied knowing and cognitive neuroscience has demonstrated that affective experiences play a key role in reasoning and decision-making processes. Damasio writes that the emotions point to the "sector of the decision-making space where our reason can operate most efficiently. . . . Well-tuned and deployed emotion, as I see it, is necessary for the edifice of reason to operate properly."[54] While scholars have critiqued Damasio for oversimplifying complex cognitive

---

51 Damasio, "A Second Chance for Emotion," 12.
52 Edmund T. Rolls, *Emotion Explained* (New York: Oxford University Press, 2005), 51–52.
53 Damasio, *Looking for Spinoza*, 29. Here Damasio corrects previous thinking about the relationship between the emotions and feeling: "The centrality of feeling obscures the matter of how feelings arise and favors the view that somehow feelings occur first and are expressed subsequently in emotions. That view is incorrect, and it is to blame, at least in part, for the delay in finding a plausible neurobiological account for feelings. It turns out that it is feelings that are mostly shadows of the external manner of emotions" (29).
54 Damasio, "A Second Chance for Emotion," 14.

processes and for placing too much attention on the biological basis of emotion at the expense of the social context, his basic point that emotions are not at odds with reason and they play a significant role in cognitive processes are points that are well taken and widely acknowledged.[55]

Various regions of the brain are associated with the processing of emotion. One of them, the limbic system, is a so-called primitive area of the brain that plays a role in a range of functions related to memory and sensory perception.[56] While neurologists debate exactly what the limbic system includes or how it operates, it is clear that it connects by a complex system of networks to the pre-frontal cortex which is the site where higher levels of cognitive reasoning occur, including understandings of the self.[57] Sensory data not only move from the limbic system to the prefrontal cortex, they can also be moderated by it since there is a rich two-way communication between these regions of the brain. Many studies of emotion and the brain have an evolutionary emphasis and highlight the strong biological predispositions that humans have to expressing fear in given situations, however it would be incorrect to draw the conclusion that even strong emotions like fear can be understood solely as biologically determined.[58]

Even neuropsychologists, whose descriptions of emotion as largely physiological processes and who are often critiqued for universalizing and/or over-determining human experiences, take care to note that emotions are not uniformly experienced and that not all individuals

---

55   See Daniel Gross's important discussion, *The Secret History of Emotion: From Aristotle's "Rhetoric" To Modern Brain Science* (Chicago: University of Chicago Press, 2006), 21–39. Gross critiques Damasio as having an operative understanding of emotion as "behaviorist and mechanistic" – ironically not unlike the understanding of emotion held by Descartes which he sought to critique (34, n. 4).

56   The limbic system includes regions like the amygdala and hippocampus, and according to some, the precuneus—an understudied region of the brain that is thought to play a role in vivid egocentric episodic memories. The processes governed by the precuneus are discussed in chapter 4.

57   Geertz, "Brain, Body and Culture," 306. Further discussion of primary and secondary emotion processes and emotion's role in memory construction may be found in chapters three and four respectively.

58   The evolutionary understandings of emotion are associated with Charles Darwin, *Expression of the Emotions in Man and Animals* (New York: Appleton and Company, 1899), and Paul Ekman, *Emotion in the Human Face* (Cambridge: Cambridge University Press, 1982).

share a common capacity for affective experiences. Biological approaches to emotion acknowledge its variability and social construction; critical points that cohere with affective research in other fields of the humanities and social sciences. Nevertheless, tensions between biological and cultural understandings persist and offer important opportunities for refinement. Daniel Gross, a political theorist, critiques what he perceives to be a flaw in Damasio's theoretical view, namely the expectation that emotions are universally experienced, differing only in degrees. Gross writes: "Throwing a temper tantrum or fuming or muttering curses under one's breath might strike us as a lesser degree of the same emotion exercised by a vengeful tyrant who forces a defiant subject to eat his own son for dinner, but it would not strike Aristotle so."[59] For certain communities like the one that Aristotle experienced, certain emotions would not have been available to all persons– such an egalitarian assumption reflects a post-enlightenment worldview. Certain emotions would have been reserved for individuals who enjoyed a certain class or status. In contrast to the majority of modern biological perceptions of emotions, the ancient world rightly understood emotions as socially and rhetorically constructed and variable given a person's status and rank in society—elites were not expected to experience the same range and intensity of emotions as those holding a lesser social status. Barbara Rosenwein speaks of various emotional communities in her study of the social history of emotions:

> I postulate the existence of 'emotional communities': groups in which people adhere to the same norms of emotional expression and value—or devalue—the same or related emotions. More than one emotional community may exist—indeed normally does exist—contemporaneously, and these communities may change over time. Some come to the fore to dominate our sources, then recede in importance. Others are almost entirely hidden from us, though we may imagine they exist and may even see some of their effects on more visible groups.[60]

---

59 Daniel Gross, *The Secret History of Emotion*, 5.
60 Barbara H. Rosenwein, *Emotional Communities in the Early Middle Ages* (Ithaca: Cornell University Press, 2006), 2. For examples of this research into the social history of emotions, see Daniel Gross, *The Secret History of Emotion*; S. McNamer, *Affective Meditations*.
    Emotions' cultural variability has been further researched in Anna Wierzbicka's pointed critique of modern scholarly discussions of emotion as not only displaying a western bias, but also suffering from biases specific to an English-speaking worldview. Anna Wierzbicka, *Emotions Across Languages and Cultures: Diversity and Universals* (Cambridge: Cambridge University Press, 1999).

The cultural context and social history of emotions is critical for understanding emotions. While cultural theorists have critiqued biological studies of the emotions as being overly deterministic, neuropsychological descriptions of emotion as physical processes remain useful for understanding the instrumental role that emotions play in the performance or outward display of affect within ritual contexts.[61]

The hodayot describe religious experiences of transformation with language about the body. Detailed and dramatic references to the speaker's experiences of physical and psychological anguish are expressed in bodily terms. These dramatic references to the body of the speaker in the hodayot succeed in constructing a lyrical subject whose body is capable of phenomenal and sensory experiences but which is not based on an actual person's specific experiences. Such a body can be called imaginal, a terminology that is often associated with the French History of Religions scholar, Henry Corbin (1907–1978), who used the term to distinguish experiences that are both phenomenal and spiritual but not based in empirical realities.[62] According to Jeffrey Kripal, "Corbin understood the imaginal to be a noetic organ that accessed a real dimension of reality whose contours and content were nevertheless shaped and formed by what he called the 'creative imagination,' an empowered form of what most people experience in its simpler and unenlightened

---

For example, she explains that the common English expression to describe emotional states as "feeling upset" reflects an expectation that the normal state is to be composed or in control, but such an expectation could not be said to be typical for all non-English-speaking European cultures (19). It should be noted here that the majority of biological approaches to emotion is done by English-speaking scholars.

61   In other words, my primary interest in biological understandings of emotion is an interest in the outwardly expression of emotion as displayed in a performance; I do not wish to commit to affirming the deterministic claims that biological studies have upon the human experience of emotions.

62   Please note that my use of this term 'imaginal' is restricted to the phenomenal aspects of this body's experiences; I do not share Corbin's understanding of it as a normative measure. See Henry Corbin, *Temple and Contemplation* (London: KPI in association with Islamic Publications, 1986), 263–390. He uses the term 'imaginal' to speak of the phenomenal experience of the Temple (*Imago Templi*). See Elliot R. Wolfson's discussion of Corbin in "*Imago templi* and the Meeting of the Two Seas," *RES* 51 (2007): 121–135; also Frances Flannery, with Nicolae Roddy, Colleen Shantz, and Rodney A. Werline, "Introduction: Religious Experience, Past and Present," *Experientia*, 1–10, esp. 4–5. More will be said about imaginal in chapter two.

state as the imagination or 'the imaginary.'"[63] This imaginal body is the constructed body of the speaker of the hodayot and, as such, is the site for extraordinary experiences: both the excruciating experiences of physical and psychological distress and the extraordinary transformative encounters with God. Because this study will focus on the particular religious experience of transformative ascent and otherworldly spatial experiences like being in the company of angels, the imaginal body that is constructed is that of a visionary. Chapter two discusses how embodiment language and the rhetorical construction of an imaginal body function to engender a religious experience for the ancient reader by offering an imitable script to be performed.[64] In this chapter, I present the theoretical foundations for a model of performative reading that lie in post-structuralist understandings of embodiment and subjectivity. The ancient reader, through the performative reading of texts and the reenactment of the bodily emotions that are described, could hope to create the subjectivity of a visionary and recreate the religious experience of ascent and communion with angels for himself.

III. The Theoretical Post-Structural Framework of Performance Theory and Ritual Studies

In the following section, I wish to foreground the current scholarship on performance theory and subjectivity, much of which has been shaped by Judith Butler, who famously applied Jacques Derrida's theory of language in "Signature Event Context"[65] to embodied experiences and un-

---

63 Jeffrey J. Kripal, "The Rise of the Imaginal: Psychical Research on the Horizon of Theory (Again)," *RSR* 22 (2007): 179–191, here 182.
64 Catherine Bell speaks about the embodied aspects of ritual experience as the "sensations experienced by the body in movement" and also "the evocation of a total, unified, and overwhelming sensory experience," Bell, *Ritual: Perspectives and Dimensions* (New York: Oxford University Press, 1997), 74.
65 Jacques Derrida, "Signature, Event, Context," trans. Samuel Weber and Jeffrey Mehlman, *Glyph: Johns Hopkins Textual Studies* 7 (1977): 172–97 is the first English translation of this essay which was originally written for a conference, Congrès international des Sociétés de philosophie de langue francaise (Montreal, August 1971) and published in French in the proceedings of that conference. It has also been repr. in Derrida, *Margins of Philosophy* (trans. Alan Bass; Chicago: University of Chicago, 1982), and Derrida, *Limited Inc* (Evanston: Northwestern University, 1988), 1–23. Citations of "Signature Event Con-

derstandings of subjectivity. The understanding that is presumed in this work is that Qumran hodayot as prayer texts are ritually performed and seek to reiterate religious events and experiences.[66]

A. Post-structuralism

In his essay, "Signature Event Context," Jacques Derrida responds to John Austin's work on performative utterances,[67] arguing against Austin's claim that it is possible to secure the intention of an original utterance. Using the example of a "signature," Derrida challenges Austin's assumption that a text, in this case a signature, always attests to the assent of the will of the signator.[68] Derrida presents Austin's position in the following way:

> By definition, a written signature implies the actual or empirical nonpresence of the signer. But, it will be claimed, the signature also marks and retains his having-been present in a past *now* or present [*maintenant*] which will remain a future *now* or present [*maintenant*], thus in a general *maintenant*, in the transcendental form of presentness [*maintenance*]. That general *maintenance* is in some way inscribed, pinpointed in the always evident and singular present punctuality of the form of the signature. Such is the enigmatic originality of every paraph. In order for the tethering to the source to occur, what must be retained is the absolute singularity of a signature-event and a signature-form: the pure reproducibility of a pure event.[69]

---

text" are taken from the Weber and Mehlman translation as it appears in *Limited Inc* (1988).

66 Many early scrolls scholars approached the hodayot as a literary and poetic collection but not as ritual texts. Nevertheless as prayer texts directed to God, this is the most immediate way of understanding them.

67 John L. Austin, *How to Do Things with Words* (Oxford: Clarendon Press, 1962).

68 The example of the signature is one that arises from John Austin himself who had used the idea of the signature as an example of a pure performative utterance. Jonathan Culler discusses Austin's position as follows: "What speech act is more serious than the act of signing a document, a performance whose legal, financial, and political implications may be enormous? Austin cites the act of signature as the equivalent in writing of explicit performative utterances with the form "I hereby. . . ," and indeed it is in appending a signature that one can in our culture most authoritatively take responsibility for an utterance. By signing a document, one intends its meaning and seriously performs the signifying act it accomplishes."Culler, "Convention and Meaning: Derrida and Austin," *New Literary History* 13 (1981): 15–30, here 26.

69 Derrida, "Signature Event Context," 20; emphasis original.

Derrida concludes his essay by questioning the presumed authorial intention of his own signature when he calls it a counterfeit. By doing so, he calls into question Austin's assertion that there is a pure relationship between the original intention and the iteration of his own signature, which is digitally reproduced at the end of the essay.[70] Derrida's challenge of the permanence of authorial intent is accompanied by his admission that signatures can function properly, but when they do it is because they rely upon the recognizability of the successive iterations and imitations of the so-called 'original' form. For Derrida, "every repetition is an alteration (iteration)" that imperfectly reproduces the original event but is recognizable as an imitation.[71] This creates a phenomenon of a typology that relies upon the resemblances among the iterations, each of which imitates imperfectly. It is important to note that for Derrida, there is no necessary generative original event, because there is nothing that connects the iteration to a so-called 'original.' The so-called 'original' event is only an aftereffect that is created by the typology derived from multiple iterations. Each iteration can always be lifted from its context and so exist as an independent citation. Derrida writes, "in order to function, that is, to be readable, a signature must have a repeatable, iterable, imitable form; it must be able to be detached from the present and singular intention of its production."[72] Culler elaborates on the example of the signature on a check or a promissory note. The signature, which is a recognizable imitation of the original, functions to validate the check even if the intention of the signator has changed since he signed the check.[73] In this sense, the successive iterations must be separable from the "*vouloir-dire*" or the authorial intent at

---

70 Derrida, "Signature Event Context," 20–21.
71 Gayatri Chakravorty Spival, "Revolutions That as Yet Have No Mode: Derrida's Limited Inc." *Diacritics* 10 (1980): 29–49, here 37. Spival goes on to say the following: "But repetition is the basis of identification. Thus, if repetition alters, it has to be faced that alteration identifies and identity is always impure. Thus iterability—like the trace structure—is the *positive* condition of possibility of identification, the very thing whose absolute rigor it renders impossible. It is in terms of iterable (rather than repeatable) identities that communication and consensus are established."
72 Derrida, "Signature Event Context," 20.
73 Culler, "Convention and Meaning," 26. Culler also offers the example of a signature stamp or any machine that replicates a signature. In such a case, the signator may not even be aware that his signature was created and thus may have never had an intention of paying (26–27).

the time of a text's production. Citationality is a crucial feature of every text. Derrida writes:

> And this is the possibility on which I want to insist: the possibility of dis-engagement and citational graft which belongs to the structure of every mark, spoken or written, and which constitutes every mark in writing be-fore and outside of every horizon of semio-linguistic communication; in writing, which is to say in the possibility of its functioning being cut off, at a certain point, from its "original" desire-to-say-what-one-means (*vou-loir-dire*) and from its participation in a saturable and constraining context. Every sign, linguistic or nonlinguistic, spoken or written (in the current sense of this opposition), in a small or large unit, can be *cited*, put between quotation marks; in so doing it can break with every given context, engen-dering an infinity of new contexts in a manner which is absolutely illimit-able. This does not imply that the mark is valid outside of a context, but on the contrary that there are only contexts without any center or absolute an-choring [*ancrage*]. This citationality, this duplication or duplicity, this iter-ability of the mark is neither an accident nor an anomaly, it is that (normal/abnormal) without which a mark could not even have a function called "normal." What would a mark be that could not be cited? Or one whose origins would not get lost along the way?[74]

For Derrida, these successive iterations are recognizable imitations of the original even though they are always broken from the event that orig-inates them. By virtue of their citationality, that is, their ability to be lifted out of context, the meaning of these successive iterations cannot be determined by the intention of the so-called 'original' event.

This review of Derrida's theory of language is worthwhile given his long-lasting influence upon modern performance theory and ritual stud-ies. His theoretical framework is mediated to these other fields through the work of Judith Butler, who applied his thinking to embodiment and gender. Thus understanding the post-structuralist framework of per-formance theory can be helpful for thinking about a model of perform-ative reading in the case of the Qumran hodayot. There are two points that emerge from Derrida's "Signature Event Context" that are of inter-est to performance theory and ritual studies. The first is Derrida's point that the so-called 'original' event is *not* what generates the iterations, but rather that this event is an illusory aftereffect of the iterations. The suc-cessive iterations of an originating event succeed in creating the effect of an 'original.'[75] Multiple and successive iterations can succeed in creating

---

74 Derrida, "Signature Event Context," 12.

75 The "original event," here discussed as the originating utterance (either spoken or written), is never recoverable because a text's citationality severs any tie to an

an "effect of norming," which suggests that the original event (a construct) is itself a normative measure. Judith Butler describes this norming of the "original event" as a "phantasmatic idealization of itself . . . that produce(s) effects that posture as grounds . . . the normative measure of the real."[76]

The second important point is Derrida's idea of supplementarity, that successive reiterations of this hypothetical 'original' will never be perfect imitations for each is always different from another in some way. The difference that arises among iterations of the original event is called 'supplementarity,' a reference to what is added to or what supplants the original.[77] Because of this, the so-called 'original' event can be neither determinative nor normative. Each iteration exists independently and is not determined in advance by the illusory 'original' event. Ultimately the generation of successive iterations creates the *illusory* effect of a normed 'original' event. Even so, this illusory effect is in no way a determined effect; it can only be understood as one of many possible effects.[78]

Derrida's theoretical discussion in "Signature Event Context" offers insights into how a strictly historical–literary understanding of the Qumran hodayot, prayer texts that reiterate the religious experiences of ascent and communion with angels, does not adequately account for elements that likely arose naturally during conditions of reiterative ritual performances. The variety of hodayot manuscripts suggest that they were performed and reenacted. These multiple iterations succeed in cre-

---

original *"vouloir-dire"* or authorial intention. According to Derrida, there is neither a necessary relationship between a text and the "original" utterance that produced it, nor a pure iteration of it.

76   Judith Butler describes the 'norming' of the 'original event' in her essay "Imitation and Gender Insubordination," in *Inside/Out: Lesbian Theories, Gay Theories* (ed. Diana Fuss; New York: Routledge, 1991), 13–31, here 21. Parts of this essay were delivered at a conference on homosexuality at Yale University in October 1989; repr. as 307–320 in *The Lesbian and Gay Studies Reader* (ed. Henry Abelove, Michèle Aina Barale, David M. Halperin; New York: Routledge, 1993). All citations to this essay are taken from the 1991 printing.

77   Culler, "Convention and Meaning," 20.

78   Butler would say that the illusory norm of 'heterosexuality' is only one effect of the typology of forms of iteration. In this case, the effect of normative heterosexuality is not determinative, allowing for the possibility of other ways of norming and construction. Butler writes, "gender is … an imitation that regularly produces the ideal it attempts to approximate;" Butler, "Imitation and Gender Insubordination," 28.

ating an illusion that there was an originating and generative experience of ascent and communion with angels. In the case of the TH, scholars have presumed that the similarities in literary style and experiences found in columns X to XVII are evidence for an actual historical person who generated them all. While a critique of the popular understanding of the TH known as the Teacher Hymns Hypothesis will be presented in chapter two, it is sufficient to state here that this understanding would not be tenable according to Derrida's theory of language which denies that an 'original' event is necessarily the generative cause for subsequent iterations.

Derrida's theory of supplementarity can also be helpful for understanding the diversity of literary forms of the hodayot manuscripts, which vary not only in the order and arrangement of units, as in the case of 4Q427 which shows a different order of CH, but also in the literary form of specific compositions as well. In a famous example of the latter, the text popularly known as SGH has been found in two different forms. This is a remarkable composition that describes a human ascent into the heavens and elevation above angelic beings. The composition is known from at least four manuscripts that are usually sorted into two distinct recensions: Recension A (4Q427 7; 1QH XXV, 34–XXVII, 3; 4Q471b + 4Q431 I) and Recension B (4Q491 11 I).[79] The majority of the studies on this text from Qumran have sought to sort out the relationship between these two recensions. The exception is the study by Florentino García Martínez, who argues strongly that the recensions should be understood independently from each other.[80] García Martínez expresses grave reservations about the relationship between the two recensions, reasoning that they cannot be "genetically related compositions. Neither can be explained by the other. Nor can either be explained by an assumed common ancestor."[81] The scholarly concern about the SGH's failure to converge into a single 'normative'

---

79 See E. Eshel, "4Q471b: A Self-Glorification Hymn," 189–91; eadem, DJD 29.421–35, at 422. Other important studies on the different recensions include M. O. Wise, "מי כמוני באלים," 173–219; Seth Sanders, "Writing, Ritual, and Apocalypse," 273–81; E. Schuller, "A Hymn from a Cave Four *Hodayot* Manuscript: 4Q427 7 i + ii," 605–28; Devorah Dimant, "A Synoptic Comparison," 157–61; John J. Collins and Devorah Dimant, "A Thrice-Told Hymn," 151–55.

80 García Martínez, "Old Texts and Modern Mirages," 105–25, esp. 111–12, 115.

81 Ibid., 115.

text is problematic because it presumes that textual pluriformity would not have been tolerated within a literary tradition. However, for a text that is performed, variation is expected, as Philip Alexander rightly notes:

> The fact that an alternative version of the Self-Glorification Hymn is found in 4Q471b, 4Q427 7 i-9 and 1QH[a] XXVI is significant. None of the other Hodayot manifest such a degree of textual variation. This suggests that the hymn was in active use within the community, and that someone felt he had the authority and the experience to vary it.[82]

Another example of literary divergence in the hodayot is the curiously named 'hodayot-like' texts which have been excluded from all major studies of the hodayot. These 'hodayot-like' texts (4Q433, 4Q433a, 4Q440) are three manuscripts that share many, but not all, literary features found in the hodayot.[83] Both the examples of SGH and the 'hodayot-like' texts demonstrate problematic ways of categorizing because they presume that there is a clear and recognizable 'original' that can be said to be normative. Such expectations that prioritize textual convergence reflect a modern printing-press context where perfect imitations can be produced rather than an ancient scribal context. The proliferation of copies of the hodayot in all of their different forms succeeds in 'norming' a single conceptualization of the hodayot. In other words, imitative writings succeed in idealizing the very event of religious experience that they seek to copy. For Derrida, the 'original' event of successive iterations is constructed from the typology of itera-

---

82 P. Alexander, *The Mystical Texts*, 89; Alexander goes on to write that mystical texts are "ergative: *they are meant to be performed*, a performance calculated precisely to assist the worshipper in appropriating and *interiorizing* the text. Even if their descriptive content originated in pure exegesis, the performance of that description completely changes the situation; it has the potential to transmute description into experience," (96, italics original).

83 Eileen Schuller, "The Classification Hodayot and Hodayot-Like (With Particular Attention to 4Q433, 4Q433 A and 4Q440)," *Sapiential, Liturgical and Poetical Texts from Qumran. Proceedings of the Third Meeting of the International Organization for Qumran Studies Oslo 1998. Published in Memory of Maurice Baillet* (ed. Daniel K. Falk, Florentino García Martínez, and Eileen M. Schuller; STDJ 35; Leiden: Brill, 2000), 182–93. Of these three 'hodayot-like' manuscripts, Schuller argues that 4Q440 (late-Hasmonean/early Herodian manuscript) is the closest to the usual hodayot collection (186–88), while 4Q433a is most dissimilar (188–190). See also the discussion in John Strugnell and Eileen Schuller, "Further *Hodayot* Manuscripts from Qumran?" 51–72, with plates.

tions. It brings with it associations of authority and normativity, but these are illusory.

Derrida's theoretical understanding of language acknowledges that there is a phenomenal experience of the multiple iterations that projects a typology, which in turn creates an expectation of a 'norming' and an 'original' event. I propose that the multiple events described in the various hodayot compositions succeed in creating the illusory effect of an 'original' visionary event. The alleged 'original' event is indistinguishable from other iterations of it and is generated by the iterations. Here I think that Corbin's understanding of the imaginal can be understood as functioning in a similar way to Derrida's notion of a constructed illusory 'original' event. Corbin uses the term imaginal to describe the phenomenal experience of the Temple (*Imago Templi*), which is not based on an actual empirical model of either the first or the second Temple, but rather on one that is constructed as an effect from multiple visionary reports such as Ezekiel's visions of the heavenly Temple.[84] Such an understanding has important implications for Qumran scholars who presume that an empirical reality of either the first or second Temple is the source that generated religious meditation and contemplation of it.[85] Corbin describes his own understanding of the word imaginal in the following way:

> It is the world situated midway between the world of purely intelligible realities and the world of sense perception; the world that I have called the imaginal world (*ālam al-mithāl, mundus imaginalis*) in order to avoid any confusion with what is commonly designated *imaginary*. . . . (It is the) meeting-place of the two seas... the place where the world of pure Ideas in the intelligible substantiality meets with the world of the objects of sense perception. It is the world where everything that appeared inanimate in the world of sense perception comes alive. . . . In short, it is at "the meeting-place of the two seas" that the *Imago Templi* reveals itself to the

---

84 Corbin, *Temple and Contemplation*, 263–390.

85 Most recently, Joseph Angel has used Corbin's conceptualization of imaginal to speak of the Temple at Qumran (*imago Templi*), offering important correctives to scholarly assumptions concerning the many references to the Temple at Qumran by critiquing Qumran scholars for presuming sociological assumptions that the empirical institution of the Temple had priority over any religious meditations upon it; as Angel asserts, quite the opposite is the case at Qumran; Angel, *Otherworldly and Eschatological Priesthood*, 83–106, here 101. In his recent monograph, Angel does well to criticize the scholarly tendency toward "reductionism and the projection of flat, one-dimensional historical assumptions onto the image of the temple in Qumran thought" (101).

visionary. . . [T]he case of the *Imago Templi* at "the meeting-place of the two seas" implies a situation which is above all speculative, in the etymological sense of the word: two mirrors (*specula*) facing each other and reflecting, one within the other, the Image that they hold. The *Imago* does not derive from empirical sources. It precedes and dominates such sources, and is thus the criterion by which they are verified and their meaning is put to the test.[86]

Corbin's point that the *Imago Templi* is not based on an actual 'original' empirical model finds agreement with Derrida's theoretical understanding in "Signature Event Context." However, Corbin's claim that the *Imago Templi* existed prior to the empirical iterations of it and that "it is the criterion by which they are verified and their meaning is put to the test" is a problematic assertion. Corbin seems to understand the imaginal to be a normative measure, a claim that Derrida would challenge, and that I also do not hold. Therefore, I wish to specify that the word imaginal is used only as a way of referencing phenomenal and spiritually sensible otherworldly experiences. The term 'imaginal body' as it is used in this study has in mind Corbin's understanding of phenomenal sensory experiences, but it does not participate in Corbin's claims of normativity and generation. Instead I wish to propose that the 'imaginal body' is a construct that is an aftereffect produced by multiple literary iterations that incorporate elements from different visionaries and seers. The reports of religious experience found in the hodayot are distinct instances of reiterating visionary traditions that claim ascent into the heavens and other phenomenal experiences, which experience I will call the 'imaginal visionary.'

Both Derrida's theory of iterations and their desire to recreate events and Corbin's understanding of the imaginal as a way of referring to phenomenal events that are constructed can be profitably used to formulate a model of performative reading that is generative and variable without being determined in advance. Texts like the Qumran hodayot, that are found in multiple and divergent literary forms suggest that there was a desire among the ancient users of these texts to reiterate the events that they describe. In the case of the SGH, each so-called 'recension' should be understood as an independent iteration which succeeded in recreating a religious experience without perfectly copying it. The reading and rereading of these texts led to the further generation of new forms of texts (Derrida's *supplementarity*). While this study will engage

---

86   Ibid., 265, 266, 267.

the specific order and arrangement of the hodayot recovered from 1QH and the reconstructed Cave 4 manuscript known as 4Q428, the other significant order and arrangement of the hodayot known as 4Q427 is evidence that the community sought to recreate the key religious experiences that the hodayot describe (i. e., ascent and communion with angels) without a concern to replicate the specific literary text. In other words, from a literary perspective, the texts of 1QH and 4Q428 are not presumed to be the normative models of the hodayot; rather, they are instantiations that will be the subject of our study.

B. Performance Theory and Ritual Studies

Judith Butler brought post-structuralist thought into performance theory by applying Derrida's understandings of language to embodied experiences of gender and subjectivity. In the works for which she is best known, Butler theorizes that the successive and multiple gendered performances of sexuality neither guarantee the existence of a norming original, nor a generative exemplar of gendered subjectivity. In one of her early essays on this topic, Butler describes the relationship between the successive iterations (performances) and the idea of an originating event, what she refers to as the 'original.'[87] She appropriates Derrida's

---

87 Butler writes: "There is no 'proper' gender, a gender proper to one sex rather than another, which is in some sense that sex's cultural property. Where that notion of the 'proper' operates, it is always and only *improperly* installed as the effect of a compulsory system. Drag constitutes the mundane way in which genders are appropriated, theatricalized, worn, and done; it implies that all gendering is a kind of impersonation and approximation. If this is true, it seems, there is no original or primary gender that drag imitates, but *gender is a kind of imitation for which there is no original*; in fact, it is a kind of imitation that produces the very notion of the original as an *effect* and consequence of the imitation itself. In other words, the naturalistic effects of heterosexualized genders are produced through imitative strategies; what they imitate is a phantasmatic ideal of heterosexual identity, one that is produced by the imitation as its effect. In this sense, the 'reality' of heterosexual identities is performatively constituted through an imitation that sets itself up as the origin and the ground of all imitations. In other words, heterosexuality is always in the process of imitating and approximating its own phantasmatic idealization of itself—*and failing.*..... Indeed, in its efforts to naturalize itself as the original, heterosexuality must be understood as a compulsive and compulsory repetition that can only produce the *effect* of its own originality; in other words, compulsory heterosexual identities, those ontologically consolidated phantasms of 'man' and 'woman,' are

concepts of iteration and the idea of an illusory norming effect from his theory of language and applies it to successive phenomenal iterations. Butler herself uses the language of "imitations" or repetitions for these iterations. Like Derrida, Butler concludes that these iterations point to the effect of an illusory "original" performance of gender, which only *appears* to be the "ground" or "the normative measure of the real."

Butler's notion of the embodied subject is one that is generated and not the source of iterations. It is through her theoretical work that Derrida's theory of language comes to exert an influence over performance studies and ritual studies. The theoretical turn to performance theory that has taken place in ritual studies has been described well by Stanley J. Tambiah, Catherine Bell, and Gavin Brown.[88] While ritual studies continues to be an interdisciplinary and continually moving area, a clear shift away from the traditional foci of myth and religion toward social scientific approaches, including performance studies, has succeeded in underscoring the generative power and dynamism that ritual experiences have within human societies. As such, the performance aspect of ritual highlights three significant features of ritual experience that are influenced by post-structuralist theory and are instructive for this study of embodied reading of the hodayot: the generative power of successive ritual performances, the concept of embodied subjectivity, and the radical indeterminacy and unpredictability of meaning. All of these points are significant for thinking about how religious experiences were experienced by people in antiquity through the activity of performative reading.

1. Generative aspects of Ritual Performance

In her work *Bodies that Matter*, Butler describes reiterative performative experiences as a generative process that produces subjectivity.

---

theatrically produced effects that posture as grounds, origins, the normative measure of the real." Judith Butler, "Imitation and Gender Insubordination," 21, (italics original).

88 Stanley J. Tambiah, "A Performative Approach to Ritual," *Proceedings of the British Academy* 65 (1979): 113–69; Catherine Bell, *Ritual Theory, Ritual Practice* (New York: Oxford University Press, 1992), 37–46; repr. in *The Performance Studies Reader* (ed. Henry Bial; 2d ed; New York: Routledge, 2007), 98–106; eadem, *Ritual*, 72–83; Gavin Brown, "Theorizing Ritual as Performance: Explorations of Ritual Indeterminacy," *Journal of Ritual Studies* 17 (2003): 3–18.

[P]erformativity cannot be understood outside of a process of iterability; a regularized and constrained repetition of norms. And this repetition is not performed by a subject; this repetition is what enables a subject and constitutes the temporal conditions for the subject. This iterability implies that 'performance' is not a singular 'act' or event, but a ritualized production, a ritual reiterated under and through constraint, under and through force of prohibition and taboo, with the threat of ostracism and even death controlling and compelling the shape of the production, but not, I will insist, determining it fully in advance.[89]

For Butler performativity is a citational process whose production of subjectivity is a ritualized one.[90] Post-structuralist theoretical insights into the bodily creation of subjectivity have been contextualized within ritual studies in what Catherine Bell refers to as the process of ritualization, a term that underscores the dynamic process of meaning-making in ritual experiences and in the production of culture.[91] Her understanding of ritualized actions is analogous to individual iterations, which for Jacques Derrida have priority over any presumed meaning intended by a hypothetical 'origin.' As a citational process, the iterative performances can be said to produce meaning and subjectivity within contexts of ritualization.

Ritualization is always contextually specific. It is instrumental in the maintaining of complex structures of power and meaning and undergoes change over time. Meaning arises from the repetition of controlled actions within a ritualized context. Bell insists that ritualization can only be understood contextually; it is specific to communities and cannot be abstracted.[92] Yet, Amy Hollywood points out an important tension between Bell's ritualization theory and Derrida's theory of language. She explains:

> Methodologically, Bell stresses the importance of the total context to understanding what counts as a ritual within a particular community, whereas Derrida emphasizes our inability to ever fully delimit the context and there-

---

89 Judith Butler, *Bodies that Matter: On the Discursive Limits of "Sex"* (New York: Routledge, 1993), 95.

90 Amy Hollywood identifies some internal tensions in Butler's use of Derrida and Austin, and also some refinements to Butler's conceptualization of performativity in "Performativity, Citationality, Ritualization," in *Bodily Citations: Religion and Judith Butler* (ed. Ellen T. Armour, Susan M. St. Ville; New York: Columbia University, 2006), 252–75.

91 Bell, "Ritualization of Texts and Textualization of Ritual in the Codification of Taoist Liturgy," *History of Religions* 27 (1988) 366–92.

92 Bell, *Ritual Theory, Ritual Practice*, 220–221.

by to fix the meanings or ritualized nature of any activity. (This may give rise to the very un-Derridian tendency, in Bell's work, to separate the performers of an action from the action and its effects. In my Derridean account the two are inseparable, for actions themselves constitute performers.) Through repetition, the movement whereby actions or marks are repeated in another time and place, subjectivities and relations between them are generated. The openness of Bell's understanding of ritualization might usefully be augmented by a crucial insight from Derrida, for repetition (at some level) is the one constraint on ritualization—the one bit of formalization that is constitutive of the process of ritualization itself. This also suggests the aspect of ritualization that establishes continuity between bodily practices and more fully ritualized activities, for both depend on iteration and hence generate meanings and constitute realities. The meaning is the constituted reality, thereby rendering ritual actions more like illocutions (in which the doing or saying, in the right conditions, is the performance) than like perlocutions (in which the proper outcome must follow from the saying or doing for it to be counted a performative). The habitus, in the sense used by Bourdieu and Butler, is made up of bodily practices and rituals (and the distinction between the two is itself a fluid one).[93]

Hollywood's critique is that Bell's understanding of ritualization can be said to over determine the process. In general, the idea of habitus as it appears in the thinking of Pierre Bourdieu, and subsequently in Butler, refers to a generative dynamic structure of transferrable and constraining set of cultural norms and expectations.[94]

The theoretical model that subjectivity is generated by iterable performativity is useful for considering ancient prayer texts like the Qumran hodayot. Religious texts used for liturgical purposes were read and reread and so appear over a period of time in diverse and divergent textual and literary traditions.[95] In the case of revelatory writing, Ehud Ben Zvi states:

---

93 Hollywood, "Performativity, Citationality, Ritualization," 268.

94 Pierre Bourdieu, *Outline of a Theory of Practice* (trans. Richard Nice; New York: Cambridge University Press, 1977), 72–95. He states that "The habitus is the product of the work of inculcation and appropriation necessary in order for those products of collective history, the objective structures (e. g. of language, economy, etc.) to succeed in reproducing themselves more or less completely, in the form of durable dispositions, in the organisms (which one can, if one wishes, call individuals) lastingly subjected to the same conditionings, and hence placed in the same material conditions of existence" (85).

95 Esther G. Chazon has proposed this feature of appearing in a variety of manuscripts over a period of time to be characteristic of liturgical texts. The text known as *4QDibHam* which appears in early and late Hasmonean texts and also Herodian can be argued to be liturgical and not literary; see Chazon,

I cannot overemphasize that prophetic books were meant to be read, re-read, meditated upon, again and again, to be read (and reread) to others who cannot read by themselves, and certainly not to be read once and then discarded. There are important implications to this seemingly simple observation. Books meant to be reread tend to show numerous instances of potential ambiguity, and lasting equivocality or polysemy at different levels. These features allow multiplicity of readings informing one another, and all together contributing to the rich tapestry of the text. These features are widely attested in the prophetic literature.[96]

The meditative reading and rereading of these texts is a bodily practice that is generative of exegetical insights in the form of new compositions that seek to re-create the experiences that the texts describe. As we will see in chapter four, in the case of the hodayah known as 1QH XI, 6–19, the ambiguity of the language can be said to have led to the exegetical generation of the new text, 1QH XIII, 22-XV, 8.

The consistent presence of the literary theme of ascent and communion with heavenly beings in the TH and second group of CH indicates that spatial and phenomenal otherworldly experiences were special concerns that received extended reflection and reiteration by the Qumran community. Visionary reports known from early Jewish literature are detailed accounts of embodied experiences that invite imitation and re-enactment. These details may include vivid descriptions of specific behaviors that the seer performed to prepare for the vision and, as I will argue in chapter two, reenactments of the specific emotions that the seer experienced. As a process, ritualization generates subjectivities and meaning. Chapter four will describe how the ritual performance of the hodayot has the capacity to generate further religious experiences and texts as a result.

"*4QDibHam*: Liturgy or Literature?" *RevQ* 15 (1992): 447–55; eadem, "On the Special Character of Sabbath Prayer: New Data from Qumran," *Journal of Jewish Music and Liturgy* 15 (1992–93): 1–21.

96 Ehud Ben Zvi, "The Prophetic Book: A Key Form of Prophetic Literature," *The Changing Face of Form Criticism for the Twenty-First Century* (ed. Marvin A. Sweeney and Ehud Ben Zvi; Grand Rapids, Mich.: Eerdmans, 2003), 276–97, here 280 n. 16; polysemy in prophetic texts is also discussed in idem, "Introduction: Writings, Speeches, and the Prophetic Books—Setting an Agenda," in *Writings and Speech in Israelite and Ancient Near Eastern Prophecy* (ed. Ehud Ben Zvi and Michael H. Floyd; SBLSS 10; Atlanta: Scholars, 2000), 1–29, here 18–19.

2. Embodied Subjectivity

The influence of post-structuralist thinking on ritual studies can be seen in the theoretical understanding that embodied practices in the form of ongoing ritualized physical practices play an instrumental role in the creation of subjectivity. Subjectivity is the aftereffect that results from successive practices: "[i]t is through bodily practices that subjectivities are formed, virtues inculcated and beliefs embodied."[97] While theoretical studies relating to performance and theatre have offered important insights into how subjectivity is created by embodied practices, how subjectivity is itself understood as agency differs among theorists.

Butler writes that "a phenomenological theory of constitution requires an expansion of the conventional view of acts to mean both that which constitutes meaning and that through which meaning is performed or enacted. In other words, the acts by which gender is constituted bear similarities to performative acts within theatrical contexts."[98] Butler is most famous for applying this theoretical framework to gender. The body is not born into a gendered state, but rather takes on a gendered subjectivity through the repeated bodily performance of gender over time.[99] Because gendered subjectivity needs to be constantly reiterated and performed, there is a sense that there is a "constitutive instability" in gendered identity.[100] The embodied subject is deeply formed by cultural norms, but not enslaved to them. Butler's understanding of performativity as a bodily experience has been described as being influenced by Michel Foucault's conceptualization of subjectivity as an emergent agency, although she improves upon it in a number of

---

97 Amy Hollywood, "Towards a Feminist Philosophy of Ritual and Bodily Practice," in *Difference in Philosophy of Religion* (ed. Philip Goodchild; Aldershot, England: Ashgate, 2003), 73–83, here 74. Here, Hollywood challenges the conventional prioritization of belief over practice in the theoretical fields of philosophy of religion by arguing that meaning is generated not by the articulation of belief statements but by the *ongoing* bodily performance of ritual actions (76).

98 Judith Butler, "Performative Acts and Gender Constitution: An Essay in Phenomenology and Feminist Theory," *The Performance Studies Reader, 2ⁿᵈ ed.* (ed. Henry Bial; New York: Routledge, 2004), 187–99, here 188.

99 Judith Butler, "Imitation and Gender Insubordination," 13–31.

100 Lois McNay, "Gender, Habitus and the Field: Pierre Bourdieu and the Limits of Reflexivity," *Theory, Culture & Society* (1999): 95–117, here 98. McNay writes, "It is this instability that can be prised open to create a space for the construction of marginal or 'abject' sexualities" (98).

ways.[101] Foucault's understanding of subjectivity as emerging from a basically docile body does not adequately explain the process of agency because the subject can be understood to be overdetermined by external forces that seek to discipline it. Instead, Butler uses Pierre Bourdieu's theoretical understanding of the embodied subject and habitus, a way of referring to a set of bodily dispositions that are shaped by an extended process of inculcation.[102] Bourdieu avoids Foucault's problematic understanding of the embodied subject as docile with the habitus theory which he appropriates from classical philosophy. The habitus is a set of bodily dispositions can point toward a particular action, thus giving the appearance of perpetuating behaviors without actually determining them. Because the habitus is dynamic and situational, allowing for the possibility of innovation, Bourdieu's conceptualization of subjectivity provides for a freedom and agency that Foucault's does not.

In the hopes of conceptualizing a model that fits the ancient context of the Qumran reader, I wish to draw attention to the important ways that post-structuralist understandings of the embodied subject and theories of performativity have been critiqued as well. Butler's performative model of the embodied subject is extremely useful insofar as it understands subjectivity to be the consequence of ongoing repeated bodily practices. At the same time, it is problematic because her model of subjectivity can be said to determine in advance scenarios that are oppositional.[103] Saba Mahmood has critiqued Butler's theoretical model of performativity as being steeped in a Western post-enlightenment and post-industrial understanding of the subject.[104] Mahmood's study of modern

---

101 Michel Foucault, *Discipline and Punish: The Birth of the Prison* (Harmondsworth: Peregrine, 1977).

102 Bourdieu, *Outline of a Theory of Practice,* 78–82; also idem, *Language & Symbolic Power* (Cambridge: Harvard University, 1994), 12.

103 Foucault theorized that all power entails forms of resistance, but notice that Butler herself denies Mahmood's charge that she has in mind a subjectivity of resistance; Butler, "Afterword," in *Bodily Citations,* 285.

104 Saba Mahmood, "Feminist Theory, Embodiment, and the Docile Agent: Some Reflections on the Egyptian Islamic Revival," *Cultural Anthropology* 16 (2001): 202–36; eadem, *Politics of Piety: The Islamic Revival and the Feminist Subject* (Princeton: Princeton University Press, 2005); eadem, "Agency, Performativity, and The Feminist Subject," in *Bodily Citations: Religion and Judith Butler,* 177–221. The anthropologist Talal Asad has also critiqued the idea of ritual as a Western cultural construct that may not be useful for examining non-Western religions and societies like Islam. See Talal Asad, *Genealogies of Religion: Dis-*

Muslim women has highlighted this oversimplification of post-structuralist models of agency—what she calls the feminist subject—and their inappropriate application to non-Western societies. Since Qumran is an ancient non-Western community, her critique is an important one to bear in mind. Like Butler, Mahmood also uses habitus theory as she constructs an analytical framework for the exterior bodily practices that become a means for interiority, but chooses to retrieve Aristotle's formulation of habitus rather than Bourdieu's, because the latter is too steeped in a post-industrial context that tends to take a largely pessimistic view of the culture to which the subjectivity is conformed. Mahmood explains:

> Apart from the socioeconomic determinism that characterizes Bourdieu's discussion of bodily dispositions, what I find problematic in this approach is its lack of attention to the pedagogical process by which a habitus is learned. In the ethnographic account I have presented of the mosque movement, the body was thematized by the mosque participants as a site of moral training and cultivation; the intentional nature of this cultivation problematizes the narrow model of unconscious imbibing that Bourdieu assumes in his discussion of habitus. Consistent with the Aristotelian conception of habitus, conscious training in the habituation of virtues itself was undertaken, paradoxically, with the goal of making consciousness redundant to the practice of these virtues. This was evident in Mona's advice to the young woman when she said that one should become so accustomed to the act of praying five times a day that when one does not pray one feels just as uncomfortable as when one forgets to eat: at this stage, the act of prayer has attained the status of an almost physiological need that is fulfilled without conscious reflection. Yet it would be a mistake to say that mosque participants believe that once a virtue has taken root in one's disposition, it issues forth perfunctorily and automatically. Since the point is not simply that one acts virtuously but also how one enacts a virtue (with what intent, emotion, commitment, and so forth), constant vigilance and monitoring of one's practices is a critical element in this tradition of ethical formation. This economy of self-discipline therefore draws attention to the role self-directed action plays in the learning of an embodied disposition and its relationship to 'unconscious' ways of being.[105]

Mahmood describes various techniques or bodily practices that can be used as means of bringing a certain type of subjectivity into being. She analyzes the embodied ritual practice of veiling as an exterior means for cultivating the interior disposition of shyness and the exterior

---

cipline and Reasons of Power in Christianity and Islam (Baltimore: Johns Hopkins Press, 1993), 56–57; also Bell, *Ritual*, 259–65.

105 Mahmood, *Politics of Piety*, 136–139, here 138–39.

bodily experience of fear as a way of cultivating the interior disposition of piety.[106] In both of these instances religious practices generate an emergent subject who then cultivates a predisposition for certain behaviors, but is never determined in advance to be modest nor pious.

Here I wish to observe that Mahmood's illustration of the emergence of the embodied subjectivity as a pedagogical process performed by ritual practices is useful for imagining how ancient Israel and early Judaism understood the body's relationship to the mind.[107] There was no mind-body dualism recognized in antiquity in the ways that later Cartesian dualism conceptualized. According to Steven Weitzman, pedagogical practices in the form of disciplining the body's parts and regimenting its sensory functions sought to cultivate an emergent embodied subjectivity that was the necessary precondition for either living under the covenant law, or being wise.[108] Such practices predisposed but did not predetermine one to be faithful to the law as can be seen Israel's ability to forget the law in the Deuteronomic history.

Mahmood's point is significant and similar to Hollywood's critique of Bell's understanding of ritualization that was discussed earlier. Both scholars are careful to avoid a situation wherein the effect is predetermined by a specific context. Significantly for our discussion of the Qumran hodayot, the created subjectivity *does not need* to be conceptualized in advance as oppositional or in resistance to something else. Mahmood specifies her critique of Butler in Butler's reliance on post-

---

106 Mahmood discusses veiling in *Politics of Piety*, 156–161, see too eadem, "Feminist Theory, Embodiment, and the Docile Agent," 212–17.

107 Certainly what is said here about the body and sensory function also applies to certain but not all forms of Christianity as well.

108 The disciplining of the sensory functions is a topic that will be examined in more detail in chapter two and the work of Steven Weitzman, "Sensory Reform in Deuteronomy," in *Religion and the Self in Antiquity* (ed. David Brakke, Michael Satlow, and Steven Weitzman; Bloomington: Indiana University Press, 2005), 123–39; Greg Schmidt Goering, "Attentive Ears and Forward-Looking Eyes: Ritualization of the Senses in the Jewish Wisdom Tradition," Paper presented at the Joint session of Ritual and Religious Experience in Early Judaism and Early Christianity at the Society of Biblical Literature Annual Meeting (Atlanta: November 2010), 1–15; and idem, *Perceiving Wisdom: Disciplining the Senses and the Construction of the Self in the Jewish Wisdom Tradition*, a monograph in progress. I am grateful to Greg for sharing a copy of his work with me. I also wish to point to other studies that are in press but were not available for me to consult as I worked on this manuscript; Yael Avrahami, *In the Biblical Sense: Sensory Perception in the Hebrew Bible* (LHBOTS; London: Continuum/T&T Clark, forthcoming in 2011).

industrialist theory as favoring an oppositional understanding of subjectivity as agency. Given the longstanding scholarly view that the Qumran cult reflects a community that was somehow in reaction to the Jerusalem Temple cult, it can be tempting to presume that the subjectivity of the visionary is one that was directly generated by the specific historical context of the second temple period.[109] However, I do not find it *necessary* to insist that the subjectivity of the visionary be understood as an expression of agency generated from the sociological and political context of resistance against the Jerusalem Temple cult—to do so would be to determine in advance the effect that is created. In other words, the human who ascends into the heavens is not a subjectivity that is necessarily generated by the second temple context and not one that is restricted to its texts. The creation of subjectivity from the repeated bodily practices of meditative reading does not need to be one that is inherently oppositional.

---

109 The thesis that the Qumran community (communities) is a cultic group disenfranchised from the Jerusalem cult is a long-standing one that is based on specific texts, most notably the Damascus Document (CD 3:12; 4:15–5:12; and 6:11–7:6) and 1QpHab 8:9–13, and the controversial text known as 4QMMT. This text published in the 1980s exerted a special impact on how scholars theorized the origins of the Qumran group. The editors refer to this text as "a polemical halakhic letter" Elisha Qimron and John Strugnell, "An Unpublished Halakhic Letter from Qumran," in *Biblical Archaeology Today: Proceedings of the International Congress on Biblical Archaeology, Jerusalem, April 1984* (ed. J. Amitai; Jerusalem: Israel Exploration Society, 1985), 400–7, here 401; Qimron and Strugnell, *Qumran Cave 4, vol. V: Miqṣat Maʿaśe Ha-Torah* (DJD 10; Oxford: Clarendon, 1994). See the discussion in John J. Collins, "The Origin of the Qumran Community: A Review of the Evidence," in *To Touch the Text: Biblical and Related Studies in Honor of Joseph A. Fitzmyer, S.J.* (ed. Maurya P. Horgan and Paul J. Kobelski; New York: Crossroad, 1989), 159–78; James C. VanderKam, "Identity and History of the Community," in *The Dead Sea Scrolls after Fifty Years: A Comprehensive Assessment* (ed. Peter W. Flint and James VanderKam; 2 Vols.; Leiden: Brill, 1998–1999), 2.507–23; Philip R. Callaway, *The History of the Qumran Community: An Investigation* (JSPSup 3; Sheffield: Sheffield Academic Press, 1988), 11–27; Hanan Eshel, *The Dead Sea Scrolls and the Hasmonean State* (Grand Rapids: Eerdmans, 2008), 1–27; John J. Collins, *Beyond the Qumran Community: The Sectarian Movement of the Dead Sea Scrolls* (Grand Rapids: Eerdmans, 2010); and Alison Schofield, "Rereading S: A New Model of Textual Development in Light of the Cave 4 Serekh Copies," *DSD* 15 (2008): 96–120; and eadem, *From Qumran to the Yaḥad: A New Paradigm of Textual Development for the Community Rule* (STDJ 77; Leiden: Brill, 2009).

3. The Radical Indeterminacy of Ritual Experiences

The third insight of performance theory that is instructive for understanding the religious experience of the hodayot is the radical indeterminacy of performances and ritual experiences. This is grounded in
Derrida's assertion that each iteration is independent and not determined by the illusory effect of an 'original' event. Richard Schechner
refers to the indeterminacy of theatre performance in the following
way: "as embodied practices each and every performance is specific
and different from every other. The differences enact the conventions
and traditions of a genre, the personal choices made by the performers,
directors, and authors, various cultural patterns, historical circumstances,
and the particularities of reception."[110] Despite the care with which visionaries recorded their experiences and the evidence for the careful
techniques to follow, there were no guarantees that a religious experience, ascent or vision, would take place. In this sense, the ritual as performance is radically indeterminate because there is no certainty that
one will be granted an experience of the otherworld. Martha Himmelfarb describes it well when she writes, "the ascent to God's throne is not
for everyone, and even those chosen human beings who enter the realm
of the angels must fear that they are intruding."[111] The expectation is
that the visionary is privileged in his otherworldly experience, but
that he is not entitled to it.

The generation of visionary experiences from the practice of reading
was unpredictable and not guaranteed. However, when it occurred, I
propose that it was recorded as an iteration of the imaginal visionary experience when it was accompanied by observable bodily signs. The result of the ongoing generation of compositions from religious meditation is phenomenon that can result in what appears to the modern
eye as the inelegant piling up of visionary reports. In other words, in
those instances when an ancient reader was successful in recreating
the religious experience and generated a new text, I propose that it
was accompanied by the bodily display of the emotions associated
with the visionary experience. It may be that the actual observance of
bodily emotion, expressed as physical distress and anguish in the reader
during the ritualized performance of the texts, actually guaranteed the

---

110 Richard Schechner, *Performance Studies: An Introduction* (2d ed.; New York:
    Routledge, 2006), 36.
111 Himmelfarb, "From Prophecy to Apocalypse," 152.

religious experience. The physical expression of emotion can be a helpful way of understanding how anonymous texts like the hodayot were authenticated. Because the physical display of affect is something that most individuals cannot consciously muster, the successful bodily performance of emotions likely functioned to elevate or secure the social status of the individual within the community. Gary Ebersole discusses the importance of the physical display of performative emotions and states that it can carry a political currency within a ritualized context.[112] In the case of the hodayot, the bodily display of emotion can be understood as a costly display which, according to evolutionary anthropologists, carries significant political power in religious communities by demonstrating commitment and authenticating religiosity.[113] Such events are status-securing experiences. These costly displays not only result in political tensions by elevating the status of the one who performs them, they also create stronger group cohesion (entitivity) among those who observe them.

The radical indeterminacy of ritual experiences indicates that the religious experiences that are described in the hodayot are not guaranteed by the simple act of reading or recitation. Instead a reader's entrance into the flow of the text demands great training of the psyche and emotions and careful preparation. A religious experience is not one that can be predictably replicated, but when it happened I propose that it could have been confirmed through the ancient reader's bodily expression of emotion.

---

112 Gary L. Ebersole, "The Poetics and Politics of Ritualized Weeping in Early and Medieval Japan," *Holy Tears: Weeping in the Religious Imagination* (ed. Kimberley Christine Patton and John Stratton Hawley; Princeton: Princeton University Press, 2005), 25–51. Further discussion of the concept of 'performative emotions' is given in chapters two and four. Also Frederick M. Smith, *The Self Possessed: Deity and Spirit Possession in South Asian Literature and Civilization* (New York: Columbia University Press, 2006), 103–106.

113 Richard Sosis, "The Adaptive Value of Religious Ritual: Rituals Promote Group Cohesion by Requiring Members to Engage in Behavior that is too Costly to Fake," *American Scientist* 92 (2004): 166–72; Joseph Henrich and Francisco J. Gil-White, "The Evolution of Prestige Freely Conferred Deference as a Mechanism for Enhancing the Benefits of Cultural Transmission," *Evolution and Human Behavior* 22 (2001): 165–196. An ancient example of this type of costly display can be inferred from the controversy behind Paul's first letter to the Corinthians; it is clear that the public performance of charismatic gifts resulted in controversy and tension which in turn disrupted the social and political well-being of the community.

Contemporary studies on the role of emotions and the body as well as the techniques to train and discipline the emotions are of interest in light of the role that emotion and language about the body enjoys in the hodayot. The arousal of strong emotions, fear and terror, are especially prominent and could have assisted an ancient reader in generating the kind of subjectivity that is predisposed to religious experiences of transformation and ascent. Each performative reading of the hodayot is "specific and different from every other" because the ancient reader has the freedom to spontaneously associate his own affective memories of personal terror as he reads.[114] As the ancient reader sought to become one with the rhetorical 'I' of the text, he fashioned for himself the subjectivity of a visionary in order to experience what the text describes. References to the body and the arousal of emotions are prominent features of the hodayot that function to assist an ancient reader in becoming deeply united with the rhetorical 'I' of these texts. This process does not guarantee a predetermined outcome of repeated bodily practices; rather, such practices are a necessary precondition for the possibility of creating the kind of subjectivity that predisposes an individual to a religious experience.

Conclusion

Post-structuralist understandings of the embodied subject offer the important insight that subjectivity is embodied and a created effect of repetitive performative practices. Repeated meditative ritual reading participates in the creation of a particular kind of subjectivity—one that is predisposed to transformative religious experience. Ritual practices demands that the participant "conform to it."[115] The expectation is that an ancient reader performed these prayer texts with a goal of reenacting the religious experiences that they describe. The ancient reader can hope to create the subjectivity of an imaginal visionary and experience transformation in the form of illumination, ascent, and communion with angels. In this way, the performative reading of the hodayot can be said to be oriented toward the heavens. The ancient reader would have read the rhetorical 'I' of the Qumran hodayot as if he were the subject of

---

114 Schechner, *Performance Studies*, 36. How this happens is the subject of chapter four.

115 Roy Rappaport, *Ritual and Religion in the Making of Humanity* (Cambridge: Cambridge University Press, 1999), 118–26, here 18.

these experiences. Ritual texts contain imitable practices, and I propose that the strongly valanced emotional experiences described in these apocalyptic texts functioned as affective scripts for an ancient reader to imitate and reenact. These performative emotions assist in the creation of subjectivity which is the necessary precondition for the reader to embark on his own religious experience and this can possibly lead to the generation of new texts, a topic that will be examined in chapter four. How the language of embodiment creates an imitable script for the ancient reader to reenact and the role of emotion in this process is the subject of the next chapter.

Chapter 2
The Imaginal Body as an Affective Script for Transformation

Who is the "I" of the Qumran hodayot? The traditional scholarly view has sought to give a historical answer to this question and to understand these compositions as autobiographical. This chapter seeks to challenge these longstanding and popular assumptions about the Qumran hodayot and proposes that the first-person voice in these texts can be understood from the perspective of performance theory as an affective script for a reader to reenact.

Critical study of the genre of autobiography identifies it as a specific cultural form that reflects a *modern* fascination with interiority. Eugene Stelzig comments that "the sense of the individual self as a private possession is associated with the emergence in the later eighteenth century of a more subjective awareness of human experience."[1] He goes on to describe autobiography as a "distinctive romantic genre."[2] Romantic models of authorship understand a vivid and dramatic literary style as an avenue for the authentic expression of the interiority of the author himself.[3] In his classic study of the Romantic Tradition, Meyer Howard Abrams writes that authors of this period privileged metaphors of authorship that highlighted the eruptive force of the creative activity.[4] Abrams writes that the iconic poet of this period, Lord Byron, uses the metaphor of the volcano to represent the eruptive force of the creative power:

---

1 Eugene Stelzig, "The Romantic Subject in Autobiography," in *Nonfictional Romantic Prose: Expanding Borders* (ed. Steven P. Sondrup and Virgil Nemoianu, in collaboration with Gerald Gillespie; Philadelphia: John Benjamins, 2004), 223–41, here 224.
2 Ibid., 224.
3 See the classic work by Meyer Howard Abrams, *The Mirror and the Lamp: Romantic Theory and the Critical Tradition* (New York: Oxford University Press, 1953).
4 Abrams, *The Mirror and the Lamp*, 47–69.

Byron introduces a volcano as analogy; poetry 'is the lava of the imagination whose eruption prevents an earthquake.' And it is also Byron who offers the interesting parallel between poetic creation and childbirth, resulting in a poetic offspring at once separable from and blended with the spirit and feelings of the father-poet (or is it the mother-poet?).[5]

The wellspring of this creative expression is tied to the individual and original experience of the author's emotions. The image of childbirth that Byron uses presumes a visible family resemblance between the artist and the art that is produced. In the case of the hodayot, the expectation is that the creative and lively literary style of the TH reflects the interiority of a creative genius—none other than the Teacher of Righteousness. The prizing of literary originality that characterizes the nineteenth century understanding of authorship can be recognized in the evaluative statements of the hodayot by the first scrolls scholars.[6] Jacob Licht's initial assessment was that the hodayot "does not seem to possess any high degree of literary merit. It is also very repetitive, to the point of monotony."[7] This telling statement speaks volumes about the negative valence assigned by the early scrolls scholars to stereotypical language and style. Gert Jeremias nuances Licht's comments by distinguishing the TH section as possessing a "lebendigen Sprache," in contrast to the rest of the hodayot scroll which makes use of "erstarrte Wendungen und monotone Wiederholungen."[8] It was common for early scholars to negatively assess the compositional techniques employed by the authors of the Community Hymns. In doing so, they privileged anachronistic models of authorship by assuming that creative writing found in the TH was authored by an creative author.[9] Such expectations privilege Romantic notions of individuality and interiority. The lively literary style and vivid imagery recognized in the TH resulted in the higher esteem grant-

---

5   Abrams, *The Mirror and the Lamp*, 49.

6   See too the discussion of the influence of Romanticism upon Hermann Gunkel and Form Criticism's understanding of the "I" in the psalms in Susan E. Gillingham, *The Poems and Psalms of the Hebrew Bible* (Oxford: Oxford University Press, 1994), 174; and Amy C. Cottrill, *Language, Power, and Identity in the Lament Psalms of the Individual* (LHBOTS 493; London: T & T Clark, 2008), 12–14.

7   Jacob Licht, "The Doctrine of the Thanksgiving Scroll," *IEJ* 6 (1956): 1–13; 89–101, here 1.

8   Gert Jeremias, *Der Lehrer der Gerechtigkeit*, 171.

9   As studies have demonstrated, prayer literature from the second temple period relies upon stereotypical 'scriptural' language; see Newman, *Praying by the Book*; Chazon, "Scripture and Prayer in 'The Words of the Luminaries,'" 25–41.

ed to this sub-collection by scholars of the Heidelberg School. Jürgen Becker writes:

> Daß ein Teil der Lieder vom Lehrer der Gerechtigkeit stamen" warden, darf man darum mit gutem Recht annehmen, weil in einigen Psalmen die hinter dem Ich des Beters stehende Person so konkret, exzeptionell und pregnant in den Aussagen zutage tritt, daß man in ihr deutlich den Lehrer der Gerechtigkeit als den Gründer der Gemeinde erkennt. Das Hauptmerkmal ist dabei die Struktur des Ichs der Psalmen.[10]

The vivid aspects of the TH were understood by scholars of the Heidelberg School as direct markers of an author with a dynamic and strong personality.[11] According to this Romantic understanding of authorship, the art form resembles the author who created it, like a child resembles his or her parent. The scholarly presumption that the Qumran hodayot should be understood as autobiographical writings was a common assessment of the TH but it reflects an anachronistic understanding of authorship by the early scholars who examined these texts.

The scholarly judgments of the Heidelberg School demonstrate the rhetorical impact that the vivid language of embodiment and the impassioned reports in the TH exert upon the reader. Carol Newsom, commenting on how underutilized rhetorical criticism is on the Qumran texts, writes the following about the rhetorical features of the hodayot: "the tradition of prayer out of which the *Hodayot* developed is one that elaborately displays the speaker's subjectivity: his humiliation and triumphs, his hopes and fears, and even the sensations of his body. It is an extraordinarily personal and intimate rhetoric."[12] Indeed, the system-

---

10 Jürgen Becker, *Das Heil Gottes*, 51.

11 For a discussion of the far-reaching influence of Romanticism on German intellectual thought of the nineteenth and twentieth centuries, see Monika Schmitz-Emans, "Theories of Romanticism: The First Two Hundred Years," in *Nonfictional Romantic Prose: Expanding Borders* (ed. Steven P. Sondrup and Virgil Nemoianu, in collaboration with Gerald Gillespie; Philadelphia: John Benjamins, 2004), 13–36.

12 The passage continues: "Even though the *Hodayot* of the Teacher take up many issues of conflict and community disaffection, the rhetoric of the *Hodayot* shifts the focus from whatever the content of the conflict was about and instead places it on the suffering but courageous persona of the Teacher. Thus the hymns invite the listener (both God and the human audience) to feel compassion for and to accept the Teacher who presents himself within them;" See Carol A. Newsom, "Rhetorical Criticism and the Dead Sea Scrolls," in *Rediscovering the Dead Sea Scrolls: An Assessment of Old and New Approaches and Methods* (ed. Maxine L. Grossman; Grand Rapids: Eerdmans, 2010), 198–214, here

atic naming of body parts, reports of their brokenness, along with anguished accounts of physical and psychological distress and extraordinary
transformation that appear in the hodayot are rhetorical elements that
succeed in constructing a persona whose experiences of suffering are
so compelling as to be imagined as real. In this study, I propose understanding the strong "I" in the hodayot as a rhetorical persona, an illusory
effect produced by repeated used of vivid embodiment language. In the
process of performative reading, I propose that an ancient reader hoped
to actualize the "I" of the text and re-experience the physical and psychological tragedies that are described by reenacting the specific emotion of fear thereby hoping to participate in transformations that these
texts describe. The strong "I" in the text and the vivid embodiment language offered a compelling affective script for actualization. In her rhetorical study of body images in the biblical Psalter, Susanne Gillmayr-
Bucher writes that the first person voice and language about the body
assist the reader in the reenactment of the text as the psalmist's body becomes imagined as the reader's own body:

> All aspects of human life, its fear, desire and joy, as well as its most intimate
> thoughts and emotions are portrayed with the help of body language and
> body images. With this kind of description the readers can hardly maintain
> a distanced point of view; rather they are forced to add their own body ex-
> periences while they hear and read the text. In this way the readers are en-
> abled to overcome the distance and to re-enact the text.[13]

Gillmayr-Bucher writes that the body in the Psalms is not a real body:
"In the Psalms the language of the body is based on an experienced reality. Nevertheless, the depiction of the body presented is a fictitious
body."[14] The experiences of the psalmist are offered to the reader as a

---

211. As I have stated elsewhere, I am critical of the attribution of authorship to
the 'teacher,' that Newsom uses here. Newsom appears to express more confidence in the identification of the speaker as the "teacher" here than in her earlier study, *The Self as Symbolic Space* (curiously, she fails to use her own suggested language for the TH, the "hodayot of the leader"). Ultimately, Newsom de-
cides that the Teacher Hypothesis can be a plausible understanding of the "I" of
the hodayot, but that it cannot be definitely proven: "I do not think that a definitive case can be made either for the hypothesis that the Hodayot of the leader be associated with the Teacher of Righteousness or the hypothesis that they
be associated with an institutional role held by successive leaders," Newsom,
The Self as Symbolic Space, 299.

13 Susanne Gillmayr-Bucher, "Body Images in the Psalms," *JSOT* 28 (2004):
301–26, here 325.

14 Ibid., 305.

script for a reader to imitate. In the practice of performative reading, Amy Hollywood writes that the reader was expected to *"feel* what the psalmist felt, to learn to fear, desire, and love God in and through the words of the Psalms themselves."[15] Jennifer Koosed's recent study makes a similar point about the fictional speaker in the book of Qohelet, an anguished character whose tragic tales have long captivated modern imaginations.[16] The rhetorical persona of the hodayot hymnist, like that of the psalmist and of Qoheleth, is generated by the language of embodiment and the strong arousal of emotion in the reader.

The emotion of fear plays an instrumental role in creating the subjectivity for religious experience in the ancient reader of the hodayot. Terror guides the reader through a series of events that ultimately lead him on a journey into the heavens. Chapter three describes how the specific order and arrangement of hodayot in 1QH (4Q428) reflects a progressive spatialization which strategically arouses fear and desolation but moves toward the heavenly realm. The affective state of fear can create within the reader a preliminary state of consciousness that can prepare him for subsequent experiences of transformation. Vivid descriptions of frightening places and episodes are reported early in the TH collection, indicating that fear played an instrumental role in bringing about the psychic preparedness needed for establishing the necessary preconditions for mystical ascent. Daniel Merkur's examination of visionary literature from the ancient period concludes that "[t]he seers also engaged in exaggerated mourning, which was the crucial psychological element of their technique for inducing an alternate psychic state."[17] Emotions, especially those related to physical and psychic suffering, surely served as a powerful means of intensify the experience of reading. The reenactment of emotions functions to create the necessary conditions of liminality that allow for the creation of the subjectivity of the visionary, which was shaped by the transformative experiences described in the text.

In this chapter, I propose that the first-person voice and constructed imaginal body function together as an affective script oriented toward transformation which an ancient reader was expected to reenact. Re-

---

15 Amy Hollywood, "Spiritual but not Religious," *Harvard Divinity Bulletin* 38 (2010): 22.

16 Jennifer L. Koosed, *(Per)mutations of Qohelet: Reading the Body in the Book* (New York: T & T Clark, 2006).

17 Merkur, "The Visionary Practices of Jewish Apocalyptists," 125.

peated emotion reenactment stimulated the generation of the appropriate subjectivity that would allow for the possibility of a religious experience. The first-person voice of the Qumran hodayot is an important rhetorical feature of these texts that allows them to be understood as affective scripts for reenactment. The intense experiences of the "I" of the hodayot texts, both the reports of devastation and the remarkable accounts of transformation, are described through a rhetorical body that is constructed from multiple early Jewish visionary traditions. I propose that during the performative readings of the hodayot, the reenactment of the specific emotions that are aroused in the text was key. Embodiment language in the hodayot strategically aroused key emotions in the reader of fear and distress. In the second part of this chapter, I discuss how the ancient reader's reenactment of these emotions can be situated within an interdisciplinary model of performative reading drawn from recent scholarship on neuropsychology and performance studies. The display of performative emotions within ritual contexts can be said to have played an instrumental role in the formation of the ancient reader's subjectivity. In the conceptualization of the ritual role of the emotions that is offered here, the imaginal body's somatic experiences, understood as the physical expressions of emotions, are understood as an affective script that an ancient reader was expected to reenact.

I. Embodiment Language and the Strong "I"

The lively literary style of the hodayot is created by the detailed references to the body and its experiences. It was described by the first generation of scrolls scholars as the strong "I" of the TH. Embodiment language made its strongest impression here in the TH compositions, which strategically aroused both fear in their laments and exhilarating relief in their reports of deliverance. The effect of this embodiment language was that some first-generation scrolls scholars, Sukenik and the Heidelberg School, understood these reports to be autobiographical accounts of an actual person's experiences. Instead of imagining these texts to have been produced by a particular historical person, I propose that this embodiment language generates the effect of a rhetorically constructed persona, an imaginal body. This constructed body simultaneously serves as the site for the intense pain of the laments and as the locus for the extraordinary religious experiences of transformation for the ancient reader. The imaginal body possesses parts, enjoys the capacity for spatial experiences like locomotion, and experiences the full range of the sensations associated with embodiment, including emotional responses. In sum, it enjoys all of the experiential aspects associated with the ordinary phenomenon of physicality, but it is also capable of exceeding it insofar as it can also access the extraordinary sensations associated with being transported to otherworldly realms.

In the following section I discuss the imaginal body in the Qumran hodayot and how it participates in the larger cultural understandings of the body in early Judaism. Practices of ritualization target the sensory functions and bodily processes and seek to create the embodied subjectivity of the visionary. Experiences of transformation understood as illumination, ascent, and communion with angels are all described by referencing the body and its parts. It is also the case that the imaginal body in the hodayot offers a script of imitable practices that are culled from the physical experiences of visionaries and seers. These imitable behaviors involve more than participating in fasting, trembling, or sleeping, they also include the reenactment of emotion. I propose that the imaginal body was an affective script for transformation.

A. Ritualizing the Sensory Functions

The hodayot's marked attention to the body and its perceptual faculties can be understood within the framework of ancient Israelite and early Jewish understandings of the physical body and reiterative pedagogical practices that seek to create a desired embodied subjectivity. In the Hebrew Bible, the body was an integrated unit. There was no presumption of a dichotomy between the mind and body that characterized Cartesian dualism. Most recent neuropsychological studies favor understanding cognition as a series of embodied functions and not as disassociated mental processes.[18] Practices that discipline the body could effect real changes in the mind and in the spirit, and in this sense, ancient Israel very much understood herself as an embodied subjectivity. This bodily

---

18 Justin Storbeck and Gerald L. Clore, "On the Interdependence of Cognition and Emotion," *Cognition and Emotion* 21 (2007): 1212–37; Much work on the study of cognition and emotion has also been conducted by Antonio Damasio, *Looking for Spinoza: Joy, Sorrow, and the Feeling Brain* (New York: Harcourt, 2003); idem, *The Feeling of What Happens: Body and Emotion in the Making of Consciousness* (New York: Harcourt, 1999); idem, *Descartes' Error: Emotions, Reason, and the Human Brain* (New York: Avon Books, 1994).

consciousness often expressed itself as a concern over the unreliability of physical sensory mechanisms and as a desire to discipline or train them. Steven Weitzman's examination of sensory function finds that the general view of the body was that it was susceptible to error and that it required instruction: "The sense failings rendered Israel vulnerable to idolatry, a bewitching of the senses in Philo's understanding of this sin. Fortunately for the Jews, Mosaic law offered a remedy, a way to retrain the senses."[19] Weitzman describes Philo's concern as one that was deeply informed by a Hellenistic worldview, yet he proposes that the book of Deuteronomy can be a fruitful case study of this understanding of the body and its senses which predates the Greek philosophy of Plato.[20] Deuteronomy's regimen for sense perception targets the eyes, the ears, and the mouth. It is by practicing techniques for disciplining the senses, Weitzman argues, that the Deuteronomic law succeeds in generating the desired subjectivity of a faithful Israel.

The strategies for disciplining the senses in Deuteronomy can also be said to be operative in wisdom literature. Greg Goering's study of the disciplining of sense perception focuses on the wisdom tradition, but his conclusions are very similar to Weitzman. Goering notes that references to the body epitomize the disciplining of the senses and the instruction of the student.[21] Drawing upon Catherine Bell's theory of ritualization, Goering argues that by means of a systematic ritualization of the senses, sapiential instruction sought to inculcate the proper use of the body's sensory perceptions.[22] Those of the eyes and ears were especially targeted since these faculties are especially susceptible to being misled when they are not properly regimented. Goering cites here the

---

19 S. Weitzman, "Sensory Reform in Deuteronomy," 123–39.

20 Weitzman (in "Sensory Reform in Deuteronomy") writes: "[t]his reading of biblical law is obviously anachronistic, projecting onto the Bible ideas borrowed from Greek philosophers like Plato. And yet there is one biblical text, predating Plato and even perhaps the pre-Socratics, that can be plausibly read as an attempt to retrain the senses—the book of Deuteronomy" (124). Weitzman discusses the common pedagogical techniques shared by Deuteronomy and Proverbs: "continuous recitation, stringing reminders to one's body, and writing things down" (132).

21 Gregory Goering, "Attentive Ears and Forward-Looking Eyes: Ritualization of the Senses in the Jewish Wisdom Tradition," and idem, *Perceiving Wisdom: Disciplining the Senses and the Construction of the Self in the Jewish Wisdom Tradition*, a monograph version of this thesis in preparation. I am grateful to him for generously sharing a copy of his paper with me.

22 Catherine Bell, *Ritual Theory, Ritual Practice*.

example of Prov 20:13 which states, "do not love sleep, lest you become impoverished; open your eyes and you will have plenty of
food;" and Prov 5:1–2, "My child, be attentive to my wisdom; incline
your ear to my understanding, so that you may hold on to prudence,
and your lips may guard knowledge."[23] Goering proposes that the successful ritualization of the senses succeeded in effecting a status transformation of the student from a novice into a sage; or, as I would describe
it, the pedagogical process of disciplining of the senses generated the
embodied subjectivity of the sage.

The way the imaginal body is evoked in the Qumran hodayot participates in these broader Israelite traditions that seek to properly train
the sensory functions for the sake of creating a desired embodied subjectivity. Susan Ashbrook Harvey writes that the engagement of the body
"through actions and through sensory awareness" was done "in order to
seek religious knowledge—knowledge of the divine and of the human
person in relation to the divine."[24] In the case of the hodayot, the body
parts and sensory functions that are regimented in the sapiential literature become sites for intimate encounters with the deity and opportunities for illumination. The speaker of the hodayot itemizes various
body organs associated with understanding but highlights God's transformation of them through a divine touch: "[How] can I know unless
I have seen this? Or (how) can I understand without you conferring understanding in me? How shall I see unless you have uncovered my eyes?
And (how) shall I hear [unless You open my ears]? My heart is astound-
ed because to the uncircumcised ear a word has been disclosed, and a
heart [of stone has understanding of wondrous things]" (1QH XXI,
4–7). The speaker of the hodayot also describes the inspired words of
prayer as divine instruction that result from God's touch: "You have
given me insight into your wonderful deeds. You put thanksgiving in
my mouth and upon my tongue (You have placed) a [psal]m" (XIX,
7–8). David Rolph Seely discusses the hodayot's use of body imagery
here and also in other Qumran texts like the *Barki Nafshi* hymns and ob-

---

23 Goering ("Attentive Ears and Forward-Looking Eyes," 5–6) cites the example
    of Prov 20:13 which states, "do not love sleep, lest you become impoverished;
    open your eyes and you will have plenty of food;" and Prov 5:1–2, "My child,
    be attentive to my wisdom; incline your ear to my understanding, so that you
    may hold on to prudence, and your lips may guard knowledge."
24 Susan Ashbrook Harvey, "Locating the Sensing Body: Perception and Reli-
    gious Identity in Late Antiquity," in *Religion and the Self in Antiquity*, 140–
    62, here 141.

serves that: "body imagery gives concreteness and vividness to the poet's description of God's involvement with the community, and the range of bodily parts alluded to creates a sense of God changing the entire person."[25] A reader is invited to imagine his own body as he reads the references to the imaginal body in the hodayot. By reenacting these experiences of the body a reader is able to participate in a religious transformation as his performative reading creates the subjectivity of the "I" within himself.

Throughout the hodayot, embodiment language is used to express extraordinary religious experiences that relate to physical luminosity, locomotion and ascension into the heavens, and communion with angels in the heavenly realm. The speaker's reports of God illuminating his face (1QH XI, 4; XII, 6, 28; XV, 27; XVII, 26) are not only in continuity with biblical accounts of the righteous as radiant light (2 Sam 23:4 and also Dan 12:3); they also evoke widely attested early Jewish traditions that describe illumination as mystical transformation and union with God, who is understood to be the source of all light.[26] In the following example, the speaker reports an experience of mystical transformation: "You have exalted my horn over all who despise me. . . You have helped my soul, and You exalt my horn ever higher. I am radiant in sevenfold light, in l[ight which] You have [esta]blished for Your glory" (XV, 25, 26–27). Another way that body is evoked in the hodayot is the speaker's report of vertical locomotion and the sensation of being lifted up (1QH XI, 20–23; XIX, 13–16; XXVI, 27–28, 35–37).[27] Reports of being in the heavenly realm and in the company of celestial beings also use the language of physicality as the speaker is "brought" into

---

25 David Rolph Seely, "Implanting Pious Qualities as a Theme in the *Barki Nafshi* Hymns," in *The Dead Sea Scrolls Fifty Years after their Discovery. Proceedings of the Jerusalem Congress, July 20–25, 1997* (ed. Lawrence H. Shiffman, Emanuel Tov, James C. VanderKam, executive editor Galen Marquis; Jerusalem: Israel Exploration Society in cooperation with the Shrine of the Book, Israel Museum, 2000), 322–331. See *Barki Nafshi's* use of these body references in 4Q434 1 i 1–4.

26 For a survey of the imagery of luminosity in the early Jewish literature, see Willem F. Smelik, "On the Mystical Transformation of the Righteous into Light in Judaism," *JSJ* 26 (1995): 122–144.

27 Cf. M. Idel, *Ascensions on High in Jewish Mysticism: Pillars, Lines, Ladders* (Budapest: CEU Press, 2005); E. R. Wolfson, "Mysticism and the Poetic-Liturgical Compositions from Qumran," 185–202; Martha Himmelfarb, *Ascent to the Heaven in Jewish and Christian Apocalypses.*

the company of angels[28] and "walks around on an endless plain,"[29]and is "positioned in place."[30] The experience of ascent into the heavens often includes the phenomenon of participating in the celestial angelic liturgy and being in communion with angels and God (1QH XI, 22–24; XII, 25–26; XIV, 15–16; XV, 33–34; XIX, 14–17; XXIII, 30; XXVI, 36).[31] These reports of religious experiences can be said to increase in intensity as the reader moves along the scroll, culminating with the SGH.

In addition to understanding the body as an access point for transformative encounters with the deity, language about the body is used to communicate experiential elements that can express the magnitude of certain events. For example, the depth of the hodayot speaker's anguish is expressed in an especially poignant way by detailing specific parts of the imaginal body's suffering from head to toe. In a sampling of the varied references to the body found in 1QH XV, the speaker reports the depths of his anguish through the language of the body:

> [(My) arm] is shattered at the shoulder, my foot sinks into the mire. My eyes are blinded from seeing (6) evil, my ears from hearing bloodshed and my hear is dismayed because of evil plotting. . . (7) all the foundations of my frame shake and my bones are rattled; my bowels heave like a ship in

---

28 לבוא ביחד עם עדת בני שמים (1QH XI, 23)

29 ואתהלכה במישור לאין חקר (1QH XI, 21; cf. XV, 17–18)

30 להתיצב במעמד עם צבא קדושים (1QH XI, 22; cf. XIX, 16). The text for other examples are given in the table in chapter one (1QH XII, 25–26; XIV, 15–16; XV, 17–18, 32–34; XIX, 14–17; XXII, 15; XXVI, 36).

31 For a discussion of how this theme appears in the scroll 1QH, see Angela Kim Harkins, "Thinking about 1QH^A Sixty Years After Its Discovery"; Esther G. Chazon, "Liturgical Communion with the Angels at Qumran," in *Sapiential, Liturgical and Poetical Texts from Qumran* (ed. Daniel K. Falk, Florentino García Martínez, and Eileen M. Schuller; STDJ 35; Leiden: Brill, 2000), 95–105; Frennesson, *'In a Common Rejoicing.' Liturgical Communion with Angels in Qumran*; Crispin H. T. Fletcher-Louis, *All the Glory of Adam: Liturgical Anthropology in the Dead Sea Scrolls* (STDJ 42; Leiden: Brill, 2002); Devorah Dimant, "Men as Angels: The Self-Images of the Qumran Community," in *Religion and Politics in the Ancient Near East* (ed. Adele Berlin; Bethesda: University Press of Maryland, 1996), 93–103. For a broader discussion of the phenomenon of ascent into the heavens, see Adela Yarbro Collins, "Ascents to Heaven in Antiquity: Toward a Typology," in *A Teacher for All Generations*, 553–72. In that essay, she distinguishes between ascents that happen in lieu of death and those that happen during the lifetime of the journeyer.

a raging (8) storm and my heart pounds noisily to the destruction (1QH XV, 5–8).[32]

The imaginal body is also the site for instruction and formation which take place through divine guidance and positioning of the body. God establishes the speaker's foot on level ground in 1QH XV, 28; God establishes the foot of the speaker on the path of God's heart in 1QH XV, 41. God opens the ears so that they can receive reports of His wonders in 1QH XV, 41. Embodiment language is used to make the experiences of the imaginal body more vivid and allows a reader to reenact the transformative experiences of healing, revelation, and ascent.

B. The Embodied Subjectivity of the Imaginal Visionary

The strong "I" of the hodayot can be said to report vivid experiences that are modeled on or imitate the striking bodily experiences of various visionaries and seers. In addition to the usual scriptural authorities that are often discussed in the context of the hodayot, other non-canonical visionaries are also evoked. Studies of how ancient visionaries achieved experiences of ascent and journeying indicate that the meditation upon established visionary reports was key. The meditative reading and re-reading of tried and true visions is one way to account for the dramatic similarities among the reports of the otherworld. Daniel Merkur writes that Jewish apocalyptic visionaries "rehearsed what they knew in order to encourage their psychic states to manifest further and unknown matters on the same topics."[33] In the case of the hodayot, the reader would have meditated upon these emotionally charged experiences in the text by reading (and rereading) them as first-person experiences. In doing so, he positioned himself as the speaker of the text and created for himself the subjectivity of a visionary.

The bodily and affective experiences of certain hodayot bear resemblance to descriptions of Daniel the apocalyptic seer. The book of Dan-

---

32 Chapter five will discuss further the mapping of experiences onto the reader's body.

33 Daniel Merkur, "The Visionary Practices of Jewish Apocalypticists," 119–48, here 141; also see Daniel Merkur, "Cultivating Visions through Exegetical Meditations," in *With Letters of Light: Studies in the Dead Sea Scrolls, Early Jewish Apocalypticism, Magic, and Mysticism in Honor of Rachel Elior* (Ekstasis 2; Berlin, de Gruyter, 2011), 62–91.

iel refers to wise teachers, משכילים (Daniel 11−12), a term that has been reconstructed throughout the hodayot collection.[34] The way Daniel prays in Daniel 6:10−11 specifies his body posture of kneeling and the frequency of his praying throughout the day.[35] Like seers in other visionary texts, Daniel reports using typical preparatory techniques by engaging in appropriate deprivations of the body, fasting, and mourning: "At that time I, Daniel, had been mourning for three weeks. I had eaten no rich food, no meat or wine had entered my mouth, and I had not anointed myself at all, for the full three weeks" (Dan 10:2−3). Such deprivation techniques are also associated with the larger phenomenon of asceticism (although such techniques cannot define asceticism). Richard Valantasis describes the techniques associated with asceticism as "performances within a dominant social environment intended to inaugurate a new subjectivity, different social relations, and an alternative symbolic universe."[36] Various ascetic practices that discipline the body are so carefully described in narratives about asceticism that Valantasis describes them as highly "imitable,"[37] such that by performing the techniques one could hope to achieve a transformation in subjectivity. Shortly after Daniel's preparatory period, he reports having a vivid visionary experience. After his encounter with heavenly beings, the seer reports:

> I, Daniel, alone saw the vision; the people who were with me did not see the vision, though a great trembling fell upon them, and they fled and hid themselves. So I was left alone to see this great vision. My strength left me, and my complexion grew deathly pale, and I retained no strength. Then I heard the sound of his words; and when I heard the sound of his words, I fell into a trance, face to the ground. . . . . While he was speaking these words to me, I turned my face toward the ground and was speechless. Then one in human form touched my lips, and I opened my mouth to speak, and said to the one who stood before me, "My lord, because of

---

34 1QH V, 12; VII, 21; XX, 7; XXV, 34; for the discussion of these reconstructed incipits, see Émile Puech, "Quelques aspects de la restauration du Rouleau des Hymns (1QH)," 39−40; also Angela Kim Harkins, "Observations on the Editorial Shaping of the so-called Community Hymns from 1QH^a and 4QH^a," *DSD* 12 (2005): 233−56.

35 So too King Darius who is said to fast and deprive himself of sleep, can be said to imitate bodily behaviors of penitence in Dan 6:18.

36 Richard Valantasis, "Constructions of Power in Asceticism," *JAAR* 63 (1995): 775−821, here 797.

37 Geoffrey Harpham, *The Ascetic Imperative in Culture and Criticism* (Chicago: University of Chicago Press, 1987), 13−16.

the vision such pains have come upon me that I retain no strength. How can my lord's servant talk with my lord? For I am shaking, no strength remains in me, and no breath is left in me."[38]

Not only are Daniel's physical acts of fasting, prayer, and mourning imitable but a reader, I propose, could also train his body to imitate the physical experiences of emotion in the form of trembling and fatigue which afflict the seer after his visionary experience in Dan 10:7–9, 15–17. This pattern of concluding a religious experience with some form of physical display is also followed by the prophet Ezekiel who responds to the inaugural vision in that book by collapsing face down in a fearful state (Ezek 1:28b-2:2). So too, Paul in the Acts of the Apostles is said to have collapsed during specific religious events (Acts 9:1–9, 22:4–8; 26:12–18). In so doing, these figures perform a typical response to being in the presence of the divine. The posture of obeisance embodies the sensations of fear and unworthiness. By imitating these physical displays and recreating these emotions of fear and unworthiness, an ancient reader of the hodayot could hope to induce within himself phenomenally the religious experiences of the "I" in the text. Such a practice of displaying bodily experiences of terror during the recitation of prayer is attested by the prophet Habakkuk who claims to be physically afflicted upon reciting his prayer in Hab 3: "I heard and my bowels trembled, my lips quivered at the sound; Rot entered into my bones, I trembled where I stood" (3:16).[39] Bodily practices are understood as a

---

38 Dan 10:7–9, 15–17
39 The book of Habakkuk has long been approached from the perspective of redaction criticism and analyzed as having various distinct parts, chs. 1–2 being distinct from ch. 3. Notably, the Qumran commentary on Habakkuk treats only the first two chapters (1QpHab). The hymn of Habakkuk is frequently analyzed with a break here at v. 16 presumably resuming the hymn's opening in 3:1–2. These frame the two-part theophany in 3:3–7 and 3:8–15 that employs many mythological themes; T. Hiebert, *God of My Victory: The Ancient Hymn in Habakkuk 3* (HSM 38; Scholars Press: Atlanta, 1986); Georg Fohrer, "Das 'Gebet des Propheten Habakuk' (Hab 3,1–16)," in *Mélanges bibliques et orientaux en l'honneur de M. Mathias Delcor* (Kevelaer: Butzon und Bercker, 1985), 159–67; W. F. Albright, "The Psalm of Habakkuk," *Studies in Old Testament Prophecy* (ed. H. H. Rowley; New York: Scribner's Sons, 1950), 1–18; S. Mowinckel, "Zum Psalm des Habakkuk," *TZ* 9 (1953): 1–23; J. H. Eaton, "The Origin and Meaning of Habakkuk 3," *ZAW* 76 (1964): 144–71; Baruch Margulis, "The Psalm of Habakkuk: A Reconstruction and Interpretation," *ZAW* 82 (1970): 409–42.

performance in which the one who prays imitates the emotions and physical responses associated with a theophanic experience.

Various scenes in the hodayot resemble snapshots of familiar episodes from the book of Daniel.[40] Visceral experiences of terror are also aroused in the short hodayah in 1QH XIII, 7–21 and reinvigorate scenes from the lion's den.[41] The reference to refining metal in a crucible to a sevenfold intensity (1QH XIII, 18) alludes to the furnace that is heated up seven times more than usual during the time of trial suffered by Shadrach, Meshach, and Abedneggo (Dan 3:19–30). The hodayot speaker reports the physical sensation of being bound in shackles and fetters in 1QH XVI, 35–36, an allusion to the trauma of imprisonment in Dan 3:23–24.

Reports of the physical experiences of fear are frequently described in great detail in visionary reports as a fearful anticipation of the otherworldly experience and deep-seated terror. I propose that these reports are so clearly described as to be considered imitable techniques of affective responses that invite the reader to follow suit. Valantasis describes such detailed descriptions of asceticism as elaborate textualized performances wherein the "rigor, strictness, and steadfastness of the ascetic's life" is idealized and dramatized. The "textualized performance constructs an imitable subject, an imitable performance. These textualized performances do not actually exist but are created of the stuff of narrative and metaphor *precisely in order to set up the illusion of a reality to be imitated.*"[42] Here Valantasis' discussion highlights the important insights from Derrida and Butler about the successive reiterations of the illusory 'original' event, in our case, experience of ascent and communion with heavenly beings.

While numerous studies of the hodayot have sought to demonstrate how they reuse scriptural material,[43] the hodayot also appeal to nonscriptural traditions associated with celebrated visionaries from the sec-

---

40 Other allusions to scenes described in the Book of Daniel appear in the composition known as 1QH XVI, 5-XVII, 36, a composition that is the subject of chapter five.

41 The discussion of 1QH XIII, 7–21 may be found in chapter three which discusses places of punishment.

42 Valantasis, "Constructions of Power in Asceticism," 799.

43 The most recent study of scriptural allusions is Hughes, *Scriptural Allusions and Exegesis in the Hodayot.* While her ultimate conclusions that the hodayot can be understood as classroom exercises for a teacher is problematic, she offers the important observation that prophetic traditions associated with Ezekiel and Jeremiah are prominent in these texts.

ond temple period.[44] Enoch's popularity and influence during the second temple period is indicated by the numerous manuscript copies of texts associated with him in Cave 4, the same Cave that housed the majority of the hodayot manuscripts. The relationship between the hodayot and Enochic traditions is one that has not been fully examined by scholars, but to be clear, this study does *not* propose that hodayot are essentially rewritings of Enochic traditions or some other known tradition.[45] James C. VanderKam's scholarship has shown well how the figure of Enoch reiterates even older images of the diviner known from ancient Mesopotamian mantic traditions.[46] There are also many points of resemblance between the traditions associated with Enoch and other visionaries like Daniel. Both Enoch and the seer Daniel make similar claims:[47] Enoch states, "And I, Enoch, alone saw the sights, the ends of all (things) and no one has seen what I have seen" (*1 En.* 19:3)[48] and Daniel similarly claims, "I, Daniel, alone saw the vi-

---

44 Other examples that postdate the hodayot include 4 Ezra where the visionary reports a schedule of fasting and weeping, e. g., 4 Ezra 5:20; 6:35–37.

45 There are a handful of studies that have sought to describe a relationship between the hodayot and the Enochic traditions; See Angela Kim Harkins, "Reading the Qumran Hodayot in Light of the Traditions Associated with Enoch," *Henoch* 32 (2010): 359–400, which was researched without knowledge of the stimulating study by Eric Miller, "The Self-Glorification Hymn Reexamined." Other important studies of the relationship between the hodayot and the Enochic traditions are by George W. E. Nickelsburg, "The Qumranic Radicalizing and Anthropologizing of an Eschatological Tradition (1QH 4:29–40)," in *Ernten, was man sät: Festschrift für Klaus Koch zu seinem 65 Geburtstag* (ed. D. R. Daniels, U. Glessmer, M. Rösel; Neukirchen-Vluyn: Neukirchener Verlag, 1991), 423–35; republished under the title, "The Qumranic Transformation of a Cosmological and Eschatological Tradition (1QH 4:29–40)," in *The Madrid Qumran Congress: Proceedings of the International Congress on the Dead Sea Scrolls, Madrid, 18–21 March 1991* (vol. 2; ed. J. C. Trebolle Barrera and L. Vegas Montaner; STDJ 11; Leiden: Brill, 1992), 649–59. Most recently, Nickelsburg explores the points of similarity between *1 En.* 61:12–13 and 1QH IX, 23–33; XI, 20–24; XIV, 9–17; XVIII, 3–14, 16–25; XIX, 30–37 in "The Parables of Enoch and the Manuscripts from Qumran," in *A Teacher for All Generations, Vol. 2*, 655–68, esp. 667.

46 James C. VanderKam, *Enoch and the Growth of an Apocalyptic Tradition* (CBQMS; Washington, D.C.: CBA, 1984); see too the recent study by Reed, *Fallen Angels*.

47 This claim of uniqueness may be part of the visionary tradition that asserts the authenticity of the visionary experience.

48 The finality of this statement is one of the reasons why many scholars see *1 En.* 19 as a conclusion to a literary unit within the Book of the Watchers.

sion" (Dan 10:7). Scholars have engaged this topic of the common elements in the Enochic and Danielic traditions.[49] Ironically, despite
claims of his own visionary uniqueness, Enoch is himself an imitation
rather than an exemplar; he reiterates the experiences of an imaginal
human visionary. It is the case that neither an actual historical figure
known as Enoch, nor an 'original' literary form of the Enochic traditions is responsible for generating these traditions. Enoch's report also
cannot be understood as the 'original' myth of ascent since it repeats
and reiterates traditions attested in even older Mesopotamian literature.
Derrida's point is well-noted here, namely that the mere presence of numerous iterations cannot be used to assist scholarly arguments in favor of
"proving" the existence of an original event in time and space. Instead
they can be used only to construct an idea of an illusory original event;
in other words, the presence of numerous iterations of the original event
(the "effect") can only point to the presumption, not to the empirical
reality, of an original event.

The visionary traditions associated with the figure of Enoch have
received the least amount of attention in the scholarship on the hodayot.
Insofar as these Enochic traditions offer clear and detailed accounts of his
visionary experiences, they can be understood as invitations for imitation that facilitate the generation of the subjectivity of a seer. As an in-
tercessory figure, Enoch mediates between the angels and God, demonstrating his capacity to relate deeply to both. In the scene describing his
meeting with the angels in *1 Enoch* 13:3–6, the angels are afraid and
seized with trembling (*1 En.* 13:3), an act which mirrors the seismic
tremors of the earth that are described in the introduction to the BW

All texts from *1 Enoch* are taken from George W. E. Nickelsburg and James C.
VanderKam, *1 Enoch: A New Translation based on the Hermeneia Commentary*
(Minneapolis: Fortress, 2004).

49 Helge S. Kvanvig, "Throne Visions and Monsters: The Encounter Between
Danielic and Enochic Traditions," *ZAW* 117 (2005): 249–72; idem, "Henoch
und der Menschensohn. Das Verhältnis von Hen 14 zu Dan 7," *StTh* 38 (1984):
101–33; Loren Stuckenbruck, idem, "Daniel and Early Enoch Traditions in
the Scrolls," in *The Book of Daniel: Composition and Reception, Vol. 2* (ed.
John J. Collins and Peter W. Flint; Leiden: Brill, 2001), 368–86; idem,
"The Throne-Theophany of the Book of Giants: Some New Light on the
Background of Daniel 7," in *The Scrolls and the Scriptures: Qumran Fifty Years
After* (ed. Stanley E. Porter and Craig A. Evans; Sheffield: Sheffield Academic
Press, 1997), 211–220; T. Francis Glasson, "The Son of Man Imagery: Enoch
XIV and Daniel VII," *NTS* 23 (1977): 82–91.

in *1 Enoch* 1:5.[50] Enoch, in turn, imitates their quaking when he is described twice as trembling with fear as he approaches the presence of God in the heavenly realm. The first time Enoch says, "Fear enveloped me, and trembling seized me, and I was quaking and trembling, and I fell upon my face" (*1 En.* 14:13–14). Enoch is said to tremble a second time at the end of *1 Enoch* 14, immediately prior to the Oracle: "Until now I had been on my face, prostrate and trembling" (14:24). Here, we can easily imagine Enoch's trembling body just prior to his audience with God as the natural pious reaction to being in the presence of God similarly described in other scriptural texts.[51] Enoch's bodily shaking performs the physical expression of fear that is reported to have been displayed by both the angels and the earth. In this way, the description of Enoch's bodily reactions mirrors a physical experience that he shares with the non-human beings. His trembling bespeaks his sensitivity to understand the fear and the suffering experienced by both the angels and the earth, and this capacity to relate deeply to the other beings befits his role as intercessor. Like the angels who weep in *1 En.* 13:9, Enoch himself weeps piteously in the Dream Visions (*1 En.* 90:39). The figure of Enoch both imitates physical reactions by non-human beings and offers itself as a model for imitation, especially in accounts of his intense emotional experiences of psychological distress, which culminates physically in his weeping of tears. Such reports of weeping are imitable practices that suggest continuity between second temple apocalyptic groups and later mystical practices.

Scholars have notably neglected the extent to which visionary traditions attached to the figure of Enoch appear in the hodayot, yet Enoch was one of the most popular visionaries of this time period and the seer of the first Jewish Apocalypse.[52] The body posture and affective experi-

---

50 The literary features of the introductory section (*1 En.* 1–5) suggest that it had a different compositional history than the following section of BW (*1 En.* 6–11); see Nickelsburg, *1 Enoch 1–36, 81–108* (Hermeneia; Minneapolis: Fortress, 2001), 129–64. It is thought to be a secondary addition to the BW; see also the literary analysis by Lars Hartman, *Asking for a Meaning: A Study of 1 Enoch 1–5* (CBNTS 12; Lund: CWK Geerup, 1979).

51 See James C. VanderKam, "The Theophany of 1 Enoch 1 3b-9," *VT* 23 (1973): 129–50 for a discussion of this pious response to theophany.

52 On the popularity of the Enochic traditions at Qumran and beyond, see James C. VanderKam, *Enoch: A Man for All Generations* (Columbia: University of South Carolina, 1995), 110–130; Annette Yoshiko Reed, *Fallen Angels*; and Gabriele Boccaccini, *Beyond the Essene Hypothesis: The Partings of the Ways between Qumran and Enochic Judaism* (Grand Rapids: Eerdmans, 1998); and

ences of the speaker of the TH can be said to mirror those of the figure Enoch. The hodayot speaker reports being seized by fear and trembling (1QH XII, 23, 34), just as Enoch himself is overcome by physical trembling in his own ascent to the heavens in *1 En.* 14: 13–14. The hodayot speaker "is pulled upright and stands tall" (1QH XII, 23, 37), just as Enoch is pulled up and made to stand tall in *1 En.* 14:24. In another TH, the hymnist reports: "My heart reels in anguish and my loins tremble. My groaning reaches the depths and completely searches out the chambers of Sheol. I am terrified when I hear of Your judgments against powerful warriors and Your dispute with the hosts of your holy ones in the heavens" (1QH XVIII, 35–37). This passage seems to allude to the events described in the Enochic Book of the Watchers (*1 En.* 15–16) that occasion the fearful trembling of the angels, the earth, and Enoch. In this same hodayah, 1QH XVI, 5-XVII, 36, the speaker reports being in an otherworldly realm, what is surely the mythical garden of Eden. There he states that he is the gardener of the otherworldly garden. Such a claim alludes to Enoch's own career as the caretaker of a mythical garden according to the *Book of Giants* and the *Book of Jubilees.*[53] In the composition just prior to the SGH, 1QH XXIII, 1- XXV, 33, other allusions to elements from the Enochic myth of the Watchers appears: "angels of eternity in judgment" (XXIV, 8–9); "bastards" (XXIV, 16); and "in contempt because all the spirits of bastards act wickedly against flesh" (XXIV, 26).

Rather than restrict the study of the body imagery in the TH to a specific figure, either the Teacher of Righteousness or any other known historical person or scriptural personality, I propose that the strong "I" of the TH is a composite persona that resembles the experiences of multiple visionaries and visionary traditions. When the TH are read synchronically with the second group of CH, the strong "I" of the texts can be seen to construct a rhetorical persona of an imaginal body that progressively experiences transformation and ascent into the heavens. The distinct literary quality of the TH arises from the vivid reports of distress and deliverance that arouse strong compelling emotions in the reader. These vivid images about the speaker's experiences in the TH

---

idem., *Enoch and Qumran Origins: New Light on a Forgotten Connection* (Grand Rapids: Eerdmans, 2005).

53 The passage about the tall trees in 1QH XVI, 10–11 can also be an allusion to the Enochic myth of the Watchers, who are depicted as tall cedars in the Damascus Document (CD 2:16–19).

rely upon descriptions of embodiment that function purposefully to allow the ancient reader to access not only the extraordinary experiences that are reported in the TH, but more importantly the progressive transformations that take place, culminating in the crescendo of the SGH. As the ancient reader reads these texts, the "I" of the compositions invites him to reenact the bodily experiences that are described. In doing so, the imaginal body and its parts become the ancient reader's body.

Derrida's thinking, as it has been appropriated by Butler to instances of non-textualized phenomenal media such as embodied performances, can be extremely helpful in thinking about the phenomenal experience of the human ascent into the heavenly realm. Here there is no 'original' human visionary who existed in time and space. The 'original' is illusory and not recoverable, even though numerous iterations of this event exist in various cultures and periods.[54] While there are many famous examples and instantiations of a human who ascends into the heavens, there is no 'original' event, according to Butler (and Derrida). Instead, a range of elements has come to be recognizably associated with the visionary figure.[55] The original event for the visionary is not based on any empirical model but instead constructed after the fact from the multiple iterations that have appeared in the divergent traditions known as Jewish and Christian apocalyptic and Hekhalot, as well as in writings from Mesopotamian, Egyptian, and Hellenistic traditions that speak of journey reports, visionary experiences, and heavenly ascent.[56] These religious ex-

---

54 See here Alan F. Segal's systematic study in *Life after Death* and the essays in John J. Collins and Michael Fishbane (eds.), *Death, Ecstasy, and Other Worldly Journeys* (Albany: SUNY Press, 1995).

55 In this way, I follow Jonathan Z. Smith's demonstration that it is not possible to locate a unique and definitive essential quality in religious phenomena; see Smith, "Fences and Neighbors: Some Contours of Early Judaism," *Imagining Religion: From Babylon to Jonestown* (Chicago: University of Chicago, 1982): 1–18.

56 A number of studies treat the broad phenomenon of visionary ascent; some representative studies are A. Y. Collins, "Ascents to the Heaven in Antiquity: Toward a Typology;" April D. DeConick (ed.), *Paradise Now*; Moshe Idel, *Ascensions on High in Jewish Mysticism*; the massive survey of literature by Alan F. Segal, *Life After Death* (New York: Doubleday, 2004); Collins and Fishbane (eds.), *Death, Ecstasy, and Other Worldly Journeys*; Ioan P. Couliano, *Out of this World: Otherworldly Journeys from Gilgamesh to Albert Einstein* (Boston: Shambhala, 1991); Carol Zaleski, *Otherworld Journeys: Accounts of Near-Death Experience in Medieval and Modern Times* (New York: Oxford University, 1987); Ioan P. Couliano, *Expériences de l'extase: extase, ascension et récit visionnaire*

periences are overwhelmingly sensory, recounting in great detail the bodily aspects of these divine encounters by emphasizing ocular, sonorous, olfactory, tactile, or gustatory elements of the otherworld. Reports of visionary experiences target specific perceptual organs, most commonly seeing and hearing, and thereby intensify the experience of reenactment for the reader who places himself as the "I" of these texts. Their descriptions underscore the importance of the "phenomenal texture of religious experience" across a broad range of communities through time and space.[57] The embodied subjectivity of the visionary is the effect that is produced after many repetitive instances of performative reading and rereading. I propose that affective experiences that are described in great detail in second temple literature also offered to ancient readers an affective script of imitable behavior for reenactment. The hodayot are not simply texts that describe extraordinary religious experiences, they invite the ancient reader to imitate and recreate the emotion experiences of the lyrical speaker. By reading and seeking to imitate the experiences described in visionary texts, an ancient reader could have hoped to generate religious experiences of his own.

The physical expression of tears found in accounts of Enoch's visionary experiences and in other seers underscore the special instrumental role of weeping and point to its efficacy as a technique for inducing religious experience. Moshe Idel's ground-breaking work on the distinct role that the practice of weeping had among mystical techniques is well-known.[58] More recently, Sarah McNamer's study of affective meditation in medieval Christian writings has examined how devotional writings invite meditation upon Christ's suffering. Texts that would strike a modern reader as exaggerated in their sentimentality carried the expectation that readers would participate in and reenact the emo-

---

de l'hellénisme au moyen âge (Paris: Payot, 1984); Christopher Rowland, The Open Heaven; Violet MacDermot, The Cult of the Seer in the Ancient Middle East: A Contribution to Current Research on Hallucinations Drawn from Coptic and Other Texts (Berkeley: University of California, 1971).

57 Elliot R. Wolfson, "Sacred Space and Mental Iconography: Imago Templi and Contemplation in Rhineland Jewish Pietism," Ki Baruch Hu: Ancient Near Eastern, biblical, and Judaic studies in honor of Baruch A. Levine (Winona Lake: Eisenbrauns, 1999): 593–634, here 593.

58 Moshe Idel, "Mystical Techniques," 438–94; see too the 'gift of tears' in later Christian traditions, see Jean Leclercq, The Love of Learning and the Desire for God: A Study of Monastic Culture (New York: Fordham University Press, 1982), 58–59.

tions of desolation.[59] Such devotional writings on suffering are highly imitable affective performance scripts intended to bring about a state of tears in their readers.

Amy Hollywood describes how meditation upon suffering can create subjectivity in the reader. In the following excerpt, Hollywood compares the particular case of Angela of Foligno and the twentieth century theorist Georges Bataille:

> The extremity of the other's suffering leads not only to his or her own dissolution but also to that of the contemplator or viewer. It is through this laceration and loss of self that communication between the self and the other occurs. The practice of dramatization or mediation is a necessary (although not sufficient) condition if one is to stand out of the self and open oneself to the other—if one is, in other words, to attain ecstasy and communication. . . . Angela and Bataille both use meditative techniques to reenact and to experience sensibly, emotionally, and viscerally the extraordinary physical suffering of another; meditation on the fragmented bodies of torture victims gives rise to the dissolution of the subject and to his or her lacerating openness to the other.[60]

Meditation on reports of vivid and visceral bodily suffering is instrumental in the generation of subjectivity. In the case of the hodayot, the vivid reports of suffering experienced by the imaginal body can be easily mapped out onto the ancient reader's actual body, offering him an affective script to reenact. The process of performative reading that I am describing is one that seeks to draw the reader into the rhetoric of the text, "into a self-understanding shaped according to the patterns embedded in the hodayot."[61]

Vivid reports of physical and psychological suffering dominate the hodayot collection popularly known as the TH. The strong arousal of emotions in these visionary reports reiterates the powerful affective experiences of fear and trembling expressed in traditions associated with the imaginal visionary. Within the context of ritualization, strong emotions also function to assist the reader in intensifying his own experience of reading during successive performances of these texts. The reiterative

---

59   McNamer, *Affective Meditation and the Invention of Medieval Compassion.*

60   Amy Hollywood, *Sensible Ecstasy: Mysticism, Sexual Difference, and the Demands of History* (Chicago: University of Chicago Press, 2002), 70–71 and 74–75.

61   Carol Newsom, "Constructing 'We, You, and the Others' through Non-Polemical Discourse," 13–21, esp. 18–20 and eadem, *Self as Symbolic Space,* 198–202.

process of reenacting these affective experiences during the performative reading and re-reading of the hodayot created within the ancient reader the subjectivity of the imaginal body. During this process, an ancient reader could have intensified his affective arousal by drawing upon his own memories of emotion-laden experiences as well.

II. Emotions in Performance Studies

The psychologist Silvan S. Tomkins describes the instrumental role of emotion as a general intensifier of experiences:

> The affect system is therefore the primary motivational system because without its amplification, nothing else matters—and with its amplification, anything else can matter. It thus combines urgency and generality. It lends its power to memory, to perception, to thought, and to action no less than to the drives.[62]

Since Tomkins' assertions in the late 1970s, emotion research has further deepened its understanding of emotion's special role in memory construction and reconstruction, a topic that will be discussed in more detail in chapter four. Emotion studies have changed much in the last century as neuropsychologists have increasingly advocated for recognizing the important role that emotion, understood strictly as bodily responses of heart palpitations and endocrine changes, plays in cognition. Such physical displays of affect are also very difficult for most individuals to display at will. Within the context of performative reading, the successful reenactment of affect can function to heighten a reader's experience of the text. The reenactment of a strong emotion such as fear can naturally result in the mind reconstructing other memories of similarly valanced emotions, and in so doing, result in the further generation of new visions.[63]

---

62 Silvan S. Tomkins, "Script Theory: Differential Magnification of Affects," *Nebraska Symposium on Motivation 1978: Human Emotion* (ed. Richard Dienstbier; Lincoln: University of Nebraska Press, 1979), 201–36.

63 This generative aspect of ritual meditation upon visionary reports is discussed in Christopher Rowland's recent study and is the subject of chapter four; see Christopher Rowland with Patricia Gibbons and Vicente Dobroruka, "Visionary Experience in Ancient Judaism and Christianity," *Paradise Now*, 41–56, esp. 50–51. Rowland emphasizes the visual and imaging aspects of memory and its relationship to visionary experiences.

Rhetorical features in the text, such as the first person voice and references to the body and its suffering, likely assisted the reader of the hodayot in reenacting the emotional experiences of the lyrical subject. The intensity of the affective experiences in the hodayot, especially in the TH, suggests that the particular emotions of fear and anxiety were especially powerful ones for the reader to reenact and experience for himself. A reader's reenactment of these affective experiences can be instrumental in generating within him a subjectivity that is predisposed to having a religious experience. While the emotions associated with fear are not the only affective experiences in the TH, they are of special interest given scholars' suggestions that mourning and weeping were pervasive techniques for ascent in early Jewish and Christian literature.

Recent theoretical work on the study of religion has proposed the need for further work in understanding how religion and aspects of embodiment relate to one another. Armin W. Geertz has highlighted the need for interdisciplinary models in which religion is understood as anchored within physical bodies and enmeshed in cultural systems, what he terms a "biocultural theory of religion."[64] In the hodayot the striking and dramatic references to the body, its brokenness and its phenomenal ecstasy, arouse both the emotions of fear and exhilaration in the reader. I propose that the imaginal body that is constructed functioned as an affective script for the ancient reader to reenact.

A. Stanislavsky's System

Method theory, an acting approach wherein emotions play an instrumental role, offers an especially helpful way of thinking about how the hodayot, texts written in the first person, might have been experienced in antiquity. This approach to acting associated with Constantin Stanislavsky (1863–1948), also known as Stanislavsky's System, has been critically reengaged in recent times.[65] The renewed interest in Sta-

---

64 Geertz, "Brain, Body and Culture," 304–21.
65 While the term 'Stanislavsky's System' projects a false impression of its coherence and theoretical cohesiveness, it was Stanislavsky's preferred way of describing his approach to performance, and so his approach will be referred to here as Stanislavsky's System. Sharon M. Carnicke writes (in *Stanislavsky in Focus: An Acting Master for the Twenty-First Century*, 2d ed. [New York: Routledge, 2009], 226) that this was "Stanislavsky's preferred word for his compendium of lures and techniques for the actor. He saw his System as an actor's 'guide'

nislavsky's System by scholars in performance theory is due to recent developments in cognitive neuropsychology's understanding of the role of
the emotions in human knowing and in the formation of subjectivity.[66]
Stanislavsky sought to train actors to discipline their affective memories
so that emotions could be aroused during key moments of a performance, with the goal of assisting the performer in becoming deeply united
with the character in the text.[67]

> The difficulty of this aspect of emotional perception is that the actor is now
> coming to his part not through the text, the words of his role, nor by in-
> tellectual analysis or other conscious means of knowledge, but through his
> own sensations, his own real emotions, his personal life experience. . . .
> This moment is what we in actor's jargon call the state of 'I am,' it is
> the point where I begin to feel myself in the thick of things, where I
> begin to coalesce with all the circumstances suggested by the playwright
> and by the actor, begin to have the right to be part of them.[68]

Read in the light of Stanislavsky's System, the hodayot's detailed reports
of the body and its experiences can be seen as a kind of affective script

---

and an acting 'grammar' that facilitates expressive communication from the
stage, not a dogmatic or required curriculum." His techniques for acting are
also cited in shorthand as the "Method" or referred to as "Method Acting."

It is important to know that Stanislavsky's work has undergone a number of
translation and transmission issues that obfuscate and confuse for any English
reader his approach to performance. These challenges are described well by
Carnicke in *Stanislavsky in Focus*. Theatre studies and techniques for acting
may be helpful in thinking about how the performance of a text is transformative for the performer. N.B. that the author's name was published as "Stanislavski" but in the scholarly literature, he is referred to as "Stanislavsky" and that is
how I refer to him. Carnicke explains the "Stanislavsky" as the typical way to
anglicize Russian names; the other variant is atypical and appears only as necessary as in the citation of this 1948 publication; this situation is briefly mentioned by Carnicke, *Stanislavsky in Focus*, xiii; and discussed in greater detail
in Sharon M. Carnicke, "*An Actor Prepares/Rabota aktera nad soboï, Chast' I*: A
Comparison of the English with the Russian Stanislavsky," *Theatre Journal* 36
(1984): 481–94.

66   Other recent engagements of Stanislavsky's work include Rose Whyman, *The
     Stanislavsky System of Acting: Legacy and Influence in Modern Performance* (New
     York: Cambridge University Press, 2008).
67   The edition of Constantin Stanislavski (Stanislavsky), *An Actor Prepares* (trans. by
     E. Reynolds Hapgood; New York: Theatre Arts Books, 1948) uses the phrase
     "emotion memory" instead of "affective memory;" again an issue of translation
     from the Russian into English, see Carnicke, *Stanislavsky in Focus*, 53–104.
68   Constantin Stanislavski (Stanislavsky), *Creating a Role* (trans. Elizabeth Reynolds
     Hapgood; New York: Theatre Arts Books, 1961), 25–26.

offered for the ancient reader to reenact and imitate. The texts known as the Teacher Hymns strongly arouse fear, an emotion that is understood to have functioned instrumentally in assisting an ancient reader in forming the appropriate subjectivity that might predispose him for a religious experience. During the process of meditative reading, an ancient reader sought to reenact the key emotions aroused by the scenes in the text by placing himself in the role of the "I." In this section, I discuss how the affective experience of fear is understood in neuropsychology and how this emotion, when situated within a performance context, can be understood to play an instrumental role in the ritual reenactment of the text.

B. Performing an Affective Script

Scholars have long observed that emotions play an instrumental role in memory construction and reconstruction, a topic that will receive further treatment in chapter four. In the case of the emotion of fear, memory's naturally associative properties will automatically reinvigorate other experiences of similar affect.[69] This otherwise subconscious bodily response can become learned behavior because of the innate capacity that humans have for imitative behavior and vicarious learning. Past research into automaticity has challenged the strict understanding of these processes as *either* conscious *or* automatic.[70] The acquisition of automaticity requires much repetition and is a relatively slow process that not all individuals readily master.[71]

---

69 Many studies on the emotion of fear approaches it from a functional Darwinian perspective: emotions help to identify behaviors and situations that are desirable for the perpetuation of the species; see Edmund T. Rolls, *Emotion Explained*, 59–62; Arne Öhman, Anders Flykt, and Daniel Lundqvist, "Unconscious Emotion: Evolutionary Perspectives, Psychophysiological Data and Neuropsychological Mechanisms," in *Cognitive Neuroscience of Emotion: Series in Affective Science* (ed. Richard D. Lane and Lynn Nadel; New York: Oxford University Press, 2000), 296–327. Nevertheless, it would be wrong to conclude that such evolutionary processes determine behavior; even compelling emotions can be over-ridden as needed; e.g., a fire-fighter must learn to overcome the strong drive to run away from flames.

70 John A. Bargh, "Conditional Automaticity: Varieties of Automatic Influence in Social Perception and Cognition," in *Unintended Thought* (ed. James S. Uleman and John A. Bargh; New York: Guilford Press, 1989), 3–51

71 John A. Bargh and Tanya L. Chartrand, "The Unbearable Automaticity of Being," *American Psychologist* 54 (1999): 462–79, here 476.

Stanislavsky's method approach to acting has been analyzed by theorists from the perspective of cognitive neuroscience and neurophysiology who are interested in how the body and emotions contribute to the formation of subjectivity.[72] Stanislavsky's System uses a set of visualization techniques that train the emotions to respond to various stimuli at key moments during a performance. Stanislavsky himself sought to associate his method with scientific understandings of the human person and he was influenced greatly by the psychologist Théodule Ribot (1839–1916) who published a study called *The Psychology of the Emotions* in 1897.[73] In that study, Ribot reports that affective memory can be aroused both spontaneously and voluntarily.[74] Whyman writes,

> Here is the central idea that Stanislavsky verified from his reading of Ribot—that *affective memory* gives veracity to acting because it is based in 'nature', that is, in 'real' experience. Stanislavsky adopts Ribot's thesis from *Affective Memory (AM)*, that emotional images as well as visual, auditory, tactile-motor, verbal images and images derived from smell, taste, internal sensations, pleasure and pain can be revived both spontaneously and voluntarily.[75]

Stanislavsky sought to teach actors how to discipline their affective memories so that they could reinvigorate them during key moments of a performance, in the hope that the performer would succeed in creating the subjectivity of the character in the script. Stanislavsky describes this type of acting approach in the following excerpt from *An Actor Prepares*:

> To play truly means to be right, logical, coherent, to think, strive, feel and act in unison with your role. . . . If you take all these internal processes, and adapt them to the spiritual and physical life of the person you are representing, we call that living the part. This is of supreme significance in creative work. Aside from the fact that it opens up avenues for inspiration, living the part helps the artist to carry out one of his main objectives. His job is not to present merely the external life of his character. He must fit his own human qualities to the life of this other person, and pour into it all of his own soul. The fundamental aim of our art is the creation of this inner life of a human spirit, and its expression in an artistic form.

---

72 Antonio Damasio, *The Feeling of What Happens*; idem, *Looking for Spinoza*; idem, *Descartes' Error*.

73 Théodule Ribot, *The Psychology of the Emotions* (New York: Scribner's, 1897); see the discussion by Whyman, *The Stanislavsky System of Acting*, 52–57.

74 Notice that Ribot uses an outdated model of memory as a static file that is retrieved at a later time. More discussion of memory is found in chapter 4.

75 Whyman, *The Stanislavsky System of Acting*, 53–54.

The goal of a successful actor is to create within himself the subjectivity of the character in the script so that it can be performed in a realistic and dynamic manner. Among the various techniques discussed in this book are the exercise of the imagination, muscle relaxation, and the isolation of specific muscles to both help the body to be receptive to stimuli and to train the mind and the body. In order for this approach to be successful, the actor also has to vividly imagine himself as the character. Dyer P. Bilgrave and Robert H. Deluty explain these techniques:

> He directed them to extract and articulate the goals of their characters from their scripts, but he also considered this extraction and articulation insufficient to produce realistic behavior on stage. He asked his actors to invest considerable time and energy into imagining vividly the relevant experiences and situational contexts of their characters – the matrix of time and place, economic background, work history, medical history, social history, and key formative experiences within which their goals were formed. In essence, Stanislavsky directed an actor both to articulate his or her character's goals and objectives and to imagine with as much vividness and detail as possible the character's raw experience that led to the coalescing of these goals.[76]

According to Stanislavsky, the appropriate behaviors and actions would emerge naturally once the actor succeeds in mastering the internal disposition of his character.

Speaking through the character Tortsov, Stanislavsky coaches the novice on how to perform a character that may be completely foreign to him by relying upon external stimuli to modulate his temperament:

> Suppose you have chosen a plot you cannot believe. It is inevitable that if you force yourself the result will be self-deception, which must disorganize your whole mood. The same is true of any other of the elements. . . . The first necessary step is the relaxation of muscular tension. What you must do is to ask: am I sure of my attitude toward this or that particular place? Do I really feel this or that action? Should I change or add to such and such imaginative detail? All these preparatory exercises test your expressive apparatus.[77]

These preparations assist the actor in focusing on the mastery of a character's emotional temperament in order to respond naturally to the situations in the script. Stanislavsky writes that when this is done well, the

---

76 Dyer P. Bilgrave and Robert H. Deluty, "Stanislavski's Acting Method and Control Theory: Commonalities across Time, Place, and Field," *Social Behavior and Personality: An International Journal* 32 (2004), 329–40, here 331.

77 Stanislavski (Stanislavsky), *An Actor Prepares*, 249, 51.

effect will be as follows: "Sometimes an objective exists subconsciously and is even carried out subconsciously without either the knowledge or the will of the actor. Often it is only afterwards that he realizes fully what it is that has happened."[78] This aspect of Stanislavsky's technique is known as "experiencing," and he understands it to be the goal of performance. Stanislavsky writes, "it is necessary to experience the role, that is to have the sensation (*oshchushchat'*) of its feelings, every time and on every repetition of creativity." This involves the repeated and extensive visualization of the character in the script to help the actor master the emotions that animate the character's thoughts and behaviors. The actor would then need to attach these emotions and affective memories to various stimuli so that they can be reinvigorated as needed during the performance. An actor's ability to train his own affective memory plays a key role in how realistically he can perform the character in a script.

In *An Actor Prepares*, Stanislavsky urges novice actors to develop and train their emotion memory, which is their capacity to construct and reconstruct compelling affective emotion memories.[79] The practice of reconstructing affective memories is one that pays special attention to the embodied sensations associated with the experience:

> By recalling all the sensory details surrounding an emotional moment from one's past, the actor can theoretically learn to revive feelings at will. Remembering the time of day, the weather, how the sun felt on her face, how his shirt clung to him, the actor revives the grief she felt at her mother's funeral, the anger that flared when his wife left him. With practice, the actor can become more and more adept, reducing the necessary time to just "one minute." By careful selection of emotional material analogous to the play, the actor can mine personal experience in the creation of character.[80]

A successful affective memory will be able to associate stimuli from the script such as physical objects or dialogue with strong emotions so that the actor can then reinvigorate the memory at the appropriate time. The objective is to create as realistically as possible the experience of the appropriate emotions and feelings within the actor. Stanislavsky writes:

> The principal feels the insult; the witness can share only sympathetic feelings. But sympathy then might be transformed into direct reaction. That is exactly what happens to us when we are working on a role. From the very

---

78 Stanislavski (Stanislavsky), *An Actor Prepares*, 255.
79 Stanislavski (Stanislavsky), *An Actor Prepares*, 154–81.
80 Carnicke, *Stanislavsky in Focus*, 127.

moment when the actor feels that change take place in him he becomes an active principal in the life of the play—real human feelings are born in him—often this transformation from human sympathy into the real feelings of the person in the part occurs spontaneously. The actor may feel the situation of the person in the part so keenly, and respond to it so actively, that he actually puts himself in the place of that person. . . . He wants to act, to participate in the situation, to resent the insult, just as though it were a matter of personal honour with him. In that case the transformation of the emotions of the witness to those of the principal takes place so completely that the strength and quality of the feelings involved are not diminished. You can see from this that we use not only our own past emotions as creative material but we use feelings that we have had in sympathizing with the emotions of others.[81]

In the method acting approach, the regulation of emotions and the ability to reconstitute them as necessary can rely upon both internal and external stimuli. Once the actor masters the affective script of the character, he has succeeded in creating a subjectivity through which the role can be performed as realistically as possible.

III. Performative Emotions in Religious Experience[82]

Stanislavsky's System offers a model for imagining how bodily practices and the training of affective experiences can create subjectivity. The question for religious studies is not whether these performative emotions can be authenticated as 'real' experiences of affect. Instead, emotions experienced in ritual contexts function in a performative way that must be situated within a larger social history of a religious tradition. With this in mind, three aspects of emotions are useful for thinking about how this model of performing the hodayot was experienced in antiquity: the physical display of performative emotions; the cultural specificity of the emotions; and the political aspects of performativity.

---

81 Stanislavski (Stanislavsky), *An Actor Prepares*, 178–79.

82 The language of 'performative emotions' that appears in the following sections and throughout the work is taken from Gary Ebersole's study of 'performative tears,' namely bodily emotions that are displayed in highly orchestrated ritual contexts; "The Function of Ritual Weeping Revisited: Affective Expression and Moral Discourse," 211–46.

A. The Physical Expression of Affect: Trembling and Tears

Stanislavsky's System has been presented here as a way of imagining how ancients may have moved from text to religious experiences. The role of the body and the expectation that repetition of behaviors can exert a tremendous influence over consciousness in Stanislavsky's System reinforces the view that reiterated affective performances result in the creation of subjectivity. In her discussion of the formation of subjectivity through ritual practices, Saba Mahmood identifies the performance of emotion, specifically fear, as playing a key role in creation of subjectivity and the cultivation of the appropriate disposition of piety.[83] External religious practices may or may not express an interiorized religiosity, but they are certainly the necessary means of acquiring it. She writes: "For the women I worked with, bodily acts (like weeping in prayer), when performed repeatedly, both in public and private, endowed the self with certain qualities: bodily behavior was therefore not so much a sign of interiority as it was a means of acquiring its potentiality."[84] Mahmood uses potentiality here in the Aristotelian sense, which "implies that in order to be good at something one undergoes a teleological program of volitional training that presupposes an exemplary path to knowledge—knowledge that one comes to acquire through assiduous schooling and practice."[85] Mahmood affirms that piety is not the precondition of the weeping religious person; it is the aftereffect that is created from the repeated performance of this practice. The bodily practices become embodied habits that create the predisposition of piety without predetermining it in advance. The arousal of fear and the performance of this emotion within ritualized contexts are the necessary preconditions for creating the subjectivity of the religious person.

In the context of ritualization, the repeated performance of emotions is vitally important. In the course of reading and rereading the ho-

---

83 Mahmood writes, "It became apparent to me that the argument that people are driven to behave piously because of the fear of hell or the promise of rewards leaves unexplained what it seeks to answer: specifically, how these emotions are acquired and come to command authority in the topography of a particular moral-passional self. In what follows, therefore, I want to attend to the specific texture of these emotions—in particular, fear—and to understand how they came to be constituted as motives for, and modalities of, pious conduct in the realization of a virtuous life," (*Politics of Piety*, 140).

84 Mahmood, *Politics of Piety*, 147.

85 Ibid., 147.

dayot, and by repeatedly reenacting the emotions of fear that are strategically aroused in the text, an ancient reader can hope to create within
himself the subjectivity of the hodayot speaker. Such an understanding
of the crucial role of performative emotions comports with the important work of Moshe Idel who was the first to propose that the physical
experience of desolation possessed a spiritual efficacy. In his examination
of emotion within Jewish mystical traditions, Idel notes: "It [weeping] is
always part of a more elaborate sequence of ascetic exercises—fasting,
mourning, self-induced suffering—and is commonly their last step. In
some instances, the mystic is actually exhausted by the time he begins
weeping; a state of falling asleep or sometimes previous fainting gives
concrete evidence of this exhaustion."[86] Idel's work is especially relevant for our consideration of the Qumran hodayot because he offers a
neurophysiological description of the visionary experience:

> [T]he hyperactivation of the oracular system represents a concentration on
> one mode of perception at the very moment when all other doors of per-
> ception are progressively being repressed. This new balance of stimuli pre-
> pares the way for paranormal states of consciousness focused upon visual
> experiences. In such cases, the ideas or concepts upon which one has fo-
> cused his intellectual and emotional activity tend to reveal themselves
> through the hyperexcited medium. From a strictly psychological point of
> view, the visions that follow a painful and sorrowful state of mind can be
> related to what Marganita Laski designated as 'desolation ecstasies'.[87]

Weeping is not the only technique used by these mystics, but it is a crucial one that is used in conjunction with other bodily practices.[88] According to Idel's study of the thirteenth century Kabbalist known as
Abraham Abulafia, techniques for inducing a religious experience speci-
fied several bodily practices. An individual was instructed to chant the

---

86 Moshe Idel, *Kabbalah: New Perspectives* (New Haven: Yale University, 1988),
     75–88, here 88; see also idem, "Mystical Techniques," 438–94, esp. 439–
     53; idem, *Ascensions on High*. There is a fine discussion of Idel's methodological
     insights by Frances Flannery, "Ascents, Apocalypses, and Neuroscience: Moshe
     Idel and the Study of Religious Experience" (paper presented at the annual
     meeting of the Society of Biblical Literature, New Orleans, 2009); see too,
     eadem, "The Body and Ritual Reconsidered, Imagined, and Experienced,"
     in *Experientia, Volume 1: Inquiry into Religious Experience in Early Judaism and
     Early Christianity* (ed. F. Flannery, C. Shantz, and R. A. Werline; Atlanta:
     Scholars, 2008), 13–18.
87 Idel, *Kabbalah*, 88.
88 See as well the study of techniques and practices by J. R. Davila in *Descenders to
     the Chariot*.

divine names, to maintain controlled breathing, and to carefully position his or her hands and head.[89] Other scholars have noted the importance of hymn singing in medieval mystical texts.[90] Unlike Idel, who benefited from having access to the many medieval manuals of Abraham Abulafia, scholars of early Jewish texts have had to infer various techniques from accounts by ancient Jewish visionaries. This literature also describes the careful manipulation of the seer's body prior to a religious experience, e.g., the eating of special herbs (4 Ezra 9:26–28). Not only do the descriptions of these techniques allow for the reenactment of the text; they physically prepare the body to assume the subjectivity of the person in the text. The expression of physical tears, which is frequently reported in early Jewish visionary texts (*2 En.* 1:2; 3 Bar 1:1–3 and *T.Levi* 2:3–4), is understood by Idel as a sign of the total physical exhaustion of the individual.[91] The reenactment of the emotion of desolation is instrumental in bringing about the ecstatic state, and can be understood as a crucial preparatory state. Daniel Merkur describes this process in psychological terms:

> The ecstatic induction technique of ancient Jewish apocalyptists was, I suggest, a further religious manipulation of the unconscious bipolar mechanism. Severely depressed moods were deliberately provoked over a period of hours, days, or weeks until the unconscious psyche manifested an ecstasy in defense against the depression. The bipolar mechanism accomplished a qualitative transformation of affect from negative to positive while conserving its quantity, so that the amount of psychic energy that had been invested in negative affect was available to be expended as elation.[92]

Fasting and sleep deprivation are practices that bring the body to culminate in this physical state of desperation (weeping). The repeated arousal of desolation within a ritual context can induce the cathartic sensation of weeping, which can be transformed into ecstasy under the right circumstances.

---

89   Moshe Idel, *The Mystical Experience in Abraham Abulafia* (trans. from the Hebrew by J. Chipman; Albany: SUNY, 1988), 13–54.

90   Alan Segal, *Life after Death*, 330–33, cites *Hekhaloth Rabbati's* directives to begin the ascent with the recitation of a certain psalm 112 times.

91   See Idel, *Kabbalah*, 75–88; and Martha Himmelfarb, "The Practice of Ascent in the Ancient Mediterranean World," in *Death, Ecstasy, and Other Worldly Journeys*, 123–37.

92   Merkur, "The Visionary Practices of Jewish Apocalyptists," 125.

Weeping prior to a visionary experience is not uncommon among early Jewish apocalyptic writings.[93] Enoch is said to be overcome by tears just prior to his encounter with heavenly beings at the beginning of *2 Enoch*. Weeping is performed prior to Ezra's reception of visions in *4 Ezra* 5:13, 20; 6:30–31, 35. So too, the speaker in *2 Baruch* reports mourning prior to receiving a revelation from God in *2 Bar* 81:2–4.[94] Like these other seers, the speaker of the Qumran hodayot reports that "my eyes (burn) like a fire in a furnace, and my weeping (flows) like rivers of water."[95] Vivid reports of weeping also appear in strategic places in the hodayot. In the TH, the speaker describes his agony in the following way: "I eat the bread of my misery and my drink is endless weeping… my bread has been turned into strife, and my drink into a master of disputes. It enters my bones, making (my) spirit stumble and finishing off (my) strength" (1QH XIII, 35–36). In the passage that is the subject of chapter five, the hodayot hymnist reports the totality of his physical devastation in the imitable form of trembling and tears: "The strength of my loins has become a disaster, my arm is shattered at the elbow [and I am un][able] to wave my hand. My [foo]t is bound in shackles, my knees buckle like water, unable to take a step. There is no sound to my footfall" (1QH XVI, 34–35). These excruciating reports of distress likely aroused similar emotions within the reader who is invited to imagine each part of his own body as he moves through the catalogue of the devastated body in the text.

In other ways, the hodayot invite the vivid re-experiencing of the text through their detailed descriptions of the body's experiences. This appeal to sensory experiences heightens a reader's ability to imagine himself in the role of the affective script. The imaginative exercise of placing onself at the scene is facilitated by the text's use of descriptive imagery and references to the body. Descriptions can either map out the reader's own physiology from head to toe, or target specific sensory organs. In these texts, special attention is given to referencing as many of the body's senses as possible. In the case of 1QH XIII, 7–21, a reader can be expected to imagine himself in the very midst of bloodthirsty

---

93   Ibid., 125–34.

94   For other examples of weeping as an induction technique from apocalyptic literature and from the Bible and Canaanite literature, see Merkur, "Visionary Practices of Jewish Apocalyptists," 125–31.

95   Here it is better to read a guttural confusion between the *ayin* and *aleph*. The scroll reads: "my eyes are *like a moth* in a furnace" (כעש), but it is better to read "my eyes (burn) like a fire in a furnace" (כאש).

lions. Meditation on the various details of the lion's mouth and teeth can also activate the imaginative application of the other senses. A reader might imagine the musty odor of the lion's den or hear the panting of the beasts and their terrifying roars. Imagining all of the physically sensible details that are associated with fearsome experiences can achieve an intense reenactment of the emotions that engages an ancient reader's own affective memory. Neuropsychological studies have demonstrated that the multiplicity of sensory stimuli an individual perceives, even when these sensations are learned by instruction and imagined in the mind without any first-hand experiencing. In such circumstances, sensory perception can become so aroused as to make imagined events seem 'real' in the body's expression of emotion.[96] Elizabeth Phelps describes this process in the following way:

> [H]aving an instructed, episodic representation of the emotional significance of a stimulus can lead to activation of the amygdala, which in turn meditates the physiological expression of fear when this stimulus is encountered. These types of fears are imagined and anticipated, *but never actually experienced*, yet they rely on similar neural mechanisms for expression as those that are learned through direct experience.[97] (emphasis mine)

The sensory processing sites of the brain and the areas responsible for cognition are connected in a rich two-way network. When this happens, an ancient reader can hope to achieve the state that Stanislavsky calls "experiencing." Such detailed and rousing descriptions could have served as cues for the reader to reenact the strong emotions of despair that culminate in the expression of tears.

The biological aspect of ritually experienced performative emotions notably highlights an important consequence of the cultural systems that rely on the physical and outward expression of affect. Performative emotions are not spontaneous displays of affect that are generated by unconscious biological responses to external stimuli; rather they are the result of careful training. This display depends upon reiterative bodily practices and can function in critical ways within ritual contexts. In his study of Japanese religious experiences, Gary Ebersole states that

---

96   Linda A. Henkel, N. Franklin, and M. K. Johnson, "Cross-modal Confusions between Perceived and Imagined Events," *Journal of Experimental Psychology: Learning, Memory, & Cognition* 26 (2000): 321–35.

97   Elizabeth A. Phelps, "Human emotion and Memory: Interactions of the Amygdala and Hippocampal Complex," *Current Opinion in Neurobiology* 14 (2004): 198–202, here 200.

performative emotions that are expressed in unambiguous bodily displays are always a part of a tightly controlled and stylized performance:[98]

> Ritualized weeping is a performative act, and instances of it must be analyzed as such. The cases of weeping we will be concerned with are stylized performances of socioculturally constructed and recognized affective displays. To put this another way, the shedding of tears in a tightly scripted program of stylized acts is a performative act, complete with actors and an audience.[99]

Within ritual contexts, the outward display of emotion in the form of tears is crucial in the performative reenactment of ritual texts.

Studies of emotion in the ancient world indicate that emotions had a performative function that reflected social and cultural hierarchies and norms. In studies of tears in the Graeco-Roman world, the display of excessive tears in rituals of mourning carried an important performative function that did not rely upon the whether or not genuine feelings of grief and sadness were present.

> Outward expressions of grief were, according to ancient social norms, necessary, right and an act of duty, against which Cicero argues in his philosophical considerations (Tusc. 3.61, 3.64). The fact that the grief was indeed a social obligation becomes clear after a look at Cassius Dio's account of the burial of the emperor Augustus in 14 A.D. All citizens participated in the ritual mourning, though many of them, Cassius Dio states, did not feel any real grief (Cassius Dio 56.43.1). . . . The citizens of Rome were obliged to express their loyalty and connection to family and patron by outward displays of grief.[100]

The external expression of emotion can be an indicator that a text was reenacted effectively by the reader. As Ebersole is careful to specify, the efficacy of performative emotions did not rely upon whether or not the emotion was 'real,' but upon whether it was physically displayed during the critical moments of the ritual.

---

98 See Gary L. Ebersole, "The Poetics and Politics of Ritualized Weeping," 25–51.

99 Ebersole, "The Poetics and Politics of Ritualized Weeping," 26.

100 Darja Šterbenc Erker, "Women's Tears in Ancient Roman Ritual," *Tears in the Graeco-Roman World* (ed. Thorsten Fögen; Berlin: W. de Gruyter, 2009), 135–60, here 138–39; also Augusto Fraschetti, *Rome et le prince* (trans. into the French by Vincent Jolivet; Paris: Belin, 1994), 94.

B. Cultural Specificity of Emotions

Emotions experienced within the context of religious experience reflect expectations that are appropriate to specific cultural contexts. In her comparison of otherworldly journey reports from the medieval period with those of modern times, Carol Zaleski has shown that the emotions experienced reflect the distinct cultural expectations of the time and the circumstances of the seer. Such culturally-specific expectations become incorporated into the vision, even though general features of the journey remain consistent across cultures and through time.[101] Certain elements of a vision will reflect the individual's socially conditioned expectations of the narrative journey to the otherworld. The journey is typically a vivid sensory experience of the otherworld, complete with elaborate details of extraordinary topography, and culminating with the transformative experience of the seer. This framework serves as a basic model that is, in turn, imitated over time, even into the contemporary period. Zaleski's study demonstrates the culturally conditioned aspects of affective expectations in the context of religious experience. So too, the recent study by Nina Azari can be said to demonstrate that the culturally conditioned affective experiences of a religious community can strongly influence the ways in which affect emerges in the context of religious experience.[102]

The model of religious experience that is presented here is one which proposes that the ancient reader reenacts the text by displaying

---

101 Carol Zaleski, *Otherworld Journeys*. Memories of fearful and terrifying scenes are seared upon the imagination of these medieval seers. In the case of Peter the Hermit, the palpable experience of fear is a typical feature for many of the visionary reports from the Middle Ages. The austere lives of these seers are thought to have functioned preemptively as a kind of purgatory lived on earth in the hopes of mitigating the time of purification needed after death (78). In contrast, there is a striking absence of the affect of fear in modern day visionary experiences which report that "subjects were left with a profound sense of serenity, humility, and wonder." (142)

102 Nina P. Azari, Janpeter Nickel, Gilbert Wunderlich, Michael Niedeggen, Harald Hefter, Lutz Tellmann, Hans Herzog, Petra Stoerig, Dieter Birnbacher, and Rüdiger J. Seitz, "Neural Correlates of Religious Experience," *European Journal of Neuroscience* 13 (2001): 1649–52. This study demonstrated the dissimilar affective experience (absence of emotional arousal) for members of a German pietistic community during states of religious experience. Such a socially reserved group can be said to have a dissimilar affect from the other groups that showed high correlation with affect and religious experience.

the appropriate performative emotions aroused by it. It is important to note that religious experience, as it is described here, is not predetermined or guaranteed to happen as a result of executing these bodily practices; rather, the reenactment of performative emotions creates the necessary preconditions for its possibility. By reenacting the lyrical body's suffering, the ancient reader can hope to re-experience the events of being in the heavenly realm and so he reads with an "I" to the heavens, with an expectation to ascend eventually into the heavenly angelic communion. When the right performative emotions are physically aroused in the reader, he can enjoy a largely scripted sensation of the religious transformations that the texts describe. The emotions that are reenacted can guide the reader to participate in the scripted religious experiences described in the text. This type of religious experience is discussed in chapter three. At the same time, the creation of the subjectivity of the visionary can allow him to generate new religious experiences that exceed these scripted affect experiences of the imaginal body. In this type of experience, the reader enjoys an intensity of greater participation in the experience. In such instances, a reader can be said to become transformed into an author who generates a new experience of his own. In the latter scenario, religious experience is understood to be generative and innovative (Derrida's principle of supplementarity).[103] This type of religious experience will be discussed in chapters four and five.

C. The Political Dimension of Performative Emotions

Much of the scholarship on strongly valenced emotions such as fear is conducted by both neuropsychologists and also social psychologists who share a cultural interest in managing negative emotions that plague individuals who suffer from debilitating phobias or depressions. Emotion researchers strongly resist the claim that individuals are predetermined to have specific emotion experiences and express the view that all affective processes can be managed over time. Nevertheless, not everyone has the same capacity for affective memory training, with few

---

103 In the case of the religious experience understood as the scripted reenactment of affect, the event is generative insofar as the embodied subjectivity is a result and it also participates in the principle of supplementarity insofar as each reenactment with be different.

people possessing the potential to exercise full mastery over their emotions and to arouse them at will. Psychologists describe this predisposition of openness to experiences as "imaginative involvement" and "absorption."[104] Suzanne Roche and Kevin McConkey write that individuals who show a predisposition to absorption also rate very high on synesthesia or sensory processing:

> [G]ood synesthetes transform, enrich, store, and encode events in a variety of sensory modalities, and the stored representations are engaging and highly involving. This suggests that high-absorption subjects elaborate internal and external events in a multimodal or cross-modal way; it also suggests that the experience of absorption involves spontaneous elaboration of a synesthetic kind. . . . Furthermore, high-absorption subjects appear to incorporate into their sensory experience events that are subtly suggested by their imaginings. Rader and Tellegen's findings highlight the need for further analysis of the relationship of absorption with cross-modal experiencing of both externally presented and internally generated events.[105]

Individuals who demonstrate a high-absorption tendency also show a high degree of facility with visualization and cross-modal processing of sensory stimuli.[106] These studies show that there is a high degree of variability of predispositions to imaginative involvement and absorption, and that not all individuals process sensory stimuli with the same degree of vividness.[107]

For the majority of people, the openness to imaginative involvement and absorption of affective experiences varies greatly with the ma-

---

104 Suzanne M. Roche and Kevin M. McConkey, "Absorption: Nature, Assessment, and Correlates," *Journal of Personality and Social Psychology* 59 (1990): 91–101. Also see Martha L. Glisky, Douglas J. Tataryn, Betsy A. Tobias, John F. Kihlstrom, and Kevin M. McConkey, "Absorption, Openness to Experience, and Hypnotizability," *Journal of Personality and Social Psychology* 60 (1991): 263–72.
105 Roche and McConkey, "Absorption," 96.
106 T. Cameron Wild, Don Kuiken, and Don Schopflocher, "The Role of Absorption in Experiential Involvement," *Journal of Personality and Social Psychology* 69 (1995): 569–79. These authors observe that many of these traits are associated with aesthetic perceptions and the arts. Ronald J. Pekala, Catherine F. Wenger, and Ralph L. Levine, "Individual Differences in Phenomenological Experience: States of Consciousness as a Function of Absorption," *Journal of Personality and Social Psychology* 48 (1985): 123–32.
107 Notably, the clinical tests that measure this are in need of refinement. Many rely upon the self-reported traits of college students, a majority of whom are female, and a representative sampling of broader ranges of range and gender are not easily accessed; Roche and McConkey, "Absorption," 99.

jority of people experiencing affective memory construction and reconstruction as a subconscious and instantaneous process. Certain individuals succeed in disciplining their affective memory by repeatedly performing certain techniques, but the disciplining of the emotions is a
skill that not all are able to master and one that requires extensive training and preparation. There is no reason to assume that the ancient reader
who sought to achieve a visionary experience from reading would have
found it to be an easy process. It is more likely that individuals who
were able to achieve a religious experience from meditative reading
were few in number.

Because performative emotions are outwardly displayed physical experiences, they enjoy a political dimension. Gary Ebersole writes that
when performative emotions are rightly reenacted within the proper ritualized contexts, they can function in important ways, including the ad-
vancement of the social status of the one who performs them.[108] This
aspect of performative emotions is what evolutionary anthropologists
describe as a costly display that can earn credibility and prestige for
the one who performs them in appropriate ritual acts.[109] In the case
of the performative emotions displayed by the ancient reader of the
Qumran hodayot, the tears that express the suffering of the rhetorical
"I" in the texts are the costly display that cannot easily be mimicked
by most individuals. Costly displays are acts that are difficult to replicate
or that require a significant expenditure of energy or express suffering of
some sort. For religious societies, the costly display can serve to authenticate the individual who performs it. The performative act demonstrates the individual's utmost and unwavering commitment to the religious community.

---

108 Ebersole, "The Function of Ritual Weeping," 187.
109 Richard Sosis, "The Adaptive Value of Religious Ritual: Rituals Promote
Group Cohesion by Requiring Members to Engage in Behavior that is Too
Costly to Fake," *American Scientist* 92 (2004): 166–72; Joseph Henrich, "The
Evolution of Costly Displays, Cooperation and Religion: Credibility Enhanc-
ing Displays and their Implications for Cultural Evolution," *Evolution and
Human Behavior* 30 (2009): 244–60; Joseph Henrich and Francisco J. Gil-
White, "The Evolution of Prestige Freely Conferred Deference as a Mecha-
nism for Enhancing the Benefits of Cultural Transmission," *Evolution and
Human Behavior* 22 (2001): 165–96; Joseph Henrich, Richard McElreach, Abi-
gail Barr, Jean Ensminger, Clark Barrett, Alexander Bolyanatz, Juan Camilo
Cardenas, Michael Gurven, Edwins Gwako, Natalie Henrich, Carolyn Lesoro-
gol, Frank Marlowe, David Tracer, John Ziker, "Costly Punishment Across
Human Societies," *Science* 312 (2006): 1767–70.

Many religious ritual actions can be considered as costly displays–circumcision, celibacy, requiring specific garments, mortification of the flesh, insistence upon knowing and using a specific ancient language. These behaviors express a high level of commitment of the members in that community or group and result in a heightened sense of entitivity among the members of that group and pro-social behavior such as cooperation to meet common goals. Richard Sosis writes that

> Adherence to a set of religious beliefs entails a host of ritual obligations and expected behaviors. Although there may be physical or psychological benefits associated with some ritual practices, the significant time, energy and financial costs involved serve as effective deterrents for anyone who does not believe in the teachings of a particular religion.[110]

While the Qumran covenanters likely shared aspects of literacy that otherwise stratified other ancient communities, texts like the Community Rule emphasize a strong hierarchical social context. The hodayot as a collection are written in the first person voice and are presumed to have been performed by a single individual, and not a group of individuals. Contrary to Carol Newsom's thesis that the hodayot were recited as initiation texts, I have suggested that the hodayot were performed by the *maskil*– an individual who reenacted the affective experiences described in the texts. The display of scripted performative emotions by the *maskil* would have served to demonstrate and renew the authenticity of his religious commitment in the eyes of the community. The reenactment of scripted emotions allows the *maskil* to generate the appropriate subjectivity that will predispose him to having his own religious experiences. Such a process can help to explain how the collection came into being over time since certain compositions are written by different authors using different orthographic systems.

The expression of performative emotions within the context of ritualized reading has a political dimension and serves to confirm and elevate an individual's status within the community and to contribute to the experience of entitivity in the group. Emotions, when rightly situated within the ritualized context of performance, can be imagined in an instrumental way as assisting an ancient reader in moving from the ritualized performance of a text to engendering his own religious experi-

---

110 Sosis, "The Adaptive Value of Religious Ritual," 169; also Joseph Bulbulia and Richard Sosis, "Signalling Theory and the Evolution of Religious Cooperation," *Religion* 41 (2011): 363–388.

ence. In so doing, the ancient reader could have also succeeded in confirming his status as a religious virtuoso within the community.

Conclusion

Texts that detail the physical and psychological horrors of the body through the first person voice demonstrate the compelling aspect of these rhetorical tools for readers. Dramatic laments and vivid language about the body in the TH figure prominently to draw the reader emotionally into the text and to allow for the affective synchronization of the reader's emotions with those described in the text. While the emotions of fear and terror (both of which are related to suffering) are not the only affective experiences in the TH, these emotions are the most compelling ones. Emotions within the hodayot function in a strategic way and influence the experience of reading. Amy Kalmanofsky's study of the rhetorical use of terror in the book of Jeremiah demonstrates well how compelling the emotion of fear was for the ancient reader. In the case of the prophetic texts, emotion functioned to motivate the reader to change his/her behavior and repent.[111] The arousal of emotions is instrumental and strategically directed towards transformation.

Carol Newsom is right to assert that the first-person speech in the hodayot functions rhetorically to draw the reader "into a self-understanding shaped according to the patterns embedded in the hodayot."[112] Language about the imaginal body and its sensory functions along with

---

111 Amy Kalmanofsky, *Terror all Around: Horror, Monsters, and Theology in the Book of Jeremiah* (New York: T&T Clark, 2008).Kalmanofsky draws upon the work of Noël Carroll when she writes that "reading is primarily an emotional experience. Emotions render texts intelligible. Texts elicit emotions that both attract and guide a reader through the narrative, enabling the reader to make sense of the presented plot," (92). Noël Carroll, "Art, Narrative, and Emotion," *Emotion and the Arts* (ed. Mette Hjort and Sue Laver; New York: Oxford University, 1997), 190–211. See also Jenefer Robinson, *Deeper Than Reason: Emotion and its Role in Literature, Music, and Art* (Oxford: Clarendon Press, 2005), 122–35. Interpretation itself relies upon emotional engagement; Robinson writes, "experiences, feelings, and responses can then form the basis for a critical reading of the work" (124); and "the emotions are ways of focusing *attention* on those things that are important" (126, italics original).

112 Newsom, "Constructing 'We, You, and the Others' through Non-Polemical Discourse,"13–21, esp. 18–20; and eadem, *Self as Symbolic Space*, 198–202.

reports of emotional experiences are the rhetorical elements in the text that construct experiences that a reader seeks to reenact. These rhetorical features allow the one who reads through the experiences of the first person "I" to participate in scripted experiences of transformation and intimate encounters with God. The activity of performative reading seeks to re-create these events with an experiential quality of lived experience in the reader and comes to expression in the body's display of emotion.

The focus of performative reading is on the transformation of the one who reads. It is in such a moment that the liminal space between the actor and the role become fused together and the "actor becomes taken over by a role" and becomes taken up into its "flow."[113] Richard Schechner describes the distinction between the performer's experience of entering wholly into his role as "transformation" and the return as "transportation."

> I call performances where performers are changed "transformations" and those where performers are returned to their starting places "transportations." "Transportation" because during the performance the performers are "taken somewhere" but at the end, often assisted by others, they are "cooled down" and reenter ordinary life just about where they went in. The performer goes from the "ordinary world" to the "performative

---

113 Richard Schechner, "Performers and Spectators: Transported and Transformed," *Kenyon Review*, n.s. 3 (1981): 83–113, here 89. Schechner is most famous for his pioneering work in environmental theater which breaks down the traditional understandings of performance space, seeking instead to envelop the audience with the performance; see *Environmental Theater* (New York: Hawthorn Books, 1973). There Schechner describes his own work in performance theory as a form of social science and not aesthetics (vii). The idea of a performance having a "flow" comes from Clifford Geertz (*The Interpretation of Cultures: Selected Essays* [New York: Basic Books, 1973], 10 and 17) who writes the following about actions and their signification: "Once human behavior is seen as (most of the time; there are *true* twitches) symbolic action—action which, like phonation in speech, pigment in painting, line in writing, or sonance in music, signifies—the question as to whether culture is patterned conduct or a frame of mind, or even the two somehow mixed together, loses sense. The thing to ask about a burlesqued wink or a mock sheep raid is not what their ontological status is. . . . . The thing to ask is what their import is: what it is, ridicule or challenge, irony or anger, snobbery or pride, that, in their occurrence and through their agency, is getting said. . . . Behavior must be attended to, and with some exactness, because it is through the flow of behavior—or more precisely, social action—that cultural forms find articulation. They find it as well, of course, in various sorts of artifacts, and various states of consciousness; but these draw their meaning from the role they play."

world," from one time/space reference to another, from one personality reference to one or more others.[114]

During the moment of "experiencing" the reader can re-experience the events described in the script that is being performed. The rhetorical "I" allows the reader to access the extreme experiences described in the prayer text, the goal of experiencing traumatic suffering is religious transformation and ascent into the heavenly realm. Such transformation is also accessible to viewers of this ritualized reading, albeit in a different way. Schechner writes, "[s]pectators at transformation performances usually have a stake in seeing that the performance succeeds. They are relatives of the performers, part of the same community. Thus in transformation performances the attention of the transported and the spectators converges on the transformed."[115] Performative reading, insofar as the ritual recitation is presumed to take place in a communal context, may result in a performance that could in turn be efficacious for viewers such that they too experience transformation, yet the two experiences remain wholly distinct.

Embodiment language and the rhetorical "I" do not report the experiences of a historical individual but rather construct an affective script of an imaginal body whose experiences an ancient reader is invited to identify as his own. A key part of this movement from the ritualized reading of a text to the religious experience of it is the ancient reader's ability to reenact the emotions of fear and desolation when he imaginatively places himself within the scenes described in the text. Details that target specific sensory perceptions of seeing and hearing are especially effective at assisting a reader in "experiencing" the text. According to the method of reading proposed here, the reader, through the performative activity of reading texts that describe religious experiences, could have come to experience the scripted moments transformations that the text describes by creating the subjectivity of the imaginal body in the text.

The social context of emotions in the ancient world did not share the modern concern to arbitrate between real and fake emotions or

---

114 Schechner, "Performers and Spectators," 91.
115 Schechner, "Performers and Spectators," 95–96. In contrast to this scenario where the community understands the performance and is tuned into the experiences of the performer who is being transported, Schechner describes the mundane viewing of modern Broadway performances as requiring very little of the spectator apart from his/her responsivity (109).

real and fake religious experiences. The bodily expressions of performative emotions did, however, confirm that an extraordinary experience took place. The physical display of affect (tears, blushing, trembling) within the context of ritual experiences serves an important purpose as a costly display. If that religious experience generated a new vision, then the outward display of performative emotions can be said to authenticate the new religious experience. The hodayot texts, anonymous writings describing extraordinary experiences of transformation, were writings that were generated over time and authenticated by the performative emotions of the body.

Chapter 3
Progressive Spatialization:
The Scripted Movement Out From Places of Punishment

Spatiality refers to the elaborate way that language about space and physical experience contributes to a reader's phenomenal experience of an event. In other words, all of the sensations of embodiment that are experienced by the imaginal body discussed in chapter two become available to the ancient reader through the language of spatiality, which not only includes aspects of embodied experiences but also the physical aspects of an individual's surroundings. This chapter provides a broad overview of the visionary aspects of the hodayot as detailed reports of progressive otherworldly bodily experiences with a clear spatial dimension. Spaces in the hodayot (TH + CH II) mark the reader's journey out from places of punishment to paradise and into the heavens. Spatial details contribute a sense of realism that likely facilitated an ancient reader's reenactment of the emotions that they arouse.[1] Critical spatial theory can help to parse how space is understood in the hodayot and how it relates to religious experience.

I. Critical Spatial Theory: Firstspace, Secondspace, and Thirdspace

Jon Berquist describes spatial and spatiality in the following way:

---

1 See Yairah Amit, *Reading Biblical Narratives: Literary Criticism and the Hebrew Bible* (trans. Y. Lotan; Minneapolis: Fortress Press, 2001), 115–25; Johan Brinkman, *The Perception of Space in the Old Testament: An Exploration of the Methodological Problems of its Investigation, Exemplified by a Study of Exodus 25–31* (Kampen: Kok Pharos, 1992); and the discussion in Françoise Mirguet, "Numbers 16: The Significance of Place—An Analysis of Spatial Markers," *JSOT* 32 (2008): 311–330, esp. 315–18.

Within the growing body of literature on critical spatiality, the terms space and spatiality refer to aspects of reality that involve concepts of distance, height, width, breadth, orientation and direction, and also human perceptions, constructions and uses of these aspects.[2]

Religious texts construct elaborate spatial worlds and also reuse familiar spaces in significant ways. Critical spatial theorists call the descriptions of spaces of the world as we know it empirically as 'Firstspace' or ordinary geography.[3] In contrast, spaces constructed by religious texts are called

---

2   Jon L. Berquist, "Critical Spatiality and the Construction of the Ancient World," in *Imagining Biblical Worlds: Studies in Spatial, Social, and Historical Constructs in Honor of James W. Flanagan* (ed. David M. Gunn and Paula McNutt; London: Sheffield Academic Press, 2002), 14–29, here 15. Berquist discusses critical spatiality's indebtedness to Marx and various social theories. Important foundational work on spatial theory and biblical studies was done by James W. Flanagan, "Ancient Perceptions of Space/ Perceptions of Ancient Space," in *The Social World of the Hebrew Bible: Twenty-Five Years of the Social Sciences in the Academy* (Semeia 87; ed. R. A. Simpkins and S. L. Cook; Atlanta: Society of Biblical Literature, 1999), 15–43; idem., "Space" in *Handbook of Postmodern Biblical Interpretation* (St. Louis: Chalice Press, 2000), 239–44; idem., "Mapping the Biblical World: Perceptions of Space in Ancient Southwestern Asia," in *Mappa Mundi: Mapping Culture/Mapping the World* (ed. Jacqueline Murray; Working Papers in the Humanities 9; Windsor: Humanities Research Group at the University of Windsor, 2001), 1–18; See also the recent collection in honor of James Flanagan: David M. Gunn and Paula McNutt, (eds), *Imagining Biblical Worlds: Studies in Spatial, Social, and Historical Constructs in Honor of James W. Flanagan*; also Jon L. Berquist and Claudia V. Camp (eds), *Constructions of Space I: Theory, Geography, and Narrative.* New York: Continuum, 2008.

3   Berquist in "Critical Spatiality and the Construction of the Ancient World," explains this terminology, which is taken from the theorist Edward W. Soja: "Soja writes of three spaces: Firstspace (geophysical realities as perceived), Secondspace (mapped realities as represented) and Thirdspace (lived realities as practiced)" (20); see Edward W. Soja, *Thirdspace*, whose work is indebted to Henri Lefebvre, *The Production of Space*. It is also necessary to refer here to the slightly different but analogous model of spatiality described by Michel Foucault (trans. Jay Miskowiec), "Of Other Spaces," 22–27. Here see the discussion of these post-modern theorists by Flanagan, "Ancient Perceptions of Space/Perceptions of Ancient Space," 27–30 and Philip R. Davies, "Space and Sects in the Qumran Scrolls," in *Imagining Biblical Worlds*, 81–97. More recently, see the excellent discussion of critical spatiality outlined by Christl M. Maier, *Daughter Zion, Mother Zion: Gender, Space, and the Sacred in Ancient Israel* (Minneapolis: Fortress Press, 2008), 10–29; and Alison Schofield, "Re-placing Priestly Space: The Wilderness as Heterotopia in the Dead Sea Scrolls," in *A Teacher for All Generations: Essays in Honor of James C. VanderKam* (JSJS 153/I; ed. Eric F. Mason et al; Leiden: Brill, 2012), 470–90.

'Secondspace' or religious geography, wherein "theological imagination and religious cosmology play an active role in representing geographical space."[4] While Secondspace experiences and events reference or reuse elements familiar from ordinary experience, they should not and cannot be equated with ordinary geography. The realm of Secondspace is phenomenal and experiential but it does not rely on any single empirical reality as its model; in fact, no actual site is used as a model and it occupies no physical place. Secondspace accounts are constructed by communities to serve political and religious purposes.[5]

The idea of Secondspace is analogous to Michel Foucault's notion of utopia, which he calls "a placeless place."[6] In his example of the mirror, Foucault describes how the mirror functions as a utopia because it offers a glimpse into a virtual space that occupies no place.[7] He writes:

---

4   Thomas B. Dozeman, "Biblical Geography and Critical Spatial Studies," in *Constructions of Space I: Theory, Geography, and Narrative* (ed. Jon L. Berquist and Claudia V. Camp; New York: Continuum, 2008), 87–108, here 88; also R. W. Stump, "The Geography of Religion—Introduction," *Journal of Cultural Geography* 7 (1986): 1–3.

5   While they doesn't use the language of critical spatial theory, the analysis of the geography in *Jubilees* as serving a larger theological and political purpose and not reflecting actual ordinary geography is proposed by James C. VanderKam, "Putting them in their Place: Geography as an Evaluative Tool," in *Pursuing the Text: Studies in Honor of Ben Zion Wacholder on the Occasion of his Seventieth Birthday* (ed. John C. Reeves and John Kampen; JSOTSup 184; Sheffield: Sheffield Academic Press, 1994), 46–69; repr. in *From Revelation to Canon: Studies in the Hebrew Bible and Second Temple Literature* (JSJS 62; Leiden: Brill, 2000), 476–99; page citations are from this repr; and Daniel Machiela, "'Each to His Own Inheritance': Geography as an Evaluative Tool in the Genesis Apocryphon," *DSD* 15 (2008): 50–66.

6   See Michel Foucault (trans. Jay Miskowiec), "Of Other Spaces," 24. It is not necessary to attach only positive ideas to this idea of utopia, they are placeless spaces but do not carry an intrinsic positive value.

7   Here, note that Foucault uses the idea of "space" differently from "place" which is more concrete and precise. Peter Johnson writes the following in his essay, "Unravelling Foucault's 'Different Spaces,'" *History of the Human Sciences* 19 (2006): 75–90: "As is often remarked, there are complex and subtle relational differences in English and French between space [*espace*] and place [*lieu*]. Augé provides a helpful and succinct distinction. 'Space' is much more abstract than 'place'. The former term can refer to an area, a distance and, significantly in relation to Foucault's concept of heterotopia, a temporal period (the space of two days). The latter, more tangible term, refers to an event or a history, whether mythical or real" (76–77). Here he cites M. Augé, *Non-Places: Introduction to an Anthropology of Supermodernity* (London: Verso, 1995), 81–4.

Utopias are sites with no real place. They are sites that have a general relation of direct or inverted analogy with the real space of Society. . . .
The mirror is, after all, a utopia, since it is a placeless place. In the mirror,
I see myself there where I am not, in an unreal, virtual space that opens up
behind the surface; I am over there, there where I am not, a sort of shadow
that gives my own visibility to myself, that enables me to see myself there
where I am absent; such is the utopia of the mirror.[8]

Even though the word carries an overwhelmingly positive association in
common parlance, Foucault's utopia need not be idealized as referring
to only positive places. The idea of Secondspace or Foucault's utopia
is the phenomenal world of the imaginal speaker described in chapter
two and refers to richly detailed experiences that are constructed imaginatively by the text, none of which exist in real space and time. Secondspace is, I propose, a helpful framework for understanding the phenomenal religious geography constructed by the text of the hodayot,
into which a reader can enjoy embodied scripted experiences through
an imitative reenactment of the text. When a reader performatively
reads the hodayot and imagines himself in these secondspatial terrains,
he engages in a scripted reenactment of the experiences of transformation that these texts describe.

Beyond these two spaces, there is another place called the 'Thirdspace,' which is the realm of lived experience where the creative process
of transformation is possible and power is reconfigured. Thirdspace is a
liminal realm that reaches into the interstices of lived existence. For the
theorists most closely associated with this conceptual triad of spatiality,
Henri Lefebvre and Edward Soja, Thirdspace is primarily a place of resistance where alternative realities come into being. Both scholars envi-
sion Thirdspace with a strong Marxist lens.[9] This oppositional aspect,

---

8   Foucault, "Of Other Spaces," 24.
9   Thirdspace is also associated with what are known as Post-marxism approaches
     which include thinkers like Michel Foucault whom we will discuss shortly (see
     Peter Beilharz, "Post-Marxism" in the *Encyclopedia of Social Theory, Vol. 1* [ed.
     George Ritzer; Thousand Oaks: Sage, 2005], 581) and other theoretical studies
     in identity and power, including post-colonialism. For a summary of these so-
     cial theories, see Elizabeth King Keenan and Dennis Miehls, "Third Space Ac-
     tivities and Change Processes: An Exploration of Ideas from Social and Psycho-
     dynamic Theories," *Clinical Social Work Journal* 36 (2008): 165–75; H. K.
     Bhabha, *The Location of Culture* (London: Routledge, 1994) and G. E. Anzal-
     dúa, *Borderlands/La Frontera: The New Mestiza* (San Francisco: Aunt Lute
     Books, 1999). Keenan and Miehls describe Thirdspace as "thresholds where ex-

however, is not inherent in the idea of Thirdspace and I am reluctant to introduce a necessary condition of opposition into the idea of Thirdspace experiences, since doing so can pre-determine experiences in Thirdspace as resistance and restrict full participation as lived experience. Instead, I find Michel Foucault's concept of heterotopia to be helpful.[10] Peter Johnson argues that Foucault's understanding of heterotopia does not carry an inherent idea of resistance to a dominant culture.[11] Returning to the idea of the 'placeless place' occupied by the mirror, Foucault explains how the mirror can simultaneously function as a heterotopia insofar as it is grounded in actual experiential phenomena:

> But it [i.e., mirror] is also a heterotopia in so far as the mirror does exist in reality, where it exerts a sort of counteraction on the position that I occupy. . . . The mirror functions as a heterotopia in this respect: it makes this place that I occupy at the moment when I look at myself in the glass at once absolutely real, connected with all the space that surrounds it, and absolutely unreal, since in order to be perceived it has to pass through this virtual point which is over there.[12]

Foucault's heterotopia is a space of simultaneity because it includes the full range of sensations and the freedom of movement that comes with experiential physicality. Such experiences are phenomenally real but elusive. Foucault writes that heterotopias "always presuppose a system of opening and closing that both isolates them and makes them penetrable. In general, the heterotopic site is not freely accessible like a public

---

isting perspectives are dissembled, other perspectives are considered, and new understandings emerge" (166).

10 See the discussion by Soja, *Thirdspace*, 15–16; according to Soja, Lefebvre called the Thirdspace "lived spaces of representation." Foucault, "Of Other Spaces," 22–27; referred to these spaces as "heterotopias," the "space in which we live, which draws us out of ourselves, in which the erosion of our lives, our time and our history occurs" (here 23, see also 24–27). I find Foucault's description of heterotopia to be more amenable than the understanding of Thirdspace, but I will use the two terms interchangeably.

11 P. Johnson ("Unraveling Foucault's 'Different Spaces,'" 81–82) writes: "[t]he supposition here is that Foucault's 'different spaces' are sites for resistance to the dominant culture. This may be one interpretation, but it is actually difficult to find anyone who explicitly makes a sustained case for it. Hetherington asserts that the term has been used to identify 'sites of marginality that act as postmodern spaces for resistance and transgression—treating them in many ways as liminal spaces' but the references he provides are not substantive;" Kevin Hetherington, *The Badlands of Modernity: Heterotopia and Social Ordering* (London: Routledge, 1997), 41.

12 Foucault, "On Other Spaces," 24.

place. Either the entry is compulsory, as in the case of entering a barracks or prison, or else the individual has to submit to rites and purifications. To get in, one must have a certain permission and make certain gestures."[13] Heterotopias are liminal real world experiences and so they have real world consequences and it follows that those who experience these 'other spaces' might benefit from changes in status as a result.

Experiences of heterotopias can be generated by ritual practices. A fine example of the constructed, not actual, understandings of the Land in the apocalypse of *2 Baruch* is offered by Liv Ingeborg Lied who writes:

> [T]his study maintains that *2 Baruch*'s descriptions of the locations of the Land are fuzzy and fluid, and that locations may be rejected and replaced. This does not mean that the Land is not considered to have a location. The Land is always located and, therefore, always has a territory associated with it, but since praxis is given priority, no single geographical spot is, *per se*, considered to be the Land. The status 'Land' is not inherent to a territory, but dependent on the transformative ability of righteous praxis.[14]

Here Lied demonstrates how the very idea of the land in *2 Baruch* is generated by the community's religious practices. The ongoing conceptualizations of the land throughout time are responsive to the lived experience of the righteous communities that generate them. Land as a Thirdspatial reality is one created by lived praxis and as such it can be recreated as well.[15]

For our discussion of the hodayot, the body and the material text function as the real world places for heterotopia; both are firmly planted in the ordinary world of lived experiences. Like Foucault's mirror, the text as material object is a kind of heterotopia because it is a physical portal to a world constructed by the religious imagination that has the potential to lead to fully participatory and transformative Thirdspace experiences. The reader's embodied encounter with the scroll as a material object insists upon a linear directional movement from right to left without the freedom of random access. Because of this movement from beginning to end, a scroll enjoys unique elements of physical spatiality; and, like the mirror, it simultaneously provides entry points into scripted events imagined in Secondspace and potentially access to the

---

13 Foucault, "Of Other Spaces," 26.
14 Liv Ingeborg Lied, *The Other Lands of Israel: Imaginations of the Land in 2 Baruch* (SJSJ 129; Leiden: Brill, 2008), 17.
15 Lied, *The Other Lands of Israel*, 313.

lived experience of Thirdspace. For our discussion of spatiality the phenomenon of reading a material text– the scroll– and of reenacting the affective experiences described therein provides the physical and real world experience of place that allows for access into the heterotopic space.

The general categorical distinctions between Secondspace and Thirdspace are helpful for distinguishing between what I propose are two fundamentally different types of religious experiences, both of which can be experienced by the ritualized practices of performative reading. Secondspace experiences of events offer an affective script for an ancient reader to reenact in ritual contexts. In this type of religious experience, the language of embodiment and the emotions experienced by the imaginal body in the text, provide a guide for the kind of experience the reader seeks to have. In other words, when the reader positions himself as the "I" in the text, he seeks to generate the subjectivity of the "I" with the aim of accessing the extraordinary experiences of transformation that the texts describe. In this synchronic understanding of the hodayot, all of the spatial and phenomenal reports can be understood to be affective scripts to be used in a Secondspatial reenactment of religious experience.

At the same time, it is possible to consider the hodayot diachronically and consider how certain hodayot were generated as a result of this practice of ongoing performative reading and rereading. Such is the topic of chapter four. Variations in the orthography in 1QH indicate that the hodayot were composed at different times by different authors. The collection is one that emerged over a period of time. Some hodayot show signs that a different type of religious experience has taken place, one that I wish to describe as a Thirdspatial event. In this scenario, performative reading could generate an experience where a reader moved away from the scripted experiences in the text that he was reenacting and became transformed into an author of a substantially new religious experience. In this sense, Thirdspatial experiences can be characterized as having a transformative and generative aspect. Texts that report Thirdspatial events notably record extraordinary phenomenal and spatial experiences from a vivid episodic egocentric perspective. According to this diachronic understanding, certain hodayot compositions can be understood to have been generated from religious experiences of Thirdspace by different anonymous authors.

Borrowing the basic spatial schema from theoretical conceptualizations of space, Thirdspace experiences can be distinguished from Secondspace ones by the fullness of the lived-experience that is reported in them. Secondspatial events also offer perceptual sensations of embodiment that are no less real for the readers who reenact them but the critical difference is that Secondspatial sensations are guided by the text. Texts that report Thirdspace experiences can in turn function as Secondspace scripts for subsequent readers. This process is illustrated well by Kathryn M. Lopez's application of spatial theory to apocalyptic texts.[16] According to Lopez, apocalyptic writings present alternative constructions of religious geography that can be said to emerge from Secondspace constructions of religious geography insofar as they challenge and reinterpret ideas of space imposed by other Jewish groups or hegemonic foreign rulers. When understood in this way, apocalyptic writings can be understood diachronically as having originated as reports of Thirdspace experiences:

> Often described as literal journeys in the narratives of the apocalypses, they created an alternative space that could successfully resist the Secondspace definitions of other Jewish groups as well as those placed upon the region as a colony. The intention of the apocalypse as political writings was to help the 'real –and-imagined' become a livable and lived space for these apocalyptic communities.[17]

Lopez is right to describe apocalyptic writings as presenting alternative realities against externally imposed understandings of space, nevertheless, I hesitate to highlight the oppositional aspect as that which distinguishes Thirdspace from Secondspace because I find that it can potentially over-determine apocalyptic worldviews to consist of *only* resistance. The routinization of apocalyptic texts, what may have been generated from a Thirdspace experience, can then be experienced as the constructed apocalyptic worlds of Secondspace that can be revisited and enculturated. Lopez writes:

> Apocalyptic writings reflect unique constructions of space and time, and the corresponding social phenomenon of apocalypticism, I would contend, indicates that these writings helped normalize the apocalyptic worldview and were, therefore, real for the groups that produced them. The writings

---

16   Kathryn M. Lopez, "Standing Before the Throne of God: Critical Spatiality in Apocalyptic Scenes of Judgment," in *Constructions of Space II: the Biblical City and Other Imagined Spaces* (ed. Jon L. Berquist and Claudia V. Camp; New York: T & T Clark, 2008), 139–55, here 140.

17   Lopez, "Standing Before the Throne of God," 143.

are 'not simply a second-order ideological expression(s) . . . of a pre-given political subject.'[18]

For the purposes of this discussion of the hodayot, I wish to propose understanding the distinctive aspect of Thirdspatial religious experience as a fully participatory experience of events that have been generated by religious practices of performative reading. Rather than resistance, however, I propose distinguishing Thirdspace experiences as significant departures from the scripted experiences of Secondspace. Thirdspatial experiences resemble lived-experience in that participants in Thirdspace are given the creative freedom to challenge, expand, and innovate; engagement is not confined to simply opposition or resistance. Every description of religious geography, either apocalyptic or hegemonic, can function, I propose, as a Secondspace construction that offers a reader a scripted experience of spatiality to reenact. The bodily practice of performative reenactment of these Secondspace experiences can also function as a portal to Thirdspace experiences wherein a reader can hope to generate a religious experience of his own. When this happens, the reader becomes transformed into a full participant in the constructed world of the text and an author of a new religious experience of his own.[19]

In the case of Thirdspace readings of the hodayot, I propose two distinctive aspects of Thirdspatial events. The first is its capacity to transform an ancient reader from an imitator of scripted Secondspace experiences into a full participant in an event. The second is its ability to generate entirely new experiences of the otherworld thus transforming the reader into an author. Both of these functions rely upon ritual practices of performative reading which create an embodied subjectivity in the reader and the necessary predisposition for religious experience. In Thirdspace scenarios, experiences and events are no longer scripted and imitated; they are created anew. Experiences in Thirdspace are liminal experiences that are grounded in ordinary physical spatiality that are transformative and generative. Because they are generated by religious practices, Thirdspace experiences have 'real' public and political consequences in this world insofar as they can be accepted or rejected by a community. Their political impact lies in their potential to alter the real status enjoyed by the elite individuals who experience them.

---

18 Lopez, "Standing Before the Throne of God," 140.
19 How the practice of performative reenactment of affect can generate texts is the topic of chapter 4.

The body of the reader displays the evidence that a Thirdspatial experience has taken place. The anonymous hodayot, unlike other writings from the second temple period, are not authenticated by a pseudonymous attribution system but by the costly displays of affect performed by the body of the reader himself.

I propose that the collection known as 4Q428, when understood synchronically, reflects a general and intentional progression in spatiality that guides an ancient reader from fearful places of punishment to paradise and into the heavens. Similar journey sequencing that moves from punishment to paradise appears in otherworldly visionary texts.[20] In these Secondspace realms, a reader can experience moments of transformation by reenacting the scripted emotions described in the text. In doing so, he positioned himself as a viewer of the events as they are described through the subjectivity of the "I" in the text. The religious experience that takes place in these Secondspace texts is a scripted reenactment of affect; the ancient reader of the hodayot aimed to re-experience the phenomenal sensations of the imaginal body in a religiously constructed world. The imaginal body of the speaker functions as the vehicle through which the ancient reader moves through the constructed terrain of religious geography of the hodayot through the subjectivity of "ancient textualized persons."[21] In contrast to this, Thirdspace or the realm of lived religious experience, are events that are generated during the practice of performative reading when an ancient reader has been phenomenally transformed into a participant in a new visionary experience. This chapter is concerned to describe the religious geography (Secondspace) that is constructed by the text of the hodayot and its goal is not to detail how Thirdspace experiences occur. That is a topic reserved for chapters four and five.

---

20 Texts that demonstrate this sequencing of sites include Enoch's journeys in the Book of the Watchers, and John's visions in Rev., among others; Kelley Coblentz Bautch discusses these two locales of punishment and paradise, in her excellent essay, "Mythic Geography," *The Eerdmans Dictionary of Early Judaism* (ed. John J. Collins and Daniel C. Harlow; Grand Rapids: Eerdmans, 2010), 673–74. The author uses the term "mythic geography" to refer to "sites, topography, regions, or realms that have a legendary quality to them and are in some manner ordinarily inaccessible to humankind" (673). Instead of adopting the language of "mythic geography," I prefer to refer to these sites constructed from religious texts and traditions more generally as "religious geography," or Secondspace.

21 Claudia Camp, "Storied Space, or, Ben Sira 'Tells' a Temple," in *Imagining Biblical Worlds*, 64–80, here 77.

II. The Secondspace Terrain of the Hodayot

The texts of the hodayot describe a detailed religious geography (Secondspace) that reflects a general movement out from places of punishment to places of paradise and eventually bring the reader into the heavens. Such places have physical elements that are familiar to our ordinary perceptions of the world and arouse bodily responses in the form of emotions, but they themselves are realms that are constructed rhetorically from religious texts and traditions. As such, they do not map onto a consistent image of space and occupy no actual place in ordinary geography.

In the biblical example of Ezra's penitential prayer in Nehemiah 9, the retelling of the Exodus wanderings and the accounts of the settlement of the land are Secondspace reports that use familiar geographical markers of the Sea of Reeds (יַם־סוּף), Mount Sinai (הַר־סִינַי), Egypt (מִצְרַיִם), and wilderness (מִדְבָּר). These details give the story a sense of realism and authenticity, yet the exact location of these events in ordinary geography is not clear and not recoverable.[22] These vivid descriptions of Secondspace realms are illusory insofar as they cannot be synchronized with actual (Firstspace) maps of the ancient near east.[23] Like the locales described in visionary reports, the sites in Secondspace defy modern attempts to lay them out in a consistent spatial paradigm. In her discussion of the otherworldly sites visited by the seer Enoch, Kelley Coblentz Bautch discusses the confounding way that the clear physical markers of these places of punishment recorded in Enoch's various journey reports resist fitting into a common conceptual geography with each other and with other geographic systems known from antiquity. She writes:

> From this brief examination of Second Temple period works, we see that no one work replicates exactly the cosmology or geographical interests of 1 Enoch 17–19, though the Hebrew Apocalypse of Elijah certainly comes

---

22 Lied comments on this similar technique in *2 Baruch*, that familiar and clearly recognizable elements are introduced in order to "make that presentation recognizable, meaningful, and a source of comfort to its audience" (*The Other Lands of Israel*, 309).

23 See the discussion by James W. Flanagan, "Ancient Perceptions of Space/Perceptions of Ancient Space," 38–39. Here he engages Peter Machinist, "Outsiders or Insiders: The Biblical View of Emergent Israel and Its Contexts," in *The Other in Jewish Thought and History: Constructions of Jewish Culture and Identity* (ed. Laurence J. Silberstein and Robert L. Cohn; New York: New York University Press, 1994), 35–60, here 54.

close. Even within the Enochic corpus itself, the cosmos as well as sacred sites are often transformed—as one finds in 1 Enoch 108's depiction of an eastern place of punishment beyond the edges of the earth—or reflect other paradigms, such as the multiple heaven schema in portions of the Similitudes. Yet we should not expect to find many texts which consistently maintain or slavishly follow 1 Enoch 17–19's cosmology or sense of geography.[24]

Not only is this the case for places of punishment, Secondspace descriptions of paradise also conflate mythical and familiar details from known geographies of this world. The occasional reference to landmarks from ordinary geography lend a quality of authenticity and realism to these descriptions of paradise that are otherwise impossible to locate in real space and impossible to reconcile with one another.[25]

Secondspatial reports are so vividly described with attention to the physicality of the experience that they succeed in simulating actual experiences. For example, the speaker sees the fiery rivers of Belial and the burning mountains in 1QH XI, 20–37 in the Secondspace landscape and also imagines himself in the den of ferocious lions in 1QH XIII, 7–21. Such spaces have clear experiential dimensions, but they do not map onto a single system with clear coordinates. In the case of the den of lions in column XIII, the space does not need to be empirically verified for it to arouse fear. The realism of these spaces helps a reader to phenomenally reenact the bodily experiences of being in those spaces by arousing the physical emotions that are scripted in the text. The reiterated practice of this performative reading can then create

---

24 Kelley Coblentz Bautch, *A Study of the Geography of 1 Enoch 17–19: "No One Has Seen What I Have Seen"* (JSJS 81; Leiden: Brill, 2003), 272. Coblentz Bautch largely engages the work of Peter Gould and Rodney White, *Mental Maps* (2d ed.; Boston: Allen & Unwin, 1986) who argue that mental geography reflects individual perceptions of place which are shaped by key identity markers of social location, preferences, language etc.; on identity issues in religious mapping. Kevin Hetherington describes the political aspect of spatiality in the following way: "space and place are seen to be situated within relations of power and in some cases within relations of power-knowledge. Power is said to be performed through spatial relations and encoded in the representation of space or as 'place myths'" in *The Badlands of Modernity*, 20. See too Berquist, "Critical Spatiality and the Construction of the Ancient World," 24.

25 Martha Himmelfarb, "The Temple and the Garden of Eden in Ezekiel, the Book of the Watchers, and the Wisdom of ben Sira," in *Sacred Places and Profane Spaces: Essays in the Geographics of Judaism, Christianity, and Islam* (ed. Jamie Scott and Paul Simpson-Housley; Westport, Conn.: Greenwood, 1991), 63–78.

within the reader the necessary subjectivity to predispose him to having
the kind of religious experience that is described in the text. The placement of terrifying scenes at the beginning of the collection is a sign of
purposeful redaction because it creates the effect of an incremental
building of affect, eventually moving the reader from one type of consciousness into another. This chapter discusses the Secondspatial places
of terror in the hodayot scroll that appear in columns X–XV which depict several terrifying spaces associated with punishment and entrapment. The spaces in the hodayot scroll shift from places of imprisonment to paradise, a garden situated on the threshold of the heavens.
Chapter five discusses the garden scene is mentioned briefly in 1QH
XIV 15–22 and the extended discursive report of the religious geography of paradise that appears at 1QH XVI, 5–27 in the composition
known as 1QH XVI, 5-XVII, 36. Thereafter, a clear spatial change occurs at the full blank line in 1QH XVII, 37 which can be said to mark
the reader's movement into the heavens. It is at this point that reports of
phenomenal experiences in the heavens appear, along with a marked
change in the affective cadence which has now shifted to the jubilant.

The movement out from places of punishment to paradise and into
the heavenly realm can be detected in other visionary literature which
suggests that ancient visionaries read and reread other visionary reports
and were familiar with this general spatial progression. Tzvi Abusch reports that ancient Mesopotamian visionary journeys follow a cyclical
pattern which reflects the course of natural phenomena.[26] Passageway
between the world of the living and the netherworld was routine and
followed a cyclical course that resembled the circuits of heavenly bodies.[27] In his examination of a particular series of incantation texts known
as the *Maqlû*, Abusch writes that the liminal space between the cosmic
realms of the netherworld and the heavens was marked by a place of imprisonment which held fearsome witches:

> The celebrant must approach Bēlet-ṣēri at the border between the heavens
> and the netherworld, where a passageway or crossing (*nēbiru*) serves as an
> entry point from the netherworld into the heavens. Here, where the two
> worlds meet, there is a place to imprison and hold back those who wish
> to follow a cosmic circuit but who must now not be allowed to go either
> forward into the inhabited world (and then on into the netherworld) or

---

26 Tzvi Abusch, "Ascent to the Stars in a Mesopotamian Ritual: Social Metaphor
    and Religious Experience," in *Death, Ecstasy, and Other Worldly Journeys* (ed.
    John J. Collins and Michael Fishbane; Albany: SUNY, 1995), 15–39.
27 Abusch, "Ascent to the Stars," 15.

backward, like the planets, into the netherworld. The speaker must ensure that the dead witches who had ascended during the festival of the dead be confined for trial at a point between heaven and the netherworld and not permitted to return to the netherworld, whence they could reascend in subsequent years.[28]

The pattern of visiting places of imprisonment first may reflect this ancient mythological presumption that the otherworldly journey begins by crossing this liminal boundary. This general pattern of beginning an otherworldly journey with a visit to places of punishment is attested in the Enochic Book of the Watchers. While it is difficult to reconcile the details of the different journey reports in *1 En.* 17–19 and 20–36, it is clear that in both, Enoch visits places of punishment first and then moves on to paradise. So too in the Apocalypse of John, the seer reports first the scenes of judgment and then the mythical garden Eden as the New Jerusalem.

While the spatial progression from punishment to paradise may be a recurring literary pattern that is consciously imitated by the hodayot author, the affective cadence that it produces can be said to create a script for the psychological journey of the ancient reader. In addition to reflecting general mythological patterns about visionary journeys, the arousal of fear generated by visiting places of imprisonment is especially compelling and can play an instrumental role in creating the necessary subjectivity of a visionary. Because the spatiality of these places of punishment is so vividly described, it can simulate real experiences of these Secondspaces that result in actual bodily responses of the scripted emotion. As an ancient reader positioned himself as the "I" of these hodayot, the imaginative visualization of these otherworldly places facilitated his affective reenactment of these events. This chapter proposes that the hodayot collection follows a clear and linear progression of locales that begins with places of punishment and moves on to places of paradise. The reading of the hodayot, however, is ultimately oriented toward entry into the heavens.

A. Spatial Orientation to the Collection TH+CH II

The hodayot collection that is formed from the TH material and the second group of CH reflects features that indicate that it was shaped

---

28 Abusch, "Ascent to the Stars," 19–20.

with an editorial concern. The composition known as 1QH IX, 1-X, 4 can be considered to be an introduction to the collection.[29] The themes that it engages make it a fitting introduction for a collection that is oriented toward the heavens. In this hymnic praise of God's creative power, the hymnist describes two realms. He begins with a description of the celestial realm and then offers an account of the earthly one, giving greater attention to the former. In the description of the heavens, he includes details about the various angelic beings and the mysterious orbits of the celestial bodies.

> You have stretched out the heavens (12) for Your glory,
> All [] You ha]ve established according to Your will
> And spirits of might according to their statutes
> Before (13) they became angels of h[oliness]
> Became eternal spirits in their dominions,
> Luminaries according to their mysteries,
> (14) Stars according to [their] circuits,
> [and all the stor]m [winds] according to their duty
> Meteors and lightning bolts according to their work
> and storehouses (13) designed according to the[ir] purposes
> [   ] according to their mysteries. *vacat*[30]

The celestial details in this passage anticipate what I propose is the heavenly orientation of the hodayot scroll. Here the idea of the heavenly journey is presented as following a natural cyclical pattern. As expected, shortly after this glimpse of the heavenly realm, there is a report of the speaker's self-conscious awareness of his unworthiness, passages that scrolls scholars call the *Niedrigkeitsdoxologien*.[31] The *Niedrigkeitsdoxologien* appear with some frequency throughout the hodayot scroll. I proposed

---

29 This composition was first suggested as an introduction to the TH collection by Eileen Schuller, "The Cave 4 Hodayot Manuscripts: A Preliminary Description." This composition contains many wisdom themes, and it can be divided into seven units which are formed by six *vacats* (so too, 1QH XV, 9–28 can be divided into seven smaller units).

30 1QH IX, 11–13

31 There is a recurring image of the speaker's depraved and unworthy state but its appearance in the TH and CH II collections that we are examining together in this study differs slightly from the formulation that is found in the first group of CH. The image of the speaker's embodiment as "a creature of clay, kneaded with water" (ואני יצר החמר ומגבל המים) makes an appearance in this hodayah. The exact same formulation, appears later in XI, 24–25. The phrase, "a creature of clay" (יצר חמר) also appears in 1QH XII, 30 and in 1QH XX, 29. Notice that a slightly different formulation of this appears in the CH I: "edifice of dust kneaded with water" (מבנה עפר ומגבל מים), appears in 1QH V, 30.

elsewhere that the *Niedrigkeitsdoxologien* should be coupled with these glimpses of the heavenly realm which are scattered throughout the TH and the second group of CH, in a manner not unlike the realization of unworthiness that Isaiah experiences immediately after seeing the heavenly throne in Isa 6.[32] Later in this introductory composition, the hodayah hymnist offers an extended meditation upon the divine origins of the heavenly liturgy of praise (1QH IX, 29–33).[33] In the places where the *Niedrigkeitsdoxologien* are especially pronounced, in XI, 20–37; XII, 6-XIII, 6; and XVI, 5-XVII, 36, they follow immediately after reports of heavenly ascent and communion with angels.[34]

The phenomenon of reading a scroll imposes a linear progression upon the hodayot compositions that would not otherwise be necessary in a codex that could be randomly accessed. The Secondspace sites in the hodayot appear in a progressive order that begins with places of punishment and moves on to places of paradise. The Secondspace geography of these otherworldly scenes is depicted with stock images that typically appear in a mythic landscape. In addition to referencing these familiar terrifying landmarks, the hodayot in columns X-XV employ a rhetoric of binding and entrapment. A clear shift takes place with the report of the well-watered paradise in 1QH XVI, 5-XVII, 36 as the

---

32 See A. K. Harkins, "A New Proposal for Thinking about 1QH^A Sixty Years after Its Discovery," 101–34. Jürgen Becker says the following about the presence of the *Niedrigkeitsdoxologien* in the CH in his *Das Heil Gottes: Heils-und Sündenbegriffe in den Qumrantexten und im Neuen Testament* (SUNT 3; Göttingen: VandenHoeck & Ruprecht, 1964): "Diese Aussagen sind ferner alles andere als Darstellung subjektiver Verzweiflung, sondern dienen innerhalb der Bekenntnislieder dazu, Gott nur noch höher zu preisen, daß er selbst dieser Ausweglosigkeit Herr wurde. Weiter dürfen diese Bekenntnisse nicht als bewußte Übertreibung aufgefaßt warden, sondern sie wollen in sachlicher Weise den tatsächlichen Zustand schildern" (137–38).

33 "You created breath on the tongue, You know its words, You determined the fruit of the lips prior to their existence. You placed words on the line, and the breath of the lips pour forth in measure. You make the measuring lines go out according to their mysteries, and the utterances of spirits according to their calculation, in order to make known Your glory, in order to recount Your wonders in all the works of Your truth and Your righteous jud[gments], in order to praise Your name with the mouth of all those who know You. According to their understanding they shall bless You forever [and ever]" (1QH IX, 29–33).

34 Sarah Tanzer comments that the *Niedrigkeitsdoxologien* are more detailed in these compositions, see her "Sages at Qumran: Wisdom in the Hodayot," 143–149, here 149; see the discussion in A. K. Harkins, "Thinking about 1QH^A Sixty Years after its Discovery," 106–22.

reader is transported to the mythical garden of Eden, the subject of
chapter five. The scroll culminates with the setting of the heavenly angelic liturgy and the SGH functions as an experiential crescendo.
Table II charts the various shifts in affect and spatiality.

B. Places of Punishment and Entrapment: The Religious Geography of Terror in the TH

Descriptions of religious geography frequently contain features that reiterate scenes known from other cultures and traditions, and this is especially the case for descriptions of the netherworld. In the case of otherworldly places of punishment, stock images frequently populate the
landscape and bring with them psychological aspects of terror. The hodayot that will be discussed here, 1QH X, 22–32; XI, 6–19 + 20–37;
XII, 6-XIII, 6; and XIII, 7–21, were chosen because they offer the
clearest and most sustained descriptions of Secondspace realms. The religious geography in these compositions arouses the terror of physical
punishment and the psychological experience of being trapped and imprisoned. Other affective states of fear and anxiety are generated by allusions to warfare, either besiegement or attacks. The proposal that was
made in chapter two is that the arousal of fear is an instrumental state
that creates the necessary preconditions for religious experience. How
bodily fear is experienced in the reader is discussed in chapter four.

Elaborate Secondspace sites are constructed in the apocalyptic *Book
of the Watchers* and experienced through the character of Enoch. These
punitive spaces are set aside for the disobedient angels.[35] The vague resemblance of these sites to ancient near eastern and Hellenistic mythic
geography is clear but cannot be mapped with any consistency onto
them.[36] Stock features include regions like those reserved for the dead

---

35 The best study on this topic is K. Coblentz Bautch, *A Study of the Geography of 1
    Enoch 17–19*.

36 Observed by R. H. Charles, *The Book of Enoch* (Oxford: Clarendon Press,
    1893), 87; Albrecht Dieterich, *Nekyia: Beiträge zur Erklärung der neuentdeckten
    Petrusapokalypse* (Leipzig: B. G. Teubner, 1893), 217–19; T. Francis Glasson,
    Greek Influence in Jewish Eschatology (London: SPCK, 1961); G. W. E. Nickels-
    burg, *1 Enoch 1*, 62; P. Grelot, "La géographie mythique d'Hénoch et ses sour-
    ces orientales," *RB* 65 (1958): 33–69.

Table II
Progressive Spatialization in the Hodayot

1QH Unit	Emotion	Secondspace realm of Punishment, Paradise, or Heaven	Hodayot Passage labeled according to the Secondspace realm it describes (place of punishment, paradise, heaven)
IX, 1–X, 4		Introductory composition that anticipates the heavenly trajectory of this collection	"You created breath on the tongue, and You know its words. You determined the fruit of the lips prior to their existence. You placed words on the line and the breath of the lips pour forth in measure. You make the measuring lines go out according to their mysteries, and the utterances of spirits according to their calculation, in order to make known Your glory and to recount Your wonders in all the works of Your truth and Your righteous judg[ments] and in order to praise Your name with the mouth of all those who know You. According to their understanding and they shall bless You forever [and ever]" (IX, 29–33)
X, 5–21	Fear	Entrapment Imagery	"You make my feet stand in the domain of wickedness; so that I become a trap for the rebellious but a healing for all who turn away from rebellion" (X, 10–11)
		Places of Punishment (the abyss? and the Pit)	"The assembly of the wicked is seething against me. They roar like a gale on the seas, when their waves churn; they spew forth slime and mud" (X, 14–15)
			"[And all] the men of deceit roar against me, like the sound of the thunder of mighty waters. [All] their thoughts are the plots of Belial. And they throw the life of a man into the Pit." (X, 18–19)
X, 22–32	Fear	Entrapment imagery and the Pit	"You protect me from all the snares of the Pit. Because ruthless men seek my soul." (X, 23)
	Fear	Onslaught of War	"Mighty men have encamped against me, they have surrounded me with all their weapons of war. Arrows burst forth without remedy, and the flashing blade of their spear is like a fire consuming trees. Like the roar of mighty waters is the uproar of their voice; a tempest and a rainstorm to destroy many. Wickedness and worthlessness shall explode as high as the stars when their waves pile up." (X, 27–30)
	Fear	Abyss	"They spread out a net for me, but it shall capture their own feet; and they hid snares for my soul (but) they themselves fall in them" (X, 31)
	Fear	Entrapment imagery	
X, 33–XI, 5	Fear	Pit	"A pit for all my offspring[." (X, 40)
XI, 6–19	Fear	Entrapment	Numerous images of binding and entrapment appear here (see discussion in the body of the chapter);
		Sheol	"She delivers a male through the crashing waves of death; and through the snares of Sheol," (XI, 10)
		Pit	"Shattering pain of the Pit" (XI, 13)
		Abyss	"Foundations of the wall tremble like a ship on the surface of the water, and the clouds thunder with a tumultuous noise! Those who dwell on the dust, like those who go down to the seas, are terrified by the roar of the seas; and all of their sages are like sailors on the deeps. For all their wisdom is confused by the roaring of the seas: When the abyss boils up against the freshwater springs, then waves are tossed up to towering heights, and crashing waves of waters are (heard) in the tumult of their noise and during their churning, Sh[eo]l and [Abaddon] shall open [along with al]l the arrows of the Pit. With their step to the abyss, they will make their noise heard." (XI, 14–18)
		Sheol Abaddon	
		Pit and Abyss	
		Pit	"The gates of [eternity] will open up [under] the doors of the serpent; and they shall shut the doors of the Pit behind the one pregnant with iniquity and eternal bars will be behind all the spirits of the serpent." (XI, 18–19)

Table II
Progressive Spatialization in the Hodayot (Continued)

1QH Unit	Emotion	Secondspace realm of Punishment, Paradise, or Heaven	Hodayot Passage labeled according to the Secondspace realm it describes (place of punishment, paradise, heaven)
XI, 20–37		Heavenly Ascent from Pit/Sheol Abaddon to a heavenly height	"You have redeemed my soul from the Pit; From Sheol Abaddon You have lifted me up to an eternal height, so that I might walk about (ואתהלכה) on an endless plain" (XI, 20–21).
		Heavenly Scene	"You have cleansed a perverted spirit from a great transgression, so that (he) might be stationed in position with the host of the holy ones (צבא קדושים); so that (he) might enter into communion with the congregation of the sons of heaven (בני שמים)" (XI, 22–23; cf. XXIII, 30).
	Fear	Pit	"When all the traps of the Pit are opened, and all the wicked traps and the net of the wretched ones are spread out upon the surface of the water; When all the arrows of the Pit fly out without return and shoot forth without hope. When the measuring line falls against judgment . . . and the snares of death restrain without escape" (XI, 20–29).
		Entrapment	
	Fear	Onslaught of War	". . . then the rivers of Belial will flow over all the high river banks, like a consuming fire in all their channels (?), finishing off every tree, green and dry, from their canals. It spreads by tongues of flame, until all who drink from them (are) gone. It devours the foundations of clay and the expanse of dry land. The bases of the mountains are set aflame, and the roots of flint become torrents of pitch. And it shall consume as far as the great deep (תהום רבה)" (XI, 30–33).
		Abyss	
XI, 38–XII, 5	Fear? Extremely fragmentary composition	Imprisonment	"threats of destruction" (XI, 39) "iron bars" (XI, 40).
XII, 6–XIII, 6	Fear	Punishment in the form of exile	"for he has banished me from my land, like a bird from a nest; and all of my friends and my relatives have been banished from me" (XII, 9–10).
		Conspiracy	"They are mediators of a lie and seers of deceit. They have plotted Belial against me; to exchange Your Torah which You impressed upon my heart, into flattering words for Your people" (XII, 10–12).
		Entrapment	"They withhold the drink of knowledge from thirsty ones, and for their thirst they give them vinegar to drink, in order to gaze upon their error; reeling wildly at their festivals, capturing (them) in their traps" (XII, 12–13).
		Conspiracy and entrapment	"They are liars who plot the plan of Belial and they seek You with a double heart; they are not firm in Your truth. . . They have put their own stumbling block of iniquity in front of themselves and they come seeking You" (XII, 14–15, 16).
		Entrapment	"So that those who devote themselves away from Your covenant may become ensnared by their own schemes" (XII, 20).
	Positive expectation		"Those who are like you shall stand before you forever; . . . I, when holding fast to You, I pull myself upright and stand tall over those who have rejected me"
	Fear		"But as for me, fear and trembling have seized me and all ᵐʸ bones are shattered. My heart melts like wax before a fire, and my knees buckle like water rushing down a slope . . ." (XII, 34–35).
	Positive emotion		"With the abundance of Your mercies, I was helped up and I stood up (ואקומה) and my spirit grew strong in (my) station before affliction." (XII, 36–37).

Table II
Progressive Spatialization in the Hodayot (Continued)

1QH Unit	Emotion	Secondspace realm of Punishment, Paradise, or Heaven	Hodayot Passage labeled according to the Secondspace realm it describes (place of punishment, paradise, heaven)
XIII, 7–21	Fear with the hope of escape	Entrapment	"You put me in a dwelling with many fishermen who spread out (their) net on the surface of the water" (XIII, 9–10)
	Fear	Conspiracy and Entrapment	"All their plans for abduction are the venom of serpents; they lie in wait but they have not opened their mouths against me because You are my God" (XIII, 12–13)
	Fear	Den of lions as a prison	"You rescued my pour soul from a den of lions who sharpen their tongue like a sword" (XIII, 15) There is extensive lion imagery in this hodayah see the text in chapter three.
	Fear with hope of escape	Entrapment	"You deliver the soul of the oppressed like a bir[d from a trap and] like prey from the mouth of lions" (XIII, 20–21)
XIII, 22– XV, 8	Positive emotion	Heavenly scene being at the feet of God (in the presence of God):	"[I give thanks to You] Blessed are you, O Lord, for you have not abandoned the orphan and you have not despised the destitute one, for your strength is witho[ut en]d and your glory without measure. And wonderful warriors are your servants, but a humble people (has a place) in the mud of yo[ur] feet [together] with those who are eager for righteousness so that all the faithful poor may be lifted up from the mire together." (XIII, 22–24)
	Fear	Entrapment and Ambush	"The wor[ds of]Belial unlease a lying tongue; like the poison of serpents darting out continuously. Like those who crawl in the dust, they lash out in order to ambu[sh] The p[oisons] of vipers have no remedy." (XIII, 29–30)
	Fear	Ambush	"They overtook me in narrow straits without shelter" (XIII, 31)
	Despair	Imprisonment	"For I am bound by ropes that cannot be loosened, and with fetters which cannot be broken. A strong wall [around me] and iron bars and doors of [bronze that have no] [opening.] My jail cell is with the abyss; and {I am} considered without a[and the torrents of]Belial engulf my soul without [es]c[ape]
		Vision of angelic beings	"The people of Your council are in the midst of the sons of Adam, in order to recount Your wonders to successive generations an [med]itate on [Your] mighty works without rest. ... For You have brough[t [] and Your secret to all the men of Your council, and in the lot together with the angels of presence, without a mediator between [Your] h[oly ones to] reply according to the spirit" (XIV, 14–17)
		Garden of Eden	"And they will repent at Your glorious word, and they shall become Your princes in the [eternal l]o[t and] their [shoot,] a flower will bloom as a blo[ssom for] eternal glory to raise up a shoot to the branches of an eternal planting (מטעת עולם). And it will cast shade over the entire world and its branches will be as far as the clou[ds]and its roots will be to the deeps. All the rivers of Eden [shall w]ater] its [b]r[an]ches, and it shall become seas wi[thout] measure. And they shall strengthen themselves over the world without end and as far as Sheol." (XIV, 17–20).
	Fear	Judgment; War imagery and besiegement	"For the stranger may not enter her [gat[es; armored doors with no entrance; and strong bars which will not shatter. A troop may not enter with its weapons of war; and army (may not enter) to finish off all the arrows of wars of wickedness. Then the sword of God will hasten at the moment of judgment. And all the sons of His truth shall awaken to cut off wickedness, and not of the sons of guilt will be any longer. The warrior shall draw his bow, and open up the fortresses of the heavens as an endless plain without end. And (open up) the eternal gates to bring out the weapons of war, and they shall be mighty from one end of the world to the other and arrows shall rain down.... There is no escape for all the warriors of wars." (XIV, 31–36)

Table II
Progressive Spatialization in the Hodayot *(Continued)*

1QH Unit	Emotion	Secondspace realm of Punishment, Paradise, or Heaven	Hodayot Passage labeled according to the Secondspace realm it describes (place of punishment, paradise, heaven)
XV, 9–28	Relief	Fortified Tower	"You have strengthened me before the wars of wickedness, and despite all their devastation, You have not (let me be frightened) from Your covenant. You made me like a strong tower; like a high wall. Upon a rock You have established my frame, and foundations are my foundation. All of my walls are a tested wall, which does not shake" (XV, 10–12)
	Confidence	Space of Glory	"Straightening my steps toward the paths of righteousness, so that (I) may walk about in Your presence in the domain of [the liv]ing to paths of glory [and life] and peace without t[urning and] with[out] ceasing forever" (XV, 16–18)
	Confidence	Space of Glory / Journey upward	"You have exalted my horn over all who despise me, and the entire[rem]nant of the men at battle against me are sc[attered.] Those who disputed me are like chaff before the wind, and my dominion is over those who scorn me because [You] are my God! You have helped my soul, and You exalt my horn ever higher. I am radiant in sevenfold light in l[ight which] You have [established for Your glory. . . . You establish my foot upon level[l ground forever]" (XV, 25–28)
XV, 29–36		Heavenly space;	"all the sons of Your truth You bring before You in forgiveness, cleansing them from their rebellions with the multitude of Your goodness, and with the abundance of Your m[e]rcies, making them stand before You forever and ever" (XV, 32–34)
XV, 37–XVI, 4	Confidence	Spatial movement into the presence of God	"[You] br[ing] me into the abundance of Your mercies...(XV, 38)
		Bodily image of participation in God's Glory	"[You have established my foot on the path of Your heart. And You have opened my ears to the reports of Your wonders (so that) my heart understands] Your truth" (XV, 41)
XVI, 5–XVII, 36	Confidence	Paradise: Garden of Eden	Extended description of the Garden of Eden, for a complete text, see chapter five: "You set me by a flowing fountain in a dry land, a spring of water in a parched land, and a watered garden and a pool. The field- a planting of juniper and elm together with cypress for Your glory. Trees of life hidden at the secret spring, among all the trees by the water. They will make a shoot sprout for the eternal planting...." Descriptions of the garden continue throughout col. XVI until line 27.
	Confidence	Glory of Eden	"Glory and [everlasting] splen[dor] belong to Eden." (XVI, 21)
	Strong arousal of Fear/Display of Performative Emotions	Sheol	"the breakers of death and Sheol are over my couch. My bed raises up a lament, [and my pallet] a sound of misery. My eyes (burn) like a fire in a furnace, and my weeping (flows) like rivers of water" (XVII, 4–5)
	Confidence	Entrapment and war imagery	"my adversary will not prevail against me for a stumbling block to []; [A]ll the men of wa[r against me and the leaders of strife against me have a sh]amed face". (XVII, 21–22)
	Confidence	Bodily images of glory	"The contempt of my enemies will become my glorious crown; and my stumbling (will become my) eternal strength. For by [Your] insight [You have instructed me] and my light shines forth by means of Your glory. For You make light shine from darkness for (me); [to heal] my wounds; for my stumbling, a wonderful strength; an infinite space for the distress of [my] soul" (XVII, 25–27)

Table II
Progressive Spatialization in the Hodayot (Continued)

1QH Unit	Emotion	Secondspace realm of Punishment, Paradise, or Heaven	Hodayot Passage labeled according to the Secondspace realm it describes (place of punishment, paradise, heaven)
XVII,37			A full blank line
XVII, 38–XIX, 5	Awe	In the heavenly space	"B[less]ed are Yo[u, O Lord], for [] You have increased without num[ber]. [and to prai]se Your name when doing exceedingly wonderful things [with]out ceasing [] . ." (XVII, 38)
	Awe	The rhetoric of visual perception ("Behold!"); in the presence of God	"Behold! You are the chief of angels and king of the glorious ones. Lord of every spirit and ruler over every creature...." (XVIII, 10)
	Awe		"And who among all the great creatures of Your wonder can maintain the strength to position himself before Your Glory?" (XVIII, 12–13)
XVIII, 15			A full blank line
	Awe	Entry into the heavenly scene; blessing	"Blessed are You, O Lord, God of compassion [and great] in kindness, For you have made [th[e]se things] known to me so that I might declare Your wondrous works, and not keep silent day and night" (XVIII,16)
	Awe	Rhetoric of visual perception indicates being in the physical presence of the deity	"When I gaze upon Your glory, I shall recount Your wonders" (XVIII, 22)
	Fear		"My heart reels in anguish and my loins tremble (פחד רעש). My groaning reaches the depths and completely searches out the chambers of Sheol. I am terrified when I hear of Your judgments with powerful warriors (גבורי כח) and Your dispute with the hosts of Your holy ones in the heavens (קדושי שמים)." (XVIII, 35–37)
XIX, 6–XX, 6	Confidence	Tripartite blessing formula; anticipating an extended description of the heavenly space in XX, 7–XXII, 42	"vacat Blessed are You [O Lord, t]hat You have given to Your servant the insight of knowledge to understand Your wonders and a [rel[p]]y of the tongue to] recount the abundance of Your kindness. Blessed are You, O God of compassion and grace. . .." (XIX, 29–32). "Blessed are Yo[u] O Lord, for you have worked these things, and You place p[sal[ms] of thanksgiving in the mouth of Your servant." (XIX, 35–36)
XX, 7–XXII, 42		Description of the Heavenly Space and visions of celestial orbits and circuits	(7) [For the Instruct]or: thanksgivings and a prayer, to cast oneself down and supplicating unceasingly at all times; with the coming of light (8) for [its] domin[ion], at the appointed times of the day according to its order, in accordance with the statutes of the great luminary. At the turning of evening when the fading of (9) light (marks) the beginning of the dominion of darkness during the period of nighttime, it is within in its appointed time until the turning of morning. At the end of (10) its (i. e., darkness) gathering into its dwelling place before the light for the departure of night and the arrival of the day. Continually in all (11) the birthings of epochs, the foundations of seasons, and the appointment of festivals are (set) in their order by their signs; (12) their dominion is over everything and is an order faithful to the command of God. It is a testimony of that which exists and that which shall be. (13) There is nothing other than it. Apart from it, nothing exists nor will be otherwise. Because the God of kn[o]wl[e]dge (14) has determined it and there is no other besides Him. vacat (XX, 7–14)
		Blessings	"[and] I shall open [my] mouth [to bles]s Your name, [] (XXI, 18)....

Table II
Progressive Spatialization in the Hodayot (*Continued*)

1QH Unit	Emotion	Secondspace realm of Punishment, Paradise, or Heaven	Hodayot Passage labeled according to the Secondspace realm it describes (place of punishment, paradise, heaven)
		(Text is very fragmentary here but can be understood to presume the spatial context of the heavens in the presence of the deity)	"Blessed are You, O God of knowledge, for You have determine[d]" (XXII, 34)
XXIII, 1– XXV, 33		Reference to communion with angels Language that references angelic judgment that alludes to the Myth of the Watchers	"…angels in order to unite with the sons of heaven (ליחד עם בני שמים אלים)" (XXIII, 30) "You cast down the heavenly beings (אלים) from [Your holy] place, [and they could no longer se]rve you in Your glorious dwelling" (XXIV, 11–12). "for angels of eternity in judgment (לאלי עולם לד במ]שפט)"(XXIV, 8–9) "… bastards… (ממזרים)" (XXIV, 16) "in contempt because all the spirits of bastards cause wickedness against flesh (בעבור בוז כול רוחי ממזרים יחוללו רשעה על בשר)." (XXIV, 26)
XXV, 34– XXVII, 3	SGH	References to occupying the same physical space of the heavenly realm as angelic beings; utterance of blessing formulae	"Who is like me among the divine beings?" (XXVI, 4–5) "Give praise in the holy dwelling! (במעון [קדש)" (XXVI, 10 =4Q427 7 i, 14–15) "Blessed is God who works wonders" (XXVI, 31a= 4Q427 7 ii 12) "with the divine beings in the assembly of the community of … " (עם ביחד אלים) (XXVI, 28=4Q427 7 ii, 9) "Declare and say: Blessed be God the most high who stretches out the heavens by his might and establishes all their structures by his strength!" (XXVI, 41=4Q427 7 ii 12) – – – – – "a throne of power in the congregation of the divine beings" (כסא עוז בעדת אלים) at 4Q491 11 I, 12 "I am reckoned with the divine beings, my dwelling is in the holy congregation" (ונחשבתי אני עם אלים מעוני בעדת קודש) (Recension B = 4Q491 1 14)
XXVII, 4– XXVIII, ?	CH II		

which are familiar from Hellenistic traditions.[37] There are also aspects of natural geography that become transformed into what Martha Himmelfarb describes as apocalyptic visionary "environmental punishments."[38] Features familiar from the ordinary geography are used to construct a religious geography of the otherworld, complete with terrifying fiery waterways (*1 En.* 17:5; Dan 7:10) and smoldering mountains. Such aspects underscore the fact that the seer has journeyed to an inhabitable region. Sensory experiences related to sight and sound are especially prominent and smells can also be inferred as well. Sulfur, smoke, and brimstone, presumably from such fiery elements, are all associated with punishment in apocalyptic texts like the Book of Revelation.[39] Other common netherworld regions, referred to in the religious geography of the Hebrew Bible as the Pit or Sheol, have the uncomfortable quality of dark damp mire and muck, presumably bringing the odors that are associated with such places from lived experience.[40]

The Qumran hodayot reiterate a sequence attested in other visionary journeys which moves out from places of punishment places to paradise. Reports of experiences associated with entrapment and imprisonment are densely concentrated in the eight compositions found in columns X-XV.[41] The sequencing of this religious geography leads the ancient reader on a progressive journey through the hodayot collection that leads to the heavenly space. The emotion of fear is an especially compelling one and its arousal plays an important instrumental role. The brain and body's expression of fear is similar to other negative emotions like desolation and anger.

Hodayot that vividly describe a religious geography of punishment stimulate the body's affective response of fear. The more detailed these Secondspace descriptions are, the more intense the arousal. The speaker of the hodayot describes a spatial setting whose terrain not only has

---

37 James C. VanderKam, *Enoch and the Growth of an Apocalyptic Tradition,* 136 n. 94; 137–38 n. 100.

38 Martha Himmelfarb, *Tours of Hell: An Apocalyptic Form in Jewish and Christian Literature* (Philadelphia: Fortress Press, 1983), 106–126.

39 Brimstone is referenced in Rev. 9:17, 18; 14:10; 19:20; 20:10; 21:8; Smoke appears in Rev. 8:4; 9:2, 3, 17, 18; 14:11; 15:8; 18:9, 18; 19:3; see Himmelfarb, *Tours of Hell,* 113–115 n. 45.

40 Himmelfarb, 107; N. J. Tromp, *Primitive Conceptions of Death and the Nether World in the Old Testament* (Rome: Pontifical Biblical Institute, 1969).

41 1QH X, 5–21, 22–32; X, 33-XI, 5; XI, 6–19, 20–37; XI, 38-XII, 5; XII, 6-XIII, 6; XIII, 7–21; XIII, 22-XV, 8.

depth and contours, but also sights and sounds, allowing for a fully phenomenal experience of an otherworldly site. In these hodayot, when a
religious geography landscape is described, it is depicted with references
that commonly appear in other visionary texts. For example, the fiery
rivers mentioned in column XI are stock features from visions of the
otherworld. Frequently, a layering effect results from the many reports
of experiential aspects of embodiment, with specific attention given to
organs associated with sensory functions, namely the eyes and ears. The
multiplication of perceptual details contributes a quality of realism to the
descriptions of the otherworld and can assist in the process of visualization and reenactment. These hodayot also utilize idiomatic language
that depends upon the phenomenal experience of entrapment and the
sensations of being confined. The "snares of the Pit" (X, 23), "snares
for my soul" (X, 31), "cords of death that bind" (XI, 29) all arouse emotions of fear and anxiety.

Many of the extensive reports of danger appear in 1QH X–XIII, although fleeting references take place outside of these compositions.
This section examines how these locales for punishment and the vivid
imagery of imprisonment appear in the hodayot. Their positioning in
columns X–XV succeeds in creating the effect of a mounting fear
which, I propose, aims to arouse the *pathos* of fear in the reader.
These are discussed with special attention given to the ways in which
certain terrifying elements in the hodayot resemble those found in
other visionary traditions, specifically those associated with the figure
of Enoch and the Daniel traditions.

1. Entrapment and Enemy Attacks: 1QH X, 22–32

In the hodayah known as 1QH X, 22–32, the arousal of fear appears in
the form of references to the Pit, the experience of entrapment, and also
references to war and weaponry. The terror of entrapment and confine-
ment is a theme that recurs in 1QH X–XIII.

The Text of 1QH X, 22–32

(22) I give thanks to You, O Lord, For You have placed me in the bundle
of the living (בצרור החיים) (23) And You protect me from all the snares of the
Pit (מכול מוקשי שחת). Because violent men seek my soul (כ[י]א עריצים בקצו נפשי).[42]

---

42 Cf. Ps. 86:14 and Ps 54:5 where the same phrase, עריצים בקשו נפשי, appears in both
    places; John Elwolde favors seeing this as a direct citation of scripture; see El-

In my holding fast (24) onto Your covenant. And they are a worthless council, the congregation of Belial; They do not know that my position is from You; (25) You saved my life with Your kindnesses for my way is from You. They, because of You, they attack (26) me so that You may be honored by the judgment of the wicked ones. And you are strengthening me against the sons (27) of Adam, for my standing is in Your kindness.

And I myself have said, "Mighty men have encamped against me; they have surrounded me with all (28) their weapons of war, (their) arrows burst forth without remedy (ויפרו חצים לאין מרפא),[43] and (their) brandished blade (flashes) like a fire consuming wood (ולהוב חנית כאש אוכלת עצים).[44] (29) Like the roar of mighty waters is the uproar of their voice (וכהמון מים רבים שאון קולם);[45] a tempest and a rainstorm to destroy many (נפץ זרם להשחית רבים).[46] Wickedness and worthlessness shall explode as high as the stars when their waves pile up (למזורות יבקעו אפעה ושוא בהתרומם גליהם)."[47] But as for me, when my heart melts like water, then my soul holds fast to Your covenant. (31) But as for them, they spread out a net for me, but it shall capture their own feet, and they hid snares for my soul (but) they themselves fall in them. *vacat* And "my foot stands on level ground. (32) Far from their congregation I will bless Your name" (Ps. 26:12) *vacat*

The composition begins by describing thankful deliverance from a grave situation. The speaker begins with an image of binding with the declaration he has been "*bundled* with the living" (X, 22), an expression cited in 1 Sam 25:29 that expresses confidence in the Lord's care and protection in a life or death situation.[48] Presumably the danger is the threat of physical harm by unnamed assailants, "violent men seek my soul" (עריצים בקשו נפשי). The ex-

---

wolde, "The Hodayot's Use of the Psalter: Text-critical Contributions (Book 3: Pss 73–89)," *DSD* 17 (2010): 159–79, here 172–73

43 Cf. 1QH XI, 28 "all the arrows of the Pit fly out without return" (בהתעופף כול חצי שחת לאין השב).

44 Cf. 1QH XI, 30 which states, "in a *fire consuming* all of their hatred, finishing off every tree, green and dry" (כאש אוכלת בכול שאביהם להתם כל עץ לח ויבש); Here the image of a consuming fire is also part of an otherworldly scene of an apocalyptic fiery destruction. Following M. Delcor, *Les Hymnes de Qumran (Hodayot),* I favor reading the preposition as "like" and not as an instrumental *beth* which is proposed by the editors of DJD 40; cf. J. Licht who does not read any preposition here; *The Thanksgiving Scroll,* [Hebr, 87]; cf. also Isa 30:30 (ולהב אש אוכלה).

45 Cf. 1QH XI, 14 (בקול המון); XI, 15 (מהמון מים); Isa 17:12–13 "Woe, the thunder (המון) of many peoples, they thunder like the thundering of the sea! Woe! The roar of nations, they roar like the roaring of mighty waters (מים רבים)!"

46 Cf. Isa 30:30 (נפץ וזרם).

47 Cf. 1QH XI, 16 (ויתרגשו לרום גלים).

48 In 1 Sam 25:29, the phrase appears within Abigail's express desire that the LORD protect David in the face of life-threatening circumstances.

pression of being "*bundled* with the living" bears a positive connotation, but the sensation of being *tied-up*, as it appears in the remainder of the composition, is extremely negative. The threatening image of being bound appears in the imagery of physical entrapment with phrases like the "snares of the Pit" (X, 23); "net" (רשת פרש לי) in X, 31; "traps" (פחים טמנו לנפשי) in X, 31; and "they spread out a net for me" (והם רשת פרשו לי) in X, 31; and "they hid snares for my soul" (ופחים טמנו לנפשי) in X, 31.

Vivid imagery that appeals to the reader's sense of sight appears in a passage that looks like a quote at X, 27.[49] The dominant fear-inducing imagery can be situated in the stock imagery of terror, the military siege. The speaker reports that warriors have surrounded him on all sides, wielding weapons of war, firing poisonous darts with no cure, and brandishing a blade whose edge flashes like a fire devouring wood (חנו עלי גבורים סבבום בכל כלי מלחמותם ויפרו חצים לאין מרפא ולהוב חנית כאש אוכלת עצים). These graphic references to an onslaught are described in such a way as to intensify the fear of physical pain, death, and dismemberment since the speaker is said to be surrounded on all sides. Descriptions that appeal to the reader's sense of hearing is also given when the speaker compares the voice of the enemies to the deafening roar of mighty waters in a tempest storm. Like the waters, their verbal threats can be destructive. Accompanying these visual and auditory descriptions are references to the phenomenal aspects of the speaker's embodiment in X, 30: "his heart melts like water" (במוס לבי כמים), and his soul clings tightly to God's covenant (ותחזק נפשי בבריתך). The limb of locomotion, the foot, is evoked first as the enemies' foot which will become ensnared by their own devices, and later contrasted with the speaker's own foot which is planted "firmly on level ground" (X, 31). All of these bodily references contribute to the construction of sensory experience in this composition. Visceral references to embodied experiences assist the reader in experiencing the text and reenacting the powerful emotions that it describes.

In addition to the reference to the Pit (שחת) in X, 23, the churning waters can easily be imagined as the chaotic waters of the primordial waters (תהום) since they stimulate the sensation of hopelessness and pose the

---

49   The speaker appears to be quoting himself when he begins by saying "And I myself have said…" in X, 27, but this is not, as far as I know, a quote of a known passage. Many allusions and much phraseology familiar from the psalms appear in this hodayah; for a discussion of them see Kittel, *The Hymns of Qumran*, 33–55.

same threat, although they are not named as such. The churning and threatening waters continue as a vivid image in column XI but there they appear to be embedded in more otherworldly context. Many of the experiences of physical and psychological terror that are encountered in this composition—besiegement, hopelessness, imprisonment, and entrapment—continue on as dominate themes through column XIII.

2. 1QH XI: Specific Allusions to Enochic Places of Punishment

Column XI of the hodayot scroll from Cave 1 makes use of a number of spatial elements familiar to visionary traditions, in particular those associated with the figure of Enoch and construct an elaborate phenomenal religious geography. Even though Hartmut Stegemann proposed understanding 1QH XI, 6–19 and 20–37 as two distinct compositions, they are discussed together in this section because they share many features.[50] Both compositions make reference to Secondspace sites associated with punishment: the Pit (שחת) at XI, 13, 17, 19, 20, 27, 28; Sheol Abaddon (שאול אבדון) at XI, 17, 20;[51] and also to the watery chaos (תהום) at XI 18, 32, 33.

The specific image of "flying arrows of the Pit" (חצי שחת) mentioned in 1QH XI, 17 and 28 are reminiscent of Enoch's visit to the terrifying place of imprisonment during the beginning of his journey to the northwest (1 En. 17:1–8): "And I saw the place of the luminaries and the treasuries of the stars and of the thunders, and to the depths of the ether, where the bow of fire and the arrows and their quivers (were) and the sword of fire and all the lightening" (1 En. 17:3).[52] Column XI describes Secondspace locales that have aspects of liminality and arouse images of incarceration. This is the realm with "gates of eternity"

---

50 H. Stegemann, "The Number of Psalms in 1QHodayotᵃ and some of their Sections," in *Liturgical Perspectives: Prayer and Poetry in Light of the Dead Sea Scrolls. Proceedings of the Fifth International Symposium of the Orion Center for the Study of the Dead Sea Scrolls and Associated Literature, 19–23 January, 2000* (ed. Esther G. Chazon, Ruth Clements, Avital Pinnick; STDJ 48; Leiden: Brill, 2003), 191–234. The text and notes for this column are given in chapter four because they are discussed in detail there with 1QH XIII, 22-XV, 8.

51 This construction, "Sheol Abaddon," appears only in Prov. 27:20. The word "Abaddon" appears alone in XI, 33

52 Enoch's vision combines references to celestial bodies with language associated with weaponry in a way that is reminiscent of the hodayot's reference to the flying "arrows of the Pit."

which open to receive the evildoers and "eternal bars" (וברִיחֵי עוֹלם) that
slam shut behind them (1QH XI, 18–19). Such scenes are comparable
to the terrifying reports of the place of the eternal imprisonment of the
celestial beings, briefly mentioned in *1 En.* 10:12–13[53] and reiterated
later in the Book of the Watchers. Enoch sees a prison for the watchers
in the form of an abyss with pillars of fire (*1 En.* 18:11; 19:1–2 and also
1 En. 21:7–10). In these journey sequences, the antediluvian patriarch
passes into terrifying Secondspace regions that are hitherto restricted
from humans.[54] Expressions like, "cords of death bind with no (hope
of) escape" (וחבלי מות אפפו לאין פלט) (1QH XI, 29) suggest that the terrain
is a netherworld space.[55]

The hodayah's description of the otherworldly locales continues
with specific details about the amazing contours of this religious geography, details which convey a foreboding quality as the reader moves
along column XI. Himmelfarb describes the horrifying transformations
of otherwise natural geographical elements into burning punitive ones as
environmental punishments.[56] The author of 1QH XI, 20–37 fills this
religious geography with stock images of the netherworld frequently
observed in other visionary reports. According to 1QH XI, 30, at the
eschatological moment, the fiery rivers of Belial will bubble over the
riverbanks (XI, 30) and consume as far as Abaddon (XI, 33).[57] The journey reports in *1 En.* 17–18 are an interesting point of comparison here.
Enoch recounts the following landscape in *1 En.* 17:5: "And I came to

---

53 As identified by Helmer Ringgren, *Handskrifterna från Qumran* (Symbolae Bib-
    licae Upsalienses 15; Uppsala: Wretmans, 1956); Holm-Nielsen, *Hodayot*, 60.
54 Kelley Coblentz Bautch, "The Heavenly Temple, the Prison in the Void and
    the Uninhabited Paradise: Otherworldly Sites in the *Book of the Watchers*," in
    *Other Worlds and Their Relation to This World: Early Jewish and Ancient Christian
    Traditions* (ed. Tobias Nicklas, Joseph Verheyden, Erik M. M. Eynikel, Floren-
    tino García Martínez; Leiden: Brill, 2010), 37–53. There she describes the in-
    accessibility of otherworldly sites, particularly the heavenly temple, the prison of
    the angels, and paradise, to be a characteristic feature of the locales that Enoch
    visits: "The three sites are presented in the Book of the Watchers as unambig-
    uously located beyond the inhabited earth and the three appear unavailable to
    people" (38).
55 Cf. 1QH XIII, 41
56 Himmelfarb, *Tours of Hell*, 106–26.
57 This passage was read largely through the lens of biblical allusions by Helmer
    Ringgren, "Der Weltbrand in den Hodajot," in *Bibel und Qumran: Beiträge
    zur Erforschung der Beziehungen zwischen Bibel-und Qumranwissenschaft. Festschrift
    für Hans Bardtke* (Berlin: Evangelische Haupt-Bibelgesellschaft, 1968), 177–
    182.

the river of fire, in which fire flows down like water and discharges into the great sea of the west." Both references in column XI, at 30 and 33, and Enoch's report describe a burning landscape but the specific details of these landscapes do not map cleanly onto each other.[58] Another passage from Enoch's journeys that relates here is his climactic entrance into the heavenly throne room (*1 En.* 14) where he relays his exciting glimpse into the architecture of the heavenly house and its amazing fixtures.[59] According to this report, fire can be seen flowing underneath God's throne (*1 En.* 14:19). A similar account in Dan 7:10 describes a single burning river flowing under the throne of the ancient of days (נהר די־נור). According to the formulation in Dan 7:10, there is only a single river while the description in the older Book of the Watchers specifies that there is more than one river: "from beneath the throne issued *rivers* of flaming fire" (emphasis mine, *1 En.* 14:19).[60] The fiery contours of the religious geography in the hodayah at XI, 30–35 resemble features from the religious geography of other visionary traditions but never perfectly replicate them.

Column XI culminates in a terrifying mention of God's holy dwelling (XI, 35). A similar spatial progression to the abode of the deity also takes place in *1 En.* 14 which describes Enoch's entry into the throne room. The fear that seizes the seer at that moment is palpable: "Fear en-

---

58 Kelley Coblentz Bautch proposes that the burning river in *1 En.* 17:5 is a permanent feature of the netherworld scenery, while the hodayah anticipates that the rivers will ignite at a future eschatological moment of conflagration; see Coblentz Bautch, *A Study of the Geography of 1 Enoch 17–19*, 82–83; see also 82 n. 59. In this sense, the fiery river is like that known from Greek mythology, the Pyriphlegethon (Πυριφλεγέθων); see Plato, *Phaedo* §112e-113c.

59 The contours of this visionary scene are indebted to biblical passages like Isa 6, Ezek 1–2, and have also influenced later accounts like that preserved in Dan 7. The citation in *1 En.* 14:19 is thought to have greater antiquity than the Dan reference; see Martha Himmelfarb, *Tours of Hell*, 111–112, also n. 34; although a recent study by Ryan E. Stokes challenges this traditional thinking, "The Throne Visions of Daniel 7, 1 Enoch 14, and the Qumran Book of Giants (4Q530): An Analysis of Their Literary Relationship," *DSD* 15 (2008): 340–58. The priority of *1 En.* to Daniel is not an essential aspect of my discussion since it seems clear to me that the hodayah is thinking of many fiery rivers, like the account in *1 En.* See too Kelley Coblentz Bautch's discussion of the echoes of Ezekiel traditions in this vision of the heavenly temple in her essay, "Otherworldly Sites in the *Book of the Watchers*," 41–42.

60 Unfortunately, 4Q204 VI, 30 ends just shortly before this description of the rivers of flaming fire (// Book of the Watchers 14:16) so it is not possible to check what the Qumran text would have read.

veloped me, and trembling seized me, and I was quaking and trembling, and I fell upon my face" (*1 En.* 14:13–14). Such details serve as a road sign and a reminder to the ancient reader that at this point, Enoch has spatially moved *very* close to the divine presence. Enoch's visit to the space of God's dwelling appears just prior to the judgment oracle in *1 En.* 15–16. The composition known as 1QH XI, 20–37 shows a similar spatial progression when the movement toward God's holy dwelling (XI, 35)[61] is followed by a mention of God's terrifying judgment (XI, 35–37). The hodayah's conflation of fiery rivers, God's holy dwelling, and the anticipation of God's terrifying judgment is strongly reminiscent of extraordinary and memorable scenes reported in *1 En.* 14–16.

The hodayah states that the conflagration will consume the mountain bases reaching all the way down to the very foundations of the earth's surface, even unto the great deep (תהום) (XI, 32): "It devours the foundations of clay and the expanse of dry land. The bases of the mountains are set aflame, and the roots of flint become torrents of pitch. And it shall consume as far as the great deep." Immediately after this mention, the hodayah author adds a memorable reference to the deafening howls of horror in the description of the otherworldly scene of conflagration, "the schemers of the deep shall roar with a clamor of those who spew mire" (XI, 33).[62] The hodayah description in 1QH XI, 31–32 presumes that the earth is a land mass that floats atop the primordial waters (תהום) and that at the time of wrath, the interior of the earth will be thoroughly ignited. The hodayot speaker's access to what is taking place deep within the foundations of the earth recalls Enoch's special claim to have seen for himself the foundations of the earth in *1 En.* 18:2.

The strong and terrifying imagery of the conflagration are referenced in two other places in the second hodayah which refers to the things of this world as "melting away" (ויתמוגגו). The first of these appears in XI, 35 where it says that all the things on the earth will melt away in the great

---

61 A biblical allusion to Isa 63:15 (מזבל וראה קדשך).

62 The reference to mire and slimy mud is one that is more commonly associated with descriptions of Hades found in traditions of Orphism. See Himmelfarb, *Tours of Hell*, 107 n. 10. There she references Plato, *Republic* §363c–d; and *Phaedo* §69c. See also the reference to the loud sound of the raised voices of the heavenly hosts in 1QH XI, 36.

destruction.[63] In the next line, the hodayah goes on to state that "the foundations of the world shall melt and tremble" (וְיִתְמוֹגְגוּ וִירְעֲדוּ אוֹשֵׁי עוֹלָם in 1QH XI, 36), and here we see a description of an imitable response to the great conflagration. The word in the hodayah for "trembling" (רעד) appears as a form of the Greek verb τρέμων. This constellation of elements in the hodayah echoes the classic cosmic response to the proximity of God that is familiar from biblical descriptions of theophanies which also makes its way into the introduction of the Book of the Watchers in *1 En.* 1:5–6.[64] This detail about the foundations of the earth in 1QH XI, 36 is especially reminiscent of the description in the introduction to the Book of the Watchers (*1 En.* 1:5–6): "All the ends of the earth will be shaken, and trembling and great fear will seize them (the watchers) unto the ends of the earth. The high mountains will be shaken and fall and break apart, and the high hills will be made low and melt like wax before the fire." The earth's response to the presence of God resembles that of the angels who in turn were "seized with *trembling* and fear" (ἔλαβεν αὐτοὺς τρόμος καὶ φόβος)" as they anticipate God's judgment (*1 En.* 13:3). A very similar phrase appears in the description of Enoch's own terror just as he entered into the heavenly house: "Fear enveloped me, and *trembling* seized me, (φόβος με ἐκάλυψεν καὶ τρόμος με ἔλαβεν) and I was quaking and trembling (καὶ ἤμην σειόμενος καὶ τρέμων), and I fell upon my face" (*1 En.* 14:13–14).[65] In the corre-

---

63 The antecedents for this verb in 1QH XI, 35 is taken to be both the earth's schemers who shake, and those who live on the earth who will go insane (XI, 34).

64 See James C. VanderKam's discussion of this theophany in *1 En.*, "The Theophany of Enoch I 3B-7, 9" 129–50; repr. in *From Revelation to Canon*, 332–53. All citations of this article are taken from the reprint edition. Note too that in the Qumran copies of the Dream Visions, the verbs for trembling and fear (רע[ד]ין וּדְחֹל[ין מן קודמוהי) is used to describe the response of the animals before the "Lord of the flock," again a theophanic context for the verbs; see 4Q205 2 ii 30. Michael Segal also discusses this Enochic passage as a theophanic episode and compares it to the Exodus events, "Text, Translation, and Allusion: An Unidentified Biblical Reference in *1 Enoch* 1:5." Nickelsburg also discusses this scene from *1 En.* 1:3–9 in light of 1QH XII, 6-XIII, 6 in "The Qumranic Radicalizing and Anthropologizing of an Eschatological Tradition (1 QH 4:29–40)," 423–35; and republished as "The Qumranic Transformation of a Cosmological and Eschatological Tradition (1QH 4:29–40)," 649–59.

65 The verb τρέμων is also used in *1 En.* 14:24; see the transcription of the Gizeh text by M. Black, *Apocalypsis Henochi Graece* (Leiden: Brill, 1970), 27–28. The discussion by VanderKam underscores the traditional nature of this language and its classic association with theophanies in the LXX, "The Theophany of

sponding passage from 4Q204 VI, 27, the verb has been reconstructed here (ר[עד) to describe Enoch's trembling just before he fell on his face (*1 En.* 14:14). The Greek equivalent for the verb רעד found in 1QH XI, 36 "tremble" (τρέμων) appears at key moments in the Book of the Watchers.[66] The presence of this language in the hodayah is one that uses traditional theophany language and joins the strong emotions of fearful anticipation to imitable trembling. The behaviors are scripted insofar as the visible response of trembling in the face of a theophanic event is widely attested in the literature of this time period.[67] David Aune describes such scenarios as "theophanic salvation-judgment speeches" in which an account of some form of physical expression of fear is detailed as a part of the description of the theophany.[68]

The hodayot cite familiar features from the landscape of the otherworld known from visionary traditions like the Book of the Watchers. Doing so lends an aspect of realism and authenticity to the Secondspatial terrain that is being described in column XI, making it more credible and compelling to an ancient reader. This examination of the hodayot's appeal to familiar and extraordinary emotionally-charged scenes from the Book of the Watchers can also suggest an imitative practice of meditating upon known visionary journeys.[69] It may also be that the fright-

---

Enoch," 346–47, esp. 347 n. 62 where he lists Exod 15:15, 16; Deut 11:25; Isa 19:16; Hab 3:16; Judith 2:28, 15:2.

66 In the two accounts preserved in *1 En.* 21, Enoch experiences bodily manifestations of fear which are expressed in his trembling (*1 En.* 21:1, 7–9).

67 See VanderKam for a review of this literature, "The Theophany of Enoch."

68 David E. Aune, *Prophecy in Early Christianity and the Ancient Mediterranean World* (Grand Rapids: Eerdmans, 1983), 118–121. In the theophany in *1 En.* 1:3–9 the physical expression of fear takes the form of trembling by the earth and the angels; in the theophany in 4 Ezra 6:18–28 the physical expression of fear is untimely births, the emptying of full storehouses, and the senescence of rivers.

69 Other allusions to the Enochic traditions appear apart from these spatial references. Because they allude to similar experiences of embodiment between the speaker of the hodayot and the figure of Enoch, it appropriate to mention them here briefly. In 1QH XVIII, 36 when the hodayah speaker states, "I am terrified when I hear of Your judgments against powerful warriors" which can be an allusion to the judgment scene of the watchers. The terror here matches Enoch's own fear and trembling in *1 En.* 14:24–25 just prior to God's Oracle. The speaker is said to be helped or made to stand upright, (1QH XII, 23 and 37; XXII, 15;) just as Enoch was made to stand upright with the assistance of an angel (*1 En.* 14:24). In the fragmentary sections in 1QH XXIV, 6–25 (= col. XXIV + frg. 45) mention is made to "angels of eternity in judgment," "imprisonment," "bastards," and the phrase "to condemn all the spirits of bastards with

ening scenes and motifs from Enochic traditions were so vividly experienced that they left a searing imprint on the mind of the hodayot author, contributing to their lasting power. Whether or not the author consciously intended to rewrite these Enochic traditions is not the focus of this examination, and many of the details in those Enochic visions are themselves reused images from other sources. What should be noted is that certain vivid details of the otherworld known from visionary journeys to Secondspace realms reappear in the Qumran hodayot. The hodayot in column XI recounts terrifying places and mythical characters in a strikingly graphic way. As the Qumran reader of the hodayot engaged in a performative reading of these texts, these graphic details construct a religious geography of these places of punishment and give an experiential quality to the text. This can assist a reader who seeks to reenact the text to respond with similar fear and trembling.

3. Entrapment (1QH XII, 6–XIII, 6)

Glimpses of punishment and entrapment appear in the composition known as 1QH XII, 6–XIII, 6.[70] This is a text that was associated with the experiences of the Teacher of Righteousness known from other texts by early scrolls scholars.[71] A reference that appears there: "he has banished me from my land like a bird from a nest" (1QH XII, 9–10) was understood as an allusion to the experience of exile taken as a historical event from the autobiography of the Teacher of Righteousness. The composition goes on to elaborate the theme of en-

---

flesh" (frg. 45). These images in the second group of CH reiterate familiar events from the myth of the watchers traditions. The assemblage of details indicates that established visionary traditions, particularly the popular and widespread traditions associated with the visionary Enoch, may have been imagined during the composition of the hodayot. The visions of the otherworld found in the hodayot were aided by meditations on previous otherworldly experiences. The reading and rereading of visionary reports determined in advance the contents of the revelation; see Christopher Rowland, *The Open Heaven*, 215–28; see also Christopher Rowland, with Patricia Gibbons and Vicente Dobroruka, "Visionary Experience in Ancient Judaism and Christianity," *Paradise Now*, 41–56.

70 Further discussion of this hodayah and Nickelsburg's discussion of it appears in chapter four.

71 For a discussion of the unusual orthography that appears in this composition, see Angela Kim Harkins, "Who is the Teacher of the Teacher Hymns? Re-Examining the Teacher Hymns Hypothesis Fifty Years Later," in *A Teacher for All Generations*, 452–54.

trapment in XII, 13 which describes the speaker's enemies as "reeling widely at their festivals, capturing (them) in their traps."

4. The Lion's Den (1QH XIII, 7–21)

Themes of entrapment and punishment familiar from other visionary traditions continue in the hodayot that follow the two apocalyptic compositions in 1QH XI. The imagery in the relatively short hodayah in 1QH XIII, 7–21 describes sites of punishment and experiences associated with the seer Daniel.

(7) I give thanks to You, O Lord!

For You did not forsake me when I sojourned among a foreign people [ ] according to my guilt (8) You judged me. Nor did You forsake me to the wickedness of my inclinations; but You have helped my life from destruction.

You have given me [es]cape in the midst of (9) "the king of beasts" (לביאים); Lions (אריות) (who) are appointed for the children of guilt, the mighty ones who grind bones; The warriors who drink blo[od].

You put me [–––] (10) in a dwelling with many fishermen who spread out (their) net on the surface of the water;[72] with those who hunt for the children of injustice. There (11) you have established me for judgment, You have encouraged in my heart the counsel of truth, From this is a covenant for those who seek it.

You shut the mouth of the young lions (ותסגור פי כפירים); whose (12) teeth are like a sword (אשר כחרב שניהם); whose fangs are like a sharp spear (ומתלעותם כחנית חדה). All their plans for abduction are the venom of serpents. They lie in wait but they have not (13) opened their mouths against me.

For You are my God! You have concealed me from the sons of Adam; Your Torah You have hidden in [me] until the moment of (14) the revealing of Your salvation to me. For during my soul's distress You did not forsake me; You heard my anguished cry in the bitterness of my soul; (15) You recognized the tune of my woes in my groaning; You rescued my poor soul from a den of lions who sharpen their tongue like a sword (ותצל נפש עני במעון אריות אשר שננו כחרב לשונם).

(16) You are my God! You shut their {tongues} teeth lest they shred the soul{s} of the poor and destitute; Their tongue is dawn in (17) like a sword into its scabbard; So that the life of Your servant is not [cut o]ff. In order that You might magnify [me] before the sons of Adam. You have dealt wonderfully (18) with the oppressed. You have brought him to the te[st like g]old

---

72 Another allusion to the theme of entrapment appears here. Cf. Jer 16:16; the fishermen, like the lions, are also agents of divine judgment.

being worked by fire, like silver being refined in the crucible of the silver-smiths to a sevenfold purity.[73]

(19) But the wicked of the peoples rush against me with their afflictions, all day long they crush my soul. *vacat.*

(20) You are my God! You turn ~~my soul~~ a storm into stillness;[74] You de-liver the soul of the oppressed like a bir[d from a trap and] like a prey from the mouth of lions.

As many as three different words for lions appear in this hodayah: לביאים, אריות, and כפירים; alongside numerous descriptions of their terrifying maw. The composition dramatizes the terror that these majestic beasts arouse and makes the danger that they pose more vivid and graphic. The beasts spare the speaker but attack his accusers in a manner that re-sembles Daniel's encounter (Dan 6:17–25). The lions in this hodayah ultimately function as God's agents who are said to execute divine jus-tice against the children of guilt. The ambiguous role of the majestic beast presumed here, which balances the terror associated with wicked-ness and the equally terrifying experience of divine justice, is a fairly pervasive trope in ancient near eastern texts and other Jewish and Chris-tian traditions.[75]

The role of the lions in the Qumran hodayah shares a resemblance to the part that they play in the Daniel traditions. Daniel is thrown into the lion's den and sealed within it for the night. His survival is under-stood as a divine miracle. His rivals are then thrown into the pit where they meet a certain death and Daniel is exalted in his position in the king's court, and similarly in Bel and the Dragon.[76] John J. Collins describes the motif of the lion's den as an independently circulating el-ement that was reused by the authors of these Danielic tales.[77] Karel van der Toorn identifies a number of stereotypical elements in the story of

---

73 Cf. Ps 12:7; Dan 3:19; 1QM XVII, 5–9; and also 1QH XV, 27.

74 The scribe has made deletion marks around the words "my soul."

75 See the exhaustive study of leontomorphic imagery by Brent Strawn, "Why Does the Lion Disappear in Revelation 5? Leonine Imagery in Early Jewish and Christian Literatures," *JSP* 17 (2007):37–74.

76 Here, the story specifies that there are seven lions who were accustomed to eat-ing two humans and two sheep a day. Daniel is thrown in with these ravenous beasts, but is unharmed due to divine protection.

77 John J. Collins, *Daniel: A Commentary on the Book of Daniel* (Hermeneia; Min-neapolis: Fortress, 1993), 263–64, n. 15 where he cites: Augustinus Kurt Fenz, "Ein Drache in Babel: Exegetische Skizze über Daniel 14, 23–42," *SEÅ* 35 (1970): 12.

the lion's den which he traces in Babylonian literary traditions which he refers to as the Tale of the Vindicated Courtier.[78] The Babylonian traditions and the Danielic tales about lions share certain features: the protagonist suffers from the attacks of rivals whose sharp accusations produce injury likened to physical wounds from the mouth of these terrifying beasts. The protagonist survives the threat of danger represented by the lions' den, is vindicated and eventually exalted.[79] Van der Toorn describes the Danielic reuse of these Babylonian literary traditions in the following way:

> In the Babylonian tradition, however, the lions are not real lions; they stand for human adversaries. The "pit of lions," in its sole Babylonian occurrence, is a metaphor for the hostility and competition among the scholars at court. The biblical author inherited the motif of the lions' pit from the Babylonian tradition, but when he incorporated it into the story of Daniel, he turned the metaphor into a literal description.[80]

Van der Toorn comments that the Danielic traditions, unlike the Babylonian traditions, introduce an especially high level of visual detail and other experiential elements. This compositional style, common among apocalyptic writings, I propose, intends to arouse a strong emotional response in the reader.

The presentation of the lions' den motif in 1QH XIII, 7–21, is rich in visual and sonorous details which allow for the cross-modal experiencing of entrapment and imprisonment. The fear of being consumed is aroused by the opening references to vicious animals who "grind bones" and "drink blood" (XIII, 9), all of which generates a palpable fear in the reader.[81] The theme of entrapment found in other hodayot appears here in fleeting but poignant scenes of a fishermen's net (1QH XIII, 10), an ambush of venomous vipers (XIII, 12), a bird caught in a trap (XIII, 20). Terror has a spatial aspect as the speaker describes himself in the lair of lions (XIII, 15). The physicality of the lion's maw is described with detail to the teeth and tongue which are likened

---

78 Karel van der Toorn, "In the Lions' Den: The Babylonian Background of a Biblical Motif," *CBQ* 60 (1998): 626–40; see especially his discussion in about the literary elements shared with the Babylonian wisdom text, *Ludlul bēl nēmeqi*.

79 These are the formal elements of the tale of the Vindicated Courtier; K. van der Toorn, "In the Lion's Den," 626–27.

80 K. van der Toorn, "In the Lions' Den," 627.

81 Cf. Mal 3:2–3 where vicious imagery of devouring flesh is used as a metaphor for the wicked leaders of the house of Israel.

to sharp swords and spears. The visual image of the lion's fangs bleed into imagery of a serpent's fangs and the poisonous venom carried by its bite (XIII, 13). The weaponry of the mouth is a fitting image for the verbal accusations that the speaker endures (XIII, 13). Sonorous elements are related in the speaker's report of his own anguished cries which he describes as a woeful melody (XIII, 14–15). One can easily imagine the terrifying roar of the lions and also the musty smell of their den.

The extensive and detailed references to the predator's maw in this composition, I propose, aim to excite within the ancient reader a palpable experience of fear so as to simulate the physical sensation of being in a den of lions. The magnification of fear that is created by the sensuous details in this composition is then transformed to relief as the ancient reader imagines himself plucked from the predator's jowls by God himself (1QH XIII, 20). Near the end of this composition, a striking image for the transformation is offered; suffering is presented as a time of trial after which the speaker is said to be refined to a seven-fold purity. The imagery of purifying metal alludes to Ps 12:7: "The words of the LORD are pure words, silver purged in an earthen crucible, refined sevenfold." The crucible is like the furnace which is fired up to a seven-fold intensity in Dan 3:19 and also anticipates the later reference to seven-fold illumination that appears in 1QH XV, 27.

The next hodayah in 1QH XIII, 22-XV, 8 continues the theme of imprisonment and entrapment. This composition will be discussed in greater detail in chapter four. Here I wish to observe briefly that scenes of ambush by serpents appear in 1QH XIII, 28–30 and the imprisonment of the speaker is reported in XIII, 38–41. Imagery of enemy onslaught and besiegement appear in XIV, 28–36. After column XV, there are occasional references to imprisonment and punishment but none compare to the steady and vivid reports found in columns X-XV. There is a fleeting reference to traps and snares appear in fragment 3 (1QH XXI, 21–22) and a brief mention of imprisonment appears in 1QH XXIV, 8–9; but neither of these passages are as developed and as vividly recounted as the extended meditations upon the places of punishment that are found in columns X-XV.

Conclusion

This chapter has proposed that critical spatial theory can be useful in identifying a progressive development in the hodayot collection (TH + CH II) that moves generally from places of imprisonment and punishment to places of paradise. Embodiment language and descriptions that target specific sensory functions found in columns X–XV function rhetorically to re-create cross-modal experiences of terrifying fear. The experiences are so vividly described as to stimulate actual sensory experiences of fear expressed bodily in the form of heart palpitations and endocrine changes. Because fear is such a compelling emotion, its arousal is especially instrumental in generating the desired subjectivity of the visionary.

The phenomenal experiences of space and sensation that have been described in this chapter have been presented as Secondspatial events that offer a reader an affective script to reenact by which he can also participate in the moments of transformation that are described in the texts. The reader's movement out from places of punishment pauses in paradise at the threshold of the heavens. The scripted reenactment of affect can eventually carry a reader into the celestial realm of divine beings.

Chapter 4
The Thirdspace Terrain of the Hodayot: The Arousal of Fear and the Exegetical Generation of Texts

The dynamic events described in the Qumran hodayot are set in richly detailed spaces that follow a progressive movement from places of punishment to places of paradise. In this chapter, I wish to examine how the reenactment of affect can account for a diachronic understanding of how certain hodayot were generated. The reader's reenactment of Secondspace descriptions of otherworldly places of punishment can generate the appropriate subjectivity that can provide the opportunity for Thirdspatial experiences. In such an experience, the ancient reader is transformed into a full participant in his own experience and simultaneously becomes an author of his own visionary experience of the other world.

The Secondspace realm of terror constructed by the text in column XI arouses strong emotions of terror. The practice of performative reading whereby an ancient reader is expected to reenact the events in columns XI by arousing the emotions of fear is a practice that could have led to the generation of new texts. Under the right circumstances such reading was capable of generating a religious experience in which elements from a reader's own emotion memory became incorporated into the text being used for meditation, resulting in the generation of a new Thirdspatial experience. I propose that 1QH XIII, 22-XV, 8 is a Thirdspace report of an experience that was generated by the strategic arousal of emotions in 1QH column XI. This newly created text shows signs of being based on the text used for meditation, but also clearly incorporates specific elements that the ancient reader's memory which were naturally reinvigorated and actualized as he performed the text. By successfully fashioning for himself the subjectivity of a visionary, an ancient reader could hope to be transformed into a participant in a new visionary experience and became an author.

Places associated with punishment are frequently visited in reports of visionary experiences, and often are the first stop in otherworldly journey sequences. Seth L. Sanders describes one journey report from the 7th c. B.C.E. known as the "Underworld Vision of an Assyrian Crown Prince,"[1] an account in which a human traveler experiences the sensations of being in an otherworldly locale. Sanders observes that themes of judgment and punishment are prominent in this near eastern report. The religious geography of this Secondspace can also function as a portal into another sacred realm, and facilitate the journey into Thirdspace religious experience where participatory transformation occurs.[2] These moments of transformation may be seen in the various rhetorical changes that take place during the course of the tale. In this text, a series of terrifying sites of the netherworld are beheld by a crown prince named Kummay who has a visionary experience. Kummay engages in various imitable activities involving incense and weeping, to induce another journey into the netherworld.[3] Here, the difference in the visionary experiences may be detected by the shifts in vocabulary used to describe them. Sanders writes that the earlier dream vision, called a *šuttu* is qualitatively different from the *tabrītu* which is a vision had during a waking state.

> The prince awakes, cursing the dream and weeping, and makes the mistake of praying to her again. He then experiences a full-blown vision of the netherworld. This time his experience is referred to as a *tabrītu* rather than merely a *šuttu*. While these two terms occasionally appear in the same context, they are sharply differentiated. While a *šuttu* is simply a dream, *tabrītu* appears frequently in the vocabulary of Sennacherib and Essarhaddon to describe building projects—actually existing physical objects. It refers to awe-inspiring things seen with the eye. Far from a strictly mental event, numerous Sargonid occurrences of *tabrītu* refer to material things seen in daylight. They way this vision is narrated emphasizes its reality.[4]

The distinction that Sanders points out between the two different types of visionary experiences, the *šuttu* and *tabrītu,* approximates the difference between Secondspace and Thirdspace experiences. Thirdspace experiences like the *tabrītu* are qualitatively different; they enjoy all of the phenomenal sensations of lived experience which can include a percep-

---

1   Seth L. Sanders, "The First Tour of Hell: From Neo-Assyrian Propaganda to Early Jewish Revelation," *JANER* 9 (2009): 151–69.
2   Sanders, "The First Tour of Hell," 152.
3   Sanders, "The First Tour of Hell," 157.
4   Sanders, "The First Tour of Hell," 158.

tual intensity and an agency which experiences in Secondspace may lack. Thirdspace experiences have a quality of simultaneity insofar as they are otherworldly experiences that occur in a real bodily lived experience; the visionary is fully aware of the sentient aspects of his physicality and also experiences the Thirdspace with the freedom of lived experience. Another rhetorical shift that occurs is that between narrative and first person report. The human visionary culminates in physical trembling and collapse before the deity.[5] Sanders writes, "[t]he text is formally intriguing and creative in several ways. It is narrated in the third person, but the vision breaks this frame and switches without warning into a first-person confession, and in an exquisite narratological twist, the story itself becomes its narrator's expiation for the sin that the vision condemns."[6] Similar shifts in language appear in apocalyptic literature which moves from the rhetoric of narrative to direct speech.[7]

This chapter begins by discussing the text of 1QH column XI which contains a richly detailed Secondspatial landscape that was the text used for meditation and performative reading. In this text appear images of distress that, I propose, become actualized and intensified in a subsequent composition: a birthing woman, a ship on the sea, and a city under siege. The rhetorical "I" in this text can be said to function instrumentally within a practice of affective reenactment in a generative way. Reenacting the performative emotion of terror that is aroused by column XI can create a subjectivity that predisposes an ancient reader to have a religious experience of the text. I propose that the composition known as 1QH XIII, 22–XV, 8 is an account of the new experience that

---

5   Sanders, "The First Tour of Hell," 152. Sanders makes the case that this Assyrian text is the oldest precursor to apocalyptic visionary journey genre. Sanders' essay is useful for establishing the full historical and literary context of the Assyrian text, for the purpose of comparative study; his approach is an improvement to the typical use of these texts as simply ancestors to later Jewish and Christian apocalyptic; see "The First Tour of Hell," 151, 156–69. To clarify, Sanders' diachronic analysis of these visionary tales is not a conclusion that this study shares since this study understands the hodayot to be reiterating visionary experiences with no desire to map out directional lines of influence.

6   Sanders, "The First Tour of Hell," 156.

7   See the discussion of this phenomenon by Edith M. Humphrey, *And I Turned to See the Voice: The Rhetoric of Vision in the New Testament* (Grand Rapids: Baker Academic, 2007), 31–102. Humphreys comments that rhetorical criticism is underutilized in New Testament apocalyptic vision reports (35); this is similar to Newsom's comments about the use of rhetorical criticism in Dead Sea Scrolls research, Newsom, "Rhetorical Criticism and the Dead Sea Scrolls," 200.

was generated. This composition exegetically develops the three images used for meditation from column XI.

I. The Anthropologizing "I" and the Process of Actualization

Terrifying images in the Qumran hodayot are intensified by the process of *anthropologizing*. George Nickelsburg was the first to use the language of *anthropologizing* to describe the literary maneuver of taking an event and applying it to the speaker himself through the use of the first person "I".[8] Nickelsburg proposed that the text in 1QH column XII had appropriated images about the theophany described in *1 En.* 1:3–9 in a distinctive way by *anthropologizing* them. In other words, the watchers' physical response and the earth's "cosmic reactions to God's judgment" are appropriated by the hodayot speaker in the form of the first person "I" and subsequently presented as if they were his own experiences. The Enochic text reports:

> (5) All the watchers will fear and <quake>,
> and those who are hiding in all the ends of the earth will sing.
> All the ends of the earth will be shaken,
> and trembling and great fear will seize them (the watchers)
> unto the ends of the earth.
> (6) The high mountains will be shaken and fall and break apart,
> and the high hills will be made low
> and melt like wax before the fire.
> (7) The earth will be wholly rent asunder,
> and everything on the earth will perish,
> and there will be judgment on all.
> (8) With the righteous he will make peace,

---

8   George W.E. Nickelsburg, "The Qumranic Radicalizing and Anthropologiz-
     ing of an eschatological tradition (1QH 4:29–40)," 423–35, also republished
     as "The Qumranic Transformation of a Cosmological and Eschatological Tra-
     dition (1QH 4:29–40)," 649–59. In these essays, Nickelsburg uses the older
     system of numbering for the hodayot that is based on the critical edition pub-
     lished by E. Sukenik. In that system, the composition that is today known as
     1QH XII, 30–41 was numbered as 1QH IV, 29–40. The numbering of the
     hodayot in this essay follows the system of columns and lines found in DJD
     40, which differs by a few lines from the widely accessible text found in Flor-
     entino García Martínez and E. J. C. Tigchelaar (eds), *Dead Sea Scrolls Study Ed-
     ition* (2 vols.; Leiden: Brill, 1999).

and over the chosen there will be protection
And upon them will be mercy.[9]

Nickelsburg discusses this imagery in light of the following passage in 1QH XII, 34–36:

> But as for me, trembling and quaking have seized me, and all my bones rattle; my heart melts like wax before the fire,
> and my knees buckle (35) like water rushing down a slope,
> for I recall my guilty acts together with the unfaithfulness of my ancestors,
> when the wicked rose up against Your covenant (36) and
> the deceitful ones against Your word.

In these two passages, the speaker of the hodayah reports his own expression of the physical manifestations of fear, namely bodily trembling and shaking, in the watchers and the earth; and like the Enochic text, the hodayah passage appears within the context of judgment and mercy. The body of the hodayah speaker can be said to be an imitation or mimesis of the non-human experiences recounted in *1 Enoch*.

Although Nickelsburg did not develop the question of how this anthropologizing technique functions within the larger context of the hodayot, I wish to take up his concept of an anthropologizing "I" by examining how this actualization technique appears in 1QH XI, 7–8. Three anthropologizing statements are made about extraordinary events, two of which are not human and one which would not share the same gender as the reader of the text. All three are presented as if they were the experiences of the speaker himself through the strategic use of the first-person "I." The application of the rhetorical "I" to these non-human experiences effectively produces a script for a reader to perform, one in which the reader imagines himself to be the woman, the ship, and the city. The anthropologizing "I" serves a rhetorical purpose and succeeds in intensifying the affective experiences of the one who meditates upon this text, and allows him to perform the text in a mimetic fashion. I propose that this anthropologizing technique, especially when it is used to arouse emotions of fear and terror within the reader, could have assisted in the further generation of visionary texts. The compositions in 1QH XI and in XIII, 22-XV, 8 are offered as illustrations of this process.

These apocalyptic compositions share a number of elements that link them to each other in a meaningful way, and they were likely

---

9   *1 En.* 1:5–8

read in sequence. Both compositions share common Secondspace locales associated with punishment and the netherworld discussed previously in chapter three. In addition to these Secondspace locales, similar
language recurs in both which link XI, 6–19 and XI, 20–37: the verb
'shake' in the *hiphil* form וירישו (רעע- II), which appears in both 1QH XI,
13 and 34;[10] constructions related to the imagery of binding appear
throughout column XI in the phrases "snares of Sheol" (ובחבלי שאול in
XI, 10) and "snares of death" (וחבלי מות in XI, 29).[11] A Secondspace experience of terror is constructed by the two compositions in column XI.
There is an appeal to the auditory horrors of terrifying sounds (בהמון קולם
in XI, 17 and בהמון כוחו in XI, 33) and an arousal of dreaded anticipation
of cosmic destruction, expressed in the form of the churning waters (XI,
14–18) and molten rivers (XI, 30–33), all of which heighten the reader's psychological experience of terror and confusion.

It should be emphasized from the outset that the first half of column
XI, lines 6–19, is remarkable among all of the hodayot for its many and
striking literary devices. Because of this, the discussion in the annota-
tions to this composition is more detailed than those given for other hodayot in this book. No other hodayah comes close to this text's use of
wordplays and images, although double-entendres are not totally absent
in the second half of column XI.[12] Scott B. Noegel's recent study has
highlighted the important role that puns and other wordplays play in
the ancient understanding of revelatory literature.[13] While words and

---

10   See the corresponding note to the translation of this verb in 1QH XI, 13 in my
     translation found in this chapter.
11   The lexeme "cords" (חבלי) appears several times in column XI in other con-
     structions that express the experience of being "seized" or "gripped" by
     sharp pain. In total, the lexeme appears numerous times in column XI at 9,
     10 (2xs), 12, 13, 29.
12   See 1QH XI, 20 in my translation and the note there.
13   Scott B. Noegel, *Nocturnal Ciphers: The Allusive Language of Dreams in the An-
     cient Near East* (AOS 89; New Haven: American Oriental Society, 2007), who
     argues that wordplay and puns were crucial characteristics of dream literature
     and their interpretations throughout the ancient near east. Studies that have
     highlighted this feature in the hodayot are M. Rand, "Metathesis as a Poetic
     Technique in Hodayot Poetry and Its Relevance to the Development of He-
     brew Rhyme," *DSD* 8 (2001): 51–66; J.E. Harding, "The Wordplay between
     the Roots כשל and שכל in the Literature of the Yahad," *RevQ* 19 (1999): 69–82.
     For a recent examination of the esoteric literature at Qumran, see Samuel I.
     Thomas, *The "Mysteries" of Qumran: Mystery, Secrecy, and Esotericism in the
     Dead Sea Scrolls* (SBLEJL 25; Atlanta: Society of Biblical Literature, 2009).
     Note also Ehud Ben Zvi's comments about revelatory literature, "The Prophet-

phrases serve to link the first composition in this column (XI, 6–19) with the second one (XI, 20–37), the many examples of polysemy found in XI, 6–19 is unlike any other composition in the scroll. The richness of the similes and metaphors as well as the complex chiastic structure of the hymn also contributes to the artistry of this composition.[14] Ambiguous words that can signify a wide range of meanings are used to describe the dramatic events of the eschatological moment. This feature is striking and similar to prophetic texts, which "show numerous instances of potential ambiguity."[15] It is impossible to use stereotypical equivalents for words that appear multiple times in XI, 6–19 because each instance may demand its own rendering. The reader should also remember that even though one word is given in the translation, the ancient Qumran reader would have heard a pun immediately or associated one lexeme with a visual lexical-doppelganger. In my translation of column XI, I discuss the pun or second meaning of words in the notes and provide the Hebrew word in parentheses in the translation. Words in XI, 6–19 that participate in word plays are גבר, חבל, משבר, בכור, and אפעה; and much of this discussion appears in the notes to the translation.

Three stock references to terror are introduced near the beginning of column XI as *anthropologized* images through the use of the first person 'I': a ship in the depths of the sea (כאוניה ב[מ]צולות ים), a fortified city before an enemy siege (וכעיר מבצר), and a woman in labor (ואהיה אשת לדה כמו בצוקה) (1QH XI, 7–8). While three images are evoked in these opening lines of this hodayah, two of them, the pains of a birthing woman and the terror of a ship tossed on a stormy sea, take on an acute intensity as the composition continues. The speaker describes the pounding pain that racks the woman writhing in labor (1QH XI, 8–13), and the sea becomes an increasingly ominous setting as it comes to be described as "tumultuous and roaring waters with towering waves and crashing breakers" in 1QH XI, 14–17. Emotions of fear and terror are further intensified by the descriptions of cataclysmic annihilation and the reli-

---

ic Book," 276–97 and idem, "Introduction: Writings, Speeches, and the Prophetic Books," 1–29.

14 Although I don't agree with the author's conclusions concerning the identification of the figures in the hodayah, Christopher G. Frechette's essay remains the best treatment of the literary structure of this composition; see Frechette, "Chiasm, Reversal and Biblical Reference in 1QH 11.3–18 (= Sukenik Column 3): A Structural Proposal," *JSP* 21 (2000): 71–102.

15 E. Ben Zvi, "The Prophetic Book," 280 n. 16.

gious geography of fiery rivers and smoldering mountains (XI, 34–37).

The Text of 1QH XI, 6–19 and 20–37

(6) [I thank you, O my Lord, for] your mouth is [tru]th, And you have delivered me from [a worthless counsel] and from [   ]! (7) You hav[e saved] [my] soul [because] they have reckoned me [a reproach and a taun]t.

They have made [my] soul like a ship in the depths of the sea, (8) like a fortified city before its [enemies]. And I was in distress like a woman laboring (אשת לדה)[16] for her firstborn (מבכריה).[17] When her pains have overwhelmed her, (9) excruciating labor-pain (וחבל נמרץ) is upon her cervix (משבריה),[18] causing the firstborn (בכור)[19] of the pregnant one (הריה) to writhe; for children arrive at the shattering-pains of death.[20] (10) And she who is

---

16 Cf. Jer 13:21 (הלוא חבלים כמו יאחזוך אשת לדה) "Will labor pains not seize you like a woman in labor?"

17 Cf. Jer 4:31 (כי קול כחולה שמעתי כמבכירה צרה), "When I heard a sound like one who trembles, afflicted like one bearing her first child."

18 The word is משבריה which some translate as "her cervix" or "her womb-opening." The word משבר appears here in 1QH XI, 9 and later in XI, 10, 11, 12, 13, 17. The root meaning of this word is "to shatter" or "to break." The nominal form of the word with the *mem*-prefix appears as either "womb-opening," the "breakers," or "shattering pain." For a discussion of this word, see also Claudia Bergmann, *Childbirth as a Metaphor for Crisis* (BZAW 382; Berlin: de Gruyter, 2008), 131–33. The first appearance of this word is here in line 9 where the hymnist intends the former meaning of the word: "Her labor pains overwhelm and sharp pangs are upon her womb-opening (משבריה) causing the firstborn of the pregnant one to writhe." Immediately following this, there appears to be a scriptural quotation that is triggered by this word משבריה taken from Isa 37:3 // 2 Kgs 19:3 "because children have arrived at the birth," (כי באו בנים עד משבר). This Isaian text (// 2 Kgs 19:3) clearly references more than one child (בנים) but mentions only a single womb-opening (משבר). Perhaps the hymnist sought to improve upon this grammatical irregularity and made the word for "womb-opening" plural (משברים). In doing so, he conflated it with the "shattering-pain of death" (משבר מות) that is mentioned in 2 Sam 22:5. It is worth noting that the hymn of praise that appears immediately after David's victory in 2 Sam appears to be cited or alluded to in other places in this hodayah. The hymn is also reproduced in Ps 18. The hodayot hymnist is more likely thinking of the version in 2 Sam 22 because in the corollary in Ps 18, a variant reading appears, חבלי מות, which is probably the psalmist's harmonization of this phrase with the phrase חבלי שאול that appears in the next line in Ps 18:6.

19 Here the rendering "first born" is chosen to bring out the link with the hymnist's reference to Jer 4:31 in 1QH XI, 8. See also Frechette's discussion in "Chiasm, Reversal and Biblical Reference," 86–88.

20 Here a quotation from Isa 37:3 and 2 Kgs 19:3, כי באו משבר עד בנים, is conflated with the text in 2 Sam 22:5 משברי מות.

pregnant with a man-child (והרית גבר) is bound by her labor-pains (בחבליה). When she delivers a male (תמליט זכר)[21] through the shattering-pains of death (במשברי מוח) and through the cords of Sheol (ובחבלי שאול).[22] A wonderful counselor (פלא יועץ)[23] bursts forth with his might (עם גבורתו) (11) from the womb (כורא)[24] of the pregnant one; and a man-child (גבר) erupts from the shattering-pains (ממשברים) by the one who is pregnant with him. All (12) cervixes (משברים) tremble! And excruciating labor pains (וחבלי מרץ) are at their births and a horror (ופלצות) for those who give birth to them. And at the moments of his birthing (ובמולדיו)[25] all birth pangs (כול צירים) will overwhelm (13)in the crucible (בכור)[26] of the pregnant one!

But the one pregnant with a serpent (אפעה)[27] experiences an excruciating pain (לחבל נמרץ)[28] and the shattering-pain of the Pit (שחת ומשברי) are for all

---

21 Cf. Isa 66:7 "Before labor pain comes upon her, she delivers a male" (בטרם יבוא חבל והמליטה לה זכר).

22 Cf. 2 Sam 22:6 and also Ps 18:6 "Cords of Sheol bound me" (חבלי סני שאול) and Jon 2 (see Bergmann, *Childbirth as a Metaphor for Crisis*, 127–31). It is especially worthwhile imagining an allusion here to the poetic text in Jon 2:1–11, which also imagines the birthing womb as an underwater tomb (belly of a fish) that encloses itself around the prophet, ibid., 146–52.

23 Isa 9:5.

24 According to Jastrow, the word כורא may possibly be a euphemism for the female pudenda; Jastrow, 625.

25 Read מולד according to Jastrow as "moment of travail."

26 The Hebrew word בוכב may be read simply as the word "first-born" or as rendered here as the preposition ב- prefixed to the noun כור. The latter noun can mean either "fiery furnace" or "crucible." Later Hebrew uses this word as a slang reference to the female genitalia (cf. 1QH XI, 11). The entire range of meanings may be intended in this hodayah. The hymnist affixes the prepositional prefix מ- in XI, 11 where he writes, "A wonderful counselor bursts forth with his might from the womb (מכור) of the pregnant one." Notice too that the hymnist uses the word בכור in a later hodayah that makes strong claims for the speaker's own experience of purification in the crucible: "you manifest your greatness/ in me/ before the sons of Adam . . . you placed him [like go]ld in the cruci[ble] to be worked by fire, and like purified silver in the furnace of the smiths to be refined seven times" (XIII, 18). See too 1QapGen ar VI, 1: ובכור הורתי יעית לקושט and 4Q416 2 III 17 (4Q418 9+9a-c 18): כור הורוכה; see Hughes, *Scriptural Allusion and Exegesis in the Hodayot*, 193 n. 41.

27 The Hebrew word, אפעה, appears here in XI, 13, and also in 1QHᵃ X, 30; XI, 13, 18, 19 and does not appear anywhere else in the scrolls. This word may mean "groaning" (Isa 42:14). In later Hebrew the word may also mean "viper," and in later Rabbinic Hebrew the word may mean "leopard" or "hyena"; two flesh-eating animals (I am grateful to J. Angel for bringing this to my attention).

The context does not help to suggest which meaning is preferable, but within the immediate context of the so-called TH the translation of "serpent" fits best

doers of horror (מעשי פלצות). And (14) the foundations of the wall shake (ויריעו אושי קיר)[29] like a ship upon the surface of the water (כאוניה על פני מים). And the clouds thunder (ויהמו)[30] with a tumultuous noise (בקול המון)! And the ones who dwell on the dust, (15) like those who go down to the waters,[31] are terrified by the tumultuous waters (מהמון מים). And all of their (כ̇ל̇מ̇ו)[32] sages (וחכמיה)[33] are like sailors on the deeps (כמלחים במצולות), for (16) all of their wisdom is confused by the roaring of the seas (בהמות ימים).

---

the hymnist's description of his enemies as serpentine (תנינים); see 1QH[a] XIII, 12, 29. In favor of the serpentine imagery, see the extensive discussion by Michael Fishbane, "The Primordial Serpent and the Secrets of Creation," in *Biblical Myth & Rabbinic Mythmaking* (Oxford: Oxford University, 2003), 273–92; see also Ioan P. Couliano (*Out of this World*, 175; also idem, *Expériences de l'extase*, 13–14) who discusses the union of serpentine wind imagery (male) and primordial waters (female), resulting in the generation of a son (Nous) in Gnostic otherworldly texts. There are clearly vibrant traditions about primordial creatures that survive in the Zohar and Gnostic traditions that are worthy of discussion in light of the imagery as it appears in this hodayah, but unfortunately that stands outside the scope of this study.

28 This expression appears in Mic 2:10 (וחבל נמרץ).

29 Here, I read this verb as וריע, as the *hiphil* of רעע-II, which according to Jastrow (1488) can mean "to shake or impair"; contra the editors of DJD 40 who identify it as a *hiphil* of the verb רוע which results in the odd translation, "the foundations of the wall *groan* like a ship on the surface of the water." The DJD eds. presume a form of the root רוע ("groan"), but this is a peculiar verb to use with the foundations of a building. In the notes to this, the editor of DJD 40 argue that "groan" is preferred in light of the literary context: "we would expect a term for oral expression to parallel the following: בקול המן . . . ויהמו" (DJD 40.150). This reasoning does not make sense, however, because the more immediate and clearer parallel is to the comparison with "a ship on the surface of the water" (כאוניה על פני מים). The parsing that I propose makes better sense of the visual image of both the subject of the verb, "the foundations of the wall," and the image that is being used in comparison, "a ship on the surface of the water." This rendering also fits well the other three instances of this verb in 1QH including one that appears in XI, 34 and especially 1QH XV, 7 (וריעו כול אושי מבניתי ועצמי יתפרדו), where the verb in question appears in a nice parallelism with the next verb: "All the foundations of my frame *shake* and my bones *are rattled*."

30 The basic meaning of this verb ויהמו is "to roar" or "to groan." It is translated here as "thundered" to fit the subject "clouds" (שחקים).

31 Cf. *1 En.* 97:7 "Woe unto you, sinners, who are in the midst of the sea and on the dry land."

32 The more poetic ending מו- appears here as it does in 1QH[a] XII, 8, 9, 27.

33 Douglas suggests that the antecedent for the ה- suffix is the feminine, Jerusalem; however, given the 3 m. pl. suffix on כ̇ל̇מו it is likely that this is a scribal error for what should have been וחכמיהם; hence so the suggestion by M. Martin, *The Scribal Character of the Dead Sea Scrolls vol. 2* (Louvain: Université de Louvain/ Institut Orientaliste, 1958), 476.

When the ocean-depths boil over water springs, waves are tossed up to towering heights, (17) crashing breakers of water (ומשברי מים) are [heard] in the tumult of their noise (בהמון קולם). And with their raging, Sheol and Abaddon and all of the arrows of the Pit shall open up, (18) with their step to the ocean-deep (להתום), they shall make their noise heard.[34] And the gates of [eternity][35] will open up [under] the deeds of the serpent (מעשי אפעה).

(19) And they shall shut the doors of the pit (דלתי שחת) behind the one pregnant with iniquity (הרית עול), and eternal bars (ובריחי עולם) will (close) behind all the spirits of the serpent (כול רוחי אפעה).

(20) I give thanks to You, O Lord for You have redeemed my soul from the Pit; And from Sheol Abaddon (21) You have lifted me up to an eternal height, so that I might walk on an endless plain (ואתהלכה במישור לאין חקר).[36] And I know that there is a ritual bath (מקוה)[37] for him whom (22) You created from dust for the eternal council. You have cleansed a perverted spirit from a great transgression, so that (he) might be stationed in position with (23) the host of the holy ones, so that (he) might enter into communion with the congregation of the sons of heaven (להתיצב במעמד עם צבא קדושים ולבוא ביחד עם עדת בני שמים).[38] And for man, You have cast an eternal lot with the spirits (24) of knowledge, so that he might praise Your name in a single joyous shout (להלל שמכה ביחד רנה),[39] so that he might recount Your wonders before all Your creatures.

But I am a creature of (25) clay. What am I? One kneaded with water! For whom am I to be reckoned? And what strength do I have? For I have posi-

---

34   Ezek 27:30 והשמיעו בקולם עליך.

35   Thus the proposed reconstruction by Schuller, DJD 40.151; cf. 1QH XIV, 34.

36   Cf. Gen 5:22, 24 where a form of the verb התהלך is used for Enoch (2x's) and also for Noah in Gen 6:9. Other interesting parallels include Ode 36 of the Odes of Solomon, "the Spirit of the Lord rested on me, and it lifted me up to the high place, and set me on my feet in the high place of the Lord, before his fullness and his glory, while I was praising (Him) by the composition of His Odes," as trans. by Gerald R. Blaszczak, *A Formcritical Study of Selected Odes of Solomon* (HSM 36; Atlanta: Scholars, 1985), 9.

37   Fletcher-Louis (*All the Glory of Adam*, 109–10) rightly identifies this word (מקוה) as a double-entendre that means both "hope" as it is frequently translated. Fletcher-Louis is correct to translate this as "*miqveh*," a pool for ritual bathing given the context of the passage. Also another word for hope (תקוה) appears later in this text in XI, 28; cf. XIV, 35.

38   Cf. 1 Chr 23:28 where the expression מעמד is used for the Levites and 2 Chr 35:15 where the same expression appears with the singers. Both of the phrases for angels that appear here in l. 23 (קדושים and בני שמים) are used as a reference to the watchers; cf. *1 En.* 9:3 and *1 En.* 6:2 respectively. J. Fitzmyer (*The Genesis Apocryphon of Qumran Cave 1: A Commentary, 2nd rev. ed.* [Rome: Biblical Institute, 1971], 84) proposes that "sons of heaven" is a substitute for the "sons of God" in Gen 6:2, 3.

39   This phrase demands a cultic context.

tioned myself in the domain of wickedness, (26) and in the lot with the wretched ones. The soul of the oppressed dwells amidst tumults of the multitude; destruction (and) disaster accompany my steps.

(27) When all the traps of the Pit are opened, and all the wicked traps and the net(s) of the wretched ones are spread out upon the surface of the water; (28) when all the arrows of the Pit fly out without return and shoot forth without hope (תקוה); when the measuring line falls against judgment and the lot of wrath (falls) (29) upon those who are forsaken, and the outpouring of wrath (falls) upon the deceivers; and the time of anger belongs to all of Belial, and the snares of death shall restrain without escape; (30) then the rivers of Belial will flow ^{over} all the high river banks (וילכו נחלי בליעל ^{על} כול אגפי רום),[40] like a consuming fire in all their channels (?), finishing off every tree, green and dry, from their canals. (31) It spreads by tongues of flame,[41] until all who drink from them (are) gone.[42] It devours the foundations of clay (32) and the expanse of dry land. The bases of the mountains are set aflame, and the roots of flint become torrents of pitch. And it shall consume as far as the great deep (והאוכל עד תהום). (33) Then the torrents of Belial shall burst forth to Abaddon, and the schemers of the deep shall roar with a clamor of those who spew mire.

The earth (34) will cry out against the destruction that is coming upon the world! All of her schemers shake (וכול מחשביה ידיעו),[43] and all who (live) on her will go insane. (35)They shall melt away in the gr[ea]t destruction (ויתמוגגו בהווה גד[ו]לה).

For God will thunder with the tumult of His power and His holy dwelling shall roar forth with the truth of His glory (כיא ירעם אל בהמון כוחו ויהם זבול קודשו באמת כבודו)![44] (36) And the heavenly hosts shall raise their voice (וצבא השמים יתנו ²קולם) and the foundations of the world shall melt and tremble (ויתמוגגו וירעדו אושי עולם).[45] And the war

---

40 Cf. *1 En.* 14:19 which states "from beneath the throne issued rivers of flaming fire" and Dan 7:10 "a river of fire streamed forth before Him."

41 The antecedent here for this verb and the other f. s. verbs in lines 31 and 32 is the "consuming fire."

42 The antecedent here is the rivers of Belial.

43 Again disagreeing with the reading found in DJD 40, which translates וכול מחשביה ידיעו as "all its structures scream." I understand the parallelism here to be between living beings "all of her (the earth's) schemers" (מחשביה) and "all those who are on (or 'against') her." The rendering of מחשביה as "structures" doesn't seem to fit the parallelism because it introduces the idea of things and not beings.

44 Isa 63:15 מזבל וראה קדשך.

45 Cf. "All the ends of the earth will be shaken (σεισθήσονται), and trembling and great fear (τρόμος καὶ φόβος μέγας) will seize them (the watchers) unto the ends of the earth. The high mountains will be shaken and fall and break apart and the high hills will be made low and melt like wax before the fire (καὶ σεισθήσονται καὶ πεσοῦνται καὶ διαλυθήσονται ὄρη ὑψηλά, καὶ ταπεινωθήσονται βουνοὶ ὑψη-

of the mighty ones (37) of heaven shall spread into the world
(ומלחמת גבורי שמים תשוט בתבל) and it will not relent until (the) annihilation. It
has been determined for eternity, and (there will be) nothing like it! *vacat*

The three images that are *anthropologized* in 1QH XI, 7–8 (a ship on a
sea, a city under siege, and a woman in labor) are all images of terror and
political defeat that are familiar from the Hebrew Bible.[46] While each
image is well attested in early Jewish literature, their appearance together is uncommon. This is one reason why their reappearance in 1QH
XIII, 22-XV, 8 suggests an exegetical link. Scholars of the hodayot
have observed that the relationship between the three images is not
readily apparent. It is the case that all three of the images are powerful
examples of life-threatening danger and all are grammatically feminine.[47]
Amy Kalmanofsky describes the aim of the rhetoric of horror as intent
on drawing out specific emotional responses from the reader.[48] Kalmanofsky, in her discussion of the specific image of the writhing woman in
labor, writes that the prophetic literature employs such images to deepen
the horror that would be experienced by the mostly-male readerly audience. She writes:

> In summary, the image of a woman writhing in childbirth demonstrates the
> power and genius of the prophetic rhetoric of horror. The physical char-
> acteristics of labor—screaming, panting and writhing—describe the mani-
> festations of the fear and panic of invasion. The emotional experience of
> childbirth—feelings of being overwhelmed, vulnerable and weak—also in-
> forms the image and reflects the emotional experience of invasion. Further-
> more, the image introduces an element of irony that identifies and exagger-
> ates the futility of the situation for the vanquished. The image of the
> woman who labors for naught serves to convey the suffering of those
> who labor in vain and await death. The gendered image that describes de-
> feated male warriors also exaggerates the irony and futility of their situation.
> Pregnant women can writhe, pant and scream, but in the end, they labor
> for naught. Finally, the image serves as a rhetorical strategy of cross-gender
> identification. The prophets want their male audience to identify as
> women and to experience shame. Perhaps the rhetorical strategy of

λοὶ τοῦ διαρυῆναι ὄρη, καὶ τακήσονται ὡς κηρὸς ἀπὸ προσώπου πυρὸς ἐν
φλογί" (*1 En.* 1:5–6).

46   A direct quotation of Jer 13:21; see too the other allusions in this hodayah to
Jer 4:31; 1 Sam 4:19; Mic 2:10; Isa 37:3; 2 Sam 22:5 (2x's); Isa 66:7; 2 Sam
22:6; Isa 9:5; see Newsom, *Self as Symbolic Space*, 246–50.

47   Newsom, *Self as Symbolic Space*, 242; Hughes, *Scriptural Allusions and Exegesis*,
190.

48   Amy Kalmanofsky, "Israel's Baby: The Horror of Childbirth in the Biblical
Prophets," *Biblical Interpretation* 16 (2008): 60–82.

cross-gender identification will lead to reformation and restoration. By in-
sulting their manhood, the prophets hope to convey the pain and shame of
Israel's demise and inspire repentance.[49]

The rhetorical force of these images is to persuade the mostly male audience to repent and to reform their ways. While these three images
(ship, city, and laboring woman) may appear to be distinct and unrelated
images to the modern eye, they would have evoked deep psychological
associations of fear and political defeat for the ancient reader.

Imagery of entrapment or ensnarement, a theme discussed in the
previous chapter, is conveyed by the words chosen to describe the birthing pangs. The Hebrew word חבל appears in XI, 9, 10, 12, 13. The
range of meanings associated with this word is related to the root meaning, which is "to seize" or to bind. A variety of nouns are formed from
this root: "labor-pains," "rope," "pledge," and "sailor." Many of these
nouns are related to the image of holding tightly onto something: the
"labor-pains" that seize the pregnant woman, "cords" that grip tightly,
and the "pledge" that binds one to a vow.[50] In this composition this
word, along with ציר, can refer to the suffering pains of labor; however,
it also carries additional nuances. When it appears with the root מרץ the
connotation seems to be the sharpness of the pain or the acuteness of the
suffering that seizes the victim. The word חבל may also be "cords" or
"ropes" as it is frequently translated when coupled with the word
שאול, as we see in 2 Sam 22:6 and in its parallel in Ps 18:6.[51] The root
conveniently carries the additional connotation of "sailor" as we see
in Ezek 27:8, 27, 28, 29, and Jon 1:6. Such nautical overtones also fit
the dramatic aquatic imagery that drives the second half of the hodayah.

The bodily experience of being seized by physical pain is associated
with the birthing imagery that dominates much of the hodayah in XI,
6–19. The image of birthing is a stock image of terror from the reper-
toire of the biblical prophets that functions to underscore the pain and
fear that is oftentimes associated with experiences of warfare and military defeat. As a metaphor in apocalyptic literature, it serves too as a
marker of the eschatological moment or of the appointed time, such
as the moment of the enthronement of the chosen one. Such a moment
is assumed in the Enochic booklet known as the *Similitudes* when it

---

49 Kalmanofsky, "Israel's Baby," 74.
50 Bergmann offers a discussion of this word as expressing the personal crisis of
     being "entangled and surrounded" in *Childbirth as a Metaphor for Crisis*, 127–31.
51 Cf. Jon 2.

states: "And pain will come upon them as (upon) a woman in labor, when the child enters the mouth of the womb, and she has difficulty in giving birth" (*1 En.* 62:4).

In the case of the biblical prophetic texts, instances of the woman in labor are exceedingly negative and are associated with weakness and military defeat. The pains of the birthing woman are appropriated by the hodayot hymnist who declares himself to be in labor. Through this use of the first person "I" the reader could imagine the violent contractions that rack the body of the pregnant woman as moving through him while he utters the conflated verses from Jer 13:21. The ancient reader can be imagined as participating in the intense emotional and physical experiences of the subjectivity of the pregnant woman as he *anthropologizes* the experience of birthing by couching it in the language of first person experience. The hodayah in XI, 6–19 begins with the speaker making a brief opening quotation from the prophet Jeremiah: "And I am in distress like a birthing woman" (ואהיה בצוקה כמו אשת לדה; cf. Jer 13:21 which reads הלוא חבלים יאחזוך כמו אשת לדה). In this allusion to Jeremiah, the author of the Qumran text anthropologizes the Jeremian passage by positioning himself in the role of the laboring woman. It is curious that after this quotation the Jeremian term of "birthing woman" (אשת לדה) is abandoned in favor of the referent "pregnant woman" (הריה). This word for the "pregnant one" (הריה) then reappears several times in this column at lines 8, 9, 10 (2 x's), 12, and 18; and in the overlapping text from fragment 4Q428 4:1. Apart from these hodayot citations from column XI, the lexeme never appears elsewhere in the Qumran corpus. This point would not be unusual apart from the fact that "birthing" and "laboring" actually seem to describe the experiences of the two mysterious women in the hodayah better than the lexeme for "pregnant."[52] While the image of a laboring woman can easily generate a graphic image of anguish and serve as a fitting stock image of fear for an ancient reader,[53] the deliberate choice of the refer-

---

52 The highly elusive language of the two births and the clear literary shift from the Jeremian reference may suggest that the two birth texts belongs to an excerpted apocalyptic text that is being expanded by the hymnist.

53 The imagery of childbirth is a stock image of the horrors of political defeat. The imagery associated with childbirth appears in terrifying passages like Deut 28, which details the terrors of political destruction if Israel fails to follow the Law: "women will eat the fruit of her womb, the very flesh of her own sons and daughters," during the dire straits of enemy siege. In the story of the capture of the ark of the covenant by the arch enemy, the Philistines,

ent "pregnant woman" may aim more at the deep-seated terror that this seeks to arouse since a pregnant woman was particularly vulnerable to horrific violence during times of warfare and enemy siege.

While the metaphor of childbirth has a broad range of meanings, including the expression of dismay and defeat in battle, the image of the pregnant woman (הריה) is a far more horrifying image of the atrocities of warfare, and this may explain why the hodayah prefers this term.[54] The violence directed at expectant mothers was especially cruel during the brutal regimes of the Assyrians and later Babylonians.[55] Descriptions of violence against pregnant women appear in both of the eighth century prophets, Hosea and Amos, whose prophecies can be understood as reporting some of actual horror of warfare. The northern prophet Hosea addresses his own people who were suffering at the hands of the much larger Assyrian empire. The following is a report of violence directed against women during times of warfare: "Samaria shall bear her guilt, because she has rebelled against her God. They shall fall by the sword, their little ones shall be dashed into pieces, and their pregnant women ripped open (וְהָרִיּוֹתָיו יְבֻקָּעוּ)" (Hos 14:1). A similar wartime tactic against pregnant women is cited in the book of Amos in the opening "Oracles against the Nations."[56] There, in his catalogue of war crimes,

---

news of the political defeat and the death of her husband and father-in-law in battle bring on the labor pains of the wife of Phinehas who gives birth and dies after having given the ominous name of "Ichabod" to her son, "the glory has departed from Israel" (1 Sam 4:19–22).

54 Much has been written about the metaphor of birthing in the Hebrew Bible and the ancient near eastern literature; some representative studies include: Amy Kalmanofsky, "Israel's Baby, 60–82; Bergmann, *Childbirth as a Metaphor for Crisis*; Marten Stol, *Birth in Babylonia and the Bible: Its Mediterranean Setting* (Groningen: Styx Publications, 2000); Athalya Brenner and Fokkelien van Kijk-Hemmes, "Traces of Women's Texts in the Hebrew Bible," *On Gendering Texts: Female & Male Voices in the Hebrew Bible* (with A. Brenner; Biblical Interpretation Series 1; Leiden: Brill, 1996), 94; Katheryn Pfisterer Darr, "Like Warrior, like Woman: Destruction and Deliverance in Isaiah 42:10–17," *CBQ* 49 (1987): 560–71;

55 Amos 1:13; 2 Kgs 8:12; 15:16; Ps 137:9; Isa 13:16–18; Hos 10:14; Nah 3:10. The Hosea passage is particularly significant for Pitre's discussion of the apocalyptic appropriation of the image of pregnancy and birthing in Luke 23:28–31; *Gos. Thom.* 79b; Mark 13:17–19, Pitre, "Blessing the Barren and Warning the Fecund: Jesus' Message for Women Concerning Pregnancy and Childbirth," *JSNT* 81 (2001): 59–80, esp. 69–74.

56 On the geopolitical aspects of this condemnation of the Ammonites, see the discussion by Daniel L. Smith-Christopher, "Engendered Warfare and the Am-

the prophet indicts the Ammonites who "have ripped open pregnant women in Gilead (עַל־בִּקְעָם הָרוֹת הַגִּלְעָד) in order to enlarge their territory" (1:13). So too in 2 Kgs 8:12, the prophet Elisha describes what will befall the Israelites by the hand of Hazael, who later becomes king of the Arameans, during the enemy seige: "You will burn their fortresses, you will slay their youth with the sword, you will dash their little children to pieces, you will rip open their pregnant women (וְהָרֹתֵיהֶם תְּבַקֵּעַ)." Menaham's attack on Tiphsah occasions a similar report of violence against pregnant women (2 Kgs 15:16). These horrific episodes underscore the brutality of the targeted violence against pregnant women and may explain why this referent, הריה, appears in 1QH XI, 9, 10,11, 13, 19—it was more suitable for the purpose of arousing the emotion of fear.[57]

The image of a fortified city is one that may be understood as both metaphorically feminine in addition to being grammatically feminine. As Christl Maier has shown, the conceptualization of cities as feminine date back to an ancient tradition of personifying cities in relationship to a sovereign deity.[58] Maier has discussed the iconographic traditions of the ancient near east that depict a mural crown as a headdress of a goddess and its resemblance to a walled city.[59] After the initial appearance of

---

monites in Amos 1.13," in *Aspects of Amos: Exegesis and Interpretation* (ed. Anselm C. Hagedorn and Andrew Mein; New York: T & T Clark, 2011), 15–40.

57 The violence against the unborn during times of Assyrian warfare was also consistent with the military tactics of the later Babylonian empire against infants. In the oracle concerning Babylon in the book of Isaiah (13:1–22) the prophet writes, "[t]heir infants will be dashed to pieces before their eyes; their houses will be plundered, and their wives ravished. Their bows will slaughter the young men; they will have no mercy on the fruit of the womb; their eyes will not pity children." The moving words of the psalmist that lament the loss of the land and the exile in Psalm 137 conclude with this gruesome cry of vengeance against Babylon and Edom: "O Daughter Babylon, you devastator! Happy shall they be who pay you (the Edomites) back what you have done to us! Happy shall they be who take your little ones and dash them against the rock!" (vv. 7–9).

58 Christl Maier, *Daughter Zion, Mother Zion*, 60–93.

59 Maier, *Daughter Zion, Mother Zion*, 64–69. Also discussed in eadem, "Daughter Zion as Queen and the Iconography of the Female City," in *Images and Prophecy in the Ancient Eastern Mediterranean* (ed. Martti Nissinen and Charles E. Carter; Göttingen: Vandenhoeck & Ruprecht, 2009), 147–62; Urs Winter, *Frau und Göttin: Exegetische und ikonographische Studien zum weiblichen Gottesbild im Alten Israel und in dessen Umwelt* (OBO 53; Freiburg, Schweiz: Universitätsverlag; Göttingen: Vandenhoeck & Ruprecht, 1983); also Aloysius Fitzgerald, "The

a fortified city in 1QH XI, 8, it is mentioned briefly in line 14 where it is connected with the image of the ship on the tumultuous waters: "and the foundations of the wall moan like a ship on the surface of the water." Consistent with the author's use of double entendres throughout the composition, elements of a fortified city such as locked doors and secured city gates also possess a range of meanings. The imagery of enclosure is one that resonates with the theme of imprisonment. The association between the image of a fortified city and the feminine is one that has been examined by Cynthia Chapman in her study of reliefs depicting the brutality of Assyrian warfare.[60] In Isa 1:8, daughter Zion is compared to a city under siege.[61] In this passage, the religious geography of the city, twice described as a desolate space (שממה) in 1:7 constructs political devastation as the experience of a woman's violation by using language that is applied to raped women (e. g., Tamar in 2 Sam 13:20).[62] References to a fortified city's door or walls can also function as veiled references to the female genitalia. In biblical texts like Cant 5:4–6, references to city fortifications become double entendres alluding to a sexual encounter.[63] So too, the fortification of both doors and walls in Cant 8:9 serves as an expression of protecting the chastity of the little sister against unwanted advances.

In the Bible, the phrase a 'fortified city' is usually a foreboding one that anticipates a military invasion, and it is not a phrase that is uniquely applied to Israel. Such is the case in Ps 60:9 (=108:10), which antici-

---

Mythological Background for the Presentation of Jerusalem as Queen and False Worship as Adultery in the Old Testament," *CBQ* 34 (1972): 403–16, but he relies heavily on later Hellenistic data and assumes that the city is deified; see the critiques of Fitzgerald by Peggy L. Day, "The Personification of Cities as Female in the Hebrew Bible: The Thesis of Aloysius Fitzgerald, F. S. C.," in *Reading from this Place, Vol. 2: Social Location and Biblical Interpretation in Global Perspective* (ed. Fernando F. Segovia and Mary Ann Tolbert; Minneapolis, 1995), 283–302.

60   Cynthia Chapman, *The Gendered Language of Warfare in the Israelite-Assyrian Encounter* (HSM 62; Winona Lake: Eisenbrauns, 2004). Her study begins by noting that gendered language is used to describe power relationships, especially asymmetrical ones, 3–13.

61   Maier, *Daughter Zion, Mother Zion*, 74–77.

62   Maier, *Daughter Zion, Mother Zion*, 76; see too Lam 1:13 discussed at 146.

63   See Marvin Pope, *Song of Songs*, (AB; Garden City, N.Y.: Doubleday, 1977), 678–83; Carey Walsh, *Exquisite Desire: Religion, the Erotic, and the Song of Songs* (Minneapolis: Fortress, 2000), 112–13; Carol Meyers, "Gender Imagery in the Song of Songs," in *The Feminist Companion to the Bible* (10 vols.; Sheffield: Sheffield Academic, 1993) 1. 201–4.

pates an attack against Bozrah the capital of Edom. And so, in light of the dual meaning of secured doors and reinforced walls in the Canticle of Canticles, Chapman argues well that the account of the conquest of the city of Nineveh in Nah 2:7 and 3:13 is also capable of functioning with sexual overtones. The invasion of the city in Nah 2:6–7 and the opening of her floodgates to her enemies in Nah 3:13 are references to the dreaded experience of political conquest that may also be seen as gendered descriptions that tap into the deep psychological experiences of terror. The fleeting reference to "a fortified city [before (its) enemy]" that appears in 1QH XI, 7 is a feminine metaphor that further heightens the experience of distress and fear.

Each of these three instances where the hodayah author *anthropologizes* images of psychological and physical terror presents striking scenes. The extensive details given about the woman in labor and the ship on the sea in particular contribute to the ease with which they can be visualized, thus imparting an experiential quality to these otherworldly events. They appear alongside other references of sonorous events that could intensify the arousal of fear and anguish, as can be seen by the reference to the deafening howls of horror in the vision of the otherworldly conflagration: "the schemers of the deep shall roar with a clamor of those who spew mire" (XI, 33).[64] These sensuous details provide a vivid quality that can facilitate the arousal of fear within a reader.

The anthropologizing of these non-human experiences onto the body of the hodayot hymnist localizes and intensifies the affective experiences for the one who is reading these compositions. The first person speech and vivid dramatic language are rhetorical features that allows the reader who performs these texts access to the powerful experiences that they describe. The embodied practice of the ritual reading of these prayer texts has the capacity to generate within the reader a particular state of mind that would have allowed him to embark on a religious experience. I propose that the intensity of the events described in the text would have induced strong negative emotions in the reader. This psychological state would then create within him the predisposition to experience his own religious experience, which I propose is recounted in 1QH XIII, 22-XV, 8. The efficacy of these rhetorical features is suggested by the

---

64 The reference to mire and slime is one that is more commonly associated with descriptions of Hades found in traditions of Orphism. See M. Himmelfarb, *Tours of Hell*, 107, n. 10. There she references Plato, *Republic* §363c-d; and *Phaedo* §69c.

speaker's reports that he finds himself in the company of angels and able to see otherworldly sites (1QH XI, 20–21; XIV, 9–22).

II. The Role of the Emotions in the Generation of New Visionary Compositions

Recent studies on the role of the emotions in cognitive processes and the techniques to train and discipline them can shed light on the role that emotion and language about the body enjoys in the hodayot. The arousal of strong emotions, fear and terror, are especially prominent and could have assisted an ancient reader in becoming one with the imaginal body in the text. In the process of performative reading, the ancient reader would have naturally reinvigorated his own affective memories of personal desolation during his reenactment of the emotions in the hodayot in column XI. In chapter two I discussed how visionary reports, texts that describe religious experiences, are themselves detailed accounts that make many references to the experiences of the seer's body or to specific bodily practices that a reader can then imitate and reenact. These details may include vivid descriptions of the specific behaviors that the seer performed to prepare for the vision and, I propose, the specific emotions that the seer experienced.

Texts like 1QH column XI are richly detailed scripted Secondspatial experiences that invite participation through imitation. In the ritualization of meditative reading, the reader of the hodayot performs the prayers as an affective script to be reenacted. As discussed in chapter one, the repetitive process of ritualization can form within the reader a subjectivity that is predisposed to religious experience, without predetermining one.[65] Descriptions of terrifying experiences in column XI are described with special reference to the body and the sensory organs of seeing and hearing. These literary and rhetorical elements of the text provide scripted cues for an ancient reader to reenact. In column XI the reader's senses are targeted by the specific ways that terror is described. Descriptions that pinpoint the reader's seeing and hearing faculties facilitate the actualization of terror in the reader's body and so help to create the subjectivity of the lyrical speaker. Body imagery and the use of the first person voice are the rhetorical features that facilitate the actualization and

---

65 Hollywood, "Performativity, Citationality, Ritualization," 268. Also Bell, *Ritual Theory, Ritual Practice*, 220–221.

reenactment of the scripted emotions.[66] The sensory parts of the brain are stimulated by the richly detailed scenes of the otherworld that are imagined in the mind's eye. Seething and churning waters (XI, 14–17), a fiery terrain of molten rivers and burning mountains (XI, 30–33), tremors of the earth (XI, 34–36), and the opening of the infernal gates of eternity (XI, 18) paint visual scenes of the terrifying apocalyptic moment of annihilation. Even the fleeting reference to the heavenly expanse described in 1QH XI, 21–24 can arouse fear since the experience of being in the celestial realm is associated with terror. The experience of hearing is targeted by descriptions of crashing waves (XI, 15–17) and "roars of those who spew mire" (XI, 33). A reader is invited to hear the cries of a woman convulsed in excruciating pain as she labors. So too, the reader's ears are invited to hear the "joyous shout" of the angelic praise described in XI, 23–24. Body language in the hodayot is directed towards facilitating the reader's actualization of the text, adding depth to the perceptual experience and multiplying the number of senses that are engaged.

Studies of how ancient visionaries achieved experiences of ascent and journeying indicate that the mediation upon established visionary reports were key. This meditative reading and rereading of visions is one way to account for the dramatic similarities among the reports of the otherworld. Daniel Merkur writes that Jewish apocalyptic visionaries meditated upon tried and true visionary traditions; rehearsing "what they knew in order to encourage their psychic states to manifest further and unknown matters on the same topics."[67] In the case of the hodayot, the reader's meditation upon the emotionally charged experiences described in column XI resulted, I propose, in the exegetical generation of a new text that shows signs of associative memory reconstruction (1QH XIII, 22-XV, 8). My proposal is that the emotions that are aroused in the ritual process of meditative reading assist the reader in becoming the "I" in the text and fully participating in the vision.

---

66 Gillmayr-Bucher, "Body Images in the Psalms," 301–26.
67 Daniel Merkur, "The Visionary Practices of Jewish Apocalypticists," 141. In a more recent essay, Merkur elaborates more upon these practices to include later Jewish and Christian mystical traditions, "Cultivating Visions through Exegetical Meditations," 62–91.

A. Neuropsychological Processes

Fear is a crucial component in many ancient and medieval reports of religious experience. This is reflected in visionary literature's general pattern of beginning with visits to terrifying secondspatial realms, and this may serve an instrumental purpose. Neuropsychologists have observed that fear-inducing stimuli elicit powerful bodily responses. From an evolutionary perspective these negative emotions associated with fear and anxiety may be more compelling because they are necessary for survival.[68] Visionary literature with its detailed descriptions of terrifying topography and other scary spatial experiences that are reported in the first person voice simulates first-hand experiences of events that can elicit a powerful emotional response in the reader. Meditation upon fearful events through the reading and rereading of visionary texts describing terrifying scenes and situations can activate areas of the brain such as the limbic system and pre-frontal cortex that are associated with emotion and sensory perception, memory, and consciousness. This neural activity may also be responsible for generating visionary experiences.

Psychological research into the emotions in the twentieth century has had to address the dominant view that emotions are subjective conscious cognitive processes, akin to what is commonly referred to as feelings today. This theory, made popular by William James in the late nineteenth century, has been scrutinized and rejected in recent years.[69] Recent scholars are reluctant to merge emotion and feeling into the same category, preferring to distinguish between these two processes of affect: the first being the primary emotion processes governed by the primitive limbic system, and the secondary being the higher-order cognitive processes that occur in the precuneus and the higher cortical areas which are the regions for reasoning, visual imaging, and understandings of the self. The limbic system, a primitive center for emotion processing in the brain, is not yet fully understood.[70] Neuropsychological studies of brain-damaged individuals and improved brain-imaging technology have illuminated some of emotion's neuro-

---

68   Rolls, *Emotion Explained*.
69   William James, "What is an Emotion," *Mind* 9 (1884): 188–205.
70   Pierre Philippot and Alexandre Schaefer, "Emotion and Memory," in *Emotions: Current Issues and Future Directions* (ed. Tracy J. Mayne and George A. Bonanno; New York: Guilford Press, 2001), 82–122.

circuitry although there is much about these processes that is not known. The limbic system is one of the neurological regions for emotion processing. It is connected in a complex series of networks to other regions of the brain that govern the processing of higher level cognition.[71] "These subcortical structures evolved early and may carry out limited operations that are essentially preconscious, compared with the elaborate human cortex at the top of the brain, which is involved in conscious emotional feelings."[72] While the emotion responses of fear associated with the amygdala were thought to occur prior to conscious reasoning, the most recent studies argue strongly that these processes should be understood on a continuum and that the body's processing of emotion (fear) never occurs independently from cognitive processing.[73] When "the amygdala performs emotional evaluation, it does so within the cognitive system. This could explain why it has been so difficult to dissociate emotional from cognitive processing in humans."[74] The areas used in the processing of emotion are known to be connected in a complex series of bidirectional networks to the regions of the brain that govern the processing of higher level cognition known as the pre-frontal cortex, the site where higher-order cognition takes place.[75] It has

---

71 In a series of studies of the emotion of fear in rats, LeDoux observes that the brain's responses to stimuli that are fearful remain in operation even after those areas thought to be responsible for processing them are removed; see the study by Joseph E. LeDoux, "Emotion: Clues from the Brain," *Annual Review of Psychology* 46 (1995): 209–35. More recently, J. LeDoux, "The Emotional Brain, Fear, and the Amygdala," *Cellular and Molecular Neurobiology* 23 (2003): 727–38.

72 Piotr Winkielman and Kent C. Berridge, "Unconscious Emotion," *Current Directions in Psychological Science* 13 (2004): 120–23, here 122.

73 Storbeck and Clore, "On the Interdependence of Cognition and Emotion," 1212–37.

74 E. Halgren, "Emotional Neurophysiology of the Amygdala within the Context of Human Cognition," in *The Amygdala: Neurobiological Aspects of Emotion, Memory, and Mental Dysfunction* (ed. J. Aggleton; New York: Wiley-Liss, 1992): 191–228. See too the discussion of the amygdala by Storbeck and Clore, "On the Interdependence of Cognition and Emotion," 1214–17.

75 Damasio discusses the different sites associated with the pre-frontal cortex and writes that these areas of the brain are intimately connected to the limbic system. He cites the presence of the chemical receptors for serotonin, a neurotransmitter that inhibits the expression of aggressive behavior, in both regions of the primary and secondary emotion processing centers, *Descartes' Error*, 52–79, esp. 76–77. See also K. C. Berridge, "Pleasures of the Brain," *Brain and Cognition* 52 (2003): 106–28; and Joseph E. Le Doux, *The Emotional*

become increasingly clear that higher-level cognitive and emotion processes never operate completely independently from the limbic system,[76]
with the most recent psychological studies emphasizing the "unity and
interrelatedness of cognitive and affective processes."[77]

Studies on emotions and the processes that govern them indicate
that the arousal of fear, a primary emotion response, is especially compelling because of its evolutionary function. Fear is processed at multiple
levels by many different neurological processes.[78] Even studies that are
reluctant to strictly relegate the automatic processing of fear in the
amygdala prior to cognition, observe that this so-called primitive area
of the brain is especially sensitive to fear stimuli.[79] Neuropsychologists
are typically interested in studying the processing of negative emotions,
largely due to a cultural concern in the West to treat these somatic responses.[80] Many of their findings, while not intended for the study of
ancient visionary practices can be useful in illuminating the cognitive
processes related to visionary experiences.

The hodayot describe terrifying otherworldly spaces related to imprisonment and entrapment that function to arouse fear in the reader.
As Secondspace regions they occupy no actual space in ordinary geography but they effectively simulate highly stimulating terrifying scenarios through the elaborate creation of a textualized world. The spatialization of visionary reports provides rich sensory details of depth and distance targeted at the reader's visual and auditory faculties. Visual de-

---

Brain: The Mysterious Underpinnings of Emotional Life (New York: Simon &
Schuster, 1996).

76 See the discussion by Philippot and Schaefer, "Emotion and Memory," 97.

77 Storbeck and Clore, "On the Interdependence of Cognition and Emotion,"
1213; also see H. L. Roediger, D. Gallo, and L. Geraci, "Processing Approaches to Cognition: The Impetus from the Levels-of-Processing Framework," Memory 10 (2002): 319–32.

78 The region known as the amygdala is one site that is distinctly involved in the
primary processing of the emotion of fear, however studies of responses in individuals who have a damaged amygdala indicate that this site never operates
independently from other areas of the brain. Many studies of fear focus on
the amygdala because it is a relatively easy part of brain to isolate physically.
In contrast, the precuneus is more difficult to access and isolate.

79 Storbeck and Clore ("On the Interdependence of Cognition and Emotion,"
1225) write, "These results suggest that valence is not automatically processed
by the amygdala, but the amygdala may be sensitive to arousing stimuli such as
fearful faces."

80 Neuropsychological studies favor the view that negative emotions can be managed and controlled over time.

scriptions coupled with narrations of sonorous events simulate a multi-sensory experience that stimulates actual sensory processing of fear in the amygdala and other regions which results in the body's physical display of emotion.

Even though the hodayot are textualized spatial reports, they have the capacity to stimulate actual bodily responses of fear. Psychological studies have shown that the process of layering multiple sensory stimuli can lead individuals to perceive an event as being 'real' even if the event may not have been experienced first-hand.[81] A powerful expression of primary emotion indicates that the sensory faculties of the brain have been stimulated, imparting a quality of realism to the event that is being imaged. Psychologists refer to this phenomenon of "confusing thoughts, associations, and imaginations with actual perceptions," as one type of a variety of different source errors or source confusions.[82] In the summary discussion of this phenomenon, Karen Mitchell and Marcia Johnson write:

> For example, participants sometimes claim to have seen pictures that they only imagined . . ., and good imagers are more likely to misattribute imaginations to perceptions . . . . Neuroimaging evidence converges with this behavioral evidence in suggesting that rich self-generated perceptual information induces source errors. For example, one study compared source memory for imagined and seen pictures . . . . Imagined pictures that participants later erroneously claimed to have seen showed greater activity in precuneus during encoding than imagined items later correctly identified as imagined. This area is involved during other types of imagery tasks, supporting the idea that perceptual information either generated via active imagination or imported from one item to another . . . lends a sense of vividness to people's false memories of having seen the imagined items.[83]

---

81 Here, notice that for the social- and neuropsychologists, the labeling of events as 'real' or 'fake' follows the conventions of those disciplines. The same judgments are not being made about religious experience.

82 Karen J. Mitchell and Marcia K. Johnson, "Source Monitoring 15 Years Later: What Have We Learned from fMRI About the Neural Mechanisms of Source Memory," *Psychological Bulletin* 135 (2009): 638–77, here 654.

83 Mitchell and Johnson, "Source Monitoring 15 Years Later," 654; they cite the following works: F. T. Durso and M. K. Johnson, "The effects of orienting tasks on recognition, recall, and modality confusion of pictures and words," *Journal of Verbal Learning and Verbal Behavior* 19 (1980): 416–29; I. E. Hyman and J. Pentland, "The Role of Mental Imagery in the Creation of False Childhood Memories," *Journal of Memory and Language* 35 (1996): 101–17; B. Gonsalves, P. J. Reber, D. R. Gitelman, T. B. Parrish, M.-M. Mesulam, K. A. Paller, "Neural Evidence that Vivid Imagining can Lead to False Remembering,"

The part of the brain mentioned above, the precuneus, functions with the prefrontal cortex and other regions of the brain during the processing of vivid visual images. The precuneus is also active during the reconstitution of episodic memory, a type of memory that includes vivid egocentric experiences of spatiality.[84] Unlike the more primitive region of the amygdala, the precuneus is found in a part of the brain that is highly developed in humans. Because it is physically difficult to access, the precuneus has been the subject of fewer studies than the amygdala which, in comparison, is relatively easy to isolate in the brain. In conjunction with the prefrontal cortex, the precuneus is thought to be the processing site for visual sensory stimuli and consciousness. Psychological studies have demonstrated that negative emotions are experienced more intensely when accompanied by detailed mental visualization than without it.[85] Detailed and repetitive practices of visualizing frightening Secondspatial events; either the terrifying religious geography of fiery rivers and conflagration in 1QH XI, 31–37, or the events of birthing, military besiegement, and sailing during a tempest (1QH XI, 7–19); can arouse actual bodily responses of fear. The *anthropologizing* "I," or the first-person narration of these events, can facilitate the egocentric construction of mental images, making events seem more 'real' to the individual.[86]

When those experiences are reconstituted during subsequent re-readings of the text, the bodily response of fear is used to construct and reinforce this vivid quality during the remembering process. "[I]f a person's memory for an imagined event has qualities typical of per-

---

Psychological Science 15 (2004): 655–60; J. M. Lampinen, C. R. Meier, J. D. Arnal, J. K. Leding, "Compelling untruths: Content Borrowing and Vivid False Memories," *Journal of Experimental Psychology: Learning, Memory, and Cognition* 31 (2005): 954–63; K. B. Lyle and M. K. Johnson, "Source Misattributions May Increase the Accuracy of Source Judgments," *Memory & Cognition* 35 (2007): 1024–33.

84 Episodic memories or vivid experiential memories, are distinguished from semantic memories that are knowledge based memories of factual information; Andrew R. Mayes, Daniela Montaldi, Tom J. Spencer, and Neil Roberts, "Recalling Spatial Information as a Component of Recently and Remotely Acquired Episodic or Semantic Memories: An fMRI Study," *Neuropsychology* 18 (2004): 426–441; here, 426.

85 Emily A. Holmes and Andrew Mathews, "Mental Imagery and Emotion? A Special Relationship?" *Emotion* 5 (2005): 489–97.

86 Elizabeth A. Kensinger and Suzanne Corkin, "Memory Enhancement for Emotional Words," *Memory & Cognition* 31 (2003): 1169–80.

ceived events, such as a high degree of vividness of sensory-perceptual detail or little information about the cognitive processes involved in generating the memory, then he or she may be fooled into believing that the event had been perceived."[87] This suggests that the stimulation of the region of the brain responsible for sensory processing of fear (the amygdala), even when the stimuli are simulated, can create compelling experiences that can arouse *actual* bodily emotions in the limbic system. The psychological studies by Linda Henkel, Nancy Franklin, and Marcia Johnson targeted visual and auditory functions and exposed individuals to either actual or simulated stimuli for common events.[88] They found that simulated visual stimuli, when coupled with sonorous sensory stimuli resulted in a greater likelihood of being remembered as being 'real' events.[89] The practice of visualization, whether from the processing of actual perceived images or the construction of mental images is instrumental in the reinvigorating of memories.

The hodayot are texts that would have been read and re-read. Due to their textual form, an ancient reader would have had to rely upon his construction of mental images, yet, this cannot be said to lessen the impact of their terror. Studies by Elizabeth Kensinger and Suzanne Corkin have demonstrated that negatively valanced words were perceived similarly to negative images in so far as they were remembered with greater detail and more vividly than neutral ones.[90] Reading negative textual

---

87 Henkel, Franklin, Johnson, "Cross-Modal Source Monitoring Confusions Between Perceived and Imagined Events," also Karen J. Mitchell and Marcia K. Johnson, "Source Monitoring 15 Years Later," 638–77; M. K. Johnson, S. Hashtroudi, D. S. Lindsay, "Source Monitoring," *Psychological Bulletin* 114 (1993): 3–28. Notice that the language of 'true' or 'false' is characteristic of the social and natural science disciplines; such an arbitration of experiences is not advocated here in the study of religious experiences in antiquity.

88 Henkel, Franklin, and Johnson, "Cross-Modal Source Monitoring Confusions," 322. "[P]articipants saw, heard, imagined seeing, and imagined hearing common events, such as a *balloon popping*, a *toilet flushing*, or a *basketball bouncing*. On a given trial, an event was experienced from one of four sources (visual perception, auditory perception, visual imagery, or auditory imagery), and over the course of the trials, some events were experienced from two different sources. Some were, for example, visually imagined and at some other point were actually heard, and others were actually seen and at some other point were auditorily imagined" (322).

89 They report that the greatest likelihood for source confusion occurred when events were visually imagined but actually heard; Henkel, Franklin, and Johnson, "Cross-Modal Source Monitoring Confusions," 331.

90 Kensinger and Corkin, "Memory Enhancement for Emotional Words," 1169.

stimuli can have a similar effect as viewing negative images, and result in vivid experiencing of the event. The practice of reading spontaneously generates mental imaging of the event that is being described. This is most certainly why Aristotle, in the *Poetics*, identifies the visual aspects of a tragedy to be the least important, since the mind is able to visualize on its own without assistance from props. Tragedy does not *need* to be performed as a spectacle since its ability to move an audience to the desired affective states of pity and terror was understood to be carried by the rhetorical force of the text alone.[91] The ancient mind's capacity to visualize a terrifying scene from a verbal description may even have been enhanced by the fact that it was not bombarded by visual media in the same ways that we are today. Terrifying Secondspatial scenes of the netherworld are highly detailed and leave memorable impressions on the mind. This may explain why certain literary elements describing doom and judgment appear again and again in visionary texts—simply put, such scenes were unforgettable. In the case of Enoch's visions of the otherworldly places of punishment, their graphic and terrifying quality made these descriptions more memorable and facilitated the reconstitution of these details by subsequent authors, with the most memorable details in Enoch's visions being those reused from other known visionary experiences. The ancient mind remembered these poignant descriptions because the body's actual emotional response of fear constructed a lasting memory of them. Kensinger's and Corkin's study of the powerful impact of negative visuals, both texts and images, is especially significant for the study of ancient texts, like the hodayot that would have been read and recited.

In the case of the terrifying Secondspace descriptions found in column XI, an ancient reader can simulate intense experiences of emotion from reading these descriptions of terror that target his visual and audi-

---

91 In this section of the *Poetics* (§VI.1450), Aristotle is at pains to highlight the features of tragedy and enumerates each one according to the importance of their function. He writes that the most important is plot (ὁ μῦθος), followed by character (τὰ ἤθη), followed by thought (ἡ διάνοια), followed by diction (ἡ λέξις), He writes the following about spectacle (ἡ ὄψις) or the actual visual elements of the masks and costumes: "The Spectacle, though an attraction, is the least artistic of all the parts, and has least to do with the art of poetry. The tragic effect is quite possible without a public performance and actors; and besides, the getting-up of the Spectacle is more a matter for the costumier than the poet," (VI. 1450b15) as translated by Ingram Bywater in *The Basic Works of Aristotle* (ed. Richard McKeon; New York: Random House, 1941), 1460.

tory faculties. The layering of sensory stimuli can contribute an aspect of realism that can convince a reader that he experienced the things that are described in the text. Modern neuropsychologists and social psychologists are concerned to describe actual bodily experiences of imagined events as "source error" or "source confusion" because the contemporary context has inherited a set of presuppositions about memory and experience. Such evaluative judgments, however, are conventions for those disciplines and not useful judgments for discussing religious experience in antiquity. The expression of emotion within a performative context can be instrumental and should be recognized as 'real' if it produces the bodily sensations of an actual event even if said event was not experienced first-hand. Performative emotions, those states of affect experienced in ritual contexts, are actual bodily experiences with lasting implications for the creation of subjectivity. The fact that they are scripted experiences does not lessen their experiential impact. The supposition that performative emotions are artificial experiences and of a lesser quality is one that has been long held in religious studies which should be critically assessed. The preeminent sociologist of religion, Emil Durkheim, described emotions expressed within religious contexts as inauthentic in his classic work, *The Elementary Forms of the Religious Life* (1915). Durkheim's evaluative statements suggest a deceitful motive on the part of the religious participant and prioritize spontaneous experiences as being more 'true' or 'authentic' than scripted ones. He writes:

> One initial fact is constant: mourning is not the spontaneous expression of individual emotions. If the relations weep, lament, mutilate themselves, it is not because they feel themselves personally affected by the death of their kinsman. Of course, it may be that in certain particular cases, the chagrin expressed is really felt. But it is more generally the case that there is no connection between the sentiments felt and the gestures made by the actors in the rite. If, at the very moment when the weepers seem the most overcome by their grief, some one speaks to them of some temporal interest, it frequently happens that they change their features and tones at once, take on a laughing air and converse in the gayest fashion imaginable. Mourning is not a natural movement of private feelings ounded by a cruel loss; it is a duty imposed by the group. One weeps, not simply because he is sad, but because he is forced to weep. It is a ritual attitude which he is forced to adopt out of respect for custom, but which is, in a large measure, independent of his affective state.[92]

---

92 Emile Durkheim, *The Elementary Forms of the Religious Life* (New York: Free Press, 1915; repr. 1965), 442–43.

Current readers are right to be suspicious of Durkheim's judgments that spontaneous religious experiences are more 'authentic' than scripted ritualized experiences, especially since early Judaism was highly ritualized, even in its apocalyptic expression. Such valences say more about modern assumptions and attitudes about institutionalized religion than anything inherent in religion generally. Findings in neuropsychology demonstrate that the body and its behaviors can exert a tremendous influence over consciousness and reinforce the theoretical view that repeated bodily practices shape and powerfully influence meaning. Pedagogical techniques that arouse emotions result in long-lasting imprints on the mind. These studies of how the body experiences emotion and cognition are of interest in light of theoretical inquiries into the effect that ritualization practices have upon the formation of subjectivity.[93]

B. Emotion and Memory in Performance Theory and Neuropsychology

Emotion plays a significant role in memory construction and reconstruction. Those who study these processes recognize that emotion and sensory reactivation play a critical role in the reconstruction of compelling memory. Memory is not understood as a static file that is retrieved at will through the stimulation of memory, but rather, understood to be reinvigorated or reconstituted anew.[94] Emotion's role in memory construction and reconstruction plays an instrumental role in the performance theory associated with Constantin Stanislavsky. Stanislavsky's System can offer insights into how emotion processes including automatic memory construction can be trained to serve the purpose of a performance. While many neuropsychological processes are not yet thoroughly understood, it is possible for certain individuals to discipline

---

93 G. Brown, "Theorizing Ritual as Performance," 3–18.

94 See Craig E. L. Stark, Yoko Okado, and Elizabeth F. Loftus, "Imaging the Reconstruction of True and False Memories Using Sensory Reactivation and the Misinformation Paradigms," *Learning & Memory* 17 (2010): 485–88. Many of the studies of emotion and its role in memory construction are concerned with 'false memories.' Again, as discussed earlier, the labeling of certain experiences as 'true' or 'false' is common in the social sciences, but it is always the case that for the individual, the phenomenal experience of remembering is embodied and really felt. Stark, Okado, and Loftus write, "False memories, although inaccurate, are often just as compelling as true memories," (485).

the processes of memory construction and reconstruction over time. Stanislavsky's System offered various techniques for actors to discipline or train their emotion memories to respond as needed by the script.

While scholars readily agree that emotion plays a role in memory processes, the exact neurological processes for these operations are not yet fully understood. Emotion's role in memory construction and reconstruction is a topic that has historically been overlooked by scholars of emotion theory, but one that has received increasing attention since the 1990s.[95] While the construction of affective memories occurs spontaneously, neuropsychological studies show that they can be learned. When these secondary processes of emotion take place, they are never entirely independent from the limbic system. In other words, even learned emotional responses can be experienced with the force of spontaneously experienced emotions of fear. Research in neuropsychology confirms Stanislavsky's presumption that an actor can, over time, train his emotions to imitate the scripted emotions through repeated practices of visualization and the performance of certain bodily actions. During the process of memory construction, emotions are used in an instrumental way in the coding of these experiences.

Studies on memory construction and reconstruction show that negative affective memories are more readily invigorated than positive ones. According to Elizabeth A. Kensinger, the higher the negative valence of the event and the greater the arousal of the individual's own emotions, the more easily he or she is able to construct the memory.[96] Emotion's arousal during a vivid visualization of an event, in turn, is instrumental

---

95 The literature on emotion and memory is characterized by a methodological divide between social psychology approaches and cognitive neuropsychological ones. An interdisciplinary approach is preferable; see the helpful discussion by Kevin Ochsner and Daniel L. Schacter, "Remembering Emotional Events: A Social Cognitive Neuroscience Approach," *Handbook of Affective Sciences* (ed. Richard J. Davidson; Klaus R. Scherer; H. Hill Goldsmith; New York: Oxford University Press, 2003), 643–60.

Magda B. Arnold is among the earliest scholars to examine the relationship between emotion and memory in a systematic way: see "An Excitatory Theory of Emotion," in *Feelings and Emotions* (ed. M. L. Reymert; New York: McGraw-Hill, 1950), 11–33; eadem., *Emotion and Personality* (New York: Columbia University Press, 1960); and eadem., "Perennial Problems in the field of Emotion," in *Feelings and Emotions* (ed. M. B. Arnold; New York: Academic Press, 1970), 149–85.

96 Elizabeth A. Kensinger, "Remembering Emotional Experiences: The Contribution of Valence and Arousal," *Reviews in the Neurosciences* 15 (2004): 241–53.

in the construction of a memory of that event. While emotion's role in memory construction and reconstruction has been recognized for a long time, strongly valanced negative emotions like fear, appear to have a significant impact and is directly related to a memory's vivid qualities and aspects of realism. The region in the limbic system known as the amygdala is one of the key regions for the primary processing of fear and also where sensory functions are regulated. The stimulation of the amygdala during the arousal of fear apparently contributes to the construction of more vivid memories. As Elizabeth Kensinger's research has shown, the arousal of negative emotions is especially likely to heighten the visual specificity of memory.

> A strong correlation between the amount of activity in the right amygdala and in the right fusiform gyrus during the encoding of negative items later remembered with specific visual detail suggests that interactions between these regions may underlie this enhancement. There is abundant evidence that the amygdala can influence processing throughout the ventral visual processing stream enhancing the processing of emotionally relevant stimuli . . . . Fusiform activity often is greater during the processing of fearful faces compared to neutral faces . . ., and correlations have been noted between the amount of activity in the amygdala and the amount of activity in the fusiform cortex during viewing of emotional information . . . . Based on the speed of the anatomical connections between the amygdala and visual processing regions, there is reason to believe that at least part of the modulation occurs via the amygdala's influence on sensory processing . . . . Moreover, a neuroimaging study examining fusiform activation to fearful facial expressions in patients with varying amounts of damage to the amygdala showed a correlation between the amount of amygdalar preservation and the amount of fusiform activity.[97]

---

97   Elizabeth A. Kensinger, Rachel J. Garoff-Eaton, Daniel L. Schacter, "How Negative Emotion Enhances the Visual Specificity of a Memory," *Journal of Cognitive Neuroscience* 19 (2007): 1872–1887. She makes reference to the studies by Y. Sugase, S. Yamane, S. Ueno, and K. Kawano, "Global and Fine Information Coded by Single Neurons in the Temporal Visual Cortex," *Nature* 400 (1999): 869–73; D. G. Amaral, J. L. Price, A. Pitkanen, and S. T. Carmichael, "Anatomical Organization of the Primate Amygdaloid Complex," in *The Amygdala: Neurobiological Aspects of Emotion, Memory and Mental Dysfunction* (ed. J. Aggleton; New York: Wiley-Liss, 1992), 1–66; P. Vuilleumier, J. L. Armony, J. Driver, and R. J. Dolan, "Effects of Attention and Emotion on Face Processing in the Human Brain: An Event-related fMRI study," *Neuron* 30 (2001): 829–41; H. C. Breiter, S. L. Rauch, K. K. Kwong, J. R. Baker, R. M. Weisskoff, D. N. Kennedy, et al, "Functional Magnetic Resonance Imaging of Symptom Provocation in Obsessive-Compulsive Disorder," *Archives of General Psychiatry* 53 (1996): 595–606; J. S. Morris, C. D. Frith, D. I. Perrett, D.

Because of emotion's associative role in memory construction and re-construction, other experiences of similarly valanced emotions can spontaneously be brought to the fore.

Research into the emotions and their role in cognition provides a helpful context for understanding how emotion and memory operate within the performance theory associated with Stanislavsky which em-phasizes the role of the physical body and the emotions. In the case of a strongly valenced negative emotion, Damasio states that once the emo-tion and the conscious feeling of that emotion is present, the brain will naturally reconstitute thoughts and memories that resemble that affect. He states that "[t]his is because associated learning has linked emotions with thoughts in a rich two-way network. Certain thoughts evoke cer-tain emotions and vice versa. Cognitive and emotional levels of process-ing are continuously linked in this manner."[98] Because of the rich inter-connectedness of emotion processing regions of the brain and regions associated with higher forms of cognitive processing, emotions can be modulated by physical behaviors of the body. Once an emotion is ex-perienced, the associative processes of learning will spontaneously lead the individual to reinvigorate other memories of a similar valance. In general the relationship between emotion and memory construction is a spontaneous and subconscious process that happens automatically, but through much repetition these processes can become learned and constructed at will.

Stanislavsky's system of acting employs a set of techniques for phys-ical relaxation and visualization that facilitate emotion memory training so that the necessary affective memories can be reconstituted with some degree of automaticity at key moments during a performance.[99] Stani-slavsky emphasized the mastery of a character's emotions as a way of re-

---

Rowland, A. W. Young, A. J. Calder, et al, "A Differential Neural Response in the Human Amygdala to Fearful and Happy Facial Expressions," *Nature* 31 (1996): 812–15; P. Vuilleumier, M. P. Richardson, J. L. Armony, J. Driver, R. J. Dolan, "Distinct Influences of Amygdala Lesion on Visual Cortical Acti-vation during Emotional Face Processing," *Nature Neuroscience* 7 (2004): 1271–1278. Most recently, see Katherine R. Mickley and Elizabeth A. Kensinger, "Emotional Valence Influences the Neural Correlates Associated with Remem-bering and Knowing," *Cognitive, Affective, & Behavioral Neuroscience* 8 (2008): 143–52.

98 Damasio, *Looking for Spinoza*, 71.

99 The method theory approach to acting, associated with Constantin Stanislavsky, has been critically reengaged by recent scholars. See Sharon Carnicke, *Stanislav-sky in Focus, 2nd ed*; and Rose Whyman, *The Stanislavsky System of Acting*.

enactment of a role. An actor was expected to know how his character would react and respond emotionally to different scenarios. While reinvigorating emotions at will is not a skill that comes easily for most people, these bodily processes can become learned behavior due to the innate capacity that humans have for imitative behavior and vicarious learning. It is important to note, however, that the acquisition of automaticity requires much repetition and is a relatively slow process.[100] Automaticity is understood as processing without conscious thought or effort.[101] According to psychologists, individuals express automatic affective responses to stimuli, which responses have bearing on later cognitive, emotion, and behavioral processes.[102] While studies on the specific role that affect plays in automatic cognitive processing have not fully understood the relationship between the two, the intensity of the valence of the emotion is thought to be critical, with negative emotions being the most compelling.[103] Like the acquisition of automaticity in other cognitive processes, the automatic processing of affect requires frequent exposure to and familiarity with the process, akin to what psychologists call 'overlearning.'[104]

Being able to familiarize oneself with specific affective experiences so as to reconstitute them as needed in a later performance is a crucial aspect of Stanislavsky's system. Eventually, the frequent practice of rehearsing specific emotions makes the process automatic. The synchronization of the actor's interior emotional state with the character that he is playing can be strengthened by having a vivid memory bank of personal emotional experiences and by routinely reenacting palpable memories of personal experiences. Stanislavsky writes:

> [I]t appears that there are many degrees of power in emotion memory and both its effects and combinations are varied. On this point he said: "imagine that you have received some insult in public, perhaps a slap in the face,

---

100 Bargh and Chartrand, "The Unbearable Automaticity of Being," 476.
101 Alice M. Isen and Gregory Andrade Diamond, "Affect and Automaticity," in *Unintended Thought* (ed. James S. Uleman and John A. Bargh; New York: The Guilford Press, 1989), 124–52.
102 John A. Bargh, "The Automaticity of Everyday Life," in *Advances in Social Cognition, vol. 10* (ed. R. S. Wyer; Mahwah: Lawrence Erlbaum Associates, 1997), 1–61.
103 See R. Fazio, D. M. Sanbonmatsu, M. C. Powell, and F. R. Kardes, "On the Automatic Activation of Attitudes," *Journal of Personality and Social Psychology* 50 (1986): 229–38, here 236.
104 Isen and Diamond, "Affect and Automaticity," 138–39.

that makes your cheek burn whenever you think of it. The inner shock was so great that it blotted out all the details of this harsh incident. But some insignificant thing will instantly revive the memory of the insult, and the emotion will recur with redoubled violence. Your cheek will grow red or you will turn pale and your heart will pound. If you possess such sharp and easily aroused emotional material you will find it easy to transfer it to the stage and play a scene analogous to the experience you had in real life which left such a shocking impression on you. To do this you will not need any technique. It will play itself because nature will help you."[105]

Stanislavsky describes the strong imprint that highly charged emotional experiences leave in human memory. While these types of memory may lack accurate details or may even fade so as to become seemingly forgotten, a similar subsequent experience can spontaneously generate the reconstruction of a memory that has a great deal of emotional force. Neuropsychological studies have demonstrated that experiences that are strongly valenced as negative are more readily and vividly reinvigorated. Such powerful experiences of fear, anger, and sadness from personal memory are then easily reconstituted as needed at a later time. In another example Stanislavsky describes an actor who dined with old friends whom he had not seen for some time. In the course of the meal, the actor asked about the couple's son whom he had forgotten had died tragically since he last saw them. The emotions then experienced by the actor when he saw the reaction of his friends, "the frightened expression on the face of a man across the table, the glazed eyes of the woman next to him, and the cry that broke from the other end of the table," left a powerful imprint in his emotion memory that he was later able to use as needed during the appropriate time in his performance on stage.[106] The method acting approach emphasizes the role of the physical body and the emotions in the performance of a script. Techniques of visualization and rehearsal of strongly valenced events can, as neuropsychological studies have shown, lead the brain to spontaneously reconstitute further experiences from personal memory that correlate with that emotion.

Stanislavsky claims that the disciplined training of the emotion memory that is expected under his guidance is not possible for everyone. This comports with Damasio's assessment that generally speaking, emotions cannot be controlled:

105 Stanislavski (Stanislavsky), *An Actor Prepares*, 176.
106 Stanislavski (Stanislavsky), *An Actor Prepares*, 176.

Whatever the inducer, emotions are triggered by mechanisms we are not aware of and that we cannot control willfully. We can control, in part, the expression of some emotions, but most of us are not very good at it, and the result is that at any moment emotions are a fairly good index of how conducive the environment is to one's well-being. The nonconscious triggering of emotions also explains why they are not easy to mimic voluntarily.[107]

According to Stanislavsky, the disciplining of the emotions is a skill that few actors are able to master and it requires extensive training and preparation. There is no reason to assume that an ancient reader who sought to achieve a visionary experience from reading would have found it to be an easy process.

C. Summary of the Neuropsychology of Emotion and Performance

These studies of the role that emotions play in human cognition and in the formation of subjectivity are helpful in building a model for how meditation upon otherworldly experiences could have generated new visionary experiences. According to Stanislavsky, an individual's emotion memory can be reconstituted and merged with the temperament of the character that he seeks to perform during the actualization of the role. In the case of the hodayot, I propose that the affective script that was used for performative reading, 1QH XI, 6–37, aroused the compelling emotion of fear. The imagery in column XI provides the schema or basic framework for the meditative experience into which an ancient reader might merge elements of a similar affective valence of experiences or scenes from his emotion memory. This process of associative reconstitution and sensory stimulation is one that can result in the exegetically generated text recorded in 1QH XIII, 22-XV, 8. The three stock images of the woman in labor, the ship on a sea, and a city under siege become intensified and personalized as the hodayot reader reenacted the emotions aroused by column XI, eventually transforming him from a reader into a participant in the vision.

Humans have a strong evolutionary predisposition to respond strongly to certain emotions such as fear, and reenacting such emotional experiences can elicit powerful responses from the ancient reader. Column XI is filled with stock images of terror described in such a way as to

---

107 Damasio, "A Second Chance for Emotion," 19.

target a reader's seeing and hearing faculties. Studies on how memories are constructed and reconstituted have shown that the layering of sensory stimuli, that is the multiplication of visual, auditory, and olfactory stimuli, contributes to the strong likelihood that the mind will remember that stimuli as a 'real' experience, even when those stimuli are only simulated.[108] In other words, the successful arousal of multiple senses can effectively re-create an event so detailed as to seem real. The ancient reader could have created the semblance of a 'real' experience of being in an otherworldly locale with a text as richly detailed as 1QH XI, 6–37. By engaging in various visualization techniques, an ancient reader may have also spontaneously reconstituted memories from his own personal experiences of fear as he sought to reenact the text found in column XI. When he did so, the reader transformed himself into a participant and an author of a new visionary experience. Christopher Rowland describes the complex relationship between the reader's imagination, the text, and the recollection of memory in the following way:

> Such meditative practices have been a key part of religion down the centuries and became the cornerstone of the religious life in the late medieval period, though the practices were rooted in a long tradition. The exercise of imagination involves the visualization in the mind of objects, inspired by what is read in texts or in the external world. It has a close relationship with the visionary and the dreamlike, therefore, though in the latter the process is usually less deliberate than would be the case with an exercise of imagination.[109]

Rowland emphasizes the instrumental role of visualization in the reconstitution of memory and the dynamic process of the creation of mental images that allowed for the associative reinvigoration of a range of related memories and personal memories. Such an associative and dynamic process, he proposes, can result in exegetical creativity as well.[110] Rowland concludes by proposing that this dynamic process of meditation and

---

108 Linda A. Henkel, Nancy Franklin, and Marcia K. Johnson, "Cross-Modal Source Monitoring Confusions Between Perceived and Imagined Events," 321–35.

109 Christopher Rowland with Patricia Gibbons and Vicente Dobroruka, "Visionary Experience in Ancient Judaism and Christianity," 54.

110 Rowland, "Visionary Experience," 51. Rowland also cites Mary Carruthers and her discussion of memory and memory construction as primarily visual; Carruthers, *The Craft of Thought: Meditation, Rhetoric, and the Making of Images, 400–1200* (Cambridge: Cambridge University Press, 1998), 68–69.

memory reconstruction may explain why apocalyptic literature often contains instances where the exegete is not only a detached interpreter, but frequently a participant in the vision as well.

> Such experiences may for the visionary have their origin in an approach to texts in which the pursuit of the meaning of the text is not a detached operation but may involve the interpreter as a participant in the narrative of the biblical texts (such as John's experience of realization in his own vision of what had appeared to Ezekiel in Rev 1 and 4). Thereby he (and it was probably almost always a man) becomes a recipient of insight as the text becomes the vehicle of an imaginative transport to other realms of consciousness.[111]

Rowland's observations about apocalyptic literature such as the Book of Revelation fit well with the Qumran text of the hodayot that is being considered in this chapter. According to the method of reading proposed in this chapter, the reader, through the performative activity of reading texts that describe visionary experiences, can come to experience them for himself and at the same time, spontaneously associate his own personal affective memories with what he was reading. In doing so, he created a subjectivity of a visionary, thereby becoming himself a participant in the event and the author of a new visionary experience.

III. Moving from Secondspace to Thirdspace Experiences: Performative Reading and the Exegetical Generation of 1QH XIII, 22-XV, 8

I propose that the Secondspace descriptions of otherworldly terrors and events found in 1QH XI, 6–19 + 20–37 led to the exegetical generation of the hodayah 1QH XIII, 22-XV, 8. There are many compelling reasons why column XI can be thought to be exegetically related to 1QH XIII, 22- XV, 8. The first is the recurrence of the three literary motifs discussed above: a laboring woman, a ship on the sea, and a city under siege. The two compositions are relatively close to one another in the hodayot scroll and are attested in the oldest copy of the hodayot, 4Q428. They are separated from one another by two hodayot: the first composition, 1QH XII, 6-XIII, 6, is a text that one could argue has a different literary origin from the surrounding hodayot

---

111 Rowland, "Visionary Experience," 55.

which is not attested in 4Q428. This intervening composition has as many as five instances of supralinear *mater lectiones* in an editorial hand. These revisions can be understood as markers that reflect the desire of a later editor to integrate the secondary composition known as 1QH XII, 6-XIII, 6 into its surrounding literary context. The other intervening composition, 1QH XIII, 7−21, is a brief one that uses terrifying imagery of predatory animals to elicit a fearful response from the reader which also does not appear to be preserved in 4Q428.[112]

Three distinctive images (a pregnant woman, a ship on a sea, and a city under siege) are shared by both the hodayot; however, the composition in 1QH XIII, 22-XV, 8 appears in a significantly more expanded and more detailed format. While the Secondspatial events described in column XI contains many fantastic mythological elements, the composition in 1QH XIII, 22-XV, 8 contains several details that suggest that it reflects a Thirdspatial experience of these events. In 1QH XIII, 22-XV, 8, the speaker reports experiences that demonstrate a participatory involvement in the otherwise scripted affective events in 1QH XI, 6−37. Personal elements from the reader's affective memory that fit the emotional tenor of the script, namely extreme distress caused by anxiety and the betrayal of intimate friends (XIII, 24−27), are naturally reconstituted during the associative process of memory reconstruction and intensify the reenactment. These personal elements from the ancient reader's own memory reflect the actualization of the affective script, and find their way into the new composition that was generated (1QH XIII, 22-XV, 8). The ancient reader has become transformed into a participant in the events described in 1QH XI, 6−37, and an author of a newly conceived experience in 1QH XIII, 22-XV, 8. The speaker of 1QH XIII, 22-XV, 8 shows a participation in the abdominal pains of the pregnant woman, the fear of the city under siege, and the terror of a ship in a storm that goes beyond the scripted experiences in column XI. The appropriation of these events in 1QH XIII, 22-XV, 8, I propose, is a Thirdspatial experience that reflects aspects of the reader's lived experience.

---

112 This data about composition 1QH XII, 6-XIII, 6 and XIII, 7−21 are based on the information provided in DJD 29. I am not making the claim that the compositions in 1QH column XI and XIII, 22-XV, 8 *immediately* followed one another in 4Q428, but simply observing that the two hodayot discussed here have a relationship to one another that has greater antiquity than either of their relationships to the two intervening compositions.

In the following text of 1QH XIII, 22–XV, 8, I have highlighted in boldface print the passages that reflect a participatory transformation of the three anthropologizing images from column XI. The many lexical elements shared between these two hodayot are indicated by underlining and footnoting. It is worth noting that a number of these common words are only shared by column XI and 1QH XIII, 22–XV, 8 and appear nowhere else in the entire hodayot scroll: "pain" (ציר), "ship" (אוניה), "sailor" (מלח), "bar" (בריח); "to surround" (אפף); "city" (עיר).

Text of 1QH XIII, 22–XV, 8

(22) {I give thanks to You} Blessed are You,[113] O Lord, for You have neither abandoned the orphan, nor despised the poor! For Your strength [is without boun]ds, and Your glory (23) is without measure! Wondrous warriors are Your ministers! And with a humbled people are in the sweepings at Yo[ur] feet [together] with those impatient for (24) righteousness in order to lift (them) up from chaos together with all of those lacking grace (ועם ענוים במאטאיי רגליכ]ה יחד [עם נמהרי צדק להעלות משאון יחד כול {נמה}אביוני חסד).

But as for me, I was against [   ], for a dispute (25) and contentions to my friends. Jealousy and anger belong to those who enter into my covenant; a grumble and a complaint belong to all of my comrades. Ev[en those who ea]t my bread (26) turn their heel against me, and all those who had committed themselves to my counsel, speak perversely against me with unjust lips. The men of my [coun]cil rebel (27) and grumble round and round, about the mystery which You hid in me. They slander (me) to the children of destruction (לבני הווה)[114] because [You] have magni[fied Yourself] in me. (28) And on account of their guilt, You have concealed (the) spring of understanding and the counsel of truth. But they devise destruction (הווה) (in) their heart. And the wor [ds of] Belial unleash (29) a lying tongue like the poison of serpents darting out continuously. Like those who crawl in the dust, they lash out in order to ambu [sh.] The p[oisons] of vipers (30) have no remedy. **And it has become an incurable pain and a tormenting agony in the bowels of Your servant,** making [(his) spiri]t stumble and finishing off (31) (his) strength so that he cannot take hold of (his) station (להכשיל [רו]ח ולהתם כוח לבלתי החזק מעמד).[115] They overtook me in narrow straits without shelter, without separating from fami[ly ties   .] They clamor (32) a dispute against me on the lyre, and their grumbling is joined together with taunt-songs. **With ruin and desolation, burning pains sei[ze me] and pangs like the contractions of (33) one giving**

---

113 The scribe has made deletion marks around this word and has written the words "Blessed are You" above it.

114 The noun "destruction" (הווה) appears also in 1QH XI, 26, 34, 35, 39 and XIII, 27, 28, 33, XIV, 6, 24; XV, 4, 7, 8.

115 Cf. 1QH XI, 22 where the hodayah references the cultic term "station" (מעמד).

birth (עם שאה ומשואה זלעופות אחזוני וחבלים כצירי יולדה).[116] My heart clamors in me; I am clothed in a mourning garment, and my tongue clings to the roof of {my} mouth, for they have surrounded me with the <u>destructiveness</u> of their heart (בהוות לבם), and their desire (34) has appeared to me as bitterness. The light of my countenance dimmed into darkness, and my splendor switched into gloom. *vacat*

But You, O my God, (35) have opened a wide space in my heart! Yet they continue to grieve (me), and they enclose me all around with deep darkness, my grief feeds heartily (ואוכלה בלחם אנחתי)[117] (36) and drinks endless tears. For my eyes are weakened by anger, and my soul by daily bitterness. Misery and sorrow (37) surround me, and shame is upon (my) face. My bread has been turned into strife, and my drink into a master of disputes. It enters my bones, (38) making (my) spirit stumble and finishing off (my) strength. In accordance with the mysteries of transgression, they misconstrue the works of God in their guilt.

For I am bound by ropes (39) that cannot be loosened and by fetters that cannot be broken. A strong wall [surrounds me] and <u>iron bars</u> (ובריחי ברזל)[118] and doors of [bronze (ודלתי נחושה) that have no] (40) [opening.] My jail cell is with the <u>abyss</u>;[119] {I am}considered without (41) [and the torrents of] <u>Belial engulf my soul without (a hope of) [es]c[ape]</u>.[120]

Col. XIV Lines 1−4 are lost

(5) my heart with contempt in my mouth [   ] (6) And unfathomable <u>destruction</u> (והוה) and immeasur[able] annihilation [and You are my God] (7) You have opened my ears in the disci[p]line of those who reprove righteousness with [   ] (8) from a congregation of fraud and a council of violence. But You have brought me into the council of [the holy   ] guilt. (9) And I know there is a <u>ritual bath</u> (מקוה) for those who turn away from wicked-

---

116 The noun "pain" (ציר) only appears here and in 1QH XI, 8 and 12; Cf. 1QH XI, 8−9 which reads "And I was in distress, like a woman giving birth to her firstborn (ואהיה בצוקה כמו אשה לדה מבכריה) when contractions overwhelm (her) and excruciating labor-pain is upon her cervix (כיא נהפכו צירים וחבל נמרץ על משבריה);

117 This Hebrew idiom is translated literally here but it is expressing the idea of "my grief is insatiable."

118 The noun "bar" (בריח) appears only in col. XI at lines 19 and 40; and at XIII, 39 and XIV, 31 and nowhere else in the hodayot scroll.

119 The noun "abyss" (תהום) appears four times in column XI at 16, 18, 32, 33; and also here at XIII, 40 and XIV, 19 and 27.

120 The hebrew here is (ותחלי[בליעל אפפו נפשי לאין פ[ל]ט]). The verb "to surround" (אפף) only appears in 1QH XI, 29 and XIII, 41 and nowhere else in the scroll; Cf. 1QH XI, 29 "and the cords of death surround without (hope of) escape" (וחבלי מות אפפו לאין פלט); and 1QH XI, 30 which reads "the torrents of Belial" (ונחלי בליעל).

ness, and for those who abandon sin in [   ] <u>so that they might walk about</u> (10) in the way of Your heart without iniquity (ולהתהלך בדרך לבכה לאין עול).[121]

I am comforted against the <u>roar</u> (המון)[122] of the people and against the clamor of kingdoms when they gather themselves together [for] my [sal]vation, that (11) You will raise up a few survivors among Your people and a remnant among Your inheritance. You will refine them in order to purify (them) from guilt [and from s]in. For all (12) their deeds are by Your truth, and by Your kindness You will judge them with an abundance (המון) of mercies and much forgiveness; teaching them according to Your word (13) and establishing them according to Your upright truth in Your council for Your glory. For Your own sake [You] have worked to magnify the Torah and[   ]for [   ] (14) The people of Your council are in the midst of the sons of Adam, in order to recount Your wonders to successive generations and [med]itate on [Your] mighty works (15) without rest. And all nations shall know Your truth and all countries (shall know) Your glory.

For You have brought [   ] and Your secret (16) to all the men of Your counsel, and in the lot together with the angels of presence (ובגורל יחד עם מלאכי פנים), without a mediator between (ואין מליץ בים)[Your] h[oly ones to] reply (17) according to the spirit for [   ] And they will repent at Your glorious word, and they shall become Your princes in the [eternal] l[ot (ויהיו שריכה בגור]ל שלם) and]their [trunk] (18) sprouts like a flower blo[ssoming for] eternal glory, to raise up a shoot into the branches of an eternal planting. And it will cast shade over the entire world, and its[branches] (19) (will reach) as far as the clou[ds], and its roots (will stretch) as far as the abyss, and all the rivers of Eden [shall]w[ater] its [b]r[an]ches. And so it shall become (broad like) the <u>limitl[ess]</u> seas (והיה לימים ל]אין חקר).[123](20) And they shall be entwined over the world endlessly (והתאוֹרו על תבל לאין אפס)[124] and as far as <u>Sheol</u> (שאול);[125] [   ] [and] a spring of light shall become an everlasting font (21) without fail. In its bright flames all the child[ren of injustice] shall burn, [and it shall] become a fire burning against all the men of (22) guilt until (they are) finished off.[126]

---

121 Here a *vav* is partially visible prefixed to the infinitive of the Hebrew להתהלך. Cf. 1QH XI, 20–21, which also uses the word for a cleansing ritual bath (מקוה) joined to the imagery of "walking about" in a divine context.

122 This noun has a range of meaning, including either "abundance" or "roar" (המון). It is translated here as "roar" in order to create a parallelism with the following phrase "clamor of kingdoms" (שאון ממלכות). The noun המון appears as "noise" in 1QH XI, 14, 15, 17, 33, 35; and here at XIV, 10, but as "abundance" in XIV, 12.

123 See the discussion in the notes to this text in chapter three. Note too that "limitless" (לאין חקר) also appears in 1QH XI, 21.

124 See chapter three.

125 The noun "Sheol" (שאול) appears frequently in column XI, appearing at 10, 17, 20; here at XIV, 20.

126 1QH XIV, 15–22.

And they who joined my testimony are seduced by the medi[ators of error to] bring a stranger in the service of righteousness. (23) But You, O God, have commanded them to profit from their ways, on a path of holine[ss]on which [they walked]; but the uncircumcised, the unclean, and the violent (24) may not travel upon it. They stagger away from the way of Your heart, and in the <u>destructiveness</u> of [their] tr[ansgression] (ובהוות פֿ[שעם) they [stumble]. Belial is like a counselor (25) with their heart. [The]y [de-termine a wicked scheme and wallow in guilt.

And [as for me,] I have [become] like a sailor on a ship on the churn-ing (26) of the seas (ו]אֲנִי הִיִ[חִי כמלח באתיה בזעף ימים).[127] **Their waves and all their <u>crashing tides</u> break over me** (גֿליהם וכול משבריהם עלי).[128] A wind of dis-tortions roars [without] calm to restore a soul and without any (27) paths to a straight way on the face of the waters. The <u>abyss</u> (תהום) roars to my groaning and [my soul] approac[hes] <u>the gates of death</u> (שערי מות).[129]

I become (28) like one who enters <u>a fortified city</u> and seeks shelter be-hind a high wall until (his) escape. (ואהיה כבא בעיר מצור תעח בחומה גֿ{}ס{}גֿבה עד פלט)[130]

I lea[n] on Your truth, my God! For You (29) lay a foundation upon rock, and (lay) a beam upon the plumbline of judgment and (lay) the level of tru [th] to [m]ake tested stones for a (30) strong building that will not wobble back and forth. All who enter it shall not stagger. For the stranger may not enter her <u>gates</u> (בֿשָׁעֲרֿיֿה)! Armored <u>doors</u> (דלתי מגן) with no (31) entrance and <u>strong bars</u> (ובריחי עוז) which will not shatter. A troop may not enter with its weapons of <u>war</u> (בכלי מלחמתו);[131] an army (may not enter) to finish off all the <u>arrows</u> of (32) <u>wars</u> of wickedness (כול חצֿי מלחמות רשעה).[132]

Then the sword of God will hasten at the moment of judgment. And all the sons of His truth shall awaken to cut off (33) wickedness, and none of the sons of guilt will be any longer. The warrior (גבור) shall draw his bow, and open up the fortresses of the heavens (34) as an endless plain without end.

---

127 The noun "ship" appears only in col. XI at 7 "they have made (my) soul like a ship in the depths of the sea" (וישימו נפשֿ[י] כאתיה במֿצֿוּלות ים) and at XI, 14, "like a ship upon the surface of the water" (כאתיה על פֿנֿי מים) and here in XIV, 25 and again at XV, 7 but nowhere else in the scroll. Similarly, the noun "sailor" (מלח) appears only here in 1QH XIV, 25 and XI, 15 and nowhere else in the scroll; XI, 15 states "are like sailors on the deeps" (כמלחים במצולות).

128 For the noun "crashing waves" (משבר), cf. 1QH XI, 9 (2xs), 10, 11, 12, 13, 17.

129 The noun for "gate" (שער) only appears in col. XI and in this hodayah, but no-where else in the scroll; cf. 1QH XI, 18 "gates of eternity" (שערי] עולם); and XIV, 27, 30, 34.

130 The noun "city" (עיר) appears here and in 1QH XI, 8 (וכעיר מבצר) but nowhere else in the scroll.

131 For the noun "war" (מלחמה), Cf. 1QH XI, 36; here at XIV, 31, 32, 34, 36, 38.

132 For the noun "arrow" (חץ), all but one of the references to this noun appear in either col. XI or in this composition; Cf. 1QH XI, 17, 28; XIV, 31 and 34 (also at X, 28).

And (open up) the gates of eternity (ושערי עולם) to bring out the weapons of war (כלי מלחמות), and they shall be mighty from one end of the world to the other, and arrows (וחצי[ם])(35) shall rain down!

But there is no escape for a guilty creature. They shall be squashed to oblivion without a remnant and without hope (ואין תקוה)[133] among the abundant corpses, (36) and there is no escape for all the warriors of wars (ולכול גבורי מלחמה). vacat

For [   ] belongs to God Most High [   ](37) O you who lie in the dust, raise the standard! And the worms of the dead lift a banner for [   ] They cut[   ](38) in the battles (במלחמות) of the arrogant. And He makes the rising flood pass by; it must not enter the fortified city! [   ] (39) [   ] [   ] for plaster and as a beam for [   ] (40) truth [   ](41) [   ]

Col. XV, Lines 1–3 are lost

(4) [   ] As for me, I am speechless from their destr[uctiveness   ] (מהו[ת]מ) these things they have reviled me. (5) [my ar]m is shattered from the elbow-joint, and my foot sinks into the mire! My eyes are blinded from seeing (6) evil; my ears from hearing of bloodshed, and my heart is dismayed because of evil plotting. For Belial (בליעל) is with (them); the form of their destruction (הוותם) is revealed. (7) All the foundations of my frame shake, and my bones are rattled (וירעו כול אושי מבניתי ועצמי יתפרדו).[134] **My bowels heave like a ship in a raging (8) storm** (ותהמי עלי כאוניה בזעף חרישׁת). My heart pounds noisily to the destruction, and a whirling wind overwhelms me from the destructiveness of their rebellion (מהוות פשעם). vacat

The hodayah in 1QH XIII, 22–XV, 8 makes numerous references to the speaker's profound despair. The emotion of distress is aroused by the speaker's reports of devastating bodily pain (e. g., 1QH XV, 4–8) and experiences of betrayal (e. g., 1QH XIII, 24–41). The speaker tragically eats the bread of misery and drinks from a cup of endless weeping (1QH XIII, 35–36). As is the case with other compositions from the hodayot scroll, the speaker's experiences are described in great detail with attention to the physicality of the pain and the experiences of the body. Carol Newsom writes that "it is the description of the distraught emotional state of the speaker that truly forms the central focus of this part of the prayer. Thus the composition solicits sympathy for the speaker."[135] The bodily agonies of the speaker progress to a fever pitch with the systematic itemization of the body in 1QH XV, 5–8. In these three lines, as many as nine references to specific limbs or parts of the body are cited

---

133 The word for "hope" (תקוה) appears here and in 1QH XI, 28.
134 The word "foundation" (אוש) also appears in 1QH XI, 14, 31, 36 and here. The same peculiar root "to shake" (רעע-II) appears in 1QH XI, 13 (וירעו אושי קיר כאוניה על פני מים) and 1QH XI, 34 (וכול מחשביה ירעו).
135 Newsom, "Rhetorical Criticism and the Dead Sea Scrolls," 212.

with specific reference to an appropriate experiential activity: arm
(זרו[ע]), "from the elbow" (מקנה), "my foot" (רגלי), "my eyes" (עיני),
"my ears" (אוזני), "my heart" (לבבי), "all the foundations of my frame"
(כול אושי מבניתי), "my bones" (עצמי), "my bowels" (תכמי). The specification
of sensuous experiences lends an element of realism to the account,
thereby intensifying the arousal of emotions. The language of embodiment reflects a rhetorical imaginal body; it is not necessary to imagine
that this is a report of an actual historical person whose arm was shattered. It would, however, be important for the reader to have actively
imagined his own body limbs and extensions as they are enumerated
by the text. The rhetorical force of these references to the body facilitates the ancient reader's reenactment of the text.

I propose that the composition 1QH XIII, 22-XV, 8 is a later exegetical expansion of the hodayot in column XI. While both column XI
and XIII, 22-XV, 8 are represented among the fragments of 4Q428, the
oldest Cave 4 composite collection with both TH and CH, it may be
that the mythological imagery in 1QH XI is exceeding old and that
the exegetical composition that resulted from meditation upon this ancient text was generated as early as the middle Hasmonean period, the
dating of 4Q428. That the text in column XI is composed by a different
author from that of 1QH XIII, 22-XV, 8 can be argued based on the
striking orthographic differences between them. The orthographic system in column XI generally favors the expanded orthography for the
words כיא (8 times)/כי (twice)[136] and כול (16 times)/כל (once).[137] In contrast, the orthographic system for 1QH XIII, 22- XV, 8 consistently observes a mixed orthographic system: כיא (never)/כי (12 times) and כול (18
times)/כל (never). Because the composition in 1QH XIII, 22-XV, 8 is
considerably longer, data is also available for לא (5 times)/לוא (once). The
hodayah in what is presumably the older composition in column XI,
generally prefers the expanded orthography, although it doesn't follow
it perfectly. In contrast to this, the hodayah in what is presumably the
later exegetical composition (1QH XIII, 22- XV, 8) cannot be characterized as consistently favoring the defective orthography, as it shows a
clear and consistent preference for the expanded form of the word, כול.
There is, however, a clear divergence from 1QH XI in the consistent

---

136 The data for 1QH XI, 6–37: כיא appears 8x's at lines 6, 7, 8, 9, 10, 21, 25, 35;
      while כי appears only at lines 15 and 20.
137 The data for 1QH XI, 6–37: כול appears 16x's at lines 11, 12, 13, 16, 17, 19,
      24, 27, 28, 29, 30 (3xs), 31, 34 (2xs); while כל appears only once at line 27.

use of the defective form of כי. The orthographic divergences between
the two compositions suggest that these two hodayot were not composed by the same author.

In addition to the reappearance of the three anthropologizing images, other distinctive images and lexemes from column XI reappear
in 1QH XIII, 22-XV, 8 with such frequency that they cannot be
taken as a striking coincidence. The unusual words for walking back
and forth coupled with a ritual bath that appear together in 1QH XI,
21–22 both reappear in close proximity to one another in 1QH
XIV, 9–10. The passage from column XI reads: "You have lifted me
up to an eternal height, so that I might walk about (ואתהלכה) on an endless plain; and I know that there is a ritual bath (מקוה) for him whom You
created from dust for the eternal council." The passage from column
XIV reads: "And I know there is a ritual bath (מקוה) for those who
turn away from wickedness, and for those who abandon sin in [   ] so
that they might walk about (להתהלך) in the way of Your heart without
iniquity." Similar references to warfare can be seen in both the text
found in column XI and the hodayah in 1QH XIII, 22-XV, 8. The
"weapons of war" in 1QH XIV, 34 may be an allusion to the battle referenced in 1QH XI, 36–37. "Arrows of the Pit" which appear in 1QH
XI, 17 and 28 may be understood by the reference to arrows in XIV,
33–35.

In addition to these lexical points of contact, it is possible to observe
that the three anthropologized images from 1QH XI, 7–8 (the woman
in labor, the ship on a sea, and a city under siege) reappear and undergo
significant intensification and personalization in 1QH XIII, 22- XV, 8.
The mythical image of the speaker as a birthing woman in 1QH XI, 6–
19 has become actualized in the second hodayah as a report of excruciating
pain in his bowels in 1QH XIII, 30 (ותהי לכאוב אנוש ונגע נמאר בתכמי עבדכה),
which he later likens to the pains of one giving birth in 1QH XIII,
32–33 (שאה ומשואה זלעופות אחזוני וחבלים כצירי יולדה). So too, the stock literary image of comparing distress to a ship tossed in a stormy sea in
1QH XI, 7 (כאניה במצולות ים) and later on "like sailors on the deeps"
(כמלחים במצולות) in XI, 15 becomes personalized in the second hodayah
when the speaker reports: "and [I have beco]me *like a sailor* on a ship in
churning seas" (ו[אני היי]תי כמלח באניה בזעף ימים).[138] Similarly, the stereotypical
trope of a city under siege in 1QH XI, 8 (כעיר מבצר מלפ[ני צר]) becomes actualized in a personalized way as the speaker reports: "And I have become

---

138 1QH XIV, 25–26

like one who enters a fortified city in order to hide behind a high wall until rescue" in 1QH XIV, 27–28 (ואהיה כבא בעיר מצור תעוז תעוז בחומה נ\[ס\]{ש}גבה עד פלט). The imagery and language in 1QH XIII, 22-XV, 8 repeats these three key lexemes from 1QH XI, 6–19, but in a greatly expanded presentation that is more personalized, reflecting the emotional reenactment of the text. In each instance, the reader of 1QH XI, 6–19 has actualized the text by imagining himself as participating in the events that the anthropologizing statements describe.

In a similar way to these stock metaphors for terror, the theme of entrapment and imprisonment that is suggested by the frequent use of the expressions involving the word for "binding" (חבל) in 1QH XI, 9, 10 (2xs), 12, 13, 29 and also the reference to the "iron bars" (בריחי ברזל) at line 40 and "eternal bars" (בריחי עולם) at line 19. This language of imprisonment reappears in an experiential and personalized way in 1QH XIII, 22-XV, 8. In column XI the imagery of "binding" appears in idiomatic constructions that describe generally the experience of being seized by death or Sheol and of gripped by labor-pains. Imprisonment imagery is also conveyed by the two different constructions of "bars of" (בריחי -) in column XI. In 1QH XIII, 22-XV, 8, the idioms for "binding" and the language of "bars" become vividly imagined as an actual place of imprisonment. The speaker of that composition places himself within the image and visualizes the experience of being constrained by ropes and fetters in an actual jail cell, resulting in a report of an egocentric episodic experience of imprisonment:

> For I am bound by ropes (39) that cannot be loosened and by fetters that cannot be broken. A strong wall [surrounds me] and iron bars (ובריחי ברזל) and doors of [bronze that have no] (40)[opening.] My jail cell is with the abyss; {I am} considered without [] [] (41) [and the torrents of]Belial engulf my soul without escape (\[ותחלי \] בליעל אפפו נפשי לאין פ\[לט\]) (XIII, 38–41).

Here the actualization of the experience of being imprisoned reuses the construction of "iron bars" (בריחי ברזל) from 1QH XI, 40. Bars appear later in 1QH XIV, 31 as "strong bars that will not shatter" (בריחי עוז ללוא ישוברו). In the hodayot scroll, the lexeme "bars" appears only in column XI and in the composition that I propose is exegetically generated from meditating upon it.[139] The very end of this passage reiterates the phrase that appears in 1QH XI, 29, "and the cords of death engulf with no (hope for) escape" (וחבלי מות אפפו לאין פלט), although with a noticeable difference; in the version

---

139 Appearing in XI, 19 and 40; and twice in 1QH XIII, 22-XV, 8 at XIII, 39 and XIV, 31.

that appears in 1QH XIII, 41 has become personalized. Again, the verb אפף "to engulf" is not attested in the hodayot scroll apart from these two citations. This actualization of imprisonment, I propose, is another example of how a meditative reading of 1QH XI has generated a religious experience wherein the reader has become transformed into a participant in the event, in much the same way the three anthropologized statements from 1QH XI, 7–8 become personalized in 1QH XIII, 22-XV, 8. The egocentric episodic experiences that are produced demonstrate that a reader has become transformed into a full participant in the scene through the anthropologizing "I."

In what may be another instance of actualization, the imagery of imprisonment and the figure of the serpent (אפעה) found in column XI can be said to be exegetically glossed in 1QH XIII, 22-XV, 8. In column XI, 18–19, the ambiguous word appears with imagery associated with imprisonment:

> The gates of [eternity] will open up [under] the deeds of the serpent (אפעה); and they shall shut the doors of the Pit behind the one pregnant with iniquity and eternal bars (בריחי עולם) will be behind all the spirits of the serpent (אפעה).

In column XI, the puzzling and ambiguous word, rendered here as 'serpent' (אפעה), can also carry the meaning of 'vapor,' but the context of column XI does not immediately reveal which meaning is most appropriate. The text of 1QH XIII, 22-XV, 8 can be understood as an attempt to clarify this ambiguous word by explicating it as "the poison of *serpents*" (חמת תנינים) and "the p[oisons] of *vipers*" (מ[ב]לגות] פתנים) in XIII, 29. Here we can imagine that the author chose to use the images of 'serpent' and 'vipers' to exegetically clarify the enigmatic word אפעה found in 1QH XI, 13, 18, 19, by focusing on the meaning that is more easily visualized by the mind's eye.

Studies of emotion and their associative role in memory construction and reconstruction show that negative emotions of fear, anger, and desolation can generate a compelling reinvigoration of memory that can be experienced by the brain and expressed by the body as if it was an actual event.[140] The fear that results from the performative reading of column XI can become associated with other negative emotions like desolation, which comes to expression in the actualized text

---

140 Even if those memories are of inaccurate events, see Stark, Okado, Loftus, "Imaging the Reconstruction of True and False Memories," 485–88.

known as 1QH XIII, 22-XV, 8. This is especially apparent in passages like 1QH XIII, 22- XV, 8 that systematically detail the agony that racks the speaker's body. Following the meditation on physical pain, the speaker gives an extended lament of desolation that catalogues specific body parts, a passage in column XIII that culminates with the flowing of tears:

> **With ruin and desolation, burning pains sei[ze me] and pangs like the con-
> tractions of (33) one giving birth (**עם שאה ומשאה זלעופות אחוזי וחבלים כצירי יולדה**).** My
> heart clamors in me; I am clothed in a mourning garment, and my tongue clings
> to the roof of {my} mouth, for they have surrounded me with the destructive
> thoughts of their heart, and their desire (34) has appeared to me as bitterness.
> The light of my countenance dimmed into darkness, and my splendor switched
> into gloom. *vacat*

> But You, O my God, (35) have opened a wide space in my heart! Yet they
> continue to grieve (me), and they enclose me all around with deep dark-
> ness, so that I eat the bread of my misery, (36) and my drink is endless
> weeping. For my eyes are weakened by anger, and my soul by daily bitter-
> ness. Misery and sorrow (37) surround me, and shame is upon (my) face.
> My bread has been turned into strife, and my drink into a master of dis-
> putes. It enters my bones, (38) making (my) spirit stumble and finishing
> off (my) strength. In accordance with the mysteries of transgression, they
> misconstrue the works of God in their guilt.

This is a report of a credibility enhancing display. Embodiment language appears in an especially distressing catalogue of body parts in column XV:

> (4) [   ] As for me, I am speechless from their destr[uctiveness   ] these
> things they have reviled me. (5) [my ar]m is shattered from the
> elbow-joint, and my foot sinks into the mire! My eyes are blinded from
> seeing (6) evil; my ears from hearing of bloodshed, and my heart is dis-
> mayed because of evil plotting. For Belial is with (them); the form of
> their destruction is revealed. (7) All the foundations of my frame shake,
> and my bones are rattled (וירעו כול אושי מבניתי ועצמי יתפרדו).[141] **My bowels
> heave like a ship in a raging (8) storm.** My heart pounds noisily to
> the destruction, and a whirling wind overwhelms me from the destructive-
> ness of their rebellion. *vacat*

The great detail given to the imaginal body fully constructs a persona for a subsequent reader to embody. The body's parts and its experiential as-pects are described with precise details. In one passage, the imaginal body is the site for the divine encounter; the speaker likens himself

---

141 The same peculiar root to "shake" (רעע-II) cf. 1QH XI, 13 (וירעו אוש קיר כאתיה על פני מים)
and 1QH XI, 34 (וכול מחשביה ירעו).

to a stone edifice that does not wobble back and forth and who cannot be invaded by enemies because he leans upon God's truth.[142] Significant episodic spatial experiences of being "lifted up" (XIII, 24) and being "brought into the council of [the holy]" (XIV, 8) add an experiential depth to the composition, making it more vivid.[143] God also acts purposefully upon the imaginal body of the speaker when He "opens a wide space in my heart" (XIV, 35) and "opens my ears" (XIV, 7). When the ancient reader reenacted the strong emotion of fear that was aroused by the anthropologizing images in 1QH XI, memory's naturally associative processes could have spontaneously reconstituted other affective memories that shared a similar valence and so intensified the body's expression of distress. In contrast to the impersonal and mythical events of the Secondspatial scenes recounted in column XI, the composition known as 1QH XIII, 22-XV, 8 reflects an intensification of affect whereby fear serves to reinvigorate memories of despair and distress in a report of personal betrayal. In the newly generated text (1QH XIII, 22-XV, 8), the speaker reports his personal anguish at the hands of close friends who inflict insults, slander, and taunts:

> But as for me, I was against [   ], for a dispute (25) and contentions to my friends, jealousy and anger belong to those who enter into my covenant, a grumble and a complaint to all of my comrades. Ev[en those who ea]t my bread (26) have lifted up their heel against me, and all those who have committed themselves to my counsel speak perversely against me with unjust lips. The men of my [coun]cil rebel (27) and grumble round about the mystery which You hid in me, they slander (it) to the children of destruction, because [You] have magni[fied Yourself] in me (1QH XIII, 24–27).

The emotion of desolation reinvigorates this memory of betrayal by close friends which is reported with vivid embodiment language: friends, who had formerly "eaten bread" with the speaker, now "lift their heel" in betrayal and slander him with "unjust lips." While

---

142 1QH XIV, 28–31.

143 A possible reference to spatial locomotion that results in communion with angels may be in yet another passage, but a lacuna prevents us from confirming it: God is said to have "brought [???] and Your secret (16) to all the men of Your council, and in the lot together with the angels of presence, without a mediator between [Your] h[oly ones to] reply (17) according to the spirit…" (XIV, 15–17). The location of this reference to spatial ascent in 1QH XIII, 22-XV, 8 can also be said to imitate the basic structure in 1QH XI which situates movement upward (1QH XI, 20–24) at the heart of the composition or midway in the text.

some may wish to see actual experiences of a historical person in this passage (it may indeed reflect a memory of revolt against a person of some standing) the searing memory of being betrayed by friends is one that unfortunately is common.[144] Whether or not the memory of betrayal speaks to an actual historical event, the sensations of desolation and despair are physically experienced and intensified in the author of this text.[145] It is also possible to understand this episode of betrayal as an elaboration of a typical literary trope discussed in chapter three of the Tale of the Vindicated Courtier in which rivals are frequently depicted as attacking a protagonist who is later vindicated. Whether the episode of betrayal reflects an actual personal memory or one that was known from other literary sources, the mental process of associating experiences of desolation and anger during a highly aroused state of fear is one that can be said to take place in the body of the one who reenacts the text. What is important to observe here is how the language of the body helps to amplify and intensify the emotion of distress and despair. Through the reenactment of the affective script of fear found in column XI, an ancient reader could have been transformed into the author of a new set of experiences recorded in 1QH XIII, 22-XV, 8.

Conclusion

Contemporary studies on the role of emotions and the body as well as the techniques to train and discipline the emotions can help to illuminate the role that emotion and embodiment language plays in the hodayot. References to the body and the arousal of emotions are prominent features of the hodayot that could have assisted the reader of 1QH XI in becoming deeply united with the anthropologizing "I" of these texts. The arousal of strong emotions, fear and terror, are especially prominent in 1QH XI and assist an ancient reader in generating the subjectivity of the imaginal body of the text, allowing for the transformation of the reader into an author

---

144 Passages like this one from column XIII, are taken by some scholars who study the organization of the community to be evidence that there may have been some back-sliding among members of this splinter group to return to the older parent group (XIII, 25–27), or even that this is evidence of an actual historical leader's memory of betrayal.

145 See the discussion of the highly compelling nature of false memories in Stark, Okado, and Loftus, "Imaging the Reconstruction of True and False Memories," 485–88.

and full participant in a newly generated experience, 1QH XIII, 22-XV, 8. The ancient reader may have associated affective memories of terror from his own experience or from other sources, during his reenactment of the hodayot, thereby actualizing the text. As the ancient reader sought to become one with the rhetorical "I" of the text in column XI, he reenacted the scripted emotions aroused by the Secondspace scenes of terror, and in so doing experienced the Thirdspatial events reported in 1QH XIII, 22-XV, 5, becoming a participant in the process.

The process of generating new texts from the performative reading and rereading of existing ones that has been described in this chapter may shed light on how collections grew over time. Some collections of visions appear to the modern eye to duplicate or "pile on" compositions in inelegant ways. For the texts discussed in this chapter, both column XI and the text that I have proposed was generated as a result of performative reading, 1QH XIII, 22- XV, 8, the reader's physical display of emotion can be understood to validate the new text that was produced (XIII, 32–38; XV, 7–8).

That these two hodayot were composed by different authors is demonstrated by orthography: the author of 1QH XI preferred to use the expanded orthography for both כיא (8 out of 10 times) and כול (16 out of 17 times), while the author of 1QH XIII, 22- XV, 8 consistently preferred the *defective* form of כי (12 out of 12 instances) but the *expanded* orthography for כול (18 out of 18 times). This orthographic variation, evidence of the composite nature of the Teacher Hymns collection, is understood as a sign that the hodayah 1QH XIII, 22- XV, 8 was composed by a single author who was different from the author of the hodayah in 1QH XI. Even though both column XI and 1QH XIII, 22-XV, 8 are attested in the oldest copy of the hodayot, they were authored by different individuals. My proposal offers an explanation for why orthographic variation in the TH collection arose, an issue that previous hodayot scholarship has not addressed.

This chapter has proposed that the composition 1QH XIII, 22-XV, 8 was generated during a religious experience that was engendered by the performative reading of and meditation upon the scenes in column XI. The new composition was recorded and then added to the hodayot collection alongside other visionary reports. I propose that the guarantee of the authenticity of this experience was the visible expression of physical affect in the ancient reader himself. Signs of the appropriate bodily responses for the emotions of fear and terror (e. g., physical trembling, the weeping of real tears, uncontrollable perspiration, rapid heart rate) may have served as irrefutable evidence for the ancient community that a mystical experience had taken place in the reader. The presumption is that the body's responses to these emotions cannot be false and the ancient reader must have had an extraordinary Thirdspace experience.

Chapter 5
Paradise as a Place on the Threshold of the Heavens

The description of the primordial garden known as Eden can be considered a Secondspatial report that appeals to the body's faculties of sense perception, all of which facilitate the reenactment of the text. The text simulates a multi-sensory experience of being in a well-watered garden. A reader can easily imagine the gushing waters that irrigate this land from the sensuous description of the garden setting found in Gen 2:5–6, 10–14. The tender herbs and the many fruit bearing trees create a fragrant and visually delightful image in the mind (Gen 2:9), with the exquisite beauty of the fateful fruit referenced in Gen 3:6. Gustatory details are also provided in the narrative about the first man and the first woman, both what they were instructed to eat and to avoid (Gen 2:9, 17). Tactile impressions are left by the details of the moist earth (Gen 2:5–6), the working of the wet clay in the fashioning of the first human (2:7), and the moist breath that was breathed into his nostrils (2:7). In addition to these sensuous elements, the biblical story of the garden as told through the imaginal characters of Adam and Eve arouses strong emotions of joy, regret, and remorse.

The well-watered garden in Genesis 2–3 can be thought of as a Secondspatial realm that is constructed by recognizable landmarks from the known world that have been situated within a religiously constructed geography, resulting in a space that is impossible to reconcile with any known place in this world. Familiar details about the place and spatial features of Eden lend a quality of realism to the report and authenticate the vision of the mythical garden. The biblical account of Eden is offered by Thomas Dozeman as a classic example of how Secondspace constructs use recognizable details from Firstspace.[1] In his discussion of the mapping of Eden, he contrasts the map of this place produced according to ordinary geography (Firstpace) with that produced by religious geography (Secondspace). The Tigris and Euphrates rivers, known coordinates in the ancient near east, can be readily identified

---

1   Dozeman, "Biblical Geography and Critical Spatial Studies," 98–100.

in ordinary geography, but the other rivers cannot. Distinct challenges arise when Secondspace geographies are mapped onto a Firstspace map:

> The result of watering the ground in Gen 2 is a perfectly irrigated garden, Eden, located in the east. The river which irrigates the Garden of Eden branches into four parts: the Pishon flows to the land of Havilah, a land of pure gold and precious stones; the Gihon flows around the land of Cush; the Tigris flows east of Assyria; and the fourth, the Euphrates, receives no further description. The four rivers progress from fantastic locations (the Pishon) to a river so well known to the author that it requires no description (the Euphrates). The mixing of geographical references from the fantastic to the mundane creates a problem for interpreters, which is reflected in the representations of the Four Rivers of Paradise in Gen 2:10–14.[2]

The Secondspatial coordinates of the garden, given by the four rivers, are impossible to schematize onto a map of Mesopotamia as it is known today.

While the specific tradition of a garden named Eden is largely absent from the Hebrew Bible, depictions of a garden paradise are recounted in numerous early Jewish and Christian texts.[3] The general contours of a lush well-irrigated garden described in a multitude of early Jewish traditions create an effect that these reports are describing the same place and that they are based on a single original model yet this effect is illusory. The mythological gardens encountered in various traditions are otherworldly constructed realms that do not consistently map onto a single coordinate system—their sights are also not consistently reported.[4] The variations encountered among these numerous textual traditions suggest that the sensuous experience of being in a garden paradise was an event that ancient communities sought to re-create again and

---

2   Dozeman, "Biblical Geography and Critical Spatial Studies," 98.

3   Eibert T. C. Tigchelaar discusses the literary inconsistencies among various reports of garden paradises, including the Genesis account of Eden; see Tigchelaar, "Eden and Paradise: The Garden Motif in Some Early Jewish Texts (1 Enoch and Other Texts Found at Qumran)," in *Paradise Interpreted: Representations of Biblical Paradise in Judaism and Christianity* (ed. Gerard P. Luttikhuizen; TBN 2; Leiden: Brill, 1999), 37–62 and Veronika Bachmann, "Rooted in Paradise? The Meaning of the 'Tree of Life' in 1 Enoch 24–25 Reconsidered," *JSP* 19 (2009): 83–107. Both scholars discuss the literary inconsistencies among the garden paradise traditions. This kind of inconsistency might be expected from Secondspatial accounts.

4   The rabbis however infrequently discuss the garden; See Sandra R. Shimoff, "Gardens: From Eden to Jerusalem," *JSJ* 26 (1995): 145–55.

again. As Secondspatial experiences, gardens offer compelling affective scripts of sensual delights to reenact.

I. The Garden as Heterotopia

Elaborately described locales like the Garden of Eden (Gen 2:4–3:24) are Secondspace sites that are so vividly imagined as to seem real. According to Manfried Dietrich, the ancient Persian gardens would have been exclusive spaces, reserved for the enjoyment of the king or the deities and their priests.[5] Such lush enclosed spaces would have typically stood out from the harsh barren background of their surroundings.[6] The exclusivity of the garden space also held true for the temple and palace gardens of ancient Mesopotamia.[7]

In his essay "On Other Places," Michel Foucault identifies the garden as a classic example of the third principle of heterotopia—a space capable of simultaneity.

> [P]erhaps the oldest example of these heterotopias that take the form of contradictory sites is the garden. We must not forget that in the Orient the garden, an astonishing creation that is now a thousand years old, had very deep and seemingly superimposed meanings. The traditional garden of the Persians was a sacred space that was supposed to bring together inside its rectangle four parts representing the four parts of the world, with a space still more sacred than the others that were like an umbilicus, the navel of the world at its center (the basin and water fountain were there); and all the vegetation of the garden was supposed to come together in this space, in this sort of microcosm. As for carpets, they were originally reproductions of gardens (the garden is a rug onto which the whole world comes to enact its symbolic perfection, and the rug is a sort of garden that can move across space). The garden is the smallest parcel of the world and then it is the totality of the world.[8]

---

5   Manfried Dietrich, "Das biblische Paradies und der babylonische Tempelgarten: Überlegungen zur Lange des Gartens Eden," in *Das biblische Weltbild und seine altorientalischen Kontexte* (ed. Bernd Janowski and Beate Ego; FAT 32; Tübingen: Mohr Siebeck, 2001), 281–323, here 286.

6   Dietrich, "Das biblische Paradies und der babylonische Tempelgarten," 286.

7   Dietrich, "Das biblische Paradies und der babylonische Tempelgarten," 287; Dietrich writes that palace gardens were enclosed by the palace walls and cites the examples of the old Babylonian palace garden at Mari (18th and 17th c. BCE) and the palace garden at Ugarit (13–11 c. BCE), here 287–288. In the case of the latter, the ruler had a private entrance into the garden space.

8   Foucault, "Of Other Spaces," 25–26.

Foucault describes the garden's unique trait of simultaneity. The ancient idea of the garden is a "contradictory site" because it is a space that can contain an impossible mix of flora that would not naturally be found in the same habitat.

The breadth and variety of vegetation found in the ancient palace garden was a reflection of the social and political role that these spaces had as demonstrations of a ruler's reach and domination. Francesca Stavrakopoulou offers an elegant account of this function of garden spaces:

> Given their religious importance, gardens also played a notable ideological role in the socio-political promotion and propaganda of royalty. A number of Neo-Assyrian kings are credited with the creation of monumental gardens within or beside their palaces, which were both visually impressive and horticulturally prestigious in their collection of trees and plants gathered from the furthest reaches of the empire, demonstrating the royal mastery of other peoples, their gods, and the produce of their lands. Like their divine counterparts, these royal cultivators—or "creators"—also enjoyed strolling in their gardens. . . . In planting and cultivating gardens, these kings may have been imitating their divine counterparts, creating their own "heavens" on earth.[9]

The socio-political significance of the garden reflects the ancient conceptualization of this space as a microcosm of the created world in which the ruler stands in the place of the creator. Manfried Dietrich describes the Mesopotamian ruler as an extension of the deity. In this schema, the royal garden was designed as an expression of the divinely created world which he in turn was charged to safe-keep and to cultivate.[10] And so as "symbols of cultivated fertility, gardens were imbued with a notable religious significance, as is evident in Mesopotamian texts describing the lush gardens of the gods, which are watered by cosmic riv-

---

9 Francesca Stavrakopoulou, "Exploring the Garden of Uzza: Death, Burial and Ideologies of Kingship," *Biblica* 87 (2006): 1–21, here 6. See also M. Dietrich, "Das biblische Paradies und der babylonische Tempelgarten," 281–323; Donald J. Wiseman, "Mesopotamian Gardens," *Anatolian Studies* 33 (1983): 137–44; A. L. Oppenheim, "On Royal Gardens in Mesopotamia," *JNES* 24 (1965): 328–333.

10 M. Dietrich, "Der „Garten Eden" und die babylonischen Parkanlagen im Tempelbezirk," in *Religiöse Landschaften* (ed. Johannes Hahn and Ronning Christian; AOAT 301; Münster: Ugarit Verlag, 2002), 1–29, here 9. Dietrich refers to this as a kind of „Urbild-Abbild-Denken." Dietrich ("Das biblische Paradies und der babylonische Tempelgarten," 288) notes that the kings also enjoyed cultivating the space as guardians of the garden. See too W. Fauth, "Der Königlicher Gärtner und Jäger im Paradeisos. Beobachtungen zur Rolle des Herrschers in der vorderasiatischen Hortikultur," *Persica* 8 (1979): 1–53.

ers and stocked with fruits, spices and medicines, and references to temple gardens, in which their divine owners were believed to enjoy walking, and in which certain rituals were performed."[11] As a heterotopia, the garden was envisioned as a space where both simultaneity and liminality were possible.

As cultivated spaces, the variety of exotic specimens found in the garden was a political expression of the prestige and power of the ruler who enjoyed the status of creator in his earthly empire. The garden as a heterotopic space of contradictions sought to replicate the entirety of the created world by bringing together the exotic varieties of plant life found throughout the empire, creating a habitat that could never exist in nature. As liminal spaces designed to be adjacent to the home of the ruler within the walls of the Palace precincts, gardens mark the boundary between the ordinary realm and the ruler's private domain, and so too the transition between this world and the other world. Furthermore, they routinely served as ritual sites for royal decrees of judgment and various ceremonial activities.

Mesopotamian traditions about gardens presume that these spaces enjoy simultaneity and liminality, and these conventional understandings of gardens can be said to influence how early Jewish traditions conceptualized such spaces as well. Such verdant paradaisical settings were natural places to imagine encounters with the divine, and they were frequent stops on visionary journeys.[12] Garden traditions are prominent in the early Enochic Book of the Watchers and also play a role in the Book of Giants, although the latter is very fragmentary.[13] The garden figures

---

11 Stavrakopoulou, "Exploring the Garden of Uzza." 5.

12 E.g., the imagery of the well-watered paradise informs the mystical experiences of the Zohar, see Melila Hellner-Eshed, *A River Flows from Eden: The Language of Mystical Experience in the Zohar* (trans. by Nathan Wolski; Stanford: Stanford University Press, 2009).

13 Visions of otherworldly gardens play a role in the scenes detailed in the Book of Giants, an Enochic tradition attested in various Cave 4 texts; see Loren T. Stuckenbruck, *The Book of Giants from Qumran: Texts, Translation, and Commentary* (TSAJ 63; Tübingen: Mohr Siebeck 1997); and John C. Reeves, *Jewish Lore in Manichaean Cosmogony: Studies in the Book of Giants Traditions* (MHUC 14; Cincinnati: Hebrew Union College Press, 1992). Because the hodayah in 1QH XVI, 5–27 refers to the speaker as a gardener, one interesting tradition may be found in "Hahyah's dream" in 4Q530 II 7–12 (Stuckenbruck, *The Book of Giants*, 112–115; cf. Reeves, *Jewish Lore*, 85–90); "Mahaway's Journey to Enoch" in 4Q530 III 4–11 makes reference to gardeners who descend from heaven (Stuckenbruck, 128–34; Reeves, 102–107).

as a special otherworldly site and illustrates the aspects of simultaneity and liminality which characterize heterotopic spaces.

According to the Book of the Watchers, Enoch journeys first to the places of punishment and then on to paradaisical sites, moving from the west to the east (see *1 En.* 24:2–25). Enoch visits two different gardens, only one of which is identified as Eden. The first is an otherworldly garden at the Mountain of God, a throne-like mountain located in the center of seven mountains. Here Enoch inquires about a certain fragrant and beautiful tree. Michael, Enoch's angelic guide, discloses special details about this tree whose fruit will give life to and alleviate the sufferings of those who eat of it. This amazing cultivar has a special eschatological role on the day of the great judgment. At that time, it will be transplanted to the holy place–the house of God:

> And (as for) this fragrant tree, no flesh has the right to touch it until the great judgment, in which there will be vengeance on all and a consummation forever. Then it will be given to the righteous and the pious, and its fruit will be food for the chosen. And it will be transplanted to the holy place, by the house of God, the King of eternity. Then they will rejoice greatly and be glad, and they will enter into the sanctuary. Its fragrances <will be> in their bones, and they will live a long life on the earth, such as your fathers lived also in their days, and torments and plagues and suffering will not touch them (*1 En.* 25:4–6).

In this early Enochic tradition, the fruit of this special tree will be given to a select number at the end of days. At that time, these people will be made to dwell in the heavenly sanctuary and the era will be marked by the cessation of physical suffering. Later in the Book of the Watchers, a similar visit to an otherworldly garden takes place where Enoch is shown a certain exotic cultivar,[14] in a place further east called Jerusalem,

---

14 According to Nickelsburg, this tree will be transplanted at the end of days to this locale. Nickelsburg reasons that this tree in the Book of the Watchers is the same as the "tree of life" in Gen 2–3 because both are forbidden to humans and both offer the promise of life. Yet, it is important to note here that the two accounts do not agree on whether what is promised is a long life or an eternal one, and some have questioned whether these are in fact the same tree; see Nickelsburg, *1 Enoch 1*, 314. Cf. Veronika Bachmann disagrees and observes that this tree is not clearly named the "tree of life;" see Bachmann, "Rooted in Paradise?" also Tigchelaar, "Eden and Paradise," 37–62. Bachmann ("Rooted in Paradise?" 89) critiques this identification by Nickelsburg, whose view is influenced by the overemphasis on the eschatological aspect of the fruit to give eternal life, a misreading of the text that was first introduced by August Dill-

the center of the earth. Here in this vision, liminality is expressed by the spatial reference that positions this garden space alongside a wretched place of punishment in a valley (*1 En.* 26:1–27:5). Enoch inquires about this desolate space, and his angelic guide Sariel[15] explains that on the day of judgment the impious will be gathered and punished in the valley adjacent to the mountain. The fragrant tree and the well-irrigated garden signify the liminality of this space and are associated here with a mountainous place and God's judgment.

Enoch then journeys further east where he sees a lush garden oasis in the midst of the desert stocked with an abundance of trees and vegetation (*1 En.* 28:1–32:6). The editors of *1 Enoch* call this well-watered garden, the "Paradise of Righteousness."[16] The seer reports visiting a special site stocked with an amazing variety of fragrant trees and shrubs which do not naturally grow in the same habitat (*1 En.* 28–32). Many of these cultivars are associated with the making of incense and other ritual oils. The space of paradise is described as a well-irrigated, dew-drenched place with gushing waterways and an abundance of fragrant, fruit-bearing trees that are beautiful and pleasing in appearance. Many textual difficulties arise here in this section of *1 Enoch* due to the enumeration of specific varieties of vegetation by name. The amazing variety of vegetation evokes the aspect of gardens as a space of simultaneity. Here Enoch also encounters a certain tree that is associated with knowledge (*1 En.* 32:5–6).[17] While the different gardens in Enoch's journey reports are distinct, one being in a mountainous setting and another one further east, both are said to be holy spaces, and as can be expected,

---

mann, *Das Buch Henoch übersetzt und erklärt* (Leipzig: Wilhelm Vogel, 1853), 130.

15   Nickelsburg (*1 Enoch 1*, 319) explains that some manuscript traditions identify the angel as Uriel. He favors reading this angel as Sariel because Uriel has been mentioned already in ch. 21. Also, the function of Sariel fits well the context of this passage. Nickelsburg notes that these two angels are frequently confused in *1 En.*

16   Mention of a garden of righteousness appears briefly in *1 En.* 77:3// 4Q209 23 3–10 and 4Q210 1 ii [14]-20.

17   The translation here of the Ethiopic text yields "tree of wisdom" but the Aramaic text can also be translated as "knowledge." Thus the identification of the site as Eden can be questioned, as Tigchelaar does ("Some Remarks on the Book of the Watchers, the Priests, Enoch and Genesis, and 4Q208," in Gabriele Boccaccini, "The Origins of Enochic Judaism," *Henoch* 24 [2002], 143–45), and so *1 En.* 32 may not be referring to the tree from the Eden story in Gen 2–3. See the discussion by Bachmann, "Rooted in Paradise?" 90 n. 6.

God's garden contains some amazing cultivars, including a certain cosmic tree(s) thought to be the one associated with life, although they are not named as such.

This brief survey of the garden spaces visited during the amazing visionary journeys of Enoch in the Book of the Watchers reflects the aspects of simultaneity and liminality presumed by this early Jewish visionary tradition. As liminal spaces near the abode of the deity they contain representative specimens of the choicest variety. As is true for the ancient Mesopotamian royal garden, places of paradise in Enoch's visions are cultivated spaces associated with holy beings. In *1 En.* 24–25, the garden of fragrant trees encircles and marks a boundary around the holy place, the special seventh mountain known as the throne of God (*1 En.* 24:3–4). In this vision, reaching the garden can be understood as reaching the holy precincts and being at the threshold of the divine abode.

Another early Jewish tradition about the garden as a heterotopia is preserved in the *Book of Jubilees* which highlights the role of the garden as a cultic site and a space of liminality. According to *Jubilees*, Enoch is placed in an otherworldly paradise as a gardener. *Jubilees* interrupts the genealogy of the ancestors with a lengthy discussion of the figure of Enoch who is introduced by an allusion to the myth of the Watchers, the angels who descended to earth (*Jub.* 4:15). In this fleeting reference to the myth, the Watchers descend for honorable and not impure reasons. According to the author of *Jubilees*, Enoch is the first human to have learned and mastered the arts of writing, instruction and wisdom. He is also associated with astronomical knowledge (*Jub.* 4:17). The author of *Jubilees* introduces details here that illustrate the idea of the garden as a liminal space. Enoch was placed in the mountainous paradise known as Eden as a kind of reward to live out eternity and to conduct cultic functions:

> He was taken from human society, and we led him into the Garden of Eden for (his) greatness and honor. Now he is there writing down the judgment and condemnation of the world and all the wickedness of mankind. Because of him the flood water did not come on any of the land of Eden because he was placed there as a sign and to testify against all people in order to tell all the deeds of history until the day of judgment. He burned the evening incense of the sanctuary which is acceptable before the Lord on the mountain of incense. For there are four places on earth that belong to the Lord: The Garden of Eden, the mountain of the east, this mountain on which you are today—Mt. Sinai—and Mt. Zion (which) will be sanctified in the new creation for the sanctification of

the earth. For this reason the earth will be sanctified from all its sins and from its uncleanness into the history of eternity (*Jub.* 4:23–26).

This passage from *Jubilees* reports that Enoch was entrusted to burn the evening incense of the sanctuary.[18] The Syriac manuscript tradition for *Jub.* 4:25–26 further notes that Enoch is also the first to offer sacrifice.[19] Enoch's cultic functions, along with the Book of the Watchers tradition that this otherworldly garden was located in Jerusalem, have led some to infer that Eden served as an imaginal Temple.[20] Yet, the garden here can be said to exemplify the aspect of liminality that it possesses by virtue of its close proximity to the heavenly temple. Mesopotamian palace gardens were frequently sites for ritual activity and this tradition in *Jubilees* likewise presumes that Eden serves as a cultic space. The expectations of cultic holiness that are said to be enforced therein, is consistent with the expectation of the gradations of holiness commonly presumed by the cultic theology of Israelite religion and early Judaism. The garden is a space where rigorous observance of holiness is presumed.[21] While it lay within the holy precincts, I do not believe that it is necessary to

---

18 VanderKam, *Enoch and the Growth of an Apocalyptic Tradition*, 185–88. According to Ephrem's *Hymn on Paradise* III, 16, Adam is given the task of burning the incense in the outer sanctuary of paradise; St. Ephrem the Syrian, *The Hymns on Paradise* (trans. Sebastian Brock; Crestwood: St. Vladimir's Sminary Press, 1998), 96.

19 See E. Tisserant, "Fragments syriaques du Livre des Jubilés," *RB* 30 (1921): 73–75; VanderKam, *Enoch and the Growth of an Apocalyptic Tradition*, 186. VanderKam takes the Syriac ms to be more original and it identifies the garden as "the mountain of Paradise."

20 See Martha Himmelfarb, "The Temple and the Garden of Eden in Ezekiel," 63–78. Cf. Ps. 36:8–10 where the "fountain of life" is compared with the temple and God himself; see Fishbane's discussion in "The Well of Living Water," 5.

21 See Jacob Milgrom describes the understanding of holiness as it relates to holy places like Mount Sinai and the tabernacle as a series of concentric circles; Milgrom, *Studies in Cultic Theology and Terminology* (Leiden: Brill, 1983) 44. Menachem Haran applies the framework of concentric circles to the Temple itself: "the plans of both Solomon's temple and the tabernacle demonstrate [the pattern of] concentric circles of declining order the further they move away from the focal point of the cherubim in the inner sanctum," in Haran, *Temples and Temple-Service in Ancient Israel: An Inquiry into the Character of Cult Phenomena and the Historical Setting of the Priestly School* (Oxford: Oxford University Press, 1978), 190.

equate the garden itself with either the Temple or the Palace;[22] instead, it marked the threshold into them.

The phenomenal sensations of being in a well-watered garden in second temple literary traditions are described with such specificity that a reader can easily imagine what it is like to be there and experience it for himself. Garden spaces in visionary literature reiterate known traditions but never perfectly replicate any of them. These detailed accounts of garden paradise are written in such a way as to create a vivid Secondspatial script for reenactment. A reader can hope to experience the sensations of moving in the garden through the scripted sensory experiences in the text. The vivid spatial details in these reports simulate sensory processes in the body that are so vivid that a reader can come to experience the textualized garden as a heterotopia, thus resulting in a fuller lived-experience of this space and further visions of what this space entails.

I propose that the performative reading and visualization of a richly detailed locale like the garden paradise is capable of generating further experiences of what this space is like. The garden, when it is experienced as a heterotopia, becomes a space that can be physically re-experienced through the body which reenacts the sensations of being in that place. As a heterotopia, the descriptions of the garden can transform a reader into an author capable of generating further experiences of that space. The imaginative engagement of otherworldly settings is evidenced by the many traditions that exist concerning its terrain, spatial coordinates, and inhabitants.

II. The Garden Paradise in the Hodayot

Because descriptions of paradise are so rich in sensory detail, they compel the imagination in a way that is different from the descriptions of punishment and imprisonment discussed in chapter three. When imprisoned in a jail cell or placed in the midst of hungry lions, the body's af-

---

22 For example, Gary Anderson comments that the first man and women were chaste while in the Garden of Eden presumably because Eden functioned for them as a prototype of the Temple in "Celibacy or Consummation in the Garden? Reflections on Early Jewish and Christian Interpretations of the Garden of Eden," *HTR* 82 (1989): 121–48; it may also be that these early traditions, understood Eden to be a part of the holy precinct and that a stringent observation of holiness was expected.

fective expressions of adrenaline and heart palpitations can result in a desperate desire to flee; however when one imagines oneself in a lush verdant place, the senses are also heightened, and the effect may be to linger. Such an interpretation of the rich sensuous details of gardens overlooks the fact that in second temple Jewish literature, these spaces are overwhelmingly associated with divine judgment and the arousal of fear. The themes of discord and judgment figure prominently in the Genesis story of Eden. So too in the Enochic visionary traditions, the gardens in the journey scenes are associated with eschatological judgment. Due to their close physical proximity to the divine, gardens arouse the fear that is associated with an audience with the deity. It is also the case that a garden space anticipates judgment.

As heterotopia, scenes of paradise can function as portals into place-less spaces when the physical sensations that they stimulate are vividly reenacted in a reader. Descriptions of otherworldly gardens can be boundless in their dimensions and often contain specific details that stretch the mind's imagination, and in this sense, they can be said to embody both simultaneity and liminality. For example, the eternal tree mentioned in 1QH XIV, 15–22 is said to be "limitless" in its breadth with branches that reach as high as the clouds, stretching endlessly across the entire world (1QH XIV, 19).[23] At the same time, the religious geography of paradise in 1QH XVI, 5–27 can be extraordinarily precise, taking care to enumerate the varieties of trees that grow there and to describe the various waterways that irrigate it. The bodily experiences of being in a well-watered garden are described with such specificity that a reader can easily imagine what it is like to be there and experience it himself. The textualized imaginal body through which the sensory delights of Eden are experienced offers a sumptuous script of affective experiences for subsequent readers to reenact.

In the hodayot collection, compositions that contain detailed descriptions of garden spaces are rare but strategically located. The first ap-

---

23   See the discussion of the ancient Mesopotamian tradition of the cosmic tree known as the Mēsu-Tree, a mythological tree that may be the source tradition behind the biblical account in Ezek 31 and also Dan 4; see Andrei A. Orlov, "Arboreal Metaphors and the Divine Body Traditions in the Apocalypse of Abraham," *HTR* 102 (2009): 439–51, esp. 446 n. 24; and Silviu Bunta, "The Mēsu-Tree and the Animal Inside: Theomorphism and Theriomorphism in Daniel 4," in *The Theophaneia School: Jewish Roots of Eastern Christian Mysticism* (ed. Basil Lourié, Andrei A. Orlov, Alexander Golitzin, Bogdan G. Bucur; St. Petersburg: Byzantinorossica, 2007), 364–84.

pearance is 1QH XIV, 15–22, in the composition known as 1QH XIII, 22-XV, 8 and discussed in the previous chapter as a report of a Third-space actualization of column XI. The second occurrence is in a signif-icantly extended report in 1QH XVI, 5-XVII, 36, a composition that will be discussed in this chapter. Even though all spatial descriptions in the hodayot can be understood to function synchronically as accounts of religious geography or Secondspace, some of them, (e. g., 1QH XIII, 22-XV, 8 and 1QH XVI, 5-XVII, 36) can be understood diachronically as having been generated by Thirdspatial experiences.

The place name of Eden is used for each of the garden scenes descri-bed at 1QH XIV, 19 and XVI, 21. These two hodayot share other fea-tures, although I do not propose that they are exegetically related in the same way that I argued in favor of the relationship between column XI and 1QH XIII, 22-XV, 8 in chapter four. Nevertheless, both composi-tions share remarkable commonalities. They are of comparable length and share specific vocabulary: "incurable pain" (כאב אנוש) appears in XIII, 30 and XVI, 29; the *hendiadys* "ruin and destruction" (שאה ומשואה) appears in XIII, 32 and XVII, 6; "shoulder" (קצה) only in XV, 5 and XVI, 34; "I know that there is a ritual bath"(ואדעה כיא יש מקוה) at XIV, 9 and XVII, 14 (also XI, 21, cf. XXII, 11) and other notable phrases.[24] Based on the shared vocabulary, Michael Douglas has made the intriguing proposal that both 1QH XIII, 22-XV, 8 and XVI, 5-XVII, 36 were com-posed by the same author.[25] Furthermore, the orthography in both of these hodayot exhibits similar preferences and tendencies.[26]

This chapter proposes that the descriptions of Eden in the hodayot are reports of Thirdspace experiences that were generated from the practice of performative reading and reenactment. The first place where the otherworldly garden appears is at 1QH XIII, 22-XV, 8, a composition that has already been discussed as a report of a Thirdspace experience in chapter four. The second report of paradise appears at 1QH XVI, 5-XVII, 36 which is the focus of this chapter. I wish to pro-pose that these garden compositions can be understood as reports of het-erotopic experiences in which a reader has become transformed into an

---

24 See the list of words identified by Julie Hughes, *Scriptural Allusions and Exegesis in the Hodayot*, 176–77; also Douglas, "Power and Praise," 160–62.

25 Douglas, "Power and Praise," 162, 206.

26 Similar to 1QH XIII, 22- XV, 8, in 1QH XVI, 5-XVII, 36 there is an overall preference for the short forms of "כיא (once)/ כי (19 times) and "לוא (once)/לא (18 times)" but the long form of "כול (14 times)/כל (twice)."

author of a new experience of paradise. Furthermore, I seek to demonstrate that these descriptions of paradise appear at places in the hodayot scroll that mark boundaries into the heavenly space.

A. The Location of Paradise as a Place Above

Philip Davies describes the vertical spatialization concerns found in the Qumran literature as an ideological understanding of space.[27] The sensory experience of vertical transportation to a place of paradise is one that is found in many journey sequences that report travel to paradise.[28] George Nickelsburg makes a special point of noting Enoch's extraordinary physical agility and mobility in the Book of the Watchers in which Enoch "flies up and is lifted upward" into heaven (*1 En.* 14:8).[29] The apocalyptic seer is said to have remarkable locomotion as he approaches several spectacular sites (*1 En.* 14:9–13). These references to Enoch's amazing locomotion in the heavenly realms relate well to the terse biblical account of Enoch which comments twice that: "Enoch *walked back and forth* with the angels" (ויתהלך חנוך את האלהים; Gen. 5:22, 24). In the hodayot, spatial movement into an otherworldly place is suggested by the speaker's declaration that he is brought upwards in 1QH XI, 20–22:

---

27 Philip Davies, "Space and Sects in the Qumran Scrolls," 90–96; he writes that the "fixation on the vertical is especially apparent to readers of the Hodayoth, though it might be argued that the author(s) of these hymns may not be representative of an entire community, and the language of praise may in any case be expected to reflect the vertical dimension of communication with the deity" (95).

28 According to certain traditions, Paradise is located somewhere above in the third heaven; see *2 En.* 20; the *Apocalypse of Moses* states Adam's body will be taken up to Paradise which is located in the third heaven (37:4); Paul also mentions "third heaven" as the location where a certain man was caught up and taken to paradise (2 Cor 12:2–4). See the discussion by Erik ten Napel, "'Third Heaven' and 'Paradise'. Some Remarks on the Exegesis of 2Cor. 12, 2–4 in Syriac," in *V Symposium Syriacum 1988* (ed. René Lavenant, S.J.; Orientalia Christiana Analecta 236; Rome Pontifical Institute for Oriental Studies, 1990): 53–65, here 54 n. 4. Napel discusses the traditions that locate paradise in the third heaven and relates this to the traditions attested in Syriac texts and also in *Jubilees* that paradise is situated on a mountain place with considerable height (58–59).

29 Nickelsburg, *1 Enoch 1*, 259.

And from Sheol Abaddon You have lifted me up to an eternal height, so that I might *walk back and forth* on an endless plain.

ומשאול אבדון העליתני לרום עולם ואתהלכה במישור לאין חקר

Here, the speaker of the hodayah "walks back and forth" thereby engaging in a similar bodily activity as Enoch who "walked back and forth with 'the angels'" (Gen 5:22, 24). This hodayah passage also brings together two ideas that are present in the Enochic visionary report but not in the Genesis text: (1) the physical experience of being lifted up and whisked away (like flying) and (2) the physical experience of moving *from* the terrifying netherworld places of imprisonment *to* the paradaisical sites. In the Book of the Watchers, Enoch flies up into the heavens (*1 En.* 14:8) and journeys back and forth with his angelic guide and the journey sequences in *1 En.* 20–36 specify that Enoch visits first the places associated with punishment and then the places of paradise.

These spatial experiences of phenomenal movement upwards mark instances when the hodayot speaker reports physical passage into another realm. The presumption is that paradise is somewhere spatially above the netherworld.[30] In the instance in 1QH XI, 20–24, the movement is vertical and the speaker is said to be "positioned in his station with the host of the holy ones; brought into union with the congregation of the children of the heavens," (להתיצב במעמד עם צבא קדושים ולבוא ביחד עם עדת בני שמים) in XI, 22–23; cf. XIX, 16–17. Esther Chazon has discussed the liturgical imagery of this setting in light of the comparison that Jacob Licht has made to *1 En.* 60:2.[31] These otherworldly spatial scenes make reference to the angelic heavenly host.

---

30 James C. VanderKam describes the widespread assumption in ancient texts that the heavens lie above the earth which in turn lies above the netherworld; VanderKam, "The Angel of the Presence in the Book of Jubilees," *DSD* 7 (2000): 378–93, here 378–79 he summarizes Devorah Dimant, "מנחה לשרה in "בני שמים—תורת המלאכים בספר היובלים לאור כתבי עדת קומראן" (ed. Moshe Idel, Devorah Dimant, and S. Rosenberg; Jerusalem: Magnes Press, 1994): 97–118.

31 See too the similarities to the cultic language in 1 Chr 23:28 and 2 Chr 35:15; Esther G. Chazon, "Liturgical Function in the Cave 1 Hodayot Collection," in *Qumran Cave 1 Revisited: Texts from Cave 1 Sixty Years after Their Discovery: Proceedings of the Sixth Meeting of the IOQS in Ljubljana* (ed. D. K. Falk et al; STDJ 91; Leiden: Brill, 2010), 135–49; Jacob Licht suggested that this expression referred to the circle of heavenly beings in *The Thanksgiving Scroll* (Hebr.; Jerusalem: Bialik Institute, 1957), 84, 163. See too the discussion by Björn Frennesson, *"In a Common Rejoicing,"* 48–50. Frennesson comments that these lines in the hodayah give "the idea of a present reality and not just something that is

In the composition that lies between 1QH XIII, 22-XV,8 and 1QH XVI, 5-XVII, 36—known as 1QH XV, 9-28— vertical movement is expressed with the imagery of illumination. Michael Douglas identifies a seven-fold structure to this composition.[32] In 1QH XV, 17, the speaker uses the language of "walking about" (להתהלך) from 1QH XI, 21 and XIV, 10 but here he writes that he "walks about" in the very presence of God (להתהלך לפניך). The hodayah concludes with the spatial imagery of the speaker moving upward. "You have exalted my ray over all who despise me (ותרם קרני על כול מנאצי). . . You have exalted my ray ever higher (ותרם קרני למעלה). I am radiant in sevenfold light, in b[] You have [esta]blished for Your glory" (והופעתי באור שבעתים ב[ה]כ[נותה לכבודכה) (XV, 25, 26–27). The speaker here describes himself in terms of luminosity which he attaches to a divinely apportioned vertical movement upward.[33]

B. A Glimpse of the Garden Paradise in 1QH XIII, 22-XV,8

Chapter four proposed that column XI can be understood as reporting a series of Secondspace experiences that become actualized as Thirdspace events in 1QH XIII, 22-XV, 8. It is there in that composition, that the first explicit reference to the Garden of Eden appears at 1QH XIV, 14–22. While the text itself is broken in places, the speaker states that God

---

'vécu dans la foi et l'espérance'" as Puech, *La Croyance des Esséniens en la Vie Future: Immortalité, Résurrection, Vie Eternelle? Histoire d'une Croyance dans le Judaïsme Ancien. Vol. II. Les Donnés qumraniennes et classiques* (Gabalda, Paris, 1993), 372.

32 Douglas, "Power and Praise in the Hodayot," 139.

33 Elliot R. Wolfson, "Seven Mysteries of Knowledge: Qumran E/Sotericism Recovered," in *The Idea of Biblical Interpretation: Essays in Honor of James L. Kugel* (ed. Hindy Najman and Judith H. Newman; SJSJ 83; Leiden: Brill, 2004), 177–213. He writes: "in virtue of that vision, the priest is glorified, that is, he is transfigured into an angelic body and becomes part of the celestial retinue while remaining a leader of the *yahad* below" (200). See W. F. Smelik, "On Mystical Transformation of the Righteous into Light in Judaism," 122–44. That angels are frequently associated with a luminous and fiery appearance, like the starts is a commonly attested tradition; see the discussion by Kevin P. Sullivan, *Wrestling with Angels: A Study of the Relationship between Angels and Humans in Ancient Jewish Literature and the New Testament* (AGJU 60; Leiden: Brill, 2003), 30–32.

has brought His [glo]ry[34] and the men of God's council into the lot together with the high-ranking angels of presence. When read in series, a
reader moves from being in the presence of "holy ones" and the "children of the heavens" cited in 1QH XI, 22–23 to the "angels of the
presence" in 1QH XIV, 16. This progressive spatial movement increases
in proximity to the highest levels of angelic beings. The specific class of
angels of the presence is one of exceptionally high standing and functions in a comparable way to the presence of God Himself.[35] According
to the *Book of Jubilees*, the angels of the presence perform specific functions, including liturgical ones. In fact, they were created on the first day
already circumcised so that they could minister to God immediately
(*Jub.* 15:27–28) and observe the first festival of Weeks.[36] According
to various traditions about the angels of the presence, they have the freedom to move between the heavenly and the earthly realm and are often
dispatched on missions,[37] and so a representative from this rank of angels
is Moses' worthy interlocutor at the beginning of the *Book of Jubilees*.
The phrase is also used to refer to the archangels in *1 En.* 40:2. It is notable that this reference to communion with these esteemed angels in
1QH XIV, 16 accompanies a significant spatial shift where the speaker
of the hodayot offers a small excursus on a garden that can be identified
with Eden. The hodayah describes a garden and its mythical vegetation
in exacting detail.[38] The speaker reports in 1QH XIV, 15–22:

> For You have brought [] and Your secret (16) to all the men of Your counsel,
> and in the lot together with the angels of presence (וּבְגוֹרָל יַחַד עִם מַלְאֲכֵי פָּים), with-

34 The reconstruction of "glory" is very likely here but there is also room for an-
    other word or phrase.
35 VanderKam discusses Isa 63:9 as a possible biblical antecedent for the expression
    "angel of the presence" (see VanderKam, "The Angel of the Presence," 382–
    83); it may also be that Ezek 1:6 is another source for the development of this
    class of angels; see K. Berger, *Das Buch der Jubiläen* (Gütersloh: Gütersloher Ver-
    lagshaus Gerd Mohn, 1981), 319 n. 27a.
36 Here VanderKam summarizes Dimant's proposal that the angels of the presence
    observe the cultic laws of "circumcision, Sabbath, and the Festival of Weeks"
    which "signify the covenant between Israel and God; VanderKam, "The
    Angel of the Presence," 379. In effect, the angels of the presence are ordered,
    among heavenly beings, as Israel is ordered above the nations on earth.
37 In the *Book of Jubilees*, "the angel of the presence" is used at times in an inter-
    changeable way with the "angel of God," e.g., *Jubilees'* recounting of Exod
    14:19 says that the angel of the presence led the Israelites on their wilderness
    sojourn.
38 The full text of 1QH XIII, 22-XV, 8 appears in chapter four.

out a mediator between (ואין מליץ בנים)[Your] h[oly ones to] reply (17) according
to the spirit for [] ב[] And they will repent at Your glorious word, and they
shall become Your princes in the [eternal] l[ot (ויהיו שריכה בגור[ל עולם) and]their
[trunk] (18) sprouts like a flower blo[ssoming for] eternal glory, to raise up
a shoot into the branches of an eternal planting.[39] And it will cast shade
over the entire world, (19) (will reach) as far as the clou[ds], and its roots
(will stretch) as far as the abyss, and all the rivers and its[branches] of Eden
[shall]w[ater] its [b]r[an]ches. And so it shall become (broad like) the
limitl[ess] seas (והיה לימֹ֯ם ל[אין] חקר)[40] (20). And they shall be entwined over
the world endlessly (והתאו֯רו על תבל לאין אפס)[41] and as far as Sheol; [   ] [and]
a spring of light shall become an everlasting font (21) without fail. In its bright
flames all the child[ren of injustice] shall burn, [and it shall] become a fire
burning against all the men of (22) guilt until (they are) finished off.

In this glimpse of Eden, an excruciatingly thorough description of a certain exotic cultivar, a cosmic eternal plant, is given. Its enormity is conveyed by the spatial coordinates which are given in relation to the familiar Secondspatial region of Sheol. Its impossibly massive dimensions
lend a vivid and simultaneously mythical quality to the tree that is sug-
gestive of other Mesopotamian and early Jewish traditions about stately
trees of cosmic proportions. The *Book of Erra* 1:150–56 describes such a
tree of enormity:

---

39   Cf. the arboreal imagery that appears in the visions in the *Genesis Apocryphon*,
including a special vision of a tree in a passage that Daniel Machiela calls
"The Dream of the Garden" which is interpreted as a metaphor for Noah.
Daniel A. Machiela, *The Dead Sea Genesis Apocryphon: A New Text and Translation with Introduction and Special Treatment of Columns 13–17* (STDJ 79; Leiden: Brill, 2009), 96–104.

40   The antecedent for this verb is the trunk (נצר) introduced at the end of line 17.
The sense of the Hebrew is to express, I think, the massive diameter of the
trunk. It is also possible to interpret this as referring to the trunk (in the
sense of the roots) reaching down as far as the limitless seas, but I understand
the passage to have already spoken about the far-reaching roots which continue
as far as the abyss (see the beginning of line 19).

41   This antecedent for this verb is taken to be the branches (דליות). I took the
phrase to describe the enormity of the branch lengths. By the way, it should
be noted that lines 19 and 20 show some scribal confusion. The text moves
from the plural subject of branches (דליות) to the singular subject (discussed in
the above note) of the trunk (נצר). I think that there is a scribal confusion
over what exactly the subject of this litany of phrases is; n.b. the supralinear
'branches' between lines 18 and 19, which suggests that the scribe has also
lost track of the subject and tried to recover what he thought the subject should
be.

Where is the mēsu tree, the flesh of the gods, the ornament of the king of
the uni[verse]?
That pure tree, that august youngster suited to supremacy,
Whose roots reached as deep down as the bottom of the underwor[ld]: a
hundred double hours through the vast sea waters;
Whose top reached as high as the sky of [Anum]?[42]

Here the arboreal metaphor serves as a reference to some other being.
Visionary reports frequently specify a mythological tree of enormity
that is then said to represent certain individuals. In the visions reported
in Dan 4:10–14 and Ezek 17:22–24 the metaphor refers to a king.[43]
Abram and Sarah are also envisioned as a cedar and beautiful date
palm in Abram's dream in 1QapGen XIX.[44] The half-human offspring
of the Watchers are also described with arboreal imagery in CD 2:16–
19.

Significantly for our discussion of spatialization in the hodayot, it
worth noting here that a cosmic tree is a kind of exotic cultivar that
one might expect to find in the garden of the heavenly deity. Its dimensions are impossible to visualize and reference a space that is simultaneously limitless yet physically specific. Such a cosmic tree is said to grow
in the precincts adjacent to the Temple in Ezekiel's vision recorded in
Ezek 47:1, 12. The final visions in the Book of Revelation, showing
influence from Ezekiel's visions, mention the mythical Tree of Life in
the New Jerusalem (Rev 22:1–2). The tree described in 1QH XIII,
22-XV, 8 is found in a garden situated in close proximity to the holy
space of the heavens. The garden described in that composition marks
a liminal space. It is accompanied by extraordinary experiences of communion with celestial beings (XIV, 15–17) and the idea of divine ret-
ribution, which is imagined as an eternal fire (XIV, 21–22). While a
great deal of attention is given to the garden space and its physical features, the fantastic elements in the description ensure that the reader
knows it to be a vision of an otherworldly space.

---

42 L. Cagni, *The Poem of Erra* (SANE 1/3; Malibu: Undena, 1977), 32. This text is
    dated to sometime between the eleventh and eighth c. BCE; See the discussion
    of this tree metaphor by A. A. Orlov, "Arboreal Metaphors," 439–51,
    esp. 445–47; and S. N. Bunta, "The Mēsu-Tree and the Animal Inside,"
    364–84.
43 In addition to the usual sources discussed in light of this passage in Dan 4:10–
    14, John Collins discuss this passage in light of 4QPrNab, the *Prayer of Naboni-
    dus*; see *Daniel*, 217–18.
44 See Daniel Machiela, *The Dead Sea Genesis Apocryphon*.

Following this fleeting glimpse of paradise in 1QH XIV, 15–22, the progressive spatialization of the hodayot brings the reader fully into the Garden of Eden in 1QH XVI, 5-XVII, 36. In an intervening hodayah, the speaker reports that God "has lifted his ray ever higher" and that he shines with a seven-fold luminosity (1QH XV, 26–27). Here the reader encounters a far more extensive and discursive vision of paradise, again with precise spatial details concerning its vegetation and its waterways.

C. The Well-Watered Garden Paradise in 1QH XVI, 5-XVII, 36

The second garden scene in the hodayot is found in 1QH XVI, 5-XVII, 36 which is recognized as a single composition, also attested in 4Q428 fragment 10. This composition curiously only overlaps with the first two lines of this lengthy composition in the Cave 4 manuscript.[45] Because of the damage at the bottom of col. XVI and the top of col. XVII, early scrolls scholars were not certain if this was a single hodayah or more, yet strong literary themes that continue throughout the these columns suggest that this is a single lengthy composition. In addition to these literary features, scribal practices suggest that these two columns are part of a single composition that begins with an extended allegory of the trees.[46]

The composition 1QH XVI, 5-XVII, 36 can be easily divided into three major sections based on the imagery that appears in it.[47] The first section is a report of the religious geography of paradise (1QH XVI, 5–27) that includes details about the distinctive vegetation there and the irrigation of the land. This is followed by a detailed report of bodily anguish (1QH XVI, 27-XVII, 6) and a report of transformation (1QH

---

45 See Schuller, DJD 29.141–44. In the plates of that fragment, it is possible to see a clear *vacat* and a scribal mark in the right-hand margin at the very beginning of this composition.

46 Stegemann, "The Number of Psalms in 1QHodayot^a," 206. Stegemann observes that the Cave 4 hodayot texts now provide overlapping texts at the bottoms of columns and so it is possible to state more confidently whether or not certain compositions continue on or not. Yet the note that Stegemann has here at 206 n. 56 curiously does not actually cite Cave 4 fragments that overlap with the bottom most part of col. XVI and the transition to the very beginning lines of col. XVII.

47 See Julie Hughes, *Scriptural Allusions and Exegesis in the Hodayot*, 135–83, here 147–48.

XVII, 6–36). This composition reflects well the aspects of garden as a
heterotopia and I propose that it, like 1QH XIII, 22-XV, 8, was generated by a Thirdspatial religious experience by an anonymous individual. Its inclusion into the hodayot collection allows it to function as a
Secondspatial affective script for a subsequent reader to performatively
read and reenact. References to the body make these events compelling
and strategically arouse a reader's emotions during the scripted reenactment of the events. Through the rhetorical "I," a subsequent reader can
stand in the place of the imaginal body and imitate the speaker's experiences. This way of reading the text is assisted by the many images of
the body that heighten the reader's experience of the text and the things
described therein. Sensory experiences include references to body parts
and their spatial extension as well as their full range of motion. Experiences of both suffering and transformation are described vividly through
the rhetoric of embodiment which facilitates a reader's ability to reenact
the text. With respect to spatiality, the composition in 1QH XVI, 5-
XVII, 36 follows the reference to the speaker's vertical movement upwards in 1QH XV, 25, 26–27. When read in series, the detailed garden
vision in 1QH XVI, 5–27 can be imagined as an amazing stop on the
luminous journey upwards that was detailed in 1QH XV, 25–27 and
continues into the heavens.

The Text of 1QHᵃ XVI, 5- XVII, 36 (my translation)

(5) I give thanks [to You, O Lo]rd, for You set me at the source of flowing
waters in a dry land (כי נתתני במקור נוזלים ביבשה),[48] (at) a spring of water in a
parched land, (at) a watered (6) garden (וֹמשקי גן)[49] and (at) a pool [   ].

---

48 Here, the preposition "*at* the source," במקור denotes place and suggests close
    proximity. The preposition is distributed throughout the next three nouns.
    Note that James Charlesworth (following A. Dupont-Sommer, *Les écrits essé-
    niens découverts près de la mer morte* [4ᵗʰ ed.; Paris, 1980], 240; and J. Carmignac,
    Les textes de Qumran [Paris, 1961]) proposes the following: "(as) the *irrigator* of
    the garden;" see James H. Charlesworth, "An Allegorical and Autobiographical
    Poem by the *Moreh haṣ-Ṣedeq*," *"Sha'arei Talmon": Studies in the Bible, Qumran,
    and the Ancient Near East Presented to Shemaryahu Talmon* (ed. Michael Fishbane
    and Emanuel Tov with the assistance of Weston W. Fields; Winona Lake: Ei-
    senbrauns, 1992), 295–307, here 296–97 ns. 5 and 6.
49 The Hebr. here is "וֹמשקי גן." The image of "a watered garden" can be associated
    with Gen 2:10, which describes the river that waters the Garden of Eden, and
    with Gen 13:10, which compares the well-irrigated land of Jordan to the gar-
    den of the LORD. Cf. Charlesworth, "An Allegorical and Autobiographical
    Poem," and also Michael Daise, "Creation Motifs in the Qumran Hodayot,"

The field is a planting of cypress and evergreen together with pine for Your glory (הַשָּׂדֶה מַטַּע ברוש ותדהר עם תאשור יחד לכבודכה).[50] Trees of (7) life[51] are hidden at the secret spring, among all the trees by the water.[52] They will force a shoot to sprout for the eternal planting,[53] (8) (they will) make (it) root be-

---

in *The Dead Sea Scrolls: Fifty Years after their Discovery* (ed. Lawrence H. Schiff-man, Emanuel Tov, and James C. VanderKam; Jerusalem: Israel Exploration Society in cooperation with the Shrine of the Book, Israel Museum, 2000), 293–305, here 302.

50   These three types of trees are also mentioned in this exact sequence in Isa 41:19 in addition to other trees: "I will plant cedars in the wilderness, acacias and myrtles and oleasters; I will set cypresses in the desert, box trees and elms as well (אשים בערבה ברוש תדהר ותאשור יחדו), so that men may see and know, consider and comprehend that the LORD's hand has done this, that the Holy one of Israel has wrought it" (JPS). Notice that the precise identification of these three types of trees varies considerably among the translations. The NRSV reads curiously: "I will set in the desert the cypress, the plane (?) and the pine together." So too, this sequence of three trees appear at Isa 60:13 in a reference to the trees of the divine sanctuary, although JPS uses different names for the three: "The majesty of Lebanon shall come to you—Cypress and pine and box (ברוש תדהר ותאשור יחדו)—to adorn the site of My Sanctuary, to glorify the place where My feet rest." The Hebr. word ברוש is most certainly the cypress, a group of conifers native to the Judean mountains that can also include a kind of juniper; Michael Zohary, *Plants of the Bible* (Cambridge: Cambridge University Press, 1982), 106–107. Zohary goes on to identify the Hebr. תדהר as the Laurestinus, a flowering ornamental evergreen tree. The identification of the next tree is not clear; Zohary writes, "The only way to overcome the difficulty is to accept the reliable Aramaic translation of the *Targum Yonathan*, which renders *tidhar* as *mornian*, which is cognate with the Arabic *murran*—the only Arabic name for *Viburnum tinus*" (112).

51   Cf. Pss Sol. 14:3 which likens the holy ones to "trees of life" in the garden of the LORD: "the garden of the LORD, the trees of life, are his holy ones. Their planting is rooted forever;" Sebastian Brock, "The Psalms of Solomon," in the *Apocryphal Old Testament* (ed. H.F.D. Sparks; Oxford: Clarendon, 1984), 673; See too, "And I said, Blessed, O Lord, are those who have been planted in thy ground, and those who have a place in thy paradise, and grow up in the growth of thy trees" (*Odes Sol.* 11:18); J. A. Emerton, "The Odes of Solomon," *Apocryphal Old Testament*, 702; as noted by Julie Hughes, *Scriptural Allusions and Exegesis in the Hodayot*, 179 n. 170.

52   Licht is correct to identify this as an allusion to the allegory of the cedar tree in Ezek 31:14. Allusions to Ezekiel's allegory of the lofty cedar stand as a veiled reference to the downfall of Egypt. For the author of this psalm, the reference to the arrogant trees by the water points to the enemies of the community. Various allusions to Ezek 31:1–18 continue throughout the hodayah through line 12.

53   The Hebr. reads, "להפריח נצר למטעת עולם." In an earlier composition, the eternal planting is said to be located in Eden (1QH XIV, 18). The expectation that an

fore they force a shoot, and their roots stretch out to the strea[m]. And its stump (יזעו)[54] opens toward the living water (למים חיים) (9) which will become an eternal fountain (ויהי למקור עולם).[55] All the be[a]sts of the forest shall feed upon the shoot (growing) on it. And (the base of) its stump (shall become) a trampling place for all those who pass along the way. (10) And its branch will belong to every winged bird.[56] All the tre[es] by the water tower over it. While in their planting they grow tall, (11) they cannot extend (their) root toward the stream.[57] And he who causes the

---

eternal planting will emerge after the annihilation of wickedness from the earth appears in the Book of the Watchers 10:16. In that tradition, the eternal planting refers to Noah and his family; see Matthew Black, *The Book of Enoch or 1 Enoch: A New English Edition with Commentary and Textual Notes* (SVTP 7; Leiden: Brill, 1985), 133. There is a long tradition of interpreting this reference to an eternal shoot as a community. It may be an allusion to Isa 60:21 where God states, "And your people, all of them righteous, shall possess the land for all time; they are the shoot that I planted, my handiwork in which I glory" (cf. also Isa 11:1). An eternal planting as a community also plays a pivotal role in the Apocalypse of Weeks, in Enoch's revelation of 10 weeks or periods in human history. In the seventh week, a community of Jews "from the eternal plant of righteousness" will prevail over their opponents (93:10). Language of planting also appears in CD-A as a reference to the righteous remnant during the age of wrath (1:7). In other places in the DSS, the entire Qumran community is compared to an eternal planting in 1QS VIII, 5 and XI, 8. This allegorizing of men as plants is familiar from biblical prophetic passages like Isa 5:7, which refers to the men of Judah as seedlings; see too 60:21 and 61:3. Other relevant biblical passages include Ezek 31:1–18 and Dan 4:9–12. The metaphor of planting appears several times in *Jub.* 1:16; 16:26; 21:4; 36:6 and the wisdom text 4Q418 81:13 may also be a reference to planting.

54 Here the Hebr. יזעו should be read as an error arising from a metathesis between the first two letters; instead read גיזעו "its stump" (also appearing in the next line) which also appears as the subject of the verb ויפתח. Later in the hodayah, this word is translated as "their stump" in line 24 and "its stump" in line 25.

55 Here the "living waters" become an "eternal fount"; cf. Jer 2:13 God is the "fount of living waters" (מקור מים חיים). Also references in John 4:10–14; 6:35; 7:37–39 (ὕδωρ ζῶν); see Dale C. Allison, Jr, "The Living Water (John 4:10–14; 6:35c; 7:37–39)," *St Vladimir's Theological Quarterly* 30 (1986): 143–57; Zane C. Hodges, "Rivers of Living Water—John 7:37–39," *Bibliotheca sacra* 136 (1979): 239–48.

56 The Hebr. here is "ומבצר עליו ירעו כול ח[י]ת ח[י]ת יער ומרמס גזעו לכל עוברי דרך ודליתו לכל עוף כנף." Cf. Dan 4:9–12.

57 The Hebr. here is "ירמו עליו כול ע[צי] מים כי במטעתם יתשגשגו ואל יובל לא ישלחו שורש." Based on the translation in DJD 40 ("for in their plantation they grow tall"), the editors interpret the root of the verb יתשגשגו as the *pilp.* form of the root שגה. This may be an allusion to Isa 17:11, "Even though on the day of your planting, you make (them) grow (ביום נטעך תשגשגי) and on the morning of your sowing, you force a bud, the crop falters (נד קציר) on a day of sickness and mortal agony." In the bib-

shoot of h[o]lines to sprout into a planting of truth is hidden; (12) Because he is neither considered, nor known, his mystery is sealed.[58] *vacat*

---

lical context, the line refers to those who participate in an aberrant cult. Even though what they plant may grow initially, the entire crop will eventually come to naught. So too, within the context of this composition, the "planting that grows tall" is a reference to something that grows initially but eventually amounts to nothing because "it cannot stretch its roots to the waters." The arboreal imagery in the hodayah is very close to the myth of the Watchers which is summarized in CD 2:16–19 that specifies the offspring of the Watchers, the Giants, as tall trees: "For many have gone astray due to these; brave heroes stumbled on account of them, from ancient times until now. For having walked in the stubbornness of their hearts the Watchers of the heavens fell (נפלו עירי השמים); on account of it they were caught, for they did not heed the precepts of God. And their sons, whose height was like that of cedars and whose bodies were like mountains, fell (ובניהם אשר כרום ארזים גבהם וכהרים גויותיהם כי נפלו);" this reference is thought to be a reference to the myth of the watchers who fall from heaven (cf. *1 En.* 13:10).

58   The Hebr. here is "ומפריח נצר ק[ו]דש למטעת אמת סותר בלוא נחשב ובלא נודע חותם רזו." This line may contain more than one allusion to the prophetic corpus: Isa 53:3b "and as one from whom others hide their faces he was despised, and *we held him of no account*" (ולא חשבנהו); Isa 8:16 "Bind up the testimony, *seal* the teaching among my disciples" (צור תעודה חתום תורה בלמדי); also see Ezek 28:11, "a model example" (חותם תכנית). Michael O. Wise (*The First Messiah*) reengaged an early proposal among scrolls scholars that there is a direct relationship between the speaker of the TH and the subject of the Servant Songs. This was a view held by A. Dupont-Sommer, "Le rouleau des Hôdâyôt," 5–23 but refuted by J. Carmignac, "Les citations de l'Ancien Testament, et specialement des poems du Serviteur, 357–94, esp. 383–91. In recent days, John J. Collins has refuted Wise's thesis that there is a direct relationship between the speaker of the TH and the Servant; J. J. Collins ("Teacher and Servant," 37–50) assumes the traditional position of the Teacher Hymns Hypothesis and proposes that the author of the TH, presumably the Teacher of Righteousness, can be identified as the Servant. In addition to refuting the identification of literary parallels, Collins notes that the role that suffering has is very different in the TH from the Isaian Servant Songs. Here I think that Collins is correct that the similarities are not exact enough to be certain of an identification; however, I am not convinced that the speaker needs to be understood as the Teacher of Righteousness.

Notice that the person who is being described here is different from the speaker who uses the first person elsewhere in this psalm. Here there may be an allusion to what modern scholars refer to as the Fourth Servant Song, Isa 52:13–53:12. Both the Isaian servant and the figure in the psalm could be said to be held without esteem (cf. Isa 53:3). In the Isaian passage, the prophet describes the shoot visually as "not regarded," but here the language of the hymnist states that he is "not considered." One important distinction between the Isaian passage and this passage is this: the servant himself is the planting (Isa

But You, O [G]od, You protect its fruit all around with the mystery of powerful warriors, (13) spirits of holiness and a whirling fiery flame, lest a stra[nger approach] the spring of life ( )[59] and (14) drink the waters of holiness with the eternal trees, and bear his fruit with the planting of the heavens. For the one who sees does not perceive, (15) and the one who thinks does not believe in the source of life, and so gives away the cr[o]p of the eternal blossom.[60] But as for me, I became the insult of overflowing torrents, (16) for they expel their mire over me.[61] *vacat*

(17) But You, O my God, have placed (words) in my mouth, like rain showers for all [who thirst], and like a spring of living waters (מבוע מים חיים)[62] that

---

53:2) and the "shoot", whereas in this psalm the plant shoot is clearly distinct from the one who cultivates it. Traditional hodayot scholarship has tended to see the cultivator as the Teacher of Righteousness. Similar language is applied to the speaker of the TH in 1QHᵃ XII, 9 and XII, 24.

59 The Hebr. here is "ואתה[] א[ל] שכתה בעד פריו בסוד גבורי כח ורוחות קודש ולהט אש מתהפכת בל י[בוא ז]ר במעין חיים". This is an allusion to Gen 3:24 where God stations the cherubim and the fiery flaming sword at the entrance to the Garden of Eden to guard the fruit of the tree of life. In Arthur Everett Sekki's discussion, these two groups (גבורי כח ורוחות קודש) are understood to be angels; Sekki, *The Meaning of* Ruah[*at Qumran* (SBLDS 110; Atlanta: Scholars Press, 1989), 161−62; there he cites a similar construction used for angels attested in 4Q430 1 ii 7, "רוחות קודש קדשם."

James R. Davila proposes reading בל י[בוא ז]ר as either בל י[בוא ש]ר or בל י[בוא ש]ד. Davila argues that the word is either "prince" or "demon." He does not specify which is the case, but he is convinced that it is some supernatural being; see Davila, "The Hodayot Hymnist and the Four who Entered Paradise," *RevQ* 17 (1996): 457−78. While this reconstruction is not certain, Davila's essay is provocative as he also proposes that this hodayot played a role in a mystical visionary experience. He engages Christopher Morray-Jones, "Paradise Revisited (2 Cor 12:1−12): The Jewish Mystical Background of Paul's Apostolate, Part 1: The Jewish Sources" and Part 2: Paul's Heavenly Ascent and Its Significance," *HTR* 86 (1993): 177−217, 265−92.

60 The Hebr. here is ויתן יוב[ן] ל[פרח עולם. This imagery fits very well with the myth of the Watchers where the Watchers impart forbidden knowledge to human beings; e.g., *1 En.* 7:1; 8:1−3; 9:6, 8. In the Manichean fragments of the *Book of Giants,* the Watchers also appear in a dendromorphic form. The concern expressed in this statement fits very well the motif of the forbidden knowledge that the Watchers impart to humans (*1 En.* 7:1; 8:1−3; 9:6, 8).

61 The Hebr. reads, "כי גרשו עלי רפשם" Cf. 1QH XI, 33 "then the torrents of Belial shall burst forth to Abaddon, and the schemers of the deep shall roar with a clamor of those who spew mire" (ויבקעו לאבדון נחלי בליעל ויהמו מחשבי תהום בהמון גורשי ר[ש).

62 This living water (מים חיים) may be contrasted with the chaotic overflowing torrents of the insults endured by the speaker in XVI, 15−16. In the Hebrew Bible, "the fount of living waters," God Himself, also stands in contrast to broken cisterns that cannot even hold water in Jer 2:13. Drinking these foreign waters, here cited as the Nile and the Euphrates, is a symbol of rebellion and re-

will not fail to open. (18) The heavens will not abate. They will become a river that gushes ov[er all the trees of] water and then into immeasur[able] seas. (19) The things that are hidden away in secret will burst forth suddenly [   ] and they will become flo[od] waters (for every tree, both)(20) green and dry; a deep pool for every beast and bi[rd   ] like lead in might[y] waters,[63] [   ] (21) in sparks of fire they dry up. But the plant-ing of fruit [   ]eternal [f]ont, glory and [everlasting] splen[dor] be-long to Eden. (22) And by my hand You have opened their font with [its] ditches [   ] to turn upon the proper line, and the planting (23) of their trees is along the plumb-line of the sun [   ] for a splendid branch. When I extend my hand to dig (24) its ditches, its roots break into the flinty rock, and [   ] their stump into the earth. And so in the time of heat it maintains (25) its strength. But if I withdraw my hand, it

---

jection of the LORD (Jer 2:18–19). The comparison of the speaker's teachings to life-giving waters appears again later in the CH, 1QH XXIII, 11–14. The imagery of water as teaching or instruction also has roots in biblical traditions about the Torah as water and can be read in light of the language that is used in 1QS XI, 5–7: "For the truth of God is the rock of my steps, and his power the stay of my right hand. From the source (מקור) of His righteousness is my justification. The light in my heart stems from His glorious mysteries. My eye has seen what is everlasting: Deep wisdom which was hidden from mortal man, knowledge and clever plan hidden from the sons of man, fount (מקור) of righteousness, reservoir (מקוה) of power, with the spring (מעין) of glory from the community of flesh. But to those whom God has chosen He has given these things as an eternal possession." Trans. by Michael Fishbane in "The Well of Living Water: A Biblical Motif and its Ancient Transforma-tions," in *"Sha'arei Talmon:" Studies in the Bible, Qumran, and the Ancient Near East Presented to Shemaryahu Talmon* (ed. Michael Fishbane, Emanuel Tov, and W. Fields; Winona Lake: Eisenbrauns, 1992), 3–16. Fishbane describes the ac-count found here in 1QS XI, 5–7 in the following way: "a profound religious, perhaps even mystical, experience underlies this text" (8–9). He also discusses Ps 36:8–10 in which the image of the fountain of life (מקור חיים) appears in the context of a passage that compares the Temple of the Lord and the ultimate source of all light, God Himself. Fishbane discusses this hodayah in light of other visionary texts that associate illumination and water; 4 Ezra 14:38–41, 47; 2 Bar (Syriac) 59:7; John 7:37–38; *Odes of Solomon* 11:6–7. See too James H. Charlesworth's discussion of "living waters" as salvific waters, in Charlesworth, "Les Odes de Salomon et les manuscrits de la mer morte," *RB* 77 (1970): 522–49, esp. 534–38.

63 This is a positive image of life-threatening waters associated with the crossing of the Red Sea; cf. *1 En.* 48:9 "[f]or on the day of their tribulation and distress they will not save themselves; and into the hand of my chosen ones I shall throw them. As straw in the fire and *as lead in the water,* thus they will burn be-fore the face of the holy, and they will sink before the face of the righteous; and no trace of them will be found."

shall become like a junip[er in the wilderness] ([יהיה כערﬠֹר] במדבר).[64] Its stump is like weeds in a salt plain (וגמעו כחרלים במלחה).[65] Its ditches (26) shall produce thorns and thistles (ופלגיו יעל קוץ ודרדר);[66] briars and[weeds] (ןﬡלשמיר ושית) [on] its banks turn into worthless trees. In the presence of (27) the heat, its leaves droop and it is not rejuvenated by the spri[ng of water   ]

SHIFT: LAMENT BEGINS

[a] dwelling with sick ones, and (my) heart *m*[]' (28) in agonies. I have become like a forsaken man in grief [67] [   ]. There is no refuge for me! For my agony bursts (29) into bitterness and an incurable pain (כאוב אגוש)[68]! No strength is retained, and trou]ble was upon me like those who go down into Sheol.   And among (30) the dead my spirit searches, when [my] li[fe] reaches the Pit [   ] My soul is weary day and night (31) without rest. And it (my agony) bursts like a raging fire contained within [my] b[ones]. For days its flame consumes, (32) finishing off (my) strength to (its) limits and destroying my flesh in due time. Crashing waves soar over me, (33) and my soul sinks down in me to complete destruction, for my strength has stopped from my body. My heart is poured out like water, (34) and my flesh is melted like wax. The strength of my loins has become a disaster. My arm is shattered at the elbow, [and I am un][able] to wave my hand. (35) My [foo]t is bound in shackles. My knees buckle like water, unable to take a step. There is no sound to my footstep. (36) They bound my strong arm with fetters of hindrance. And the tongue that You had strengthened in my mouth is no longer and it is unable to raise (37) a sound and (unable) to announce teachings to revive the spirit of those who stumble, and (unable) to assist the weary with a word. The sound of my lips[69] is silenced (38) by horror.[70] The tablet of my heart is on a judg-ment line[71] [   ]   [   ]bitterness   [   ] heart [   ] dominion (39)

---

64 The Hebr. ﬠרﬠ is a reference to the Phoenician Juniper shrub that can grow into a small tree; Zohary, *Plants of the Bible*, 117.

65 This would be the saline soils near the Dead Sea, the Aravah Valley and the lower Jordan Valley. In such regions, tamarisk forests grow; M. Zohary, *Plants of the Bible*, 35.

66 Cf. Gen 3:18 "thorns and thistles shall it sprout for you" (וקוץ ודרדר תמציח לך).

67 The Hebrew here is "מגור עם חולים ﬠ[]ום בנגיﬠים לב ואהיה כאיש נﬠזוב בגוֹן". These lines may contain a brief allusion to the Fourth Servant Song (Isa 52:13–53:12). In Isa 53:3–4, the servant is described as being despised and forsaken by men. Like the speaker of the hodayah, the Servant is acquainted with agonies. See the dis-cussion by Collins, "Teacher and Servant."

68 Also at 1QH XIII, 30.

69 The phrase, מזל שפתי, also appears at XIX, 8; 4Q491 11 i17; 1QSb III, 27; 4Q511 22 3, 63–64 ii 4; 4Q416 7 3; 4Q418 222, 2; 4Q525 8 2.

70 The Hebr. reads מפלﬦוֹח. The same word that appears twice in the apocalyptic hodayah, 1QH XI, 12 and 13.

71 Here the Hebr. reads "בֹּקן משפט לוֹח לבי"; cf. 1QH XI, 28 "לאין תקוה בנפול קן על משפט" and also XIV, 29 "וכפיס על קן משפט."

among the creatur[es   ] and [I   so]ul is engulfed (40) [their] wisdo
[m   ] they are silent as one without (41) [   ] a human without
...

Col. XVII (Col. IX)
(1) [   ] darkness [   ] (2) [app]ears for disputes by night and
[   ]   (3) [   ] without compassion. In anger he stirs up mistrust and
completely [ ]   (4) The breakers of death and Sheol are over my couch.
My bed raises up a lament, [and my pallet] a sound of misery. (5) My
eyes (burn) like a fire in a furnace, and my weeping (flows) like rivers of
water.[72] My eyes fail to rest; my [strength] stands (6) far from me, and
my life has been set aside.

SHIFT: TRANSFORMATION

But as for me, from ruin to desolation (משאה אל משואה),[73] from pain to agony,
and from travails (7) to torments, my soul meditates on Your wonders.
In Your kindness You have not rejected me. Time (8) and time again my
soul deli[g]hts in the abundance of Your mercies. I give a reply to those
who confound me, (9) and reproof to those who humiliate me. I will condemn his verdict, but Your judgment I honor, for I know (10) Your truth!
I shall choose my judgment, and I am satisfied with my afflictions, because I
wait for Your kindness. You have placed (11) a supplication in the mouth
of Your servant, and You have not rebuked my life, nor have You removed my well-being, nor have You forsaken (12) my hope, but in the
face of affliction You have restored my spirit. For You have established
my spirit and know my deliberations. (13) In my distress You have soothed
me, and I delight in (Your) forgiveness. I shall be comforted for former sin.
(14) I know that there is hope in Your kindness, and an expectation in the
abundance of Your power. For no one is justified (15) in Your jud[g]ment,
and no one is bl[ameless in] Your litigation. One man may be more righteous than another, or one person may be wiser [than his fell]ow, (16) and
flesh may be honored more than a creature of c[lay], and one spirit may
surpass another spirit; but as for Your mighty str[ength], no (17) power
can compare. Your glory has no [bounds, and] Your wisdom has no
measure, and [Your] truth has [   ]; (18) and everyone who has been
forsaken has [   ] *vacat*

But as for me, in You I have [   ] (19) with me, and not   [   ]
against the men of my strife [   ] (20) And when they plot [] against
me, [   ] and if the face shows shame   [   ] (21) mine. And You
[   ] my adversary will not prevail against me for a stumbling block to

---

72   The Hebr. reads "עיני כעש בכבשן" which is literally, "my eyes (are) like a moth in a
   furnace." Here it is preferable to see this as an instance of guttural confusion
   between the *aleph* and *ayin*. I propose reading עיני כאש בכבשן "my eyes (burn)
   like a fire in a furnace."
73   Here the scribe has indicated deletion dots for the letter *aleph*; this hendiadys
   appears also at 1QH XIII, 32.

[   ][A]ll (22) the men of wa[r against me and the leaders of strife against me have a] face [that is ashamed]; and those who grumble against me have a reproach. *vacat*

(23) But You, O my God, [at] [the appointed time   ] You plead my case. For in the mystery of Your wisdom You reprove me; (24) and You hide the truth until the[moment   ] its appointed time. Your chastisement will become a joy and gladness to me, (25) and my agonies will become an et [ernal] healing and everlasting [well-being]. The contempt of my enemies will become my glorious crown, and my stumbling (will become my) eternal strength. (26) For by [Your] insight [you have instructed me] and my light shines forth by means of Your glory.[74] For You make light (27) shine from darkness for (me); [to heal] my wounds; for my stumbling, a wonderful strength; an infinite space (28) for the distress of [my] soul. [You are] my place of refuge, my stronghold, the rock of my strength and my fortress. In You (29) I take refuge from all the pain [of my soul; You save] me for an eternal escape. For You from my father (30) have known me, from the womb [You have hallowed me, from the belly of] my mother You have rendered good to me, from the breasts of she who conceived me, Your compassion (31) has been mine.[75] And in the embrace of my nurse [   ] and from my youth You have shined the insight of Your judgment on me. (32) With a sure truth You have supported me, and by Your holy spirit You have delighted me; even until this day [   ] (33) Your righteous chastisement is with my [   ] and the protection of Your peace delivers my soul. With my steps is (34) a multitude of pardons and an abundance of [mer]cies when You enter into judgment with me. Until old age You shall provide for me. For (35) my father did not know me, and my mother abandoned me to You. For You are a father to all the sons of Your truth,[76] and You rejoice (36) over them as a loving mother over her nursing child.[77] As a guardian with his embrace, You provide for all Your creatur[es]. (37) *full line vacat*

The composition 1QH XVI, 5-XVII, 36 has a notably vivid style and an experiential quality. Scholars have remarked on its mystical features. Michael Fishbane describes the garden imagery that appears here as a

---

74   The Hebr. is "ובכבודכה הופיע אורי כי מאור מחושך האירותה." On the luminosity of the speaker, see also 1QH XI, 3; XII, 6, 28; XIII, 18; XV, 26–28.

75   Here the speaker uses familial references (father, mother, nursemaid) as extremely positive metaphors for God's nurturing and compassion. This stands in sharp contrast to the way these familial terms are used in 1QH XV, 37-XVI, 4.

76   The Hebr. here is "לכול בני אמתכה." The particular formulation "sons of Your truth" appears also at 1QH XV, 32; XVIII, 29; and in the so-called SGH in XXVI, 32.

77   Here in 1QH XVII, 34–36, the speaker describes his own relationship to God using familial language.

"striking personalization of edenic imagery."[78] The lush verdant image that is painted in this composition alludes to the primordial garden, whose entrance, like the well-watered garden in this hodayah (XVI, 21), was guarded by the flaming sword of the cherubim (1QH XVI, 12–14).[79] James Davila understands this text to reflect some kind of religious experience.[80] The allegory of the trees that appears in the beginning of this hodayah (1QH XVI, 5–27) is most striking.[81] This allegory combines biblical allusions from the Garden of Eden in Gen 2:4–3:24, the parable of the trees in Ezek 31:1–18, Nebuchadnezzar's dream in Dan 4:7–14, and other prophetic passages from Jeremiah and Isaiah. It also alludes to planting imagery from visionary traditions associated with the figure of Enoch.

The hodayah begins with a description of a well-irrigated garden with two types of trees: the trees of life and the trees by the water which stand for the righteous and the wicked respectively. The general imagery of water flooding parched land is reminiscent of the biblical scenes described in Dan 4:12 and Isa 41:17–20. Water imagery appears as a metaphor for divine inspiration in a manner befitting a garden scene. Fishbane describes these waters as the "esoteric waters of wisdom and salvation."[82] The hodayah refers to mysteries that have been concealed and a special mention is made of an eternal shoot/planting which is likely an allusion to a community (see 1QS VIII, 4b–6; XI, 8). The plants rely upon a gardener who tends them by hand (1QH XVI, 22–27), and who refers to himself as being like the sweet showers that give nourishment (lines 17–21).

After the garden imagery, the hodayah shifts to an extended and powerful lament that begins at the bottom of col. XVI at line 27. Here the speaker details the totality of his suffering, both his psychological pain (XVI, 29–33) and physical brokenness (XVI, 33–36). The joining of a garden setting with eschatological judgment here follows

---

78   Fishbane, "The Well of Living Water," 9.
79   Enoch's associations with the place of Eden may be reflected in the tradition found in the Dream Visions that his wife's name was Edna, a name that shares the same consonants as Eden, 1 En. 85:3.
80   J. R. Davila, "The Hodayot Hymnist and the Four who Entered Paradise."
81   Many scholars have commented already on the broad variety of scriptural references in this composition; see Julie Hughes, *Scriptural Allusions and Exegesis in the Hodayot*, 135–83; Svend Holm-Nielsen, *Hodayot: Psalms from Qumran*; M. Delcor, *Les Hymnes de Qumran*.
82   Fishbane, "The Well of Living Water," 9.

the pattern seen in other Second Temple literature, including the Genesis Garden of Eden. The garden space as heterotopia presumes liminality and close proximity to the divine abode. Like other visionary reports
of journeys to other worlds, the hodayah anticipates a fearful emotional
response and eschatological judgment. The concluding expression of
great confidence in God also describes the covenant relationship between God and the speaker in familial terms (father, mother, nursemaid,
child). Like a parent to a child, God is both a compassionate father, loving mother, and an embracing nursemaid to the speaker. In contrast to
1QH XV, 37-XVI, 4, which speaks about the impurities associated with
being conceived in the flesh, this hodayah uses familial terms in a positive way.[83]

In the hodayah, the allegory of the trees and the scene of the well-
watered garden fades into a lengthy discussion of the speaker's own suffering, both psychological and physical. Such physical manifestations of
emotion mark a spatial movement ever closer to the divine presence. In
a striking passage, the speaker reports the burning of his eyes and the
endless flow of his tears. In several places in the early Enochic literature,
the seer reports his own experience of physical trembling and fear in the
Book of the Watchers upon seeing the various otherworldly sites and
scenes. As Enoch enters into the heavenly house, he reports his own terror: "fear enveloped me, and trembling seized me, and I was quaking
and trembling" (1 En. 14:13–14). The emphasis on fear and trembling
also recurs during key moments in the Enochic literature.[84] At the beginning of the Dream Visions Enoch reports himself "lying down in the
house of Mahalalel," his grandfather (1 En. 83:3, 6).[85] Presumably his

---

83 Cf. "[But I am] an uncl[ean per]son [and from the womb of the one who con-
    ceived me (I have lived) in faithless guilt, and from the breasts of my mother] in
    iniquity, and in the bosom [of my nurse (attached) to great impurity, and from
    my childhood in blood guilt, and unto old age in the iniquity of flesh" (1QH
    XV, 39–40; trans. from DJD 40.215). The language of nursing that appears
    here is entirely negative.

84 In the Animal Apocalypse, the animals are reported as being afraid and trem-
    bling, the earth is quaking (1 En. 86:5–6; 89:34–35).

85 The Dream Visions is known largely from the Ethiopic manuscript tradition but
    portions of the Greek for 1 En. 89:42–49 have survived and fragments from
    four Aramaic copies were identified from Cave 4 (4QEn^{c-f}). The dating of at
    least the Animal Apocalypse, quite possibly the entire Dream Visions, can be
    dated to at least 125 BCE; see the discussion by James C. VanderKam, Enoch
    and the Growth of an Apocalyptic Tradition, 160–61; Milik, The Books of Enoch,
    6, 41, 244.

extensive visions take place when he is sleeping. References to night-time visions that grieve the seer to tears appear repeatedly in the Animal Apocalypse where Enoch reports his own anguish over seeing the visions. Another reminder that Enoch's visions come to the patriarch when he is asleep is given twice at the beginning of the Animal Apocalypse when the seer begins his report by saying, "before I took your mother Edna (as my wife), I saw in a vision on my bed" (*1 En.* 85:3). A second reminder is given just prior to his recounting of the 'fall of the watchers and the violence of the giants' when the seer says, "And again, I saw with my eyes as I was sleeping. . . . I saw in the vision. . ."(*1 En.* 86:1). Near the end of the Animal Apocalypse, having seen all of the terrible visions, Enoch reports his own lament and tears several times: "I grieved exceedingly" (*1 En.* 89:67); shortly after he says this, he says, "I began to weep and lament because of those sheep" (*1 En.* 89:69); "I cried out and lamented in my sleep" (*1 En.* 90:3). The Animal Apocalypse closes with the seer saying:

> And I slept among them and awoke. And I saw everything, and this is the vision that I saw while I slept. And I awoke and blessed the Lord of righteousness and gave him glory. And after that I wept bitterly, and my tears did not cease until I could no longer endure it, but they were running down because of what I had seen; for everything will come to pass and be fulfilled, and every deed of humanity was shown to me in its order. That night I remembered the first dream. I wept because of it, and I was disturbed because I had seen the vision. (*1 En.* 90:39–42)

These descriptions of a visionary experience coming to the seer in his bed chamber and his physical responses in the form of tears is much like the speaker in the hodayot 1QH XVI, 4–5 who wails: "the breakers of death and Sheol are over my couch. My bed raises up a lament, and my pallet a sound of misery. My eyes burn like a fire in a furnace, and my weeping flows like rivers of water" (XVII, 4–5). The scenario described here is one where the visionary experiences took place during a dream state at night.

In general, human encounters with angelic and divine beings result in a specific physical response, oftentimes a complete physical collapse in fear, not unlike a pious response to a theophany.[86] Physical agony may

---

86 In various texts reporting religious experiences, the common response is fear and collapsing with the face down; Exod 3:6; 20:19; Num 22:31; Josh 5:13–15; Judg 6:23; 13:22; Ezek 1:28; 1 Chr 21:20; Matt 28:4–5; Luke 1:11–12; Acts 10:3–4; Rev 19:10; *1 En.* 14:14; *Mart. Ascen. Isa* 7:21; See the discussion by Kevin P. Sullivan, *Wrestling with Angels*, 32–33.

have been understood as an expected consequence of having an actual
visionary experience, as other seers report pain and anguish after having
seen visions. Daniel reports extreme physical effects of the vision in Dan
10:7–10. The details given here far exceed the ones given to his experience in 8:16–18, although Dan 8:27 says that the physical strain was
so overwhelming that he was incapacitated for several days. The greater
effects in chapter 10 may be due to the fact that the seer has engaged in a
three-week preparatory period of mourning and fasting, common practices for inducing a visionary experience. After his epiphany of a heavenly being described in language reminiscent of Ezekiel,[87] the seer reports being overwhelmed physically and that he slipped into a dream-
state. Daniel 10:7–10 states: "I Daniel alone saw the vision; the men
who were with me did not see the vision, yet they were seized with
a great terror and fled into hiding. So I was left alone to see this great
vision. I was drained of strength, my vigor was destroyed, and I could
not summon up strength. I heard him speaking; and when I heard
him speaking, overcome by a deep sleep, I lay prostrate on the ground."
After his dream-vision and dialogue with the man, Daniel reports:

> While he was speaking these words to me, I turned my face toward the
> ground and was speechless. Then one in human form touched my lips,
> and I opened my mouth to speak, and said to the one who stood before
> me, "My lord, because of the vision such pains have come upon me that
> I retain no strength. How can my lord's servant talk with my lord? For I
> am shaking, no strength remains in me, and no breath is left in me"
> (Dan 10:15–17).

What is notable about the post-vision report of Daniel's physical distress
is its high visibility. That something has happened to the seer is readily
visible in his physical display, even though Daniel says that "the people
who were with me did not see the vision" (10:7). Presumably Daniel
showed an unambiguous sign of bodily stress that terrified the people
who were with him and signaled to them that Daniel was experiencing
a religious vision. Later we are told that Daniel trembles physically
(10:11, 17), he collapses in a heap on the ground and needs to be assisted
into the upright position (10:9–11), and the blood drains from his face
(10:8).

The visionary experiences of Enoch, Daniel, and the speaker in the
hodayah share similar elements. There is a mention of a nighttime setting and the suggestion that religious experiences take place at night

---

87 See Collins, *Daniel*, 373–74.

during a dream-state (*1 En.* 90:3, 39–42; Dan 4:13; 10:9; 1QH XVII, 4). Significantly, the subsequent bodily effects of the religious experience for each seer are severe enough to incapacitate him. The dire lament in XVI, 27- XVII, 6 expresses the totality of the speaker's existential experience, covering all of his physical body from the mental anguish in his soul, the aches in his limbs, down to the very soles of the feet. This vivid and dramatic report of physical anguish serves, I propose, as evidence of his veridical experience. This portion of the hodayah fits well the pattern seen in other visionary reports, namely, that a visionary experience is followed by agonizing pain often accompanied by a physical collapse. Such a scenario is detailed in Dan 10:7 where Daniel's physical display communicated to the people with him that something extraordinary has happened. Notably, the vision itself was not visible to the people, only the seer's physical display. While Daniel's specific behaviors are not itemized, one can easily infer from the people's trembling that the seer's body expressed some form of physical fright.

Michael Stone has observed that "scholars are uncomfortable at the idea that the prophet is reporting something he believed had happened to him while in an alternate state of consciousness."[88] The complex literary patterns that often appear in visionary traditions do not eliminate the possibility that aspects of lived experience inform the events that are being described.[89] In the hodayah under examination, the discursive report of the physical display of performative emotion, and also the discursive report found in 1QH XIII, 22-XV, 8, can be said to record the evidence that an extraordinary experience took place. The author of 1QH XVI, 27-XVII, 6 takes pains to describe his body with care from head to toe: both the entirety of the body and its extension (tongue, arm, hands, and feet), along with the sites that connect the parts to the whole (the shattered elbows, the knees that buckle like water). These physical details are not only rhetorical elements that seek to convey a sense of realism to the report and an imaginal body for a subsequent reader to experience. This striking description of the body and its suffering can also be recognized as a record of the author's

---

88 Michael Stone, "A Reconsideration of Apocalyptic Visions," 168. This is an important essay that reiterates a key point that Stone presented in "Apocalyptic, Vision, or Hallucination?" *Milla Wa Milla* 14 (1974): 47–56, repr. in *Selected Studies in Pseudepigrapha and Apocrypha*, 419–28.
89 Stone, "A Reconsideration of Apocalyptic Visions," 178.

actual physical display. The bodily sensations, understood as endocrine changes and heart palpitations, are manifestations of emotion that can come to full expression in the form of weeping. The lament of the speaker's suffering mounts to a fever pitch at the top of 1QH XVII:

> The breakers of death and Sheol are over my couch (משברי מות ושאול על יצועי).[90] My bed raises up a lament, [and my pallet] a sound of misery (ערשי בקינה תשא ומ[טתי] בקול אנחה). My eyes (burn) like a fire in a furnace, and my weeping (flows) like rivers of water (ודמעתי כנחלי מים). My eyes fail to rest; my [strength] stands far from me, and my life has been set aside" (XVII, 5–6).

The report of a sleepless night of intense weeping may also allude to the technique of sleep deprivation.[91] Here the simile "my weeping (flows) like *rivers* of water" creates a metaphoric bridge to the first part of the hodayah that gave such rich spatial details about the irrigation of paradise: "they will become a *river* gushing ov[er all the trees of] water" (ויהיו לנחל שוטף ע[ל כול עצי [מים).[92] The tears of the speaker, like the gentle rains that fall in Eden, also possess a generative power and can effect change in status by authenticating the vision of paradise that has just been recounted. The community's acceptance of the report is evident from the inclusion of this text in the collection of prayers. Such a scenario may explain how these anonymous prayers authored by different individuals came to be transmitted as a single collection in the absence of any pseudonymous attribution.

---

90 Mention of Sheol in conjunction with endless weeping appears in Ps 6:6–7 "For there is no praise of You among the dead; in Sheol, who can acclaim You? I am weary with groaning; every night I drench my bed, I melt my couch in tears" (יגעתי באנחתי אשחה בכל־לילה מטתי בדמעתי ערשי אמסה).

91 Extended periods of weeping often accompanied other practices such as fasting and sleep deprivation etc., and could continue for several nights at a time; see Moshe Idel, *Kabbalah*, 74–88 and Elliot R. Wolfson, "Weeping, Death, and Spiritual Ascent in Sixteenth-Century Jewish Mysticism," 207–44. Note too the parallels in other ritual forms of weeping discussed by G. L. Ebersole ("The Poetics and Politics of Ritualized Weeping," 25–51) who describes a ritual practice from medieval Japan: "late-night or all-night recitative and meditative practices in dim low light, the calming and focusing of one's mind, a glittering or flickering point of light, and the shedding of tears by the reciter. Moreover, in both ritual practices, the individual weeps all night long. The shedding of tears was not, it would seem, incidental to these religious practices; they were an essential part" (38).

92 1QH XVI, 18; Ephrem too discusses various types of weeping in *Hymn* V, 13–14, the same hymn where he reports his transportation into paradise; also in *Hymn* VII, 24, XII, 9, XIII, 16, in *The Hymns on Paradise*, 107, 127.

As Daniel 10:7 indicates, ancient communities who observe religious experiences typically do not have access to the content of that vision until it is recounted to them. What can be observed is the physical display of emotion in the seer's body. It is also the case that for the community of Daniel and for the community of the hodayot, affective displays encoded in the body would have been read and interpreted by the members of that community in meaningful ways that were distinctive to that group. Psychologist Joseph Henrich calls performative emotions in ritual contexts costly practices of credibility enhancing displays which he terms CREDS.[93] Heinrich writes that certain behaviors like costly rituals convey commitment within a religious community.[94] He writes that "the more costly the displays are, the potentially deeper the degree of transmitted commitment."[95] While modern textual and literary analyses focus on the lexemes that express "weeping" and "tears," there are many embodied expressions of emotion associated with fear and terror that are communicated through subtle changes in the body that are not readily available to modern scholars. These include changes in visible perspiration, blushing, blanching, and shifts in the pitch or tone of one's voice. Such bodily displays of performative emotions would have been recognized immediately by the communities that observed them, likely resulting in changes of status and esteem for the one who displayed them. The study by Max Weisbuch and Nalini Ambady reports that bodily signs of affect are perceived and understood more rapidly and with greater accuracy for individuals who belong to that group than for individuals who stand outside of it.[96] They write that "there is substantial evidence that emotion interpretation depends crucially on

---

93   See Joseph Henrich, "The Evolution of Costly Displays, Cooperation and Religion," 244–60.

94   Henrich, "The Evolution of Costly Displays," 245.

95   Henrich, "The Evolution of Costly Displays," 245. Henrich's theory of group evolution seeks to explain the following aspects of religion: "why (1) religions are often associated with prestigious paragons of virtue who make (or made) costly sacrifices; (2) martyrdom is so persuasive; (3) religions and rituals are loaded with sacrifices of various kinds; (4) gods and ancestors want costly acts; and (5) religious leaders often take costly vows, such as those involving poverty and celibacy," (245).

96   Max Weisbuch and Nalini Ambady, "Affective Divergence: Automatic Responses to Others' Emotions Depend on Group Membership," *Journal of Personality and Social Psychology* 95 (2008): 1063–79. In this study the types of groups that they examined were racial, ethnic, cultural groups and also social groups such as basketball players and cat-lovers.

the group membership of the target and of the perceiver."[97] Such psychological studies demonstrate the multitude of ways that issues of identity and membership are inculcated in non-declarative forms. Within the context of a ritualized performance, the multiple displays of emotion can function to elevate the status of the one who performs them by demonstrating to the community that an actual experience has taken place.[98]

From a theological perspective, the bodily expression of emotion in the form of tears can effect other transformations as well, including cleansing the individual from sin[99] and moving the deity to pity. King Hezekiah sheds bitter tears in his desperate straits (2 Kgs 20:3) which God sees (2 Kgs 20:5), thus resulting in the monarch's healing and restoration. So too, the demonstration of tears in the hodayah comes prior to the transformations that are reported in 1QH XVII, 6–38. The speaker expresses confidence in God in various ways by commenting on His kindness, mercies, and right judgment (XVII, 6–18) and reports healing and restoration (XVII, 25–29). There are also a number of statements that employ familial references that emphasize the intimate relationship between God and the speaker, from the very moment of conception.[100]

---

97 Weisbuch and Ambady, "Affective Divergence," 1064; See too H. A. Elfenbein and N. Ambady, "On the Universality and Cultural Specificity of Emotion Recognition: A Meta-Analysis," *Psychological Bulletin* 128 (2002): 203–35.

98 On the ability of ritually performed emotions to effect a status change, see G. L. Ebersole, "The Function of Ritual Weeping Revisited, 185–222.

99 See Elliot R. Wolfson, "Weeping, Death, and Spiritual Ascent in Sixteenth-Century Jewish Mysticism," 209–47; idem, "Weeping, Death, and Spiritual Ascent: Jewish Mysticism," in *Religion and Emotion*, 271–303; Wolfson discusses the tradition of imagining sins recorded on one's forehead and the tears washing them away; he writes, "Karo alludes to the notion that the weeping washes off the mark of sin from one's face, an idea expressed in the *Zohar* based in part on the Talmudic reading of Ezek 9:4 to the effect that the wicked are marked by the angel Gabriel with the letter taw made from blood on their foreheads so that the angels of destruction could rule over them, whereas the righteous are marked with a letter taw made from ink. . . . in relating a story about one such individual, the *Zohar* places the following statement in his mouth: 'Each day I saw my face in a mirror, and I wept before the Holy One, blessed be He. . . on account of that very sin, and with those tears I washed my face'"(288).

100 In the previous hodayah in 1QH XV, 9–36 the speaker reports a transformation—he has become an adoptive father and a nursemaid:

The Judean desert contains within it extremes of climate, pockets of lush tropical regions such as the one surrounding Jericho, moments of extraordinary biodiversity during periodic flash floods, alongside perpetually arid conditions. Like the conceptualized garden space, the Judean desert holds the promise of simultaneity and liminality. Did the author of 1QH XVI, 5-XVII, 36 compose his text in a paradise or garden environ? It is impossible to say where the text of 1QH XVI, 5-XVII, 36 was composed. While the heterotopic site for the visionary experience in this hodayah is not recoverable, the experience of affective reenactment coupled with the bodily experience of linear reading of a scroll can be imagined as the physical experience of the textualized garden that function as the Thirdspace portal. The details in the textualized report are so vivid as to seem real, simulating the phenomenal experience of being in an actual paradise.

In the hodayah known as 1QH XVI, 5-XVII, 36, the speaker conveys an experience of the garden paradise that goes beyond the scripted experiences reported in 1QH XIII, 22-XV, 8, the events described in the garden of Eden as it is known from Gen 2-3, or any other visionary tradition about gardens. In the account of the garden in column XVI, the speaker is transformed from being a viewer into a participant in the garden scene and so comes to enjoy the freedom of lived experience in that space. The composition in 1QH XVI, 5-XVII, 36 can be understood as a report of a mystical experience, and it has the rhetorical quality of an egocentric episodic report. The speaker in 1QH XVI not only gives a detailed account of the variegated vegetation in the garden and its marvelous irrigation; he also reports a participatory role in the scene by claiming to tend the plants by watering (XVI, 17, 22) and hoeing the

---

And Yo[u] and You have made me a father to the sons of kindness (24) and a nursemaid to men of portent. They open the mouth wide like a nu[rsing infant], and like a child delighting in the bosom of (25) its nursemaid. And you have exalted my horn over all who despise me, and the entire [rem]nant of the men at battle against me are sc[attered.] Those who (26) disputed me are like chaff before the wind, and my dominion is over those who scorn me because [You] are my God! You have helped my soul, and You exalt my ray (27) ever higher. I appear in a sevenfold light, in l[ight which] You have [esta]blished for Your glory. *vacat*

Here, in the composition known as 1QH XV, 9-28, familial language is used to position the speaker in a relationship of authority where the speaker is the father of the sons of kindness (אב לבני חסד) and a nursemaid to the men or portent (וכאומן לאנשי מופת), the latter role being reminiscent of Moses himself (Num 11:12).

earth around their roots with his own hand (XVI, 23). While there are several candidates for this role as the gardener of Eden, the speaker does not perfectly follow the scripted role of any of these personalities as they are known from other visionary traditions.[101] Significantly the speaker of the hodayah reports that if he should withdrawal his care, the garden will languish and become an arid wasteland (1QH XVI, 25–27). At first glance, this appears to presume Gen 3:17–18 where the ground will no longer yield its abundance naturally, yielding instead "thorns and thistles" (קוץ ודרדר) with ease. The land must be worked, yet Eden's vegetation is never said to be reduced to this state according to Genesis. It is only outside the mythical garden that the man and the woman must toil the land (Gen 3:23), since Eden remains eternally lush and verdant.

The garden vision in 1QH XVI, 5-XVII, 36 is not simply a literary retelling of other visionary traditions. Instead, the author of this composition appears to have reconstituted memorable elements known from other garden traditions, along with his own personal memories of working the land, and generated this new vision of paradise. In other words, the fully participatory role of the speaker exceeds the conventional scenarios by introducing situations that are not mentioned in other known traditions. The fragile state of the garden, which relies upon the care of the speaker, may mirror the tenuous lived experience in the climate of the speaker's ordinary world since the speaker must dig irrigation ditches by hand, a necessary step in making land arable. Other visionary accounts of Eden do not report that this type of cultivation was needed. Instead, what is often noted is Eden's marvelous self-sufficiency as a naturally well-watered space.

---

101 Enoch is a viable candidate since he is the one who was, according to the *Book of Jubilees,* placed in Eden by God for perpetuity to minister there. Adam is known to have been banished from Eden and to have worked the land outside of paradise, however, according to the *Cave of Treasures* (4.1), Adam is placed into Paradise, inside the Garden of Eden and given the status of a cultic functionary; see Serge Ruzer, "*The Cave of Treasures* on Swearing by Abel's Blood and Expulsion from Paradise: Two Exegetical Motifs in Context," *JECS* 9 (2001): 251–71, here 257. Noah is possibly referenced in the text as the plant of righteousness, but not likely as the gardener. One should also add here, the gardener (YHWH) from the Isaian Song of the Vineyard. The allusions in 1QH XVI, 5-XVII, 36 to the book of Isaiah are well demonstrated by Julie Hughes, *Scriptural Allusions and Exegesis in the Hodayot*, 135–83. The watchers are also described in some traditions as gardeners who come from the heavens.

The text of 1QH XVI, 5-XVII, 36 can be considered a text generated from a heterotopic experience of a reader of 1QH XV, 16–22, who had become transformed into an author who has gained further knowledge about what paradise is like. The specific details about the events in this space can be understood as associative memories of garden traditions that were reconstituted by the author during a religious experience. The engagement of multiple sensory faculties is reflected in the detailed report that has been preserved. Notably, the author has placed himself in the scene, resulting in an egocentric episodic account of the events in that garden space. These details along with the subsequent excruciating laments in 1QH XVI, 27-XVII, 6 possess the quality of an egocentric episodic perspective that characterizes Thirdspatial experiences.

III. Moving On: The Spatial Progression in the Hodayot Scroll

As a heterotopia, the garden is a physical place in the ordinary world that also serves as a liminal space. The ancient conceptualization of the garden was cognizant that these spaces were designed to be within the royal precinct and adjacent to the palace. The palace garden served religious purposes by growing plants that were used in rituals themselves and serving as the space for various cultic observances.[102] As the ceremonial site for the burial of kings, palace gardens were also liminal passageways to the netherworld and simultaneously signify as well Foucault's example of the cemetery as heterotopia.[103]

These ancient conventions for garden spaces are reflected in the Enochic Book of the Watchers, which reports that the throne of God is spatially surrounded by a garden of delightful trees in *1 En.* 24–25. The role of the garden as a liminal space also characterizes traditions

---

102 See Wiseman, "Mesopotamian Gardens," 141–42. The garden was a site for various cultic activities and also for the ritual burial of kings in their function as royal mortuaries. Stavrakopoulou proposes that the garden activities described in Isa 65:3–5; 66:17 refer to the practice of garden mortuaries; Stavrakopoulou, "Exploring the Garden of Uzza," 8–21.

103 Stavrakopoulou ("Exploring the Garden of Uzza") makes the case that the Garden of Uzza was a royal cemetery garden. She discusses the function of gardens as burial sites and so gardens are liminal spaces. Foucault discusses the cemetery as a heterotopia in "Of Other Spaces," 25.

that designate a verdant region close to but just outside the Temple of the LORD. Such is the situation presumed by Ezekiel's vision of the numerous waterways that flow from the Temple and irrigate the nearby area, watering the many varieties of trees that grow there (Ezek 47). So too the Apocalypse of John envisions the New Jerusalem alongside a river of the water of life and a garden where the tree of life grows (Rev 22:1–2). The ancient near eastern practice of constructing a stately garden next to the palace of the king or the temple of the LORD, may explain why Enoch as a cultic functionary finds himself in the Garden of Eden according to the *Book of Jubilees*.

As heterotopias, the garden functioned as a liminal space that marked the boundary just outside the Mesopotamian palace or Temple. The conventional nature of their locations in the ancient near east suggests that the positioning of the garden vision in the scroll of the hodayot is strategic. The composition that includes the lengthy and detailed vision of the gardens, namely 1QH XVI, 5-XVII, 36, can be said to conceptually mark the liminal space of the threshold into the heavens which, I propose, begins just after the full blank line in 1QH XVII, 37.

The detailed report of the garden scene in 1QH XVI, 5–27 can function for a subsequent reader as a rousing description of what it is like to be in paradise. The account targets a reader's sensory registers and can succeed in stimulating his organs of perception such that he succeeds in generating the subjectivity of the rhetorical speaker of the hodayot. The reader can reenact what it is like to be an individual in the Garden of Eden. In this state, the reader can physically experience the bodily sensations that are appropriate for the experiences that he is reenacting. For individuals who exhibit high levels of synesthesia and acute sensory perceptions, focused meditation and affective reenactment of what it is like to be in a garden paradise could arouse emotion memories that disclose further details of its environs. As discussed in chapter four, areas of the brain that are responsible for sensory processing are stimulated in similar ways if the stimuli are actual events or imagined through texts. And so the composition 1QH XVI, 5-XVII, 36 contains vivid rhetorical elements of an egocentric episode experience that suggest a Thirdspace experience of paradise. The garden as heterotopias is a liminal space that allows for the simultaneous experience of real world experiences of paradise with limitless otherworldly possibilities. The composition known as 1QH XVI, 5-XVII, 36 is a report of an individual's experience of paradise, one that would have been accompanied by the expected physical displays of emotion.

The repeated reenactment of the right performative emotions is instrumental, I propose, in generating within a reader the appropriate subjectivity that would predispose him to having a lived experience of paradise. The bodily display of emotion as both physically and psychologically devastating is not so much a response to the revelations that takes place after the fact but rather an affective performance that can be said to allow for the very possibility of a religious experience. The intensity of the performance and the costly display of tears can be said to authenticate the visionary experience that takes place.[104] We might imagine that a reader meditating upon the scripted emotions in 1QH XIII, 22-XV, 8, a composition discussed in the previous chapter, subsequently generating his own vision of paradise from the glimpses given in 1QH XIV, 15–22. In such a scenario, the strong sensation of fear from meditating upon 1QH XIII, 22-XV, 8 led to the generation of a Thirdspatial account of lived experience in paradise (1QH XVI, 5-XVII, 36). And so the arousal of emotion can be said to be the instrumental technique and the necessary precondition for achieving further visionary experiences. In 1QH XVI, 5-XVII, 36, the lament of anguish is sequenced after the vision of paradise in the textualized report that has been preserved, but it may be the case that the vision and the emotional display were experienced simultaneously, with the vision being reported as prior to the physical effect in accord with the pattern seen in Daniel 10. Performative emotions secure the authenticity of these anonymous reports of what the Garden of Eden is like in the absence of an author's name, real or pseudonymous.

The composition known as 1QH XVI, 5-XVII, 36 is a report of an individual's heterotopic experience of paradise and can serve for subsequent readers as a Secondspatial affective script to reenact. A later reader of this composition can experience the religious geography of paradise through the phenomenal experiences of the first person "I" and would be compelled by the text to imagine his own body in its entirety as he read and reread the physical agonies that are mapped out. Meditation on suffering is capable of generating a powerful affective response in the reader, resulting in the creation of the subjectivity of the imaginal body in the reader himself. The hodayah enumerates the entirety of

---

104 Here I agree with Merkur that affective experiences guide the visionary's journey and experiences.

the imaginal body from head to toe. These body sites can be imagined as cues for an ancient reader who sought to reenact the emotions of fear and anguish in the trembling of his own limbs and the weeping of real tears.

With respect to the spatial progression of the hodayot, the garden in the hodayot functions in a synchronic reading as a space of simultaneity and liminality marking the progressive journey of the hodayot reader into the heavens. Simultaneity arises from traditions that gardens were artificially constructed spaces of a ruler that contained a broad representative sampling of the exotic cultivars from the various regions of his empire. The aspect of liminality arises from the spatial design of gardens in close proximity to the palace. Gardens were adjacent to the palace of the king and the temple of the deity and so anticipated encounters with them and are strongly correlated with events of judgment and fear.

According to Foucault, heterotopias do not necessarily need to resemble or correspond to experiences that are had there, but they do need to be an actual place in ordinary space and time. The linear directional experience of reading demanded by the apparatus of a scroll and the goal of re-creating the affective script of the text serve as the actual physical experiences that allow access into the garden as heterotopia. A reader of the hodayot who imagined himself as being in the Garden of Eden also understood himself as standing at the threshold of the heavenly abode, in close proximity to the space where terrifying encounters with the deity and other heavenly beings take place. The Garden of Eden, when understood as a heterotopia, demarcates a liminal space in the hodayot on the journey to the heavens.

IV. Entry into the Heavens

The reading of the Qumran hodayot is oriented towards the heavens. The rhetorical "I" and the vivid language about the body function to bring the ancient reader to the celestial realm through the highly contoured religious geography in the scroll. This chapter, along with chapters three and four, has argued that the spatial experiences described in the hodayot collection are organized in a progressive series moving out from places of punishment into places of paradise and into the heavens. Like the phenomenal experience of reading a scroll, the movement in the hodayot collection is linear and culminates with an extraordinary experience in the heavenly liturgy. A significant spatial shift into the heavenly realm is marked by the blank lines at 1QH XVII, 37 after which the spaces become situated in the celestial realm.

After the hodayot speaker offers his discursive report of the Garden of Eden in 1QH XVI, 5-XVII, 36, a scribe has recorded a full blank line appears at XVII, 37 which delineates the space of paradise from the heavenly realm. Notably it is after this point in the collection that the affective cadence of the hodayot becomes joyful. This change in affect is accompanied by a proliferation of blessing formulae throughout columns XVII to XX: they appear twice at 1QH XVII, 38 and XVIII, 16; three times in the single composition known as 1QH XIX, 6-XX, 6 at lines 30, 32, 35; and twice in XXI, 18; XXII, 34.[105] These blessing formulae occur after the blank line in 1QH XVII, 37 and can also be understood, I propose, as marking a spatial shift into the celestial realm. This final section discusses how these blessing formulae can be understood as a sign of the lyrical's speaker's entry into the heavens.

In the otherworldly journeys of Enoch, the use of the blessing formula appears as a strategy, according to Daniel Merkur, for managing unbridled terror:

> The distinctive character of the apocalyptists' prayers bears emphasis. The prayers were not petitions making requests, nor were they the acts of flattery that the terms worship, praise, and blessing might be taken to imply. They were confessions of theology. The prayers asserted doctrinal beliefs about God. In their experiential context, they articulated reasons for confidence in God. Recited until the words of confidence became heartfelt, they induced emotional states of faith; and the faith counteracted their anxieties.[106]

Merkur understands the practice of hymn singing and praising God as a technique for easing the fear that has been incrementally mounting. In the case of the journey pattern in *1 En.* 20–36, Enoch first visits places of punishment and then moves to pleasant garden scenes in a general movement from west to east. The journeys reported in *1 En.* 20–36 differ from those in *1 En.* 17–19 in that certain of the former reports show a conscious use of a literary form that includes the blessing formula.[107] Just as a blessing formula appears after Enoch's report of his jour-

---

105 Blessing formulae also appear in the first group of the CH in 1QH col. IV, 21, 29, 38; V, 15; VI, 19; VIII, 26; but the compositions in the first CH are not attested in what we presume to be the oldest copy of 1QH, namely 4Q428.

106 Merkur, "The Visionary Practices of Jewish Apocalyptists," 140.

107 There are three journeys in this part of the Book of the Watchers which correspond to a four-fold pattern: Enoch's journey to the Mountain of the Dead in

ney to the frightening places of punishment in *1 En.* 22:1–14, so too an editor has inserted a blessing formula immediately following the terrifying report in 1QH XIII, 7–21. The curious editorial addition of a blessing formula at 1QH XIII, 22 would function, according to Merkur's reasoning, as a strategy to manage the negative emotions aroused by re-enacting the fear of being in the lion's den (1QH XIII, 7–21).

In both the Enochic Book of the Watchers and in Daniel, a blessing is uttered after the seer receives a vision.[108] In the Enochic Book of the Watchers, the use of the blessing formula brings with it a notable change in the affective cadence. While the hodayot do not adhere to the specifics of the four-fold literary form followed by *1 En.* 20–36, the appearance of the blessing formula in 1QH XIII, 22 may reflect a general pattern attested to in the Book of the Watchers of concluding a terrifying vision of a place of punishment with a blessing formula of some type. In other words, the practice of including hymns and blessings in apocalyptic visionary literature may serve, as Merkur proposes, as a practical strategy for managing the affective experiences aroused by the re-enactment of these texts. Later in the hodayot scroll, a series of blessing formulae appears in the hodayah 1QH XVII, 38-XIX, 5. Similar to the instance in 1QH XIII, 22, the blessing begins the composition at 1QH XVII, 38, but here a blessing formula appears immediately after a full blank line in 1QH XVII, 37. Later, a second blessing formula appears in 1QH XVIII, 16, again immediately after a full blank line in XVIII, 15. The next composition, known as 1QH XIX, 6-XX, 6, has been called a liturgical hodayah by Esther Chazon,[109] and it contains three

---

1 En. 22:1–14; his visit to the Mountain of God and the Tree of Life in *1 En.* 24:2–25:7; and his journey to Jerusalem, the Center of the Earth and the Place of Punishment in *1 En.* 26:1–27:5. Nickelsburg describes the literary form for these visits as having the following elements: (1) Introduction to the locale; (2) Description of the vision; (3) Stereotypical dialogue between the seer and his angelic guide; and (4) a concluding praise of God, oftentimes accompanied by a blessing formula; see Nickelsburg, *1 Enoch 1*, 291–93. So too Daniel has a nighttime vision and then blesses the LORD in Dan 2:19–23.

108 So noted by Eileen Schuller, "Some Observations on Blessings of God in Texts from Qumran," in *Of Scribes and Scrolls: Studies on the Hebrew Bible, Intertestamental Judaism, and Christian Origins* (ed. Harold W. Attridge, John J. Collins, Thomas H. Tobin; College Theology Society Resources in Religion 5; New York: University Press of America, 1990), 133–43, here 142 n. 49; she cites *1 En.* 25:7; 27:5; 36:4; 81:3; 90:40; and Dan 2:19.

109 Chazon, "Liturgical Function in the Cave 1 Hodayot Collection," 135–52. It contains some lexical similarities to 1QH XI, 20–37 (137–144). The term

blessing formulae near the end (XIX, 30, 32, 35). The affective cadence of the hodayot at this point has turned firmly to rejoicing. 1QH XIX, 6-XX, 6 contains multiple references to liturgical singing and praise (XIX, 7–10; 16–17; 26–30). Other blessing formulae appear at 1QH XXII, 34 and in XXVI, 31. As in the Book of the Watchers, the use of the blessing formulae in the Qumran hodayot also coincides with a joyful affect.

While Merkur offers an intriguing proposal for understand how the blessing formulae function to manage the mounting experience of terror, I believe that it is also important to recognize how blessings signal phenomenal spatial movements into a new religious geography– the heavenly realm. Reading these formulae through the lens of critical spatial theory can complement Merkur's proposal that the blessings function psychologically. In the case of the Book of the Watchers, the journey reports in *1 En.* 20–36 conclude with a summary unit and a noticeably extended blessing passage.[110] This summary unit does not follow the typical Book of the Watchers literary form of a dialogue with an angelic intermediary. According to Nickelsburg, this section of the Book of the Watchers can be understood as a concluding summary of Enoch's journeys that also anticipates events in the later Book of the Luminaries (*1 En.* 72–82).[111] In the Book of the Luminaries, Enoch reports numerous heavenly wonders. The uncommonly dense clustering of blessings in *1 En.* 35 may mark a Secondspatial move into the heavenly space and the heavenly realia described by the Book of the Luminaries. Again, I do not wish to suggest that the hodayot were *modeled upon* the Enochic journey visions; however, I believe that the blessing for-

---

"position" (מעמד) according to Philip Alexander (*The Mystical Texts*) has "a technical sense in Qumran mysticism" denoting "one's station in heaven" (87 n. 4). Alexander writes that this word in 4Q405 20 ii-21-22, 14 refers to the position assigned to each angel in the heavenly host (87 n. 4).

110 Nickelsburg, *1 Enoch 1*, 331–32.

111 Nickelsburg and VanderKam, *1 Enoch*, 6–7. There the authors describe significant differences between the Aramaic fragments of this work and what is thought to be the much abridged version preserved in surviving Ethiopic manuscripts. Along with the Book of the Watchers, the Book of the Luminaries is considered to be among the oldest of the texts in *1 En.*, containing traditions that date back to the third century B.C.E. or possibly earlier. It is thought by many that what interrupts the transition from the Book of the Watchers to the Book of the Luminaries, namely the Book of Parables, is a much later addition. If so, it is conceivable that the Book of the Luminaries immediately followed the Book of the Watchers.

mulae in *1 En.* 22:14 and *1 En.* 27:5 offer intriguing parallels that can illuminate their function in the progressive spatialization of the Qumran hodayot.

I propose that the blessing formulae can be understood as marking spatial shifts into the heavenly realm, and they can be said to signal the phenomenal experience of a theophanic encounter with heavenly beings, when the blessing is understood with the aspect of greeting.[112] Blessing God can be contextualized within ancient social practices that recognized assymetrical relationships of power between the supplicant and the deity. One problem with Merkur's proposal is that it collapses blessing formulae together with other forms of praise and understands them solely as affect-regulating discourses,[113] overlooking the fact that blessing differs from praise in significant ways. Unlike praise, blessing has a reciprocal aspect in that it can both be received and given by God, whereas praise can only be offered to God. Christopher Frechette's examination of blessing from the perspective of its ancient near eastern context has yielded significant findings which, I propose, reflect phenomenal aspects of spatiality. He notes that the Akkadian verb *karābu* enjoys a semantic range of meaning similar to the Hebrew '*brk*' (ברך) ("bless, praise, greet") and is used in the same way insofar as the deity can be either the subject or the object.[114] According to Benno Landsberger, the Akkadian *karābu* predominantly means a greeting consisting

---

112 Notice that in the *Ma'aseh Merkavah* prayers open with a blessing addressed to God, and close with a doxology and blessing. The opening blessing functions as a salutation according to Michael D. Swartz, *Mystical Prayer in Ancient Judaism: An Analysis of Ma'aseh Merkavah* (TSAJ 28; Tübingen: Mohr Siebeck, 1992), 15.

113 Here Merkur presumes a common view proposed by Claus Westermann, *Praise and Lament in the Psalms* (Atlanta: John Knox, 1965, 1981), 25–30 who said that the two verbs for blessing and thanksgiving were closely related; yet this does not account for the distinct reciprocal aspect of the verb "to bless" which can receive God as subject and object.

114 See Christopher Frechette, "Blessing 1: Ancient Near East," in *The Encyclopedia of the Bible and Its Reception* (ed. H.-J. Klauck et al; Berlin: de Gruyter, forthcoming). Frechette gestures here to Benno Landsberger's early discussion of the Akkadian *karābu* in his essay, "Das 'gute Wort'," *Altorientalische Studien: Bruno Meissner zum sechzigsten Geburtstag am 25. April 1928* (MAOG 4/1; Leipzig: Harrassowitz, 1928), 294–321. I wish to acknowledge Christopher Frechette's generosity for providing me with an advance copy of his essay on "Blessing" and his forthcoming monograph, *Mesopotamian Ritual-prayers (Šuillas): A Case Study Investigating Idiom, Rubric, Form, and Function* (Alter Orient und Altes Testament 379; Münster: Ugarit-Verlag, forthcoming).

of a blessing gesture and formula. It presumes an asymmetrical reciprocity between the one who is greeted and the one who expresses the greeting:

> In der Bedeutung *karābu* dominiert vielmehr das Element des <<Grüssens>>, wobei sich der Gruss aus Segensgestus und -formel zusammensetzt. Nichts anderes aber als das Verharren in der Haltung des Segnenden, das ununterbrochene Sprechen frommer Formeln findet statt, wenn der Mensch der Gottheit bittend naht, häufig noch seine Bitte durch ein Geschenk unterstützend . . . . Auch dieser Bedeutung von k., die sich oft nicht anders als durch <<beten>> übersetzen lässt und in der Tat der allgemeinste Ausdruck für die Anbetung ist, geht niemals das wesentliche Moment des Grüssens, die Gegenseitigkeit, verloren: die zahlreichen Adorationsszenen zeigen die Gegenseitigkeit des Gestus zwischen Mensch und Gott.[115]

Frechette reasons on the basis of these common traits that the Hebrew verb "to bless" may also share other functional aspects of this Akkadian verb.[116] According to Frechette, situating the Hebrew ברך in its ancient near eastern context may even highlight a significant aspect of this term's social function that has been overlooked; one that reflects aspects of spatiality. In addition to its meaning as praise, "*brk*" can function as a greeting exchanged by parties of differing social status. In the ancient near east, the interaction between subordinates and superiors was closely governed by particular social conventions, which are reflected in the glyptic scenes to which Landsberger refers as *Adorazionsszenen*. Annette Zgoll terms these conventions the *Audienz-Konzept*.[117] Following Frechette, I will refer to these social contexts as an audience. Such exchanges are constituted by both asymmetry and reciprocity. These high-

---

115 Landsberger, "Das 'gute Wort'," 295.

116 Christopher Frechette, "What does 'Bless the LORD!' Mean? Interpreting Hebrew *brk* in its ANE context," Paper presented at the Catholic Biblical Association Annual Meeting (Worcester, Mass.: Assumption College, August 7, 2011). Frechette writes there that, "[w]hat Landsberger has shown for *karābu* seems applicable also to *brk*: it conveys a sense of greeting that served to recognize or to assert the existence of a favorable and reciprocal relationship with implications for the benefits and obligations proper to both parties within it."

117 Annette Zgoll draws on the non-religious story of the "Poor man from Nippur" a novella about a man who asks the city official for assistance, Zgoll, "Audienz—Ein Modell zum Verständnis mesopotamischer Handerhebungsrituale: Mit einer Deutung der Novelle vom *Armen Mann von Nippur*," *BaghM* 34 (2003): 181–99, here 189–97. See too Friedhelm Hartenstein, *Das Angesicht JHWHs: Studien zum seinen höfischen und kultischen Bedeutungshintergrund in den Psalmen und in Exodus 32–34* (FAT 55; Tübingen: Mohr Siebeck, 2008), 9.

ly structured social encounters between a subordinate and a superior reinforce the relational obligations and expectations of each to the other.
Both the supplicant and the ruler anticipate various benefits: the former
anticipates the benefit of a petition that is granted, and the latter enjoys
the public recognition of power and status.[118] Zgoll, drawing primarily
upon non-religious textual evidence, identifies ten elements of these
scenarios. In the fifth one that she identifies, the *Grußworte Bittsteller*,
the individual with lesser status offers blessings to his superior.[119] Greater
awareness of the formal social conventions that governed interactions
between subordinates and superiors can contextualize and enrich the
understanding of prayer generally in the ancient near east as an encounter that presumes asymmetrical social relationships involving the reciprocal exchange of benefits between the parties involved.[120]

The contextualization of prayer's rhetorical elements in the social
conventions of the ancient near east can help reconstruct the phenomenal experiences of certain prayers as an audience or as an encounter
with the deity.[121] According to Alan Lenzi, these rhetorical elements

---

118 Zgoll, "Tabelle 1: Vergleich profane Audienz-Zeremonie—Handerhebungsri-
    tuale," 196.
119 The "*Grußworte Bittsteller*" or the "supplicant's words of greeting" can be un-
    derstood to correspond to the hymnic invocation of the ancient Mesopotamian
    shuilla; Zgoll, "Audienz—Eine Modell zum Verständnis mesopotamischer
    Handerhebungsrituale," 196. See too the discussion by Alan Lenzi, "Invoking
    the God: Interpreting Invocations in Mesopotamian Prayers and Biblical La-
    ments of the Individual," *JBL* 129 (2010): 303–15, here 311–312 n. 20.
120 Frechette has applied the social aspects of the audience scene to his discussion of
    the ancient near eastern ritual "*Shuilla*," what is otherwise known as the 'lifting
    of the hand' ritual in Akkadian prayers; see "Shuillas," in A. Lenzi, C. Frech-
    ette, and A. Zernecke, "Introduction," in *Reading Akkadian Prayers and Hymns:
    An Introduction* (ed. Alan Lenzi; ANEM 3; Atlanta: SBL, 2011), 1–68. He
    writes: "[g]iven the lexical and visual evidence that such greetings were ex-
    changed in a reciprocal manner, this gesture would have provided a particularly
    apt ritual focus for expressing both the desire to (re-)establish such a relationship
    with the deity and the anticipation of the deity's acceptance of this relationship
    and favorable response to the petitions presented" (35).
121 Frechette ("Shuillas") writes, "[t]he basic structure of and rationale for Akkadi-
    an shuillas manifest the concept of an 'audience,' a fundamental situation of an-
    cient Near Eastern culture concerning ceremonies for a meeting in which
    someone presents a request to someone of a higher social status. Noting that
    other Mesopotamian ritual-prayers also reflect such a rationale, one scholar ar-
    gues that the shuilla-rubric itself offers a key to the distinctive rationale for these
    ritual-prayers. Preferring a literal translation of the *shuilla*-rubric, he interprets
    its idiomatic meaning as concretely grounded in a formal gesture of greeting ap-

can be understood as a formal protocol followed by parties of unequal status.[122] One example of this is found in Daisuke Shibata's study of a specific collection of *shuilla* prayers written in the Emesal-dialect of the Sumerian language. These prayers were used in ritual scenarios that reenact the return of the deity into the cultic worship space after a processional.[123] Shibata writes:

> To sum up, the evidence available so far reveals that the Šuilla-prayers were recited in processions, especially those from and to an *Akītu*-house, address-ing a deity, for whose sake the procession concerned was carried out. It be-came also clear that the prayers were recited very often during the late phase of these processions to the returning deity, although it is not exclud-ed that some prayers might have been recited during another phase in the processions, such as the beginning, as discussed below. Apparently Šuilla-prayers were performed sometimes (if not often) in the royal presence, which is also suggested by the formal blessing upon the Assyrian king ap-pended in Neo-Assyrian manuscripts.[124]

The *shuilla* ritual of a gesture and a greeting presumes an audience scene that seeks to reenact face-to-face encounters between the worshippers and the deity. In the ritual context of the *shuilla*, the supplicant's en-trance into and exit from the presence of the deity is governed by the formal social conventions that apply to all encounters between subordi-nates and superiors.[125] Asymmetry and reciprocity govern the encoun-ters between subordinates and superiors in ritual and ordinary contexts.

Studies of ancient near eastern social conventions can illuminate how Israel's rituals and prayers were phenomenally imagined and expe-

---

propriate when entering the court of a god or king and analogous to a military salute in that it demonstrates recognition of an asymmetrical relationship be-tween the subordinate who offers the gesture and the one of higher status who receives it and who may have been understood to offer a reciprocal gesture of some kind" (31). Some scholars say that the shuilla ritual and the accompa-nying greeting formula reenacts the event of being in the presence of the ruler.

122 Lenzi, "Mesopotamian Prayers and Biblical Laments," 309.

123 "Ritual Contexts and Mythological Explanations of the Emesal Šuilla-Prayers in Ancient Mesopotamia," 45 (2010): 67–85. Shibata writes, "noteworthy that in each case the prayer was recited in a very similar situation, as follows: the cultic image of the deity addressed returned from a procession to his/her cella, and then took a seat upon his/her dais" (75).

124 Shibata, "Ritual Contexts and Mythological Explanations," 74.

125 Lenzi writes that in general, the Akkadian *shuilla* texts reflect the asymmetry of a supplicant who offers his prayer to a high-ranking cosmic god. Often the peti-tion is for assistance against other deities. Lenzi, "Mesopotamian Prayers and Biblical Laments," 311.

rienced since Israel conceptualized herself vis-à-vis the deity as a vassal to a suzerain. Moshe Greenberg highlights this asymmetrical relationship between the supplicant and the deity as an operative model for ancient Israel's prayer to God.[126] Frechette proposes that the Hebrew blessing, when functioning as a greeting, should be understood with this aspect of reciprocity and asymmetry, similar to what is presumed in ancient near eastern audience scenes.[127] The element of reciprocity in the exchange of the Hebrew *brk*, indicated by its semantic range of having God either as the subject or object, is one that has not been considered adequately by previous scholars.[128] The reciprocal aspect of blessing is highlighted by specific instances in the Hebrew Bible that presume its use as a conventional greeting among unequals. Frechette discusses the use of blessing as a greeting at the beginning of Jacob's audience with Pharaoh in Gen 47:7 and as a farewell during his subsequent exit at 47:10.[129] Another clear example of the reciprocal aspect of the Hebrew *brk* is found in Ps 134:1–3, which states that the people bless God in v. 1 and that they are in turn blessed by Him in v. 3.[130] These cultural and semantic aspects of prayer and the Hebrew blessing are overlooked by scholars who wish to elide blessing into prayer. Blessings range of meanings includes functional similarities that it shares with

---

126 Moshe Greenberg, *Biblical Prose Prayer as a Window to the Popular Religion of Ancient Israel* (Taubman Lectures in Jewish Studies; Berkeley: University of California Press, 1983). He writes: "The closest human analogy to petitionary prayer will be a petitionary address to a king or some other powerful person" (20–21). That ancient Israel imagined its discourse with God in patterns analogous to asymmetrical human relationships, is also discussed in Karel van der Toorn, "Sources in Heaven: Revelation as a Scholarly Construct in Second Temple Judaism," in *Kein Land für sich allein: Studien zum Kulturkontakt in Kanaan, Israel/ Palästina und Ebirnâri für Manfred Weippert zum 65. Geburtstag* (ed. Ulrich Hübner and Ernst Axel Knauf; OBO 186; Göttingen: Vandenhoeck & Ruprecht, 2002), 265–77. See the discussion by A. Lenzi, "Mesopotamian Prayers and Biblical Laments of the Individual," 303–15.

127 Christopher Frechette, "What does 'Bless the LORD!' Mean?"

128 Frechette argues that previous scholars, notably Josef Scharbert, "*brk*," *TDOT* 2 (Grand Rapids: Eerdmans, 1977), 279–308 and Christopher W. Mitchell, *The Meaning of brk "To Bless" in the Old Testament* (SBLDS 95; Atlanta, Scholars Press, 1987), have failed to adequately draw attention to the social conventions that inform the Hebrew use of *brk*; Frechette, "What does 'Bless the LORD!' Mean?"

129 Frechette also discusses Joab blessing David in 2 Sam 14:22; and also 1 Kgs 1:47–48 in "What does 'Bless the LORD!' Mean?"

130 Frechette proposes that Ps. 134 reflects the conventions of an audience.

the Akkadian *karābu* as a social exchange that recognizes status differences among the parties involved. Its ability to also function as a greeting exchanged between a superior and a subordinate in face-to-face encounters is an aspect of reciprocity that distinguish it from other forms of praise.

This distinctive reciprocal aspect of blessing can shed light on the placement of the blessing formulae in the hodayot and how they convey spatiality. When blessing is understood with this aspect of greeting, the presence of the formula can function as a signal that the imaginal body of the speaker has entered into the audience of heavenly beings. In such a scenario, offering a blessing to God is an entirely appropriate way of greeting the deity and other heavenly beings as etiquette would demand.

Given that blessing carries the connotation of a greeting exchanged in a face-to-face encounter between unequals, the blessing formula, commonly cited as uttered in the heavenly liturgy, can be understood as a sign of the phenomenal experience of being in the real presence of heavenly beings, including the deity Himself. By joining this space, the human speaker offers a greeting in a conventional manner that imitates the recognition that the angelic beings eternally offer to Him. When the distinctive reciprocal aspect of blessing is recognized, the profusion of blessings that appear after the full blank line in 1QH XVII, 37 can be understood, I propose, as a sign that the speaker has moved into the heavenly space. At 1QH XVII, 38, the blessing, preserved in a fragmentary state, can be understood as the worshipper offering the deity a greeting of recognition and a sign of his movement into the real presence of God. There are other features that suggest that the human speaker now finds himself in the presence of esteemed heavenly beings. The compositional unit XVII, 38–14 begins with a blessing formula: "B[less]ed are Yo[u, O Lord]," which is followed predictably by sensation of unworthiness in the *Niedrigkeitsdoxologien* in 1QH XVIII, 5–9. The theological pattern of stating one's unworthiness immediately after seeing a vision of the heavenly realms resembles the prophet Isaiah's experience of the heavenly throne room in Isa 6 and his declaration that he is unclean. Immediately afterward the *Niedrigkeitsdoxologien*, this series of declarations of God's incomparable power and glory appears:

> (10) Behold (הנה)! You are the chief of angels and king of the glorious ones! Lord of every spirit and Ruler over every creature!
> (11) Apart from you nothing is done; Nor does anyone know (anything) without Your will!

There is no one except You!
(12) There is none like You in strength!
There is none comparable to Your glory!
As for Your strength, there is no price!
And who (13) among all the great creatures of Your wonder can maintain
the strength to position himself before Your glory?
(14) And what then is he who returns to his dust,
that he should maintain (his) str[en]gth?
Only for Your glory have You done all these things![131]

Here, the speaker of the hodayot expresses the phenomenal sensation of
being in the presence of God by employing the language of visual perception that frequently appears in apocalyptic visionary reports: "be-
hold."[132] According to Daniel Merkur, literary markers like this one
are a reference to a visualization process, what he calls the "meditative
act of constructing a mental image."[133] This, in addition to the litany of
praise that follows, can be understood as a report of a theophanic experience in which the blessing can be said to mark the speaker's audience
with the deity. A similar scenario can be imagined in the blessing that
appears in 1QH XVIII, 16 where shortly thereafter the speaker uses theophanic language of first-hand visual perception and declares: "I, according to my knowledge in [Your] truth, [shall sing in praise of
Your kindness], and when I gaze upon Your glory, I shall recount
Your wonders" (1QH XVIII, 22–23). Again, the perceptual language
of "gazing" suggests an experiential vision of the deity as the speaker
finds himself in the presence of God. These passages in 1QH XVII,
38 and XVIII, 16 follow the ancient rhetorical convention for visionary
reports that Edith Humphrey identifies as a *demonstratio*.[134] These ele-

---

131 1QH XVIII, 10–14
132 As Humphrey discusses in *And I Turned to See the Voice*, this is an example of the
    vividness of the visionary experience that is communicated by the rhetoric of
    seeing. These are the rhetorical elements that help to construct an event with
    experiential immediacy, L. Lieber, "The Rhetoric of Participation," 119–147.
133 Dan Merkur, "Cultivating Visions through Exegetical Meditations," 80. He in-
    cludes with the expression "behold!" and active references to seeing or gazing,
    other types of "passive constructions such as 'And he showed me' or 'said to
    me' [all of which] signified the onset of a spontaneously or autonomously un-
    folding vision, subsequent to an effort of meditation" (80). Elliot R. Wolfson
    describes this passage in 1QH XVIII, 22–23 as "knowledge of divine truth is
    equated with visually gazing at the glory, which occasions the recitation of
    God's mysteries," in "Seven Mysteries of Knowledge," 208.
134 Edith Humphrey ("To Rejoice or Not to Rejoice? Rhetoric and the Fall of
    Satan in Luke 10:17–24 and Revelation 12:1–17," in *The Reality of Apoca-*

ments describe the heavenly space as a context for a dynamic exchange of speech that presumes the speaker experientially finds himself in the real presence of the heavenly beings.

As the reader moves along in the hodayot collection, spatial descriptions of the heavenly realm become increasingly detailed, and along with them are passages that describe the transformation of the speaker in the company of angels.[135] In the composition known as 1QH XIX, 6-XX, 6, a tri-partite blessing formula appears at XIX, 30, 32, and 36.

Text of 1QH XIX, 6-XX, 6

(6) I thank You, O my God, for you have dealt wonderfully with dust, You have worked so very ^{very} powerfully with a creature of clay. As for me, what am I? For (7) You have [enlighten]ed me in the counsel of Your truth, and You have given me insight into Your wonderful deeds. You put thanksgivings in my mouth and upon my tongue (8) [a psal]m; The utterance of my lips (forms) the foundation of joyous song. I shall sing of Your kindness and I will meditate on Your strength all (9) day long. I will bless Your name continually and I will recount Your glory among the sons of Adam; in the abundance of Your goodness (10) my soul delights. As for me, I know that Your mouth is truth and in Your hand is righteousness; in Your thought (11) is all knowledge and in Your strength is all power; and all glory is with You. In Your anger are all the agonizing judgments, (12) but in Your goodness is an abundance of pardons, and Your compassion is for all the sons of Your favor. Because You have made them know the counsel of Your truth. (13) And in the mysteries of Your wonder You have given them insight. For Your glory's sake You have purified Enoch/a mortal from transgression, in order to sanctify himself (14) for You from all abominations of filth and the guilt of unfaithfulness, in order to unite wth the sons of Your truth; in the lot with (15) Your holy ones (להוחד עם בני אמתך ובגורל עם קדושכה). To raise the dead from the dust of worms up to the counsel of [Your] t[ruth]; and from a perverse spirit up to

---

lypse: Rhetoric and Politics in the Book of Revelation [ed. David L. Barr; SBLSS 39; Atlanta: SBL, 2006], 113–25) writes that the *demonstratio* was "an ancient rhetorical move in which the argument is vividly depicted before the eyes of the audience" (114); see *Ad Herrenium* IV.55.68. In the Book of the Watchers, Enoch similarly employs the rhetoric of seeing and blessing: "And when I *saw*, I *blessed*—and I shall always bless—the Lord of glory, who has wrought great and glorious wonders to show his great deeds to his angels and to the spirits of human beings, so that they might see the work of his might and glorify the deeds of his hands and bless him forever" (*1 En.* 36:4).

135 Wolfson, "Seven Mysteries of Knowledge," describes 1QH XIX, 4–6 and 10–14 as the "transformation into the angelic elite who stand before the throne ('sons of truth,' 'everlasting host,' and 'spirits of knowledge'), blessing the divine name, and utterance of hymns through which the supernal glory is recounted" (209).

Your understanding (להרים מעפר תולעת מתים לסוד א[מתכה] ומרוח נעוה לבינתכה);[136] (16) in order to position himself in place before You with the eternal hosts and spirits [of eternity] (ולהתיצב במעמד לפניכה עם צבא עד ורוחו[ת עולם]);[137] and in order to be renewed with all that i[s] (17) and will be and with those who know in a single joyous song. *vacat*

(18) [And as for me,][138] I thank You, O my God, I exalt You, O my Rock! And in the doing of wonders [ ] (19) [ ] for You have made known to me the counsel of truth; and [You have given me insight] into the myster]ies of wonder; and You have made me understand Your wondrous deeds; (20) And You have revealed to me [Yo]ur [wondr]ous works; and so I will gaze upon [ ] kindness. And I know (21) [tha]t righteousness if Yours, and by Your kindness [they] are judged [ ] and annihilation without Your compassion. (22) But as for me, a font for bitter sorrow has been opened [ ] and toil is not hidden from my eyes; (23) when I knew the inclinations of man, and I un[derstood] the response of humankind [and I recognized the lam]ent of sin and the agony of (24) guilt. They enter into my heart and penetrate my bones. [ ] and to sigh a lament (25a) and a groan on the lyre of lamentation for all grei[v]ous mourning [ ] (25) grief and bitter wailing until injustice has ceased, and the[re is no pain] and there is no affliction to make one weak. And then (26) I shall sing praises on the lyre of salvation, (on) the harp of jo[y, (on) the tambourine of rejoi]cing, (on) the flute of praise without (27) ceasing. Who among all Your creatures is able to recount al[l] Your [wonders?] All of their mouths shall praise (28) Your name forever and ever. They shall bless You according to [their] insight [and in all the end]s (of the earth) they shall declare together (29) with the sound of joyous song. There is neither grief nor groaning, and injustice [shall be found] no [longer.] You shall make Your truth shine forth (30) for eternal glory and everlasting peace. *vacat*

TRI-PARTITE BLESSING

Blessed are You, [O Lord, t]hat You have given to Your servant (31) the insight of knowledge to understand Your wonders and a [re]{p}[ly of the tongue to] recount the abundance of Your kindness. (32) **Blessed** are You, O God of compassion and grace in accordance with Your grea[t] p[o]wer and the abundance of Your truth, and the plentitu[de] (33) of Your kindness among all Your creatures. Gladden the soul of Your servant with Your truth and cleanse me (34) with Your righteousness. For just as I waited for Your goodness, so I hope for Your kindness and [Your] pardons. (35) You

---

136 This passage expresses imagery of vertical movement.
137 Cf. the language at 1QH XI, 22−23 and also XXVI, 36.
138 Stegemann reports seeing the trace of a letter at the beginning of this line, and so he understands this to be a unit continuing the hodayah; Stegemann, "The Number of Psalms," 216.

have opened up my shattering pains (פתחתה מש؟רי)[139] and You have comforted me in my grief for I have depended upon Your compassion. **Blessed** are
Yo[u] (36) O Lord, for You have worked these things, and You place p[s]al
[ms] of thanksgiving in the mouth of Your servant [   ] (37) and a supplication for favor as well as a suitable reply. And You have established for me
a wor[k of   ] (38) and I shall maint[ain strength] [   ] (39) and
You   [   ] (40) [Your] truth] (41) and I [   ] (42) [   ]

Col. XX
(1) [   ] (2) [   ] (3) [   ] (4) [   ] my soul is wide open [   ] (5) [   ]
in joy and [rejoicing and I will dwel]l safely in a ho[ly] {p[eaceful]} dwelling, [in] qui{e}tness and in ease (6) [in pea]ce and a blessing is in the tents
of glory and salvation. I will praise Your name in the midst of those who
fear You.

The cluster of blessing formulae includes spatial markers that the speaker
is physically positioned in the heavenly liturgy: "in order to be positioned in place before You with the everlasting hosts and spirits [of eter-
nity]; and in order to be renewed with all that i[s] and will be and with
those who know in a single joyous song" (1QH XIX, 16–17; cf. XI,
22–23). Elliot Wolfson describes this hodayah as referring "to the composition of liturgical poetry, which is predicated on the imaginal excursion into the theophanic realm, an excursion that breaks down the bar-
rier of angelic and human, celestial and mundane."[140] Immediately prior
to the three-fold blessing formulae, jubilant affect is expressed by a rousing description of liturgical music and praise (1QH XIX, 26–27). The
three blessings found in this composition also function well as a fitting
introduction to the lengthy and detailed description of the celestial bodies and their mysterious circuitry that begins the composition known as
1QH XX, 7-XXII, 42:

> (7) [For the Instruct]or: thanksgivings and a prayer, to cast oneself down
> and supplicating unceasingly at all times; with the coming of light (8) for
> [its] domini[on], at the appointed times of the day according to its order,
> in accordance with the statutes of the great luminary. At the turning of eve-
> ning when the fading of (9) light (marks) the beginning of the dominion of
> darkness during the period of nighttime, it is within in its appointed time
> until the turning of morning. At the end of (10) its (i.e., darkness) gather-

---

139 The word for "shattering pain" appears frequently in 1QH XI, 9 (twice), 10,
11, 12, 13, 17; also in 1QH XIV, 26 and in 1QH XVI, 32 and XVII, 4, 7;
and suggests a continuation of this imagery from col. XI.
140 Wolfson, "Seven Mysteries of Knowledge," 209. Wolfson understands the reference here to be "the experience of ontic incorporation into the divine mystery" (209).

ing into its dwelling place before the light for the departure of night and the arrival of the day. Continually in all (11) the birthings of epochs, the foundations of seasons, and the appointment of festivals are (set) in their order by their signs; (12) their dominion is over everything and is in an order faithful to the command of God. It is a testimony of that which exists and that which shall be. (13) There is nothing other than it. Apart from it, nothing exists nor will be otherwise. Because the God of kn{o}wl{-e}dge (14) has determined it and there is no other besides Him. *vacat*[141]

The heavenly space described here, which the reader is privileged to see, consists of the constellations and their orbits.[142] The blessing formulae that immediately precede this magnificent vision of the heavens can be said to mark the speaker's crossing over the threshold into the heavens.

It is in this final section of the hodayot scroll that one would expect to find the type of experiences described in the SGH, which I propose can be understood as a Thirdspace account of a person who has achieved his own fully participatory experience of the Secondspace reports of heaven. Philip Alexander describes the qualitative difference between the SGH and other Qumran ascent reports:

> There is also a striking difference between our hymn and the other ascent texts we have considered. Neither Isaiah, nor Ezekiel, nor Enoch nor Levi seem to have ascended in reality to heaven. What they experienced, strictly speaking, took place in a dream or in a vision. The language used by our hymnist here, however, strongly suggests his actual presence in heaven, in other words he made a *real*, not a visionary ascent.[143]

The speaker of the SGH has succeeded in generating a new unscripted experience of what it is like to be in the heavens. The speaker of the

---

141 1QH XX, 7–14

142 If the tri-partite blessing in 1QH XIX, 6-XX, 6 functions to introduce an extended vision of the heavens, it may also be possible to interpret the elaborate blessing sequence found at the end of the Book of the Watchers as marking Enoch's spatial shift into the Secondspace of the heavens; a celestial world that is described in the Book of the Luminaries.

143 Philip Alexander, *The Mystical Texts*, 88 (italics original). He goes on to write "[t]he Self-Glorification Hymn fizzes with real experience: it is surely not all a matter of literary convention and literary fantasy. The ascension in the Self-Glorification Hymn is not just a case of celestial tourism, viewing the wonders of heaven, and receiving a prophetic and/or priestly commission. It involves transformation—angelification, possibly even apotheosis. The ascender takes his seat in heaven above the angels. This is a classic component of mysticism: the ultimate goal of mystical experience is communion or union with the divine" (90).

SGH reports his full participation in a new and completely unexpected spatial experience of the celestial realm. The remarkable mystical composition can be understood as the literary product of a Thirdspace experience that reports ancient reader's achievement of a fully participatory and wholly new experience of the heavens. The SGH is a fitting crescendo to the spatial experiences reported throughout the hodayot scroll and should be understood in continuity with, not in isolation from, other hodayot. Even so, an understanding of the SGH as a Thirdspace account of an experience of the heavens does not preclude it from functioning as a Secondspace report for another subsequent reader.[144]

Furthermore, the speaker, finding himself in the heavenly realm, offers blessings in imitation of the celestial beings who are there already. In doing so, he assumes the practices and behaviors of the heavenly court. Biblical visions of the heavenly space commonly report that the angels utter blessing to God.[145] As can be expected, in the SGH, a composition that is clearly set in the heavenly realm, the scripted praise of God is detailed in column XXVI. First, a set of instructions directed to the heavenly beings to bless appears in XXVI, 14:

> [Sing praise, O beloved ones! Sing to the king of glory!] (10)
> Rejoice in the congre]gation of God!
> Ring out joy in the tents of salvation!
> Give praise in the holy habitation!] (11)
> Extol [together with the eternal hosts!
> Ascribe greatness to our God and glory to our king!
> Sanctify] (12) [His na]me with strong lips and a mighty tongue!
> Lift up your voice together at all times!] (13)
> Proc[laim a joyful song!
> Rejoice with an everlasting joy unceasingly!
> Worship] (14) in a common [assembly. . .
> Bless the one who wonderfully does majestic deeds and makes known his strong hand!

---

144 Here, the relationship between the different recensions of the SGH can be imagined as independently produced Thirdspace experiences from meditations on either the Secondspace reports of the heavenly realm. Because every vision of the otherworld can function as a Secondspace account, it may also be possible to imagine one recension of the SGH functioning as a Secondspace report for another recension of the SGH.

145 E.g., Ezek 3:12; Ps 103:20–21; 148:2. Not surprisingly the Qumran Songs of the Sabbath Sacrifice specify that the seven ranks of angels offer elaborate blessings and praises to God.

The following passage in 1QH XXVI, 27–34 describes a heavenly scene of the angels blessing God, can be understood as the execution of these imperatives:

> He lif[ts up the poor one from the dust to an eternal height, and to the clouds] (28) He makes him tall in stature, and (he is) with [the angels in the congregation of the *yaḥad* (ועם אלים בעדת יחד]). For an] eternal [destruction.] Those who fall to the ground He shall rai[se up at no cost. An everlasting power is with their stride] (30) and eternal joy is in t[heir] dwellings; [a perpetual glory that never ever ceases. (31a) And they shall say:
> 'Blessed is God,
> who works majestic wonders and
> who magnifies] (31) {to make known (His) power} and
> who works righte[ousness
> in the knowledge of all His creatures and
> (acts with) goodness in their presence] (32)
> in their knowledge in the greatness of His kindness [and
> of the abundance of His mercy for all the children of His truth.
> We have known You,] O God of righteousness!
> We understand [Your] tr[uth, O king of Glory!
> Because we have seen Your zeal] (34) in powerful strength; and
> [We] recognize Your judgments in the abundance of mercies and wonderful pardons.'[146]

This passage is presented here is a quotation of the blessing that the heavenly beings, along with the elect, utter to God. The speaker reiterates what the celestial beings are known to utter.

Merkur has proposed that the recital of blessings in apocalyptic visionary texts functions as a strategy for soothing terror and managing affective cadences in the reader. I agree that this may be a helpful way of understanding their function in the hodayot scroll and in other visionary journey sequences like the Book of the Watchers. At the same time, I propose that blessings mark spatial movements into the heavenly realm. In this scenario, the ancient reader was expected to imitate and reenact the discourse of the angels and to offer blessings to the LORD. When understood as a greeting offered by a subordinate to a superior, blessings signal that the speaker finds himself in the presence of heavenly beings and the deity. Frechette's proposal that the blessing marks encounters that are both asymmetrical and reciprocal according to formal conventions is helpful in understanding how the imaginal body

---

146 See too 1QH XXVI, 41: "Declare and say: Blessed be God the most high who stretches out the heavens by his might and establishes all their structures by his strength!"

of the hodayot transitions into the celestial realm. Blessings mark thresh-
olds between the religious geography of paradise described in 1QH
XVI, 5–XVII, 36 and the heavenly space that begins to be described
in 1QH XVII, 38. This journey into the heavens is anticipated by the
introductory composition in 1QH IX, 1–X, 4, which describes the
heavens and mentions the blessing that takes place there. In the hodayot,
the blessing formulae signal spatial shifts into the world of heavenly beings.

There is, however, the curious case of the editorial insertion of the
blessing formula in XIII, 22. Of the thirteen TH in the traditional TH
collection of 1QH X–XVII, the formula "I give thanks to you, O
Lord," begins twelve of them. The one exception is the composition
in 1QH XIII, 22–XV, 8 where the usual incipit, "I give thanks to
you, O Lord," appears clearly but has been deleted by cancelation
dots above and below each letter. In the place of this incipit, the phrase
"Blessed are You" has been inserted in the interlinear space above these
cancelled words.[147] This clear editorial change of an otherwise established literary pattern is generally not discussed among scholars who see a
literary unity to the TH collection. This proposal that the blessing formulae mark theophanic moments when the speaker finds himself in the
heavenly presence of the deity can also explain why an editor has added
a blessing at 1QH XIII, 22: it may be read as an editorial acknowledge-
ment that this composition includes movement into the heavenly realm.
This composition is the first hodayah in the collection that moves out
from a place of punishment, namely, a vision, albeit brief, of the Garden
of Eden in 1QH XIV, 14–22. More importantly, the speaker reports a
brief glimpse of the heavenly space in the form of a vision of various

---

147 I am not aware of anyone in the scholarship on the hodayot who has offered a
plausible explanation for this interruption of what is otherwise a consistent use
of the "I give thanks to you, O Lord," in the TH collection at 1QH XIII, 22–
XV, 8. Eileen Schuller discusses this addition of a blessing and writes that "[t]he
correction/substitution in 5:20 suggests that ברוך אתה was considered inter-
changeable with אודכה, which is attested as a biblical opening formula" see
Schuller, "Some Observations on Blessings of God in Texts from Qumran,"
134–35. Her study is primarily descriptive, and so she does not offer an any
explanation for why an editor sought to disrupt the regular use of the "I give
thanks to You" (אודכה) formula at XIII, 22. (N.B., that in this publication,
Schuller uses the older Sukenik numbering system for the hodayot; she is referring to what today is known as 1QH XIII, 22.)

celestial beings arrayed at the feet of God Himself (XIII, 23).[148] The editorial insertion of the blessing here may reflect a later editor's sensitivity to these spatial changes in the hodayot. The editorial addition of the blessing formula at 1QH XIII, 22 marks a spatial movement into the heavens and into the presence of the deity.

Conclusion

Attention to the way spatial details are presented in the hodayot collection suggests a gradual progression from places of paradise into the heavens. The garden was a space of simultaneity and liminality, representing the boundary that marks the reader's encroachment upon the deity's abode. Gardens were enjoyed and frequented by the ruler/deity whose dwelling was spatially adjacent. In literature from the second temple period, the extraordinary beauty and sensory delights of the garden made them spaces of luxuriousness. At the same time, they were associated with fear since gardens were frequently settings where the deity pronounced His judgment. As liminal spaces, the garden paradise is only a stop on the journey—not the final destination.

The entry into the heavens is marked conceptually by an editorial blank line at XVII, 37 and at XVIII, 15. The two blank lines may indicate that the hodayot that describe vivid experiential scenes of movement into the heavens were generated on different occasions. In the hodayot that report spatial experiences in the heavens, the lyrical subject expresses emotions of awe and astonishment. There is a heightened sense of visual perception (e.g., XVIII, 10 and 22) and even a report that remarks on the heavenly spaces and the celestial bodies in some detail (1QH XX, 7-XXII, 42). The language of blessing is understood here as a literary marker of a phenomenal shift in spatiality into the celestial realm which culminates with the crescendo of the SGH. The SGH

---

148 "{I give thanks to You} Blessed are You, O Lord; for You have not abandoned the orphan, and You have not despised the poor. For Your strength [is without boun]ds and Your glory (23) is without measure. Wondrous warriors are Your ministers, and a humbled people are in the sweepings at Yo[ur] feet [together] with those impatient for (24) righteousness" (1QH XIII, 22–24). Cf. the heavenly throne room vision in which the prophet reports seeing the throne of the deity surrounded by angels; Isa 6:1–2, "I saw the Lord sitting on a high and lofty throne; and the hem of his robe filled the Temple. Seraphs were standing in attendance on Him."

offers an ancient reader the extraordinary opportunity to reenact the scripted experiences of what it is like to be in the angelic communion and to experience elevation above it. The multiple orthographic systems in the CH II indicate that the compositions in TH and CH II were generated by individual anonymous readers (*maskilim*) over time. The hodayot compositions that report garden experiences can be imagined as reports of successful Thirdspatial experiences.

Conclusion

The Qumran hodayot are a collection of prayer texts from the second temple period that are attested in multiple manuscripts and show signs of several orthographic systems. How these prayers were experienced as religious texts by the community that transmitted them and how they were generated over time are two questions that this book has sought to address. This book has offered the proposal that the Qumran hodayot were read and experienced by the ancient community of covenanters within an on-going practice of performative prayer in which a reader sought to reenact the affective experiences that are described in them. I have proposed a holistic understanding of the hodayot and the extraordinary composition known as SGH based on the form of the collection known as 4Q428, one of the earliest hodayot manuscripts which contains clear evidence for only TH and CH II. The model of performative reading that has been proposed suggests that the rhetorical elements of embodiment language, the first person voice, and the strategic arousal of emotions function together to create a religious experience from reading that is oriented toward the heavens.

Chapter one discusses the major theoretical foundations for this book, post-structuralist understandings of embodied subjectivity and performance studies, and understands that subjectivity is generated by reiterative bodily practices. Chapter two proposes that the lyrical subject in the hodayot, an imaginal body, is rhetorically constructed from other known visionary traditions and that this imaginal body serves as a script for ritual reenactment. The imaginal body has fully articulated members and enjoys a complete range of phenomenal sensations, including transformation and ascent into the heavens. The language of embodiment and transformation participates in a wider sapiential tradition that seeks to regiment the sensory functions and bodily parts with the goal of transformation. In the case of the hodayot, the body is the site for intimate encounters with God. Through the practice of performative prayer the ritualization of the body takes place as an ancient reader seeks to generate the subjectivity of the speaker by reenacting scripted affective experiences. It is through the experiences of the imaginal body that an ancient reader can gain access to the transformative religious experiences of transformation and ascent described in the hodayot.

Chapter three uses critical spatial theory as a way of parsing the detailed affective and phenomenal experiences that are described in the hodayot. The affective script offered to the reader to imitate is a journey from places of punishment, through paradise, and culminates in the heavens. Critical spatial theory can be used to distinguish between experiences that are imitative and those that are innovative. Places of punishment and imprisonment arouse strong feelings of fear and terror, emotions that are instrumental in generating the appropriate subjectivity. When the hodayot are performatively read synchronically, a reader could hope to experience the phenomenal experiences of religious transformation and ascent that they describe. This type of religious experience is scripted and imitative. In this scenario, the reader uses affect to simulate his own journey to these otherworldly spaces. The ongoing practice of reading and affective reenactment can be understood from the framework of habitus theory as cultivating the necessary predisposition for religious experience. The texts construct a portal into a religious geography for an ancient reader to enter and a choreographed sequence of affective experiences to reenact.

While chapter three looked at the reading of the hodayot synchronically, chapter four proposed how critical spatial theory could be used to imagine the hodayot collection diachronically emerging over time. This chapter discussed how the performative reading of the hodayot could have induced a new religious experience, a Thirdspatial experience, and argues that 1QH XIII, 22-XV, 8 was generated from the strategic arousal of terror occasioned by mediation upon the hodayot in column XI. Here, innovative material incorporated into 1QH XIII, 22-XV, 8 and an intense personalization of experiences can be imagined as occurring during the actualization process when the reader achieves the level of "experiencing." The newly generated composition, 1QH XIII, 22-XV, 8 possesses vivid rhetorical elements that suggest an egocentric episodic experience of otherworldly spaces. There are signs of exegetically expanding upon the imagery from column XI and also the introduction of new elements like betrayal by friends that are consistent with the affective tenor. In this type of Thirdspatial religious experience, the ancient reader is transformed from a viewer who imitates scripted experiences into a full participant in the scene and thus becomes an author of a new religious experience. The text that is generated reflects a fully participatory experience that has the characteristics of lived experience.

Chapter five continues the discussion of the spaces in the hodayot and focuses on the places of paradise as they appear in the scroll. Descriptions of well-watered gardens characteristically enumerate the multiple sensory delights found within them and facilitate an affective reenactment of those texts. As is true in other garden traditions, the experiences in Eden convey a strong aspect of judgment and so arouse fear. The vision that is described in 1QH XVI, 5–27 is proposed as a fully participatory experience of being in an otherworldly Garden. It has the qualities of lived experience that suggest that it was generated from a Thirdspatial experience of the garden. As a heterotopic space, the Garden of Eden possesses simultaneity and liminality that can be conceptualized as marking the threshold into the heavens. This chapter discussed the process of generating a new text from religious experience as one in which the author's own body served to authenticate that a veridical experience took place. In the absence of any authorial attribution, the authenticity of the Thirdspatial experience was guaranteed by the dramatic report of the body's suffering in 1QH XVI, 27- XVII, 6 – such a report is also typical of other visionary texts. The hodayot collection culminates with the speaker's movement into the celestial realm which is marked by the use of the blessing formula and the intensification of the rhetoric of visual perception. These elements suggest that the imaginal body is now in the real presence of the deity and angelic beings.

When the hodayot are read synchronically, all of the spatial descriptions function as a highly contoured religious geography. The reenactment of these scripted Secondspatial experiences aim to create the appropriate subjectivity in the ancient reader, one that would allow him to experience the choreographed moments of transformation that the text describes. At the same time, certain hodayot (those discussed in chapters four and five, e.g., 1QH XIII, 22-XV, 8 and XVI, 5-XVII, 36) can be imagined as having been generated from prayerful reenactments of affect. For these hodayot, the practice of the performative reenactment of emotion offered the reader the opportunity for a fully participatory Thirdspace experience. This too is the imagined scenario for the SGH in which the speaker's claims exceed the typical expectations of being in the heavenly realm; scripted experiences found in other descriptions of the heavens are exceeded in the extraordinary report known as the SGH. The speaker claims an incomparable status for himself and claims to have a station in the heavenly space with divine beings: "as for me, my station is with the divine beings" (XXVI, 7). Imagining the SGH in this way can offer an explanation for why the experiences in the SGH resemble but also differ from what is known as Recension B (4Q491), in which even more extraordinary claims are made. All of the Thirdspatial experiences discussed in chapters four and five eventually become scripted Secondspace experiences for subsequent readers.

This book proposes that emotions, when rightly reenacted within meditative practices, could have created within the reader the necessary predisposition to generate a new religious experience. When this happened a reader was transformed from being an imitator of religious experiences to being a full participant in a new religious experience. Seth Sanders has raised an important series of questions concerning the generation of texts and its relationship to religious experience:

> Because an interpretation can produce a religious experience, do we know in any given case that it actually did? If all experience is somehow exegetical and all exegesis is somehow experiential, are all interpretations of visions themselves themselves divinely inspired? If not, how does one draw meaningful distinctions between them? In the absence of explicit native testimony as to the nature of a given religious practice and the status of a specific experience, the emphasis on exegesis risks ending up another a priori assumption.[1]

How did ancient communities make distinctions among various religiously induced exegetical experiences? In a process where new texts and events were generated from performative reenactments of prayers, this book has proposed that the bodily display of emotion could be understood to both influence changes in that individual's status and authenticate texts that were innovative in the absence of any authorial attribution.

The diachronic proposal that certain hodayot in 4Q428 were the result of Thirdspatial experiences seeks to account for the various orthographic systems present in the collection. It is clear from the various orthographic systems that the hodayot were composed at different times, by different authors, and that the anonymity of these hodayot texts was not a significant concern for the Qumran community. The appropriate display of emotion during a religious experience may be understood as a critical step needed for a community to authenticate the religious experience. A community's assent that an innovated composition reported a veridical experience was then communicated by the inclusion of the

---

1   Sanders, "Performative Exegesis," 63.

newly composed text into the pre-existing collection. This process made the innovative experience available to a subsequent reader as an affective script for reenactment. In this proposal, the body's display of performative emotions functioned to authenticate religious experiences in the absence of a system of pseudonymous attribution.

The various order and arrangement of the hodayot among the different manuscripts from Caves 1 and 4 indicate that it was a living prayer collection that grew and changed over time, and not in predictable linear ways. As a collection of prayers that was performed and reenacted, the hodayot collection shows other signs that it was a living collection. The eventual accumulation of religious experience reports over time may explain why revelatory texts are arranged in a fashion that the modern mind judges to be an inelegant piling-up of traditions. One example that was discussed in chapter five is the curious blessing formula that has been editorially inserted in 1QH XIII, 22, which disrupts an otherwise consistent literary pattern in 1QH X–XVII. The editorial insertion suggests that the proposed spatial aspects of the text outweigh any editor's desires to present a consistent literary series of "I give thanks to You." Ancient editors were not concerned to show the clean linear progression that modern minds expect, and they were not bothered by literary repetitions. In the case of the Book of the Watchers, scholars puzzle over why a text that otherwise shows clear signs of editing and redaction would also exhibit signs of clumsy literary joins and repetitions, especially in the chapters that report Enoch's visionary journeys. For example, a considerable amount of overlap appears between the locales that Enoch visits in *1 En.* 17–19 and *1 En.* 20–36. This non-linear aspect of the literary tradition of Enoch's journeys is a feature that it shares with other apocalyptic traditions. In Leonard Thompson's discussion of the literary account of the geography in the Book of Revelation, he describes the style of visionary literature as an accumulation of images that move in a circular fashion:

> In that process of circularity and accumulation, placement in the narrative sequence is a significant factor; for earlier occurrences of a term, image, or motif become a given in the narrative line, to be drawn on in the development of a later scene. That is, a secondary occurrence in the work loops back around the first occurrence of the term, image, or motif, a tertiary occurrence loops back around the first two, and so forth. There, thus, a kind

of recursive process in which an earlier usage becomes a given and provides input into the meaning of a later one.[2]

So too, the hodayot collection moves in general direction, but it cannot be said to perfectly segregate spatial experiences into places of punishment, places of paradise, and the heavens, although the general contours of these spatial regions appear. Even though this book has sought to demonstrate that a general spatial progression exists in these texts, the progression moves in fits and starts. For example, while experiences associated with punishment and entrapment are given extensive treatment in columns X–XV, later compositions (1QH XVIII, 35–37) return to these places, although they do not linger for long.

Understanding how the hodayot may have been phenomenally experienced as reenactment of affect, a process that could at times result in the spontaneous generation of new experiences and texts, can help modern scholars to understand the non-linear growth of collections and the repetitions that they contain. As Merkur suggests, the disciplined mediation upon successful visionary reports was a key practice that helped a seer to access further unknown matters. As new visionary reports were generated, they became grouped together with older established visionary texts, eventually becoming integrated into a collection that would have been used by subsequent individuals who sought to re-create religious experiences from reading. Here, the phenomenal experience of the scroll as a material object reinforces an operational experience of linear direction. The experiences described in the hodayot that move from punishment, paradise, to the heavens are consistent with the phenomenal experience of reading a textual apparatus like the scroll.

The book has proposed that the creative intertextuality found in visionary literature can be accounted for by the associative process of affective memory construction and reconstruction. The strong arousal of emotion could have led a reader to reinvigorate other memories from personal experience or other traditions. Such a proposal about how texts were generated from ritual practices of prayer and meditation helps to explain how writings imperfectly replicate other known traditions and conflate them in creative and unexpected ways. Literary stud-

---

2   Leonard L. Thompson, "Mapping and Apocalyptic World," *Sacred Places and Profane Spaces: Essays in the Geographies of Judaism, Christianity, and Islam* (ed. Jamie Scott and Paul Simpson-Housley; Westport, Conn.: Greenwood Press, 1991), 115–27, here 119.

ies that seek to trace very specific traditions and expect them to be perfectly copied in visionary traditions presume a modern phenomenal experience of textuality. In a modern printing-press culture, texts can be reproduced and copied with precision, but the ancient reiteration of religious traditions in texts generated from religious experience is creative and imprecise.

A theoretical discussion of the emotions within the context of performance studies has been presented here as a model for how ancients may have moved from text to religious experience. This model of reading can also be applied to certain early Jewish and Christian apocalyptic texts: the emotion-laden first-person reports of Enoch's journeys to the otherworld in the Book of the Watchers, the visions found in the Apocalypse of John, 4 Ezra, the *Odes of Solomon*, and Ephrem's *Hymns on Paradise*. This model can also be applied to non-apocalyptic texts in the first person that strategically arouse the emotions and also include reports of transformation, such as the "I" of the psalmist who is delivered from the consecutive episodes of sufferings, culminating in the jubilation of Pss 145–150; and the ancient hero of the Book of Job whose first person narration of suffering results in the extraordinary experience in the whirlwind, which is the theological crescendo of that book.

In closing, the model of performative reading that is proposed here for the Qumran hodayot collection known as 4Q428 has sought to understand how the first person voice, language about the body and the emotions functioned to create a religious experience from the practices of meditative reading. The bodily practices of reading that are imagined here are ones that can account for how the anonymous hodayot emerged over time by multiple authors without any anxiety for their authenticity. The costly display of emotion, expressed on the body of the ancient anonymous author, was the critical marker that a veridical experience had occurred. I hope that the proposal offered here about how the Qumran hodayot were used for meditation and prayer will stimulate a deeper appreciation of the hodayot as religious texts and contribute to the understanding of the phenomenon of reading and religious experience more broadly. While the hodayot texts did not continue to be read after the community at Qumran, the interdisciplinary analysis of the ritualized practice of performative reading that this book presents is one that can be transferred onto other texts, especially those that are written in the first person, arouse powerful emotions, and report vivid phenomenal experiences of ascent into the heavens and transformation.

Bibliography

Abrams, Meyer Howard. *The Mirror and the Lamp: Romantic Theory and the Critical Tradition.* New York: Oxford University Press, 1953.

Abusch, Tzvi. "Ascent to the Stars in a Mesopotamian Ritual: Social Metaphor and Religious Experience." Pages 15–39 in *Death, Ecstasy, and Other Worldly Journeys.* Edited by John J. Collins and Michael Fishbane. Albany: SUNY, 1995.

Albright, W. F. "The Psalm of Habakkuk." Pages 1–18 in *Studies in Old Testament Prophecy.* Edited by H. H. Rowley. New York: Scribner's Sons, 1950.

Alexander, Philip. S. "Qumran and the Genealogy of Western Mysticism." Pages 215–35 in *New Perspectives on Old Texts. Proceedings of the Tenth International Symposium of the Orion Center for the Study of the Dead Sea Scrolls and Associated Literature, 9– 11 January, 2005.* Edited by Esther G. Chazon and Betsy Halpern-Amaru in collaboration with Ruth A. Clements. STDJ 88. Leiden: Brill, 2010.

———. *The Mystical Texts: Songs of the Sabbath Sacrifice and Related Manuscripts.* London: T&T Clark, 2006.

Allison, Jr, Dale C. "The Living Water (John 4:10–14; 6:35c; 7:37–39)." *St Vladimir's Theological Quarterly* 30 (1986): 143–57.

Amar, Joseph and Edward G. Mathews, Jr.(trans.). *Ephrem the Syrian: Selected Prose Works.* Fathers of the Church series 91. Washington, D.C.: Catholic University of America Press, 1994.

Amaral, D. G., J. L. Price, A. Pitkanen, and S. T. Carmichael. "Anatomical Organization of the Primate Amygdaloid Complex." Pages 1–66 in *The Amygdala: Neurobiological Aspects of Emotion, Memory and Mental Dysfunction.* Edited by J. Aggleton. New York: Wiley-Liss, 1992.

Amit, Yairah. *Reading Biblical Narratives: Literary Criticism and the Hebrew Bible.* Translated by Y. Lotan. Minneapolis: Fortress Press, 2001.

Anderson, Gary. "Celibacy or Consummation in the Garden? Reflections on Early Jewish and Christian Interpretations of the Garden of Eden." *HTR* 82 (1989): 121–48.

Angel, Joseph L. *Otherworldly and Eschatological Priesthood in the Dead Sea Scrolls.* STDJ 86. Leiden: Brill, 2010.

———. "The Liturgical-Eschatological Priest of the *Self-Glorification Hymn.*" *RevQ* 96 (2010): 585–605.

Anzaldúa, G. E. *Borderlands/La Frontera: The New Mestiza.* San Francisco: Aunt Lute Books, 1999.

Aristotle. *Nicomachean Ethics.* Translated by W. D. Ross. Oxford: Clarendon Press, 1925.

Arnold, Magda B. "Perennial Problems in the field of Emotion." Pages 149–85 in *Feelings and Emotions*. Edited by M. B. Arnold. New York: Academic Press, 1970.

———. *Emotion and Personality*. New York: Columbia University Press, 1960.

———. "An Excitatory Theory of Emotion." Pages 11–33 in *Feelings and Emotions*. Edited by M. L. Reymert. New York: McGraw-Hill, 1950.

Asad, Talal. *Genealogies of Religion: Discipline and Reasons of Power in Christianity and Islam*. Baltimore: Johns Hopkins Press, 1993.

Augé, M. *Non-Places: Introduction to an Anthropology of Supermodernity*. London: Verso, 1995.

Aune, David E. *Prophecy in Early Christianity and the Ancient Mediterranean World*. Grand Rapids: Eerdmans, 1983.

Austin, John L. *How to Do Things with Words*. Oxford: Clarendon Press, 1962.

Avrahami, Yael. *In the Biblical Sense: Sensory Perception in the Hebrew Bible*. LHBOTS. London: Continuum/T&T Clark, 2011.

Azari, Nina P., Janpeter Nickel, Gilbert Wunderlich, Michael Niedeggen, Harald Hefter, Lutz Tellmann, Hans Herzog, Petra Stoerig, Dieter Birnbacher, and Rüdiger J. Seitz. "Neural Correlates of Religious Experience." *European Journal of Neuroscience* 13 (2001): 1649–52.

Bachmann, Veronika. "Rooted in Paradise? The Meaning of the 'Tree of Life' in 1 Enoch 24–25 Reconsidered." *JSP* 19 (2009): 83–107.

Baillet, Maurice. *Qumrân grotte 4.III (4Q482–4Q520)*. DJD 7. Oxford: Clarendon, 1982.

———. "Le volume VII de 'Discoveries in the Judaean Desert.' Présentation." Pages 75–78 in *Qumrân. Sa piété, sa théologie et son milieu*. Edited by M. Delcor. BETL 46; Paris- Gembloux: Duculot/Leuven: University of Leuven, 1978.

Bardtke, Hans. "Literaturbericht über Qumran IX. Teil: Die Loblieder (Hodajot) von Qumrân." *TRu* 40 (1975): 213–14.

———. "Considérations sur les Cantiques de Qumrân." *RB* 63 (1956): 220–33.

Bargh, John A. "The Automaticity of Everyday Life." Pages 1–61 in *Advances in Social Cognition, vol. 10*. Edited by R. S. Wyer. Mahwah: Lawrence Erlbaum Associates, 1997.

———. "Conditional Automaticity: Varieties of Automatic Influence in Social Perception and Cognition." Pages 3–51 in *Unintended Thought*. Edited by James S. Uleman and John A. Bargh. New York: Guilford Press, 1989.

Bargh, John A. and Tanya L. Chartrand. "The Unbearable Automaticity of Being." *American Psychologist* 54 (1999): 462–79.

Barros, Carolyn. *Autobiography: Narrative of Transformation*. Ann Arbor: University of Michigan, 1998.

Beck, E. *Ephräm der Syrer, Lobgesang aus der Wüste*. Freiburg: Breisgau, 1967.

——— (ed). *Des Heiligen Ephraem des Syrers Hymnen de Paradiso und Contra Julianum*. CSCO 174–75. Louvain: Peeters, 1957.

Becker, Jürgen. *Das Heil Gottes: Heils-und Sündenbegriffe in den Qumrantexten und im Neuen Testament*. SUNT 3. Göttingen: Vandenhoeck & Ruprecht, 1964.

Beilharz, Peter. "Post-Marxism." Page 581 in the *Encyclopedia of Social Theory*, *Vol. 1*. Edited by George Ritzer. Thousand Oaks: Sage, 2005.

Bell, Catherine. *Ritual: Perspectives and Dimensions*. New York: Oxford University Press, 1997.

———. *Ritual Theory, Ritual Practice*. New York: Oxford University Press, 1992. Reprinted in Pages 98–106 in *The Performance Studies Reader*. Edited by Henry Bial. 2d ed. New York: Routledge, 2007.

———. "Ritualization of Texts and Textualization of Ritual in the Codification of Taoist Liturgy." *History of Religions* 27 (1988): 366–92.

Ben Zvi, Ehud. "The Prophetic Book: A Key Form of Prophetic Literature." Pages 276–97 in *The Changing Face of Form Criticism for the Twenty-First Century*. Edited by Marvin A. Sweeney and Ehud Ben Zvi. Grand Rapids, Mich.: Eerdmans, 2003.

———. "Introduction: Writings, Speeches, and the Prophetic Books—Setting an Agenda." Pages 1–29 in *Writings and Speech in Israelite and Ancient Near Eastern Prophecy*. Edited by Ehud Ben Zvi and Michael H. Floyd. SBLSS 10. Atlanta: Scholars, 2000.

Berger, K. *Das Buch der Jubiläen*. Gütersloh: Gütersloher Verlagshaus Gerd Mohn, 1981.

Bergmann, Claudia. *Childbirth as a Metaphor for Crisis*. BZAW 382; Berlin: de Gruyter, 2008.

Berquist, Jon L. "Critical Spatiality and the Construction of the Ancient World." Pages 14–29 in *Imagining Biblical Worlds: Studies in Spatial, Social, and Historical Constructs in Honor of James W. Flanagan*. Edited by David M. Gunn and Paula McNutt. London: Sheffield Academic Press, 2002.

Berquist, Jon L. and Claudia V. Camp (ed). *Constructions of Space I: Theory, Geography, and Narrative*. New York: Continuum, 2008.

Berridge, K. C. "Pleasures of the Brain." *Brain and Cognition* 52 (2003): 106–28.

Bhabha, H. K. *The Location of Culture*. London: Routledge, 1994.

Bilgrave, Dyer P. and Robert H. Deluty. "Stanislavski's Acting Method and Control Theory: Commonalities across Time, Place, and Field." *Social Behavior and Personality: An International Journal* 32 (2004): 329–40.

Black, Matthew. *The Book of Enoch or 1 Enoch: A New English Edition with Commentary and Textual Notes*. SVTP 7. Leiden: Brill, 1985.

Blair, Rhonda. "Cognitive Neuroscience and Acting: Imagination, Conceptual Blending, and Empathy." *TDR: The Drama Review* 53 (2009): 92–103.

———. "Reconsidering Stanislavsky: Feeling, Feminism, and the Actor." Pages 249–61 in *The Performance Studies Reader, 2nd ed*. Edited by Henry Bial. New York: Routledge, 2004, 2007.

Blaszczak, Gerald R. *A Formcritical Study of Selected Odes of Solomon*. HSM 36; Atlanta: Scholars, 1985.

Block, Daniel I. "Text and Emotion: A Study in the 'Corruptions' in Ezekiel's Inaugural Vision (Ezekiel 1:4–28)." *CBQ* 50 (1988):418–442.

Boccaccini, Gabriele. *Enoch and Qumran Origins: New Light on a Forgotten Connection*. Grand Rapids: Eerdmans, 2005.

———. "The Origins of Enochic Judaism." *Henoch* 24 (2002): 143–45.

————. *Beyond the Essene Hypothesis: The Partings of the Ways between Qumran and Enochic Judaism.* Grand Rapids: Eerdmans, 1998.

Bourdieu, Pierre. *Language & Symbolic Power.* Cambridge: Harvard University, 1994.

————. *The Logic of Practice.* Translated by Richard Nice. Cambridge: Polity Press, 1990.

————. *Outline of a Theory of Practice.* Translated by Richard Nice. New York: Cambridge University Press, 1977.

Boustan, Ra'anan. "The Study of Heikhalot Literature: Between Mystical Experience and Textual Artifact." *Currents in Biblical Research* 6 (2007): 130–60.

Breiter, H. C., S. L. Rauch, K. K. Kwong, J. R. Baker, R. M. Weisskoff, D. N. Kennedy, et al. "Functional Magnetic Resonance Imaging of Symptom Provocation in Obsessive- Compulsive Disorder." *Archives of General Psychiatry* 53 (1996): 595–606.

Brenner, Athalya and Fokkelien van Kijk-Hemmes. *On Gendering Texts: Female & Male Voices in the Hebrew Bible,* Biblical Interpretation Series 1. Leiden: Brill, 1996.

Brinkman, Johan. *The Perception of Space in the Old Testament: An Exploration of the Methodological Problems of its Investigation, Exemplified by a Study of Exodus 25–31.* Kampen: Kok Pharos, 1992.

Brock, Sebastian. *The Luminous Eye: The Spiritual World Vision of Saint Ephrem the Syrian.* Cistercian Studies Series 124. Kalamazoo: Cistercian Publications, 1985, rev. ed 1992.

————. "The Psalms of Solomon." In the *Apocryphal Old Testament,* edited by H.F.D. Sparks. Oxford: Clarendon, 1984.

Brown, Gavin. "Theorizing Ritual as Performance: Explorations of Ritual Indeterminacy." *Journal of Ritual Studies* 17 (2003): 3–18.

Bulbulia, Joseph and Richard Sosis, "Signalling Theory and the Evolution of Religious Cooperation." *Religion* 41 (2011): 363–388.

Bunta, Silviu. "The Mēsu-Tree and the Animal Inside: Theomorphism and Theriomorphism in Daniel 4." Pages 364–86 in *The Theophaneia School: Jewish Roots of Eastern Christian Mysticism.* Edited by Basil Lourié, Andrei A. Orlov, Alexander Golitzin, Bogdan G. Bucur. St. Petersburg: Byzantinorossica, 2007.

Butler, Judith. "Performative Acts and Gender Constitution: An Essay in Phenomenology and Feminist Theory." Pages 187–99 in *The Performance Studies Reader, 2ⁿᵈ ed.* Edited by Henry Bial. New York: Routledge, 2004.

————. *Bodies that Matter: On the Discursive Limits of "Sex."* New York: Routledge, 1993.

————. "Imitation and Gender Insubordination." Pages 13–31 in *Inside/Out: Lesbian Theories, Gay Theories.* Edited by Diana Fuss. New York: Routledge, 1991. Reprinted as pages 307–20 in *The Lesbian and Gay Studies Reader.* Edited by Henry Abelove, Michèle Aina Barale, David M. Halperin. New York: Routledge, 1993.

Bywater, Ingram (trans.). *The Basic Works of Aristotle,* edited by Richard McKeon. New York: Random House, 1941.

Cacioppo, John T., Gary G. Berntson, Tyler S. Loring, Catherine J. Norris, Edith Rickett, and Howard Nusbaum. "Just Because You're Imaging the Brain Doesn't Mean You Can Stop Using Your Head: A Primer and Set of First Principles." *Journal of Personality and Social Psychology* 85 (2003): 650–61.

Cacioppo, John T., Gary G. Berntson and John F. Sheridan, Martha K. McClintock. "Multilevel Integrative Analyses of Human Behavior: Social Neuroscience and the Complementing Nature of Social and Biological Approaches." *Psychological Bulletin* 126 (2000): 829–43.

Cagni, L. *The Poem of Erra.* SANE 1/3; Malibu: Undena, 1977.

Callaway, Philip R. *The History of the Qumran Community: An Investigation.* JSPSup 3. Sheffield: Sheffield Academic Press, 1988.

Camp, Claudia. "Storied Space, or, Ben Sira 'Tells' a Temple." Pages 64–80 in *'Imagining' Biblical Worlds: Studies in Spatial, Social and Historical Constructs in Honor of James W. Flanagan.* Edited by D. M. Gunn and P. McNutt. JSOTS 359. London: Sheffield Academic Press, 2002.

Carmignac, Jean. *Les textes de Qumran.* Paris, 1961.

———. "Les citations de l'Ancien Testament, et specialement des poems du Serviteur, dans les hymnes de Qumran." *RevQ* 2 (1960): 357–94.

———. "Les elements historiques des 'hymns' de Qumran." *RevQ* 2 (1959/ 1960): 205–22.

Carnicke, Sharon M. *Stanislavsky in Focus: An Acting Master for the Twenty-First Century,* 2d ed. New York: Routledge, 2009.

———. "*An Actor Prepares/Rabota aktera nad soboî, Chast' I*: A Comparison of the English with the Russian Stanislavsky." *Theatre Journal* 36 (1984): 481–94.

Carroll, Noël. "Art, Narrative, and Emotion." Pages 190–211 in *Emotion and the Arts.* Edited by Mette Hjort and Sue Laver. New York: Oxford University, 1997.

Carruthers, Mary. *The Craft of Thought: Meditation, Rhetoric, and the Making of Images, 400–1200.* Cambridge: Cambridge University Press, 1998.

Chapman, Cynthia. *The Gendered Language of Warfare in the Israelite-Assyrian Encounter.* HSM 62. Winona Lake: Eisenbrauns, 2004.

Charles, R. H. *The Book of Enoch.* Oxford: Clarendon Press, 1893.

Charlesworth, James H. "An Allegorical and Autobiographical Poem by the *Moreh haṣ-Ṣedeq.*" Pages 295–307 in *"Sha'arei Talmon": Studies in the Bible, Qumran, and the Ancient Near East Presented to Shemaryahu Talmon.* Edited by Michael Fishbane and Emanuel Tov with the assistance of Weston W. Fields. Winona Lake: Eisenbrauns, 1992.

———. "Les Odes de Salomon et les manuscrits de la mer morte." *RB* 77 (1970): 522–49.

Chazon, Esther G. "Liturgical Function in the Cave 1 Hodayot Collection." Pages 135–49 in *Qumran Cave 1 Revisited: Texts from Cave 1 Sixty Years after Their Discovery: Proceedings of the Sixth Meeting of the IOQS in Ljubljana.* Edited by Daniel K. Falk et al. STDJ 91. Leiden: Brill, 2010.

———. "Scripture and Prayer in 'The Words of the Luminaries.'" Pages 25–41 in *Prayers that Cite Scripture.* Edited by James L. Kugel.

——. "Liturgical Communion with the Angels at Qumran." Pages 95–105 in *Sapiential, Liturgical and Poetical Texts from Qumran*. Edited by Daniel K. Falk, Florentino García Martínez, and Eileen M. Schuller. STDJ 35. Leiden: Brill, 2000.

——. *Qumran Cave 4: XX. Poetical and Liturgical Texts, Part 2*. DJD 29. Oxford: Clarendon Press, 1999.

——. "On the Special Character of Sabbath Prayer: New Data from Qumran." *Journal of Jewish Music and Liturgy* 15 (1992–93): 1–21.

——. "*4QDibHam*: Liturgy or Literature?" *RevQ* 15 (1992): 447–55.

Coblentz Bautch, Kelley. "Mythic Geography." Pages 673–74 in *The Eerdmans Dictionary of Early Judaism*. Edited by John J. Collins and Daniel C. Harlow. Grand Rapids: Eerdmans, 2010.

——. "The Heavenly Temple, the Prison in the Void and the Uninhabited Paradise: Otherworldly Sites in the *Book of the Watchers*." Pages 37–53 in *Other Worlds and Their Relation to This World: Early Jewish and Ancient Christian Traditions*. Edited by Tobias Nicklas, Joseph Verheyden, Erik M. M. Eynikel, Florentino García Martínez. Leiden: Brill, 2010.

——. *A Study of the Geography of 1 Enoch 17–19: "No One Has Seen What I Have Seen."* JSJS 81. Leiden: Brill, 2003.

Collins, Adela Yarbro. "Ascents to Heaven in Antiquity: Toward a Typology." Pages 553–72 in *A Teacher for All Generations: Essays in Honor of James C. VanderKam, Vol. 2*. Edited by Eric Mason, Kelley Coblentz Bautch, Angela Kim Harkins, Daniel A. Machiela. SJSJ 153/II. Leiden: Brill, 2012.

Collins, John J. *Beyond the Qumran Community: The Sectarian Movement of the Dead Sea Scrolls*. Grand Rapids: Eerdmans, 2010.

——. "Amazing Grace: The Transformation of the Thanksgiving Hymn at Qumran." Pages 75–86 in *Psalms in Community: Jewish and Christian Textual, Liturgical, and Artistic Traditions*. Edited by Harold W. Attridge and Margot E. Fassler. SBLSS 25; Atlanta: Society of Biblical Literature, 2003.

—— and Peter W. Flint (ed). *The Book of Daniel: Composition and Reception. 2 Volumes*. VTSup 83. Leiden: Brill, 2011.

——. "Teacher and Servant." In *Hommage à Marc Philonenko*. *Revue d'histoire et de philosophie religieuses* 80 (2000): 37–50.

——. *The Scepter and the Star: The Messiahs of the Dead Sea Scrolls and Other Ancient Literature*. ABRL. New York: Doubleday, 1995.

——. "A Throne in the Heavens: Apotheosis in pre-Christian Judaism." Pages 41–58 in *Death, Ecstasy, and Other Worldly Journeys*. Edited by John J. Collins and Michael A. Fishbane. Albany: State University of New York Press, 1995.

—— and Michael Fishbane (eds.). *Death, Ecstasy, and Other Worldly Journeys* Albany: SUNY Press, 1995.

—— and Devorah Dimant. "A Thrice-Told Hymn: A Response to Eileen Schuller." *JQR* 85 (1994): 151–55.

——. *Daniel: A Commentary on the Book of Daniel*. Hermeneia; Minneapolis: Fortress, 1993.

——. "The Origin of the Qumran Community: A Review of the Evidence." Pages 159–78 in *To Touch the Text: Biblical and Related Studies in*

Honor of Joseph A. Fitzmyer, S.J. Edited by Maurya P. Horgan and Paul J. Kobelski. New York: Crossroad, 1989.

Corbin, H. *Temple and Contemplation.* London: KPI in association with Islamic Publications, 1986.

Corrigan, John (ed). *Religion and Emotion: Approaches and Interpretations.* New York: Oxford University Press, 2004.

Cottrill, Amy C. *Language, Power, and Identity in the Lament Psalms of the Individual.* LHBOTS 493. London: T & T Clark, 2008.

Couliano, Ioan P. *Out of this World: Otherworldly Journeys from Gilgamesh to Albert Einstein.* Boston: Shambhala, 1991.

————. *Expériences de l'extase: extase, ascension et récit visionnaire de l'hellénisme au moyen âge.* Paris: Payot, 1984.

Culler, Jonathan. "Convention and Meaning: Derrida and Austin." *New Literary History* 13 (1981): 15–30.

Daise, Michael. "Creation Motifs in the Qumran Hodayot." Pages 293–305 in *The Dead Sea Scrolls: Fifty Years after their Discovery,* edited by Lawrence H. Schiffman, Emanuel Tov, and James C. VanderKam. Jerusalem: Israel Exploration Society in cooperation with the Shrine of the Book, Israel Museum, 2000.

Damasio, Antonio. *Looking for Spinoza: Joy, Sorrow, and the Feeling Brain.* New York: Harcourt, 2003.

————. "A Second Chance for Emotion." Pages 12–23 in *Cognitive Neuroscience of Emotion.* Edited by Richard D. Lane and Lynn Nadel. New York: Oxford University, 2000.

————. *The Feeling of What Happens: Body and Emotion in the Making of Consciousness.* New York: Harcourt, 1999.

————. *Descartes' Error: Emotions, Reason, and the Human Brain.* New York: Avon Books, 1994.

D'Aquili, Eugene G. and Andrew B. Newberg. *The Mystical Mind: Probing the Biology of Religious Experience.* Minneapolis: Fortress, 1999.

Darr, K. Pfisterer. "Like Warrior, like Woman: Destruction and Deliverance in Isaiah 42:10–17." *CBQ* 49 (1987): 560–71.

Darwin, Charles. *Expression of the Emotions in Man and Animals.* New York: Appleton and Company, 1899.

Davila, James. *Descenders to the Chariot: The People behind the Hekhalot Literature.* SJSJ 70; Leiden: Brill, 2001.

————. "Heavenly Ascents in the Dead Sea Scrolls." Pages 461–85 in *The Dead Sea Scrolls after Fifty Years: A Comprehensive Assessment.* Edited by Peter W. Flint and James C. VanderKam with the assistance of Andrea E. Alvarez. Vol. 2. Leiden: Brill, 1999.

————. "The Hodayot Hymnist and the Four who Entered Paradise." *RevQ* 17 (1996): 457–78.

Davies, Philip R. "Space and Sects in the Qumran Scrolls." Pages 81–97 in *Imagining Biblical Worlds.* Edited by David M. Gunn and Paula McNutt.

Davis, Carmel Bendon. *Mysticism & Space: Space and Spatiality in the Works of Richard Rolle, The Cloud of Unknowing Author, and Julian of Norwich.* Washington, D. C.: Catholic University of America Press, 2008.

Day, Peggy L. "The Personification of Cities as Female in the Hebrew Bible: The Thesis of Aloysius Fitzgerald, F. S. C." Pages 283–302 in *Reading from this Place, Vol. 2: Social Location and Biblical Interpretation in Global Perspective.* Edited by Fernando F. Segovia and Mary Ann Tolbert. Minneapolis: Fortress, 1995.

DeConick, April D., ed. *Paradise Now: Essays on Early Jewish and Christian Mysticism.* SBLSS 11. Atlanta: Scholars, 2006.

Delcor, M. *Les Hymnes de Qumran (Hodayot): texte hébreu, introduction, traduction, Commentaire.* Paris: Letouzey et Ané, 1962.

Derrida, Jacques. *Limited Inc.* Evanston: Northwestern University, 1988.

———. *Margins of Philosophy.* Translated by Alan Bass. Chicago: University of Chicago, 1982.

———. Signature, Event, Context." Translated by Samuel Weber and Jeffrey Mehlman. *Glyph: Johns Hopkins Textual Studies* 7 (1977): 172–97.

Dieterich, Albrecht. *Nekyia: Beiträge zur Erklärung der neuentdeckten Petrusapokalypse.* Leipzig: B. G. Teubner, 1893.

Dietrich, Manfried. "Der „Garten Eden" und die babylonischen Parkanlangen im Tempelbezirk." Pages 1–29 in *Religiöse Landschaften*, edited by Johannes Hahn and Ronning Christian. AOAT 301. Münster: Ugarit Verlag, 2002.

———. "Das biblische Paradies und der babylonische Tempelgarten: Überlegungen zur Lange des Gartens Eden." Pages 281–323 in *Das biblische Weltbild und seine altorientalischen Kontexte.* Edited by Bernd Janowski and Beate Ego. FAT 32. Tübingen: Mohr Siebeck, 2001.

Dillmann, August. *Das Buch Henoch übersetzt und erklärt.* Leipzig: Wilhelm Vogel, 1853.

Dimant, Devorah. "Men as Angels: The Self-Images of the Qumran Community." Pages 93–103 in *Religion and Politics in the Ancient Near East.* Edited by Adele Berlin. Bethesda: University Press of Maryland, 1996.

———. "בני שמים—תורת המלאכים בספר היובלים לאור כתבי עדת קומראן." Pages 97–118 in מנחה לשרה. Edited by Moshe Idel, Devorah Dimant, and S. Rosenberg. Jerusalem: Magnes Press, 1994.

———. "A Synoptic Comparison of Parallel Sections in 4Q 427 7, 4Q491 11 and 4Q471B." *JQR* 85 (1994): 157–61.

Dombkowski Hopkins, D. "The Qumran Community and 1Q Hodayot: A Reassessment." *RevQ* 10 (1981): 323–64.

Douglas, Michael C. "The Teacher Hymn Hypothesis Revisited: New Data for an Old Crux." *DSD* 6 (1999): 239–66.

———. "Power and Praise in the Hodayot: A Literary Critical Study of 1QH 9:1–18:14." Ph.D. diss., University of Chicago, 1998.

Dozeman, Thomas B. "Biblical Geography and Critical Spatial Studies." Pages 87–108 in *Constructions of Space I: Theory, Geography, and Narrative.* Edited by Jon L. Berquist and Claudia V. Camp.

Dupont-Sommer, André. *Les écrits esséniens découverts près de la mer morte.* 4th ed. Paris, 1980.

———. "Le rouleau des Hôdâyôt." *Semitica* 7 (1957): 5–23.

Durkheim, Emile. *The Elementary Forms of the Religious Life.* New York: Free Press, 1915; repr. 1965.

Durso, F. T. and M. K. Johnson. "The effects of orienting tasks on recognition, recall, and modality confusion of pictures and words." *Journal of Verbal Learning and Verbal Behavior* 19 (1980): 416–29.

Eaton, J. H. "The Origin and Meaning of Habakkuk 3." *ZAW* 76 (1964): 144–71.

Ebersole, Gary L. "The Poetics and Politics of Ritualized Weeping in Early and Medieval Japan." Pages 25–51 in *Holy Tears: Weeping in the Religious Imagination*. Edited by Kimberley Christine Patton and John Stratton Hawley. Princeton: Princeton University Press, 2005.

———. "The Function of Ritual Weeping Revisited: Affective Expression and Moral Discourse." *History of Religions* 39 (2000): 211–46. Reprinted as pages 185–222 in *Religion and Emotion: Approaches and Interpretations*. Edited by John Corrigan. Oxford: Oxford University Press, 2004.

Egger-Wenzel, Renate and Jeremy Corley (ed). *Emotions from Ben Sira to Paul*. DCLY. Berlin: de Gruyter, 2011.

Ekman, Paul. *Emotion in the Human Face*. Cambridge: Cambridge University Press, 1982.

Elfenbein, H. A. and N. Ambady. "On the Universality and Cultural Specificity of Emotion Recognition: A Meta-Analysis." *Psychological Bulletin* 128 (2002): 203–35.

Elwolde, John. "The Hodayot's Use of the Psalter: Text-critical Contributions (Book 3: Pss 73–89)." *DSD* 17 (2010): 159–79.

Emerton, J. A. "The Odes of Solomon." *Apocryphal Old Testament*. Edited by H. F. D. Sparks. Oxford: Clarendon, 1984.

St. Ephrem the Syrian. *The Hymns on Paradise*. Translated by Sebastian Brock. Crestwood: St. Vladimir's Sminary Press, 1998.

Erker, Darja Šterbenc. "Women's Tears in Ancient Roman Ritual." Pages 135–60 in *Tears in the Graeco-Roman World*. Edited by Thorsten Fögen. Berlin: W. de Gruyter, 2009.

Eshel, Esther. "The Identification of the 'Speaker' of the Self-Glorification Hymn." Pages 617–35 in *The Provo International Conference on the Dead Sea Scrolls: Technological Innovations, New Texts, and Reformulated Issues*. Edited by Donald W. Parry and Eugene Ulrich. STDJ 30. Leiden: Brill, 1999.

———. "Self-Glorification Hymn." Pages 421–35 in DJD 29. Edited by Esther Chazon et al.

———. "4Q471b: A Self-Glorification Hymn." *RevQ* 17 (1996): 189–91.

Eshel, Hanan. *The Dead Sea Scrolls and the Hasmonean State*. Grand Rapids: Eerdmans, 2008.

Fauth, W. "Der Königlicher Gärtner und Jäger im Paradeisos. Beobachtungen zur Rolle des Herrschers in der vorderasiatischen Hortikultur." *Persica* 8 (1979): 1–53.

Fazio, R., D. M. Sanbonmatsu, M. C. Powell, and F. R. Kardes. "On the Automatic Activation of Attitudes." *Journal of Personality and Social Psychology* 50 (1986): 229–38.

Fenz, Augustinus Kurt. "Ein Drache in Babel: Exegetische Skizze über Daniel 14, 23–42." *SEÅ* 35 (1970): 12.

Fishbane, Michael. *Biblical Myth & Rabbinic Mythmaking*. Oxford: Oxford University, 2003.

———. The Well of Living Water: A Biblical Motif and its Ancient Transformations." Pages 3–16 in *"Sha'arei Talmon:" Studies in the Bible, Qumran, and the Ancient Near East Presented to Shemaryahu Talmon*. Edited by Michael Fishbane, Emanuel Tov, and Weston Fields. Winona Lake: Eisenbrauns, 1992.

Fitzgerald, Aloysius. "The Mythological Background for the Presentation of Jerusalem as Queen and False Worship as Adultery in the Old Testament." *CBQ* 34 (1972): 403–16.

Fitzmyer, Joseph. *The Genesis Apocryphon of Qumran Cave 1: A Commentary, 2nd rev. ed.* Rome: Biblical Institute, 1971.

Flanagan, James W. "Mapping the Biblical World: Perceptions of Space in Ancient Southwestern Asia." Pages 1–18 in *Mappa Mundi: Mapping Culture/ Mapping the World*. Edited by Jacqueline Murray. Working Papers in the Humanities 9. Windsor: Humanities Research Group at the University of Windsor, 2001.

———. "Space." Pages 239–44 in *Handbook of Postmodern Biblical Interpretation*. St. Louis: Chalice Press, 2000.

———. "Ancient Perceptions of Space/ Perceptions of Ancient Space." Pages 15–43 in *The Social World of the Hebrew Bible: Twenty-Five Years of the Social Sciences in the Academy*. Edited by R. A. Simpkins and S. L. Cook. Semeia 87. Atlanta: Society of Biblical Literature, 1999.

Flannery, Frances. "Ascents, Apocalypses, and Neuroscience: Moshe Idel and the Study of Religious Experience." Paper presented at the annual meeting of the Society of Biblical Literature, New Orleans, 2009.

———. "The Body and Ritual Reconsidered, Imagined, and Experienced." Pages 13–18 in *Experientia, Volume 1: Inquiry into Religious Experience in Early Judaism and Early Christianity*. Edited by F. Flannery, C. Shantz, and R. A. Werline. Atlanta: Scholars, 2008.

Flannery, Frances, Colleen Shantz, and Rodney A. Werline, ed. *Experientia, Volume 1: Inquiry into Religious Experience in Early Judaism and Early Christianity*. SBLSS 40; Atlanta: Scholars, 2008.

Flannery, Frances with Nicolae Roddy, Colleen Shantz, and Rodney A. Werline. "Introduction: Religious Experience, Past and Present." Pages 1–10 in *Experientia, vol. 1*.

Fletcher-Louis, Crispin H. T. *All the Glory of Adam: Liturgical Anthropology in the Dead Sea Scrolls*. STDJ 42; Leiden: Brill, 2002.

Fohrer, Georg. "Das 'Gebet des Propheten Habakuk' (Hab 3,1–16)." Pages 159–67 in *Mélanges bibliques et orientaux en l'honneur de M. Mathias Delcor*. Kevelaer: Butzon und Bercker, 1985.

Foucault, Michel. "Of Other Spaces." Translated by Jay Miskowiec. *Diacritics* 16 (1986): 22–27

———. *Discipline and Punish: The Birth of the Prison*. Harmondsworth: Peregrine, 1977.

Frank, Georgia. "Romanos and the Night Vigil in the Sixth Century." Pages 59–78 in *Byzantine Christianity: A People's History of Christianity, vol. 3.* Edited by Derek Kreuger. Minneapolis: Fortress, 2006.

———. "Dialogue and Deliberation: The Sensory Self in the Hymns of Romanos the Melodist." Pages 163–79 in *Religion and the Self in Late Antiquity.* Edited by David Brakke, Michael L. Satlow, and Steven Weitzman. Bloomington: Indiana University Press, 2005.

Franks, David D. "The Bias Against Emotions in Western Civilization." Pages 29–34 in *Sociology of Emotions.* Edited by Catherine G. Valentine, Steve Derné, and Beverley Cuthbertson Johnson. New York: 1999.

Fraschetti, Augusto. *Rome et le prince.* Translated into the French by Vincent Jolivet. Paris: Belin, 1994.

Frechette, Christopher G. *Mesopotamian Ritual-prayers (Šuillas): A Case Study Investigating Idiom, Rubric, Form, and Function.* Alter Orient und Altes Testament 379. Münster: Ugarit-Verlag, forthcoming.

———. "What does 'Bless the LORD!' Mean? Interpreting Hebrew *brk* in its ANE context." Paper presented at the Catholic Biblical Association Annual Meeting. Worcester, Mass.: Assumption College, August 7, 2011.

———. "Blessing 1: Ancient Near East." In *The Encyclopedia of the Bible and Its Reception,* edited by H.-J. Klauck et al. Berlin: de Gruyter, forthcoming.

———. "Shuillas." In A. Lenzi, C. Frechette, and A. Zernecke. "Introduction." Pages 1–68 in *Reading Akkadian Prayers and Hymns: An Introduction.* Edited by Alan Lenzi. ANEM 3. Atlanta: SBL, 2011.

———. "Chiasm, Reversal and Biblical Reference in 1QH 11.3–18 (= Sukenik Column 3): A Structural Proposal." *JSP* 21 (2000): 71–102.

Frennesson, Björn. *'In a Common Rejoicing.' Liturgical Communion with Angels in Qumran.* Studia Semitica Upsaliensia 14. Uppsala: Uppsala University Library, 1999.

Frye, Herman Northrop. *Anatomy of Criticism: Four Essays.* Princeton: Princeton University Press, 1957.

García Martínez, Florentino. "Old Texts and Modern Mirages: The 'I' of Two Qumran Hymns." Pages 105–25 in *Qumranica Minora I: Qumran Origins and Apocalypticism.* Edited by Eibert Tigchelaar. STDJ 63. Leiden: Brill, 2007.

Geertz, Armin W. "Brain, Body and Culture: A Biocultural Theory of Religion." *Method and Theory in the Study of Religion* 22 (2010): 304–321.

Geertz, Clifford. *The Interpretation of Cultures: Selected Essays.* New York: Basic Books, 1973.

Gillingham, Susan E. *The Poems and Psalms of the Hebrew Bible.* Oxford: Oxford University Press, 1994.

Gillmayr-Bucher, Suzanne. "Body Images in the Psalms." *JSOT* 28 (2004): 301–26.

Glasson, T. Francis. "The Son of Man Imagery: Enoch XIV and Daniel VII." *NTS* 23 (1977): 82–91.

———. *Greek Influence in Jewish Eschatology.* London: SPCK, 1961.

Goering, Gregory. *Perceiving Wisdom: Disciplining the Senses and the Construction of the Self in the Jewish Wisdom Tradition.* Monograph in progress.

————. "Attentive Ears and Forward-Looking Eyes: Ritualization of the Senses in the Jewish Wisdom Tradition." Paper presented at the Joint session of Ritual and Religious Experience in Early Judaism and Early Christianity at the Society of Biblical Literature Annual Meeting. Atlanta: November 2010, 1–15.

Gonsalves, B., P. J. Reber, D. R. Gitelman, T. B. Parrish, M.-M. Mesulam, K. A. Paller. "Neural Evidence that Vivid Imagining can Lead to False Remembering." *Psychological Science* 15 (2004): 655–60.

Gould, Peter and Rodney White, *Mental Maps*. 2d ed. Boston: Allen & Unwin, 1986.

Grassie, William. *The New Sciences of Religion: Exploring Spirituality from the Outside In and Bottom Up*. New York: Palgrave Macmillan, 2010.

Greenberg, Moshe. *Biblical Prose Prayer as a Window to the Popular Religion of Ancient Israel*. Taubman Lectures in Jewish Studies. Berkeley: University of California Press, 1983.

Grelot, P. "La géographie mythique d'Hénoch et ses sources orientales." *RB* 65 (1958): 33–69.

Griffith, Sidney H. "Images of Ephraem: The Syrian Holy Man and His Church." *Traditio* 45 (1989–90): 7–33.

Gross, Daniel. *The Secret History of Emotion: From Aristotle's "Rhetoric" To Modern Brain Science*. Chicago: University of Chicago Press, 2006.

Gruenwald, Ithamar. *Apocalyptic and Merkavah Mysticism*. AGJU 14. Leiden: Brill, 1980.

Gusdorf, Georges. "Conditions et limites de l'autobiographie." In *Formen der Selbstdarstellung: Analekten zu einer Geschichte des literarischen Selbstportraits*, edited by Günther Reichenkron and Erick Hass. Berlin: Duncker & Humblot, 1956. Reprinted as "Conditions and Limits of Autobiography." Pages 28–48 in *Autobiography: Essays Theoretical and Critical*. Edited and Translated by James Olney. Princeton: Princeton University Press, 1980.

Halgren, E. "Emotional Neurophysiology of the Amygdala within the Context of Human Cognition." Pages 191–228 in *The Amygdala: Neurobiological Aspects of Emotion, Memory, and Mental Dysfunction*. Edited by J. Aggleton. New York: Wiley-Liss, 1992.

Halperin, David. *The Merkabah in Rabbinic Literature*. New Haven: American Oriental Society, 1980.

Haran, Menachem. *Temples and Temple-Service in Ancient Israel: An Inquiry into the Character of Cult Phenomena and the Historical Setting of the Priestly School*. Oxford: Oxford University Press, 1978.

Harding, J. E. "The Wordplay between the Roots כשל and שכל in the Literature of the Yahad." *RevQ* 19 (1999): 69–82.

Harkins, Angela Kim. "Who is the Teacher of the Teacher Hymns? Re-Examining the Teacher Hymns Hypothesis Fifty Years Later." Pages 449–67 in *A Teacher for All Generations: Essays in Honor of James C. VanderKam. Vol. 1*. Edited by Eric F. Mason, Samuel I. Thomas, Alison Schofield, and Eugene Ulrich. SJSJ 153/I. Leiden: Brill, 2012.

————. "The Performative Reading of the Hodayot: The Arousal of Emotions and the Exegetical Generation of Texts." *JSP* 21 (2011): 55–71.

————. "A New Proposal for Thinking about 1QH^A Sixty Years after its Discovery." Pages 101–34 in *Texts from Cave 1 Sixty Years after Their Discovery: Proceedings of the Sixth Meeting of the International Organization of Qumran Studies in Ljubljana*. Edited by Daniel K. Falk, Sarianna Metso, Donald W. Parry, and Eibert J. C. Tigchelaar. STDJ 91; Leiden: Brill, 2010.

————. "Reading the Qumran Hodayot in Light of the Traditions Associated with Enoch." *Henoch* 32 (2010): 359–400.

————. "The Community Hymns Classification: A Proposal for Further Differentiation." *DSD* 15 (2008): 121–54.

————. "Observations on the Editorial Shaping of the so-called Community Hymns from 1QH^a and 4QH^a." *DSD* 12 (2005): 233–56.

Harpham, Geoffrey. *The Ascetic Imperative in Culture and Criticism*. Chicago: University of Chicago Press, 1987.

Hartenstein, Friedhelm. *Das Angesicht JHWHs: Studien zum seinen höfischen und kultischen Bedeutungshintergrund in den Psalmen und in Exodus 32–34*. FAT 55. Tübingen: Mohr Siebeck, 2008.

Hartman, Lars. *Asking for a Meaning: A Study of 1 Enoch 1–5*. CBNTS 12. Lund: CWK Geerup, 1979.

Harvey, Susan Ashbrook. "Locating the Sensing Body: Perception and Religious Identity in Late Antiquity." Pages 140–62 in *Religion and the Self in Antiquity*. Edited by David Brakke, Michael Satlow, and Steven Weitzman. Bloomington: Indiana University Press, 2005.

————. "Spoken Words, Voiced Silence: Biblical Women in the Syriac Tradition." *JECS* 9 (2001): 105–31.

Hellner-Eshed, Melila. *A River Flows from Eden: The Language of Mystical Experience in the Zohar*. Translated from the Hebrew by Nathan Wolski. Stanford: Stanford University Press, 2009.

Henkel, Linda A., N. Franklin, and M. K. Johnson. "Cross-modal Confusions between Perceived and Imagined Events." *Journal of Experimental Psychology: Learning, Memory, & Cognition* 26 (2000): 321–35.

Henrich, Joseph. "The Evolution of Costly Displays, Cooperation and Religion: Credibility Enhancing Displays and their Implications for Cultural Evolution." *Evolution and Human Behavior* 30 (2009): 244–60.

Henrich, Joseph and Francisco J. Gil-White. "The Evolution of Prestige Freely Conferred Deference as a Mechanism for Enhancing the Benefits of Cultural Transmission." *Evolution and Human Behavior* 22 (2001): 165–96.

Henrich, Joseph, Richard McElreach, Abigail Barr, Jean Ensminger, Clark Barrett, Alexander Bolyanatz, Juan Camilo Cardenas, Michael Gurven, Edwins Gwako, Natalie Henrich, Carolyn Lesorogol, Frank Marlowe, David Tracer, John Ziker. "Costly Punishment Across Human Societies." *Science* 312 (2006): 1767–70.

Henze, Mattias. "Nebuchadnezzar's Madness (Daniel 4) in Syriac Literature." Pages 550–71 in *The Book of Daniel: Composition and Reception, Vol. 2*. Edited by John J. Collins and Peter W. Flint. VTSup 83/II. Leiden: Brill, 2001

Hetherington, Kevin. *The Badlands of Modernity: Heterotopia and Social Ordering*. London: Routledge, 1997.

Hiebert, Theodore. *God of My Victory: The Ancient Hymn in Habakkuk 3*. HSM 38. Scholars Press: Atlanta, 1986.

Himmelfarb, Martha. "The Practice of Ascent in the Ancient Mediterranean World." Pages 123–37 in *Death, Ecstasy, and Other Worldly Journeys*. Edited by J. J. Collins, and M. Fishbane.

———. *Ascent to Heaven in Jewish and Christian Apocalypses*. New York: Oxford University Press, 1993.

———. "The Temple and the Garden of Eden in Ezekiel, the Book of the Watchers, and the Wisdom of ben Sira." Pages 63–78 in *Sacred Places and Profane Spaces: Essays in the Geographics of Judaism, Christianity, and Islam*. Edited by Jamie Scott and Paul Simpson- Housley. Westport, Conn.: Greenwood, 1991.

———. "From Prophecy to Apocalypse: The Book of the Watchers and Tours of Heaven." Pages 145–65 in *Jewish Spirituality: From the Bible through the Middle Ages*. Edited by Arthur Green. New York: Crossroad, 1986.

———. *Tours of Hell: An Apocalyptic Form in Jewish and Christian Literature*. Philadelphia: Fortress Press, 1983.

Hodges, Zane C. "Rivers of Living Water—John 7:37–39." *Bibliotheca sacra* 136 (1979): 239–48.

Hollywood, Amy. "Spiritual but Not Religious: The Vital Interplay between Submission and Freedom." *Harvard Divinity Bulletin* 38 (2010): accessed on-line.

———. "Performativity, Citationality, Ritualization." Pages 252–75 in *Bodily Citations: Religion and Judith Butler*. Edited by Ellen T. Armour, Susan M. St. Ville. New York: Columbia University, 2006.

———. "Towards a Feminist Philosophy of Ritual and Bodily Practice." Pages 73–83 in *Difference in Philosophy of Religion*. Edited by Philip Goodchild. Aldershot, England: Ashgate, 2003.

———. *Sensible Ecstasy: Mysticism, Sexual Difference, and the Demands of History*. Chicago: University of Chicago Press, 2002.

Holmes, Emily A. and Andrew Mathews. "Mental Imagery and Emotion? A Special Relationship?" *Emotion* 5 (2005): 489–97.

Holm-Nielsen, Svend. *Hodayot: Psalms from Qumran*. ATDan 2. Aarhus: Universitetsforlaget, 1960.

Hughes, Julie A. *Scriptural Allusions and Exegesis in the Hodayot*. STDJ 59. Leiden: Brill, 2006.

Humphreys, Edith M. *And I Turned to See the Voice: The Rhetoric of Vision in the New Testament*. Grand Rapids: Baker Academic, 2007.

———. "To Rejoice or Not to Rejoice? Rhetoric and the Fall of Satan in Luke 10:17–24 and Revelation 12:1–17." Pages 113–25 in *The Reality of Apocalypse: Rhetoric and Politics in the Book of Revelation*. Edited by David L. Barr. SBLSS 39. Atlanta: SBL, 2006.

Hyatt, J. Philip. "The View of Man in the Qumran 'Hodayot.'" *NTS* (1956): 276–84.

Hyman, I. E. and J. Pentland. "The Role of Mental Imagery in the Creation of False Childhood Memories." *Journal of Memory and Language* 35 (1996): 101–17.

Idel, Moshe. *Ascensions on High in Jewish Mysticism: Pillars, Lines, Ladders.* Budapest: CEU Press, 2005.

———. "Mystical Techniques." Pages 438–94 in *Essential Papers on Kabbalah.* Edited by Lawrence Fine. New York: New York University Press, 1995.

———. *Kabbalah: New Perspectives.* New Haven: Yale University, 1988.

———. *The Mystical Experience in Abraham Abulafia.* Translated from the Hebrew by J. Chipman. Albany: SUNY, 1988.

Isen, Alice M. and Gregory Andrade Diamond, "Affect and Automaticity." Pages 124–52 in *Unintended Thought.* Edited by James S. Uleman and John A. Bargh. New York: The Guilford Press, 1989.

James, William. "What is an Emotion." *Mind* 9 (1884): 188–205.

Jefferson, Ann. "Autobiography as Intertext: Barthes, Sarraute, Robbe-Grillet." Pages 108–29 in *Intertextuality.* Edited by Michael Worton and Judith Still. New York: Manchester University Press, 1990.

Jeremias, Gert. *Der Lehrer der Gerechtigkeit.* SUNT 2. Göttigen: Vandenhoeck & Ruprect, 1963.

Johnson, M. K., S. Hashtroudi, D. S. Lindsay. "Source Monitoring." *Psychological Bulletin* 114 (1993): 3–28.

Johnson, Peter. "Unravelling Foucault's 'Different Spaces.'" *History of the Human Sciences* 19 (2006): 75–90.

Jordan, Pat. "Dysfunction For Dollars." *New York Times* (July 28, 2002).

Kalmanofsky, Amy. *Terror all Around: Horror, Monsters, and Theology in the Book of Jeremiah.* New York: T&T Clark, 2008.

———. "Israel's Baby: The Horror of Childbirth in the Biblical Prophets." *Biblical Interpretation* 16 (2008): 60–82.

Kensinger, Elizabeth A. "Remembering Emotional Experiences: The Contribution of Valence and Arousal." *Reviews in the Neurosciences* 15 (2004): 241–53.

Kensinger, Elizabeth A., Rachel J. Garoff-Eaton, Daniel L. Schacter. "How Negative Emotion Enhances the Visual Specificity of a Memory." *Journal of Cognitive Neuroscience* 19 (2007): 1872–1887.

Kensinger, Elizabeth A. and Suzanne Corkin. "Memory Enhancement for Emotional Words: Are Emotional Words More Vividly Remembered than Neutral Words?" *Memory & Cognition* 31 (2003):1169–80

King Keenan, Elizabeth and Dennis Miehls. "Third Space Activities and Change Processes: An Exploration of Ideas from Social and Psychodynamic Theories." *Clinical Social Work Journal* 36 (2008): 165–75.

Knohl, Israel. *The Messiah before Jesus: The Suffering Servant of the Dead Sea Scrolls.* Translated from the Hebrew by David Maisel. Berkeley: University of California Press, 2000.

Koosed, Jennifer L. *(Per)mutations of Qohelet: Reading the Body in the Book.* New York: T & T Clark, 2006.

Kripal, Jeffrey J. "The Rise of the Imaginal: Psychical Research on the Horizon of Theory (Again)." *RSR* 22 (2007): 179–191.

Kugel, James L. *Prayers that Cite Scripture.* Cambridge: Harvard University, 2006.

Kuhn, Heinz-Wolfgang. *Enderwartung und gegenwärtiges Heil: Untersuchungen zu den Gemeindeliedern von Qumran.* SUNT 4. Göttingen: Vandenhoeck & Ruprecht, 1966.

Kvanvig, Helge S. "Throne Visions and Monsters: The Encounter Between Danielic and Enochic Traditions," *ZAW* 117 (2005): 249–72.

——. "Henoch und der Menschensohn. Das Verhältnis von Hen 14 zu Dan 7," *StTh* 38 (1984): 101–33.

Lampinen, J. M., C. R. Meier, J. D. Arnal, J. K. Leding. "Compelling untruths: Content Borrowing and Vivid False Memories." *Journal of Experimental Psychology: Learning, Memory, and Cognition* 31 (2005): 954–63.

Landsberger, Benno. "Das 'gute Wort.'" Pages 294–321 in *Altorientalische Studien: Bruno Meissner zum sechzigsten Geburtstag am 25. April 1928.* MAOG 4/1. Leipzig: Harrassowitz, 1928.

Leclercq, Jean. *The Love of Learning and the Desire for God: A Study of Monastic Culture.* New York: Fordham University Press, 1982.

LeDoux, Joseph E. "The Emotional Brain, Fear, and the Amygdala." *Cellular and Molecular Neurobiology* 23 (2003): 727–38.

——. *The Emotional Brain: The Mysterious Underpinnings of Emotional Life.* New York: Simon & Schuster, 1996.

——. "Emotion: Clues from the Brain." *Annual Review of Psychology* 46 (1995): 209–35.

Lefebvre, Henri. *The Production of Space.* Translated by Donald Nicholson-Smith. Oxford: Blackwell, 1974.

Lehto, Adam. *The Demonstrations of Aphrahat, the Persian Sage.* Piscataway: Gorgias Press, 2010.

Lenzi, Alan. "Invoking the God: Interpreting Invocations in Mesopotamian Prayers and Biblical Laments of the Individual." *JBL* 129 (2010): 303–15.

Licht, Jacob. מגילת ההודיות: ממגילות מדבר יהודה. Jerusalem: Bialik, 1957.

——. "The Doctrine of the Thanksgiving Scroll." *IEJ* 6 (1956): 1–13; 89–101.

Lieber, Laura S. "The Rhetoric of Participation: Experiential Elements of Early Hebrew Liturgical Poetry." *Journal of Religion* 90 (2010): 119–47.

Lied, Liv Ingeborg. *The Other Lands of Israel: Imaginations of the Land in 2 Baruch.* SJSJ 129; Leiden: Brill, 2008.

Lopez, Kathryn M. "Standing Before the Throne of God: Critical Spatiality in Apocalyptic Scenes of Judgment." Pages 139–55 in *Constructions of Space II: the Biblical City and Other Imagined Spaces.* Edited by Jon L. Berquist and Claudia V. Camp.

Lutz, Catherine and Geoffrey M. White. "The Anthropology of Emotions." *Annual Review of Anthropology* 15 (1986): 405–36.

Lyle, K. B., and M. K. Johnson. "Source Misattributions May Increase the Accuracy of Source Judgments." *Memory & Cognition* 35 (2007): 1024–33.

MacDermot, Violet. *The Cult of the Seer in the Ancient Middle East: A Contribution to Current Research on Hallucinations Drawn from Coptic and Other Texts.* Berkeley: University of California, 1971.

Machiela, Daniel. *The Dead Sea Genesis Apocryphon: A New Text and Translation with Introduction and Special Treatment of Columns 13–17.* STDJ 79. Leiden: Brill, 2009.

———. "'Each to His Own Inheritance': Geography as an Evaluative Tool in the Genesis Apocryphon." *DSD* 15 (2008): 50–66.

Machinist, Peter. "Outsiders or Insiders: The Biblical View of Emergent Israel and Its Contexts." Pages 35–60 in *The Other in Jewish Thought and History: Constructions of Jewish Culture and Identity.* Edited by Laurence J. Silberstein and Robert L. Cohn. New York: New York University Press, 1994.

Mahmood, Saba. "Agency, Performativity, and The Feminist Subject." Pages 177–221 in *Bodily Citations: Religion and Judith Butler.* Edited by Ellen T. Armour and Susan M. St. Ville. New York: Columbia University, 2006.

———. *Politics of Piety: The Islamic Revival and the Feminist Subject.* Princeton: Princeton University Press, 2005.

———. "Feminist Theory, Embodiment, and the Docile Agent: Some Reflections on the Egyptian Islamic Revival." *Cultural Anthropology* 16 (2001): 202–36.

Maier, Christl M. "Daughter Zion as Queen and the Iconography of the Female City." Pages 147–63 in *Images and Prophecy in the Ancient Eastern Mediterranean.* Edited by Martti Nissinen and Charles E. Carter. Göttingen: Vandenhoeck & Ruprecht, 2009.

———. *Daughter Zion, Mother Zion: Gender, Space, and the Sacred in Ancient Israel.* Minneapolis: Fortress Press, 2008.

Mansoor, Menahem. *The Thanksgiving Hymns: Translated and Annotated with an Introduction,* STDJ 3. Leiden: Brill, 1961.

Margulis, Baruch. "The Psalm of Habakkuk: A Reconstruction and Interpretation." *ZAW* 82 (1970): 409–42.

Martin, Malachi. *The Scribal Character of the Dead Sea Scrolls vol. 2.* Louvain: Université de Louvain/ Institut Orientaliste, 1958.

Mayes, Andrew R., Daniela Montaldi, Tom J. Spencer, and Neil Roberts. "Recalling Spatial Information as a Component of Recently and Remotely Acquired Episodic or Semantic Memories: An fMRI Study." *Neuropsychology* 18 (2004): 426–441.

McNamer, Sarah. *Affective Meditation and the Invention of Medieval Compassion.* Philadelphia: University of Pennsylvania Press, 2010.

McNay, Lois. "Gender, Habitus and the Field: Pierre Bourdieu and the Limits of Reflexivity." *Theory, Culture & Society* (1999): 95–117.

Melki, Joseph. "Saint Ephrem le Syrien, un bilan de l'édition critique." *Parole de l'Orient* 11 (1983): 3–88.

Merkur, Daniel. "Cultivating Visions through Exegetical Meditations." Pages 62–91 in *With Letters of Light: Studies in the Dead Sea Scrolls, Early Jewish Apocalypticism, Magic, and Mysticism in Honor of Rachel Elior,* edited by Daphna V. Arbel and Andrei A. Orlov. Ekstasis 2. Berlin, de Gruyter, 2011.

———. "The Visionary Practices of Jewish Apocalyptists." Pages 119–48 in *Psychoanalytic Study of Society.* Edited by L. Bryce Boyer and Simon A.

Grolnik. Vol. 14. Hillsdale, N. J.: Analytic Press, 1989. Reprinted as pages 317–47 in *Psychology and the Bible: A New Way to Read the Scriptures, Volume Two: From Genesis to Apocalyptic*. Edited by J. Harold Ellens and Wayne G. Rollins. New York: Greenwood-Praeger Publishers, 2004.

Meyers, Carol. "Gender Imagery in the Song of Songs." Pages 201–4 in *The Feminist Companion to the Bible, Vol. 1*. 10 Vols. Sheffield: Sheffield Academic, 1993.

Mickley, Katherine R., and Elizabeth A. Kensinger. "Emotional Valence Influences the Neural Correlates Associated with Remembering and Knowing." *Cognitive, Affective, & Behavioral Neuroscience* 8 (2008): 143–52.

Milgrom, Jacob. *Studies in Cultic Theology and Terminology*. Leiden: Brill, 1983.

Miller, Eric. "The Self-Glorification Hymn Reexamined." *Henoch* 31 (2009): 307–24.

Mirguet, Françoise. "Numbers 16: The Significance of Place—An Analysis of Spatial Markers." *JSOT* 32 (2008): 311–330.

Mitchell, Christopher W. *The Meaning of brk "To Bless" in the Old Testament*. SBLDS 95; Atlanta, Scholars Press, 1987.

Mitchell, Karen J. and Marcia K. Johnson. "Source Monitoring 15 Years Later: What Have We Learned from fMRI About the Neural Mechanisms of Source Memory." *Psychological Bulletin* 135 (2009): 638–77.

Morawe, Günter. *Aufbau und Abgrenzung der Loblieder von Qumran: Studien zur gattungsgeschichtlichen Einordnung der Hodajoth*. Berlin: Evangelische Verlagsanstalt, 1961.

Morray-Jones, Christopher. "Paradise Revisited (2 Cor 12:1–12): The Jewish Mystical Background of Paul's Apostolate, Part 1: The Jewish Sources" and "Part 2: Paul's Heavenly Ascent and Its Significance." *HTR* 86 (1993): 177–217, 265–92.

———. "Transformational Mysticism in the Apocalyptic-Merkabah Tradition." *JJS* 43 (1992): 1–31.

Morris, J. S., C. D. Frith, D. I. Perrett, D. Rowland, A. W. Young, A. J. Calder, et al. "A Differential Neural Response in the Human Amygdala to Fearful and Happy Facial Expressions." *Nature* 31 (1996): 812–15.

Mowinckel, S. "Zum Psalm des Habakkuk." *TZ* 9 (1953): 1–23.

Müller, C. O. *The History and Antiquities of the Doric Race, vol. 1*. London: Oxford University Press, 1930.

Murray, Robert. *Symbols of Church and Kingdom, rev. ed.* Piscataway: Gorgias Press, 2004.

Napel, Erik ten. "'Third Heaven' and 'Paradise'. Some Remarks on the Exegesis of 2Cor. 12, 2–4 in Syriac." Pages 53–65 in *V Symposium Syriacum 1988*. Edited by René Lavenant, S.J. Orientalia Christiana Analecta 236. Rome Pontifical Institute for Oriental Studies, 1990.

Newberg, Andrew B. *Principles of Neurotheology*. Burlington: Ashgate, 2010.

Newman, Judith H. *Praying by the Book: The Scripturalization of Prayer in Second Temple Judaism*. SBLEJL 14. Atlanta: Scholars, 1999.

Newsom, Carol A. "Rhetorical Criticism and the Dead Sea Scrolls." Pages 198–214 in *Rediscovering the Dead Sea Scrolls: An Assessment of Old and*

New Approaches and Methods. Edited by Maxine L. Grossman. Grand Rapids: Eerdmans, 2010.

———. "Constructing 'We, You, and the Others' through Non-Polemical
Discourse." Pages 13–21 in *Defining Identities: We, You, and the Other in
the Dead Sea Scrolls.* Edited by Florentino García Martínez and Mladen Popović. STDJ 70. Leiden: Brill, 2008.

———. *The Self as Symbolic Space: Constructing Identity and Community at Qumran.* STDJ 52; Leiden: Brill, 2004.

Nickelsburg, George W. E. "The Parables of Enoch and the Manuscripts from
Qumran." Pages 655–68 in *A Teacher for All Generations: Essays in Honor of
James C. VanderKam, Vol. 2.* Edited by Eric Mason et al.

———. *1 Enoch 1–36, 81–108.* Hermeneia; Minneapolis: Fortress, 2001.

———. "The Qumranic Radicalizing and Anthropologizing of an Eschatological Tradition (1QH 4:29–40)." Pages 423–35 in *Ernten, was man sät: Festschrift für Klaus Koch zu seinem 65 Geburtstag.* Edited by D. R. Daniels, U.
Glessmer, M. Rösel. Neukirchen-Vluyn: Neukirchener Verlag, 1991. Republished under the title, "The Qumranic Transformation of a Cosmological and Eschatological Tradition (1QH 4:29–40)." Pages 649–59 in *The
Madrid Qumran Congress: Proceedings of the International Congress on the Dead
Sea Scrolls, Madrid, 18–21 March 1991.* vol. 2. Edited by J. C. Trebolle
Barrera and L. Vegas Montaner. STDJ 11. Leiden: Brill, 1992.

Nickelsburg, George W. E. and James C. VanderKam. *1 Enoch: A New Translation based on the Hermeneia Commentary.* Minneapolis: Fortress, 2004.

Noegel, Scott B. *Nocturnal Ciphers: The Allusive Language of Dreams in the Ancient Near East.* AOS 89. New Haven: American Oriental Society, 2007.

Ochsner, Kevin, and Daniel L. Schacter. "Remembering Emotional Events: A
Social Cognitive Neuroscience Approach." Pages 643–60 in *Handbook of
Affective Sciences.* Edited by Richard J. Davidson, Klaus R. Scherer, H.
Hill Goldsmith. New York: Oxford University Press, 2003.

Öhman, Arne, Anders Flykt, and Daniel Lundqvist. "Unconscious Emotion:
Evolutionary Perspectives, Psychophysiological Data and Neuropsychological Mechanisms." Pages 296–327 in *Cognitive Neuroscience of Emotion: Series in Affective Science.* Edited by Richard D. Lane and Lynn Nadel. New
York: Oxford University Press, 2000.

Olney, James. "Introduction." Pages 3–27 in *Autobiography: Essays Theoretical
and Critical.* Edited by James Olney.

Oppenheim, A. L. "On Royal Gardens in Mesopotamia." *JNES* 24 (1965):
328–333.

Orlov, Andrei A. "Arboreal Metaphors and the Divine Body Traditions in the
Apocalypse of Abraham." *HTR* 102 (2009): 439–51.

———. *The Enoch-Metatron Tradition.* Tübingen: Mohr Siebeck, 2005.

Parisot, J. *Aphraatis Sapientis Persae Demonstrationes I-XXII.* PS 1; Paris: Firmin-
Didot et socii, 1907.

Pekala, Ronald J., Catherine F. Wenger, and Ralph L. Levine. "Individual Differences in Phenomenological Experience: States of Consciousness as a
Function of Absorption." *Journal of Personality and Social Psychology* 48
(1985): 123–32.

Pelzer, Dave. *Moving forward: Taking the Lead in Your Life.* Center Street, 2008.
———. *The Privilege of Youth: A Teenager's Story of Longing for Acceptance and Friendship.* Dutton, 2004.
———. *Help Yourself: Celebrating the Daily Rewards of Resilience and Gratitude.* Dutton, 2000.
———. *A Man named Dave: A Story of Triumph and Forgiveness.* Dutton, 1999.
———. *The Lost Boy: A Foster Child's Search for the Love of a Family.* Health Communications, 1997.
———. *A Child Called "It": One Child's Courage to Survive.* Omaha: Omaha Press, 1993. Reprinted by Health Communications, 1995.
Philippot, Pierre and Alexandre Schaefer. "Emotion and Memory." Pages 82–122 in *Emotions: Current Issues and Future Directions.* Edited by Tracy J. Mayne and George A. Bonanno. New York: Guilford Press, 2001.
Pitre, Brant. "Blessing the Barren and Warning the Fecund: Jesus' Message for Women Concerning Pregnancy and Childbirth." *JSNT* 81 (2001): 59–80.
Polotsky, H. J. "Ephraems Reise nach Aegypten." *Or* 2 (1933): 269–74.
Pope, Marvin. *Song of Songs.* AB. Garden City, N.Y.: Doubleday, 1977.
Puech, Émile. *La Croyance des Esséniens en la Vie Future: Immortalité, Résurrection, Vie Eternelle? Histoire d'une Croyance dans le Judaïsme Ancien. Vol. II. Les Donnés qumraniennes et classiques.* Gabalda, Paris, 1993.
———. "Quelques aspects de la restauration du Rouleau des Hymns (1QH)." *JJS* 39 (1988): 38–55.
Qimron, Elisha and John Strugnell. *Qumran Cave 4, vol. V: Miqṣat Ma'aśe Ha-Torah.* DJD 10. Oxford: Clarendon, 1994.
———. "An Unpublished Halakhic Letter from Qumran." Pages 400–7 in *Biblical Archaeology Today: Proceedings of the International Congress on Biblical Archaeology, Jerusalem, April 1984.* Edited by J. Amitai. Jerusalem: Israel Exploration Society, 1985.
Rand, Michael. "Metathesis as a Poetic Technique in Hodayot Poetry and Its Relevance to the Development of Hebrew Rhyme." *DSD* 8 (2001): 51–66.
Rappaport, Roy. *Ritual and Religion in the Making of Humanity.* Cambridge: Cambridge University Press, 1999.
Reed, Annette Yoshiko. *Fallen Angels and the History of Judaism and Christianity: The Reception of Enochic Literature.* New York: Cambridge University Press, 2005.
Reeves, John C. *Jewish Lore in Manichaean Cosmogony: Studies in the Book of Giants Traditions.* MHUC 14. Cincinnati: Hebrew Union College Press, 1992.
Reike, B. "Remarques sur l'histoire de la form (Formgeschichte) des texts de Qumran." Pages 38–44 in *Les manuscrits de la mer Morte: Colloque de Strasbourg 25–27 Mai 1955.* Edited by J. Daniélou et al. Paris: Presses universitaires de France, 1957.
Ribot, Théodule. *The Psychology of the Emotions.* New York: Scribner's, 1897.
Ringgren, Helmer. "Der Weltbrand in den Hodajot." Pages 177–82 in *Bibel und Qumran: Beiträge zur Erforschung der Beziehungen zwischen Bibel-und*

Qumranwissenschaft. Festschrift für Hans Bardtke. Berlin: Evangelische Haupt-Bibelgesellschaft, 1968.

———. *Handskrifterna från Qumran.* Symbolae Biblicae Upsalienses 15. Uppsala: Wretmans, 1956.

Robinson, Jenefer. *Deeper Than Reason: Emotion and its Role in Literature, Music, and Art.* Oxford: Clarendon Press, 2005.

Roche, Suzanne M. and Kevin M. McConkey. "Absorption: Nature, Assessment, and Correlates." *Journal of Personality and Social Psychology* 59 (1990): 91–101.

Roediger, H. L., D. Gallo, and L. Geraci. "Processing Approaches to Cognition: The Impetus from the Levels-of-Processing Framework." *Memory* 10 (2002): 319–32.

Rolls, Edmund T. *Emotion Explained.* New York: Oxford University Press, 2005.

Rosenwein, Barbara H. *Emotional Communities in the Early Middle Ages.* Ithaca: Cornell University Press, 2006.

Ross, Ellen. "'She Wept and Cried Right Loud for Sorrow and for Pain.' Suffering, the Spiritual Journey, and Women's Experience in Late Medieval Mysticism." Pages 45–59 in *Maps of Flesh and Light: The Religious Experience of Medieval Women Mystics.* Edited by Ulrike Wiethaus. Syracuse: Syracuse University Press, 1993.

Rowland, Christopher. *The Open Heaven: A Study of Apocalyptic in Judaism and Early Christianity.* London: SPCK, 1992.

Rowland, Christopher with Patricia Gibbons and Vicente Dobroruka. "Visionary Experience in Ancient Judaism and Christianity." Pages 41–56 in *Paradise Now.* Edited by April D. DeConick.

Ruzer, Serge. "*The Cave of Treasures* on Swearing by Abel's Blood and Expulsion from Paradise: Two Exegetical Motifs in Context." *JECS* 9 (2001): 251–71.

Sanders, Seth L. "The First Tour of Hell: From Neo-Assyrian Propaganda to Early Jewish Revelation," *JANER* 9 (2009): 151–69.

———. "Performative Exegesis." Pages 57–79 in *Paradise Now.* Edited by April D. DeConick.

———. "Writing, Ritual, and Apocalypse: Studies in the Theme of Ascent to the Heaven in Ancient Mesopotamia and Second Temple Judaism." Ph.D. diss.; Baltimore: Johns Hopkins University, 1999.

Schäfer, Peter. *The Origins of Jewish Mysticism.* Tübingen: Mohr Siebeck, 2009.

Scharbert, Josef. "*brk.*" In *TDOT* 2, 279–308. Grand Rapids: Eerdmans, 1977.

Schechner, Richard. *Performance Studies: An Introduction.* 2d ed. New York: Routledge, 2006.

———. "Performers and Spectators: Transported and Transformed." *Kenyon Review,* n.s. 3 (1981): 83–113.

———. *Environmental Theater.* New York: Hawthorn Books, 1973.

Schmitz-Emans, Monika. "Theories of Romanticism: The First Two Hundred Years." Pages 13–36 in *Nonfictional Romantic Prose: Expanding Borders.* Edited by Steven P. Sondrup and Virgil Nemoianu, in collaboration with Gerald Gillespie. Philadelphia: John Benjamnins, 2004.

Schofield, Alison. "Re-placing Priestly Space: The Wilderness as Heterotopia in the Dead Sea Scrolls." Pages 470–90 in *A Teacher for All Generations: Essays in Honor of James C. VanderKam, Vol. 1*. Edited by Eric F. Mason et al.

———. *From Qumran to the Yaḥad: A New Paradigm of Textual Development for the Community Rule*. STDJ 77; Leiden: Brill, 2009.

———. "Rereading S: A New Model of Textual Development in Light of the Cave 4 Serekh Copies." *DSD* 15 (2008): 96–120.

Scholem, Gershom. *Major Trends in Jewish Mysticism*. 3d ed. New York: Schocken Books, 1954.

Schuller, Eileen. "Recent Scholarship on the Hodayot 1993–2010." *CBR* 10 (2011): 119–62.

———. "The Classification Hodayot and Hodayot-Like (With Particular Attention to 4Q433, 4Q433 A and 4Q440)." Pages 182–93 in *Sapiential, Liturgical and Poetical Texts from Qumran. Proceedings of the Third Meeting of the International Organization for Qumran Studies Oslo 1998. Published in Memory of Maurice Baillet*. Edited by Daniel K. Falk, Florentino García Martínez, and Eileen M. Schuller. STDJ 35. Leiden: Brill, 2000.

———. "Hodayot." Pages 69–254 in DJD 29. Edited by Esther Chazon et al.

———. "The Cave 4 Hodayot Manuscripts: A Preliminary Description." *JQR* 85 (1994): 137–50. Reprinted as "The Cave 4 Hôdāyôt Manuscripts: A Preliminary Description." Reprinted as pages 87–100 in *Qumranstudien: Vorträge und Beiträge der Teilnehmer des Qumranseminars auf dem internationalen Treffen der Society of Biblical Literature, Münster, 25.–26. Juli 1993*. Edited by Heinz-Josef Fabry, Armin Lange und Hermann Lichtenberger. Göttingen: Vandenhoeck & Ruprecht, 1996.

———. "A Hymn from a Cave Four *Hodayot* Manuscript: 4Q427 7 i + ii." *JBL* 112 (1993): 605–28.

———. "Some Observations on Blessings of God in Texts from Qumran." Pages 133–43 in *Of Scribes and Scrolls: Studies on the Hebrew Bible, Intertestamental Judaism, and Christian Origins*. Edited by Harold W. Attridge, John J. Collins, Thomas H. Tobin. College Theology Society Resources in Religion 5. New York: University Press of America, 1990.

Schuller, Eileen M. and Hartmut Stegemann, translated by Carol Newsom. *Qumran Cave 1. III. 1QHodayot^a with Incorporation of 1QHodayot^b and 4QHodayot ^a-f*. DJD 40. Oxford: Clarendon Press, 2009.

Schulz, Paul. *Autoritätsanspruch des Lehrers der Gerechtigkeit in Qumran*. Meisenheim am Glan: Verlag Anton Hain, 1974.

Sed, N. "Les hymnes sur le paradis de saint Ephrem et les traditions juives." *LM* 81 (1968): 455–501.

Seely, David Rolph. "Implanting Pious Qualities as a Theme in the *Barki Nafshi* Hymns." Pages 322–31 in *The Dead Sea Scrolls Fifty Years after their Discovery. Proceedings of the Jerusalem Congress, July 20–25, 1997*. Edited by Lawrence H. Shiffman, Emanuel Tov, James C. VanderKam, executive editor Galen Marquis. Jerusalem: Israel Exploration Society in cooperation with the Shrine of the Book, Israel Museum, 2000.

Segal, Alan F. "Religious Experience and the Construction of the Transcendent Self." Pages 27–40 in *Paradise Now*. Edited by April D. DeConick.

————. *Life After Death: A History of the Afterlife in the Religions of the West.* New York: Doubleday, 2004.

Segal, Michael. "Text, Translation, and Allusion: An Unidentified Biblical Reference in *1 Enoch* 1:5." *CBQ* 72 (2010): 464–74.

Sekki, Arthur Everett. *The Meaning of* Ruach *at Qumran.* SBLDS 110; Atlanta: Scholars Press, 1989.

Shantz, Colleen. *Paul in Ecstasy.* Cambridge: Cambridge University Press, 2009.

Shibata, Daisuke. "Ritual Contexts and Mythological Explanations of the Emesal Šuilla-Prayers in Ancient Mesopotamia." 45 (2010): 67–85.

Shimoff, Sandra R. "Gardens: From Eden to Jerusalem." *JSJ* 26 (1995): 145–55.

Smelik, Willem F. "On the Mystical Transformation of the Righteous into Light in Judaism." *JSJ* 26 (1995): 122–144.

Smith, Frederick M. *The Self Possessed: Deity and Spirit Possession in South Asian Literature and Civilization.* New York: Columbia University Press. 2006.

Smith, Jonathan Z. "Fences and Neighbors: Some Contours of Early Judaism." Pages 1–18 in *Imagining Religion: From Babylon to Jonestown.* Chicago: University of Chicago, 1982.

Smith, Morton. "Ascent to the Heavens and Deification in 4QM^a." Pages 181–88 in *Archaeology and History in the Dead Sea Scrolls: The New York University Conference in Memory of Yigael Yadin.* Edited by Lawrence H. Schiffman. JSPSup 8. JSOT/ASOR 2. Sheffield: JSOT, 1990.

Smith-Christopher, Daniel L. "Engendered Warfare and the Ammonites in Amos 1.13." Pages 15–40 in *Aspects of Amos: Exegesis and Interpretation.* Edited Anselm C. Hagedorn and Andrew Mein. New York: T & T Clark, 2011.

Soja, Edward W. *Thirdspace: Journeys to Los Angeles and Other Real-and-Imagined Places.* Malden: Blackwell, 1996.

Sosis, Richard. "The Adaptive Value of Religious Ritual: Rituals Promote Group Cohesion by Requiring Members to Engage in Behavior that is Too Costly to Fake." *American Scientist* 92 (2004): 166–72.

de Souza Nogueira, Paolo Augusto. "Ecstatic Worship in the Self-Glorification Hymn (4Q471B, 4Q427, 4Q491C). Implications for the Understanding of an Ancient Jewish and Early Christian Phenomenon." Pages 385–93 in *Wisdom and Apocalypticism in the Dead Sea Scrolls and in the Biblical Tradition,* edited by Florentino García Martínez. BETL 168; Leuven: Leuven University Press, 2003.

Spival, Gayatri Chakravorty. "Revolutions That as Yet Have No Mode: Derrida's Limited Inc." *Diacritics* 10 (1980): 29–49.

Stanislavski (Stanislavsky), Constantin. *Creating a Role.* Translated by Elizabeth Reynolds Hapgood. New York: Theatre Arts Books, 1961.

————. *An Actor Prepares.* Translated by E. Reynolds Hapgood. New York: Theatre Arts Books, 1948.

Starcky, Jean. "Les quatre étapes du messianism à Qumrân." *RB* 70 (1963): 481–505.

Stark, Craig E. L., Yoko Okado, and Elizabeth F. Loftus. "Imaging the Reconstruction of True and False Memories using Sensory Reactivation and Misinformation Paradigms." *Learning and Memory* 17 (2010): 485–88.

Stavrakopoulou, Francesca. "Exploring the Garden of Uzza: Death, Burial and Ideologies of Kingship." *Biblica* 87 (2006): 1–21.

Stegemann, Hartmut with Eileen M. Schuler, translated by Carol Newsom. *Qumran Cave 1. III. 1QHodayot^a with Incorporation of 1QHodayot^b and 4QHodayot ^{a-f}*. DJD 40. Oxford: Clarendon Press, 2009.

———. "The Number of Psalms in 1QHodayot^a and some of their Sections." Pages 191–234 in *Liturgical Perspectives: Prayer and Poetry in Light of the Dead Sea Scrolls. Proceedings of the Fifth International Symposium of the Orion Center for the Study of the Dead Sea Scrolls and Associated Literature, 19–23 January, 2000*. Edited by Esther G. Chazon, Ruth Clements, Avital Pinnick. STDJ 48. Leiden: Brill, 2003.

———. "The Material Reconstruction of 1QHodayot." Pages 272–84 in *The Dead Sea Scrolls: Fifty Years after Their Discovery: Proceedings of the Jerusalem Congress, July 20–25, 1997*. Edited by Lawrence H. Schiffman, Emanuel Tov, and James C. VanderKam, executive editor Galen Marquis. Jerusalem: IES in cooperation with the Shrine of the Book, Israel Museum, 2000.

———. Rekonstruktion der Hodajot: Ursprüngliche Gestalt und kritisch bearbeiteter Text der Hymnenrolle aus Höhle 1 von Qumran." Ph.D. diss; University of Heidelberg, 1963.

Stelzig, Eugene. "The Romantic Subject in Autobiography." Pages 223–41 in *Nonfictional Romantic Prose: Expanding Borders*. Edited by Steven P. Sondrup and Virgil Nemoianu, in collaboration with Gerald Gillespie. Philadelphia: John Benjamins, 2004.

Stokes, Ryan E. "The Throne Visions of Daniel 7, 1 Enoch 14, and the Qumran Book of Giants (4Q530): An Analysis of Their Literary Relationship." *DSD* 15 (2008): 340–58.

Stol, Marten, with a chapter by F. A. M. Wiggermann, *Birth in Babylonia and the Bible: Its Mediterranean Setting*. Groningen: Styx Publications, 2000.

Stone, Michael E. "A Reconsideration of Apocalyptic Visions." *HTR* 96 (2003): 167–180.

———. "Apocalyptic—Vision or Hallucination?" *Milla Wa Milla* 14 (1974): 47–56. Reprinted as pages 419–28 in *Selected Studies in Pseudepigrapha and Apocrypha with Special Reference to the Armenian Tradition*. SVTP 9; Leiden: Brill, 1991.

———. *Ancient Judaism: New Visions and Views*.Grand Rapids: Eerdmans, 2011.

Storbeck, Justin and Gerald L. Clore. "On the Interdependence of Cognition and Emotion." *Cognition and Emotion* 21 (2007): 1212–37.

Strawn, Brent. "Why Does the Lion Disappear in Revelation 5? Leonine Imagery in Early Jewish and Christian Literatures." *JSP* 17 (2007):37–74.

Strugnell, John and Eileen M. Schuller. "Further *Hodayot* Manuscripts from Qumran?" Pages 51–72 in *Antikes Judentum und frühes Christentum. Festschrift für Hartmut Stegemann zum 65. Geburtstag*. Edited by Bernd Hollmann, Wolfgang Reinbold, Annette Steudel. BZNW 97. Berlin, New York: de Gruyter, 1998.

Stuckenbruck, Loren T. "Daniel and Early Enoch Traditions in the Dead Sea Scrolls." Pages 368–86 in *The Book of Daniel: Composition & Reception, Volume Two.* Edited by John J. Collins and Peter W. Flint.

———. *The Book of Giants from Qumran: Texts, Translation, and Commentary.* TSAJ 63. Tübingen: Mohr Siebeck 1997.

——. "The Throne-Theophany of the Book of Giants: Some New Light on the Background of Daniel 7." Pages 211–220 in *The Scrolls and the Scriptures: Qumran Fifty Years After.* Edited by Stanley E. Porter and Craig A. Evans. Sheffield: Sheffield Academic Press, 1997.

Stump, R. W. "The Geography of Religion—Introduction." *Journal of Cultural Geography* 7 (1986): 1–3.

Sugase, Y., S. Yamane, S. Ueno, and K. Kawano. "Global and Fine Information Coded by Single Neurons in the Temporal Visual Cortex." *Nature* 400 (1999): 869–73.

Sukenik, Eliezer Lipa. אוצר המגילות הגנוזות. Prepared for the press by Nahman Avigad. Jerusalem: Magnes, 1954; Eng. *The Dead Sea Scrolls of the Hebrew University.* Jerusalem: Magnes, 1955.

———. מגילות גנוזות: מתוך גניזה קדומה שנמצאה במדבר יהודה. סקירה שנייה. Jerusalem: Bialik Foundation 1950, ★32-★50.

———. מגילות גנוזות: מתוך גניזה קדומה שנמצאה במדבר יהודה. סקירה ראשונה. Jerusalem: Bialik Foundation, 1948, ★29- ★33.

Sullivan, Kevin P. *Wrestling with Angels: A Study of the Relationship between Angels and Humans in Ancient Jewish Literature and the New Testament.* AGJU 60. Leiden: Brill, 2003.

Swartz, Michael D. *Mystical Prayer in Ancient Judaism: An Analysis of Ma'aseh Merkavah.* TSAJ 28. Tübingen: Mohr Siebeck, 1992.

Tabor, James D. *Things Unutterable: Paul's Ascent to Paradise in its Greco-Roman, Judaic, and Early Christian Contexts.* Studies in Judaism. Lanham, MD: University Press of America, 1986.

Tambiah, Stanley J. "A Performative Approach to Ritual." *Proceedings of the British Academy* 65 (1979): 113–69.

Tanzer, Sarah J. "The Sages at Qumran: Wisdom in the Hodayot." Ph.D. dissertation. Harvard University, 1987.

Taves, Ann. *Religious Experience Reconsidered: A Building-Block Approach to the Study of Religion and Other Special Things.* Princeton: Princeton University Press, 2009.

Thiel, John E. "Time, Judgment, and Competitive Spirituality: A Reading of the Development of the Doctrine of Purgatory." *Theological Studies* 69 (2008): 741–85.

Thomas, Samuel I. *The "Mysteries" of Qumran: Mystery, Secrecy, and Esotericism in the Dead Sea Scrolls.* SBLEJL 25. Atlanta: Society of Biblical Literature, 2009.

Thompson, Leonard L. "Mapping and Apocalyptic World." Pages 115–17 in *Sacred Places and Profane Spaces: Essays in the Geographics of Judaism, Christi-*

anity, and Islam. Edited by Jamie Scott and Paul Simpson-Housley. Westport, Conn.: Greenwood Press, 1991.

Tigchelaar, Eibert J. C. "Eden and Paradise: The Garden Motif in Some Early
Jewish Texts (1 Enoch and Other Texts Found at Qumran)." Pages 37–62
in *Paradise Interpreted: Representations of Biblical Paradise in Judaism and Christianity*. Edited by Gerard P. Luttikhuizen. TBN 2. Leiden: Brill, 1999.

Tisserant, E. "Fragments syriaques du Livre des Jubilés." *RB* 30 (1921): 73–75.

Tomkins, Silvan S. "Script Theory: Differential Magnification of Affects."
Pages 201–36 in *Nebraska Symposium on Motivation 1978: Human Emotion*.
Edited by Richard Dienstbier. Lincoln: University of Nebraska Press,
1979.

Toorn, Karel van der. "Sources in Heaven: Revelation as a Scholarly Construct
in Second Temple Judaism." Pages 265–77 in *Kein Land für sich allein:
Studien zum Kulturkontakt in Kanaan, Israel/Palästina und Ebirnâri für Manfred
Weippert zum 65. Geburtstag*. Edited by Ulrich Hübner and Ernst Axel
Knauf. OBO 186. Göttingen: Vandenhoeck & Ruprecht, 2002.

———. "In the Lions' Den: The Babylonian Background of a Biblical Motif."
CBQ 60 (1998): 626–40.

Tov, Emanuel. "The Copying of a Biblical Scroll." *JRH* 26 (2002): 189–209.

Tromp, N. J. *Primitive Conceptions of Death and the Nether World in the Old Testament*. Rome: Pontifical Biblical Institute, 1969.

Ulrich, Eugene (ed). *Qumran Cave 4.XI: Psalms to Chronicles*. DJD 16. Oxford:
Clarendon Press, 2000.

Valantasis, Richard. "Constructions of Power in Asceticism." *JAAR* 63 (1995):
775–821.

VanderKam, James C. "The Angel of the Presence in the Book of Jubilees."
DSD 7 (2000): 378–93.

———. "Identity and History of the Community." Pages 507–23 in *The Dead
Sea Scrolls after Fifty Years: A Comprehensive Assessment*. Edited by Peter W.
Flint and James VanderKam, 2 Vols. Leiden: Brill, 1998–1999.

———. *Enoch: A Man for All Generations*. Columbia: University of South Carolina, 1995.

———. "Putting them in their Place: Geography as an Evaluative Tool." Pages
46–69 in *Pursuing the Text: Studies in Honor of Ben Zion Wacholder on the
Occasion of his Seventieth Birthday*. Edited by John C. Reeves and John
Kampen. JSOTSup 184. Sheffield: Sheffield Academic Press, 1994. Re-
printed as pages 476–99 in *From Revelation to Canon: Studies in the Hebrew
Bible and Second Temple Literature*. SJSJ 62. Leiden: Brill, 2000.

———. *Enoch and the Growth of an Apocalyptic Tradition*. CBQMS. Washington,
D.C.: Catholic Biblical Association of America, 1984.

———. "The Theophany of 1 Enoch 1 3b-9." *VT* 23 (1973): 129–50.

Vásquez, Manuel A. *More than Belief: A Materialist Theory of Religion*. New
York: Oxford University Press, 2011.

Vuilleumier, P., M. P. Richardson, J. L. Armony, J. Driver, R. J. Dolan. "Distinct Influences of Amygdala Lesion on Visual Cortical Activation during
Emotional Face Processing." *Nature Neuroscience* 7 (2004): 1271–1278.

Vuilleumier, P. J. L. Armony, J. Driver, and R. J. Dolan. "Effects of Attention and Emotion on Face Processing in the Human Brain: An Event-related fMRI study." *Neuron* 30 (2001): 829–41.

Walsh, Carey. *Exquisite Desire: Religion, the Erotic, and the Song of Songs.* Minneapolis: Fortress, 2000.

Weisbuch, Max and Nalini Ambady, "Affective Divergence: Automatic Responses to Others' Emotions Depend on Group Membership." *Journal of Personality and Social Psychology* 95 (2008): 1063–79.

Weitzman, Steven. "Warring against Terror: The *War Scroll* and the Mobilization of Emotion." *JSJ* 40 (2009): 213–41.

———. "Sensory Reform in Deuteronomy." Pages 123–39 in *Religion and the Self in Antiquity.* Edited by David Brakke, Michael Satlow, and Steven Weitzman. Bloomington: Indiana University Press, 2005.

Westermann, Claus. *Praise and Lament in the Psalms.* Atlanta: John Knox, 1965, 1981.

Whyman, Rose. *The Stanislavsky System of Acting: Legacy and Influence in Modern Performance.* New York: Cambridge University Press, 2008.

Wierzbicka, Anna. *Emotions Across Languages and Cultures: Diversity and Universals.* Cambridge: Cambridge University Press, 1999.

Wild, T. Cameron, Don Kuiken, and Don Schopflocher. "The Role of Absorption in Experiential Involvement." *Journal of Personality and Social Psychology* 69 (1995): 569–79.

Winkielman, Piotr and Kent C. Berridge. "Unconscious Emotion." *Current Directions in Psychological Science* 13 (2004): 120–23.

Winter, Urs. *Frau und Göttin: Exegetische und ikonographische Studien zum weiblichen Gottesbild im Alten Israel und in dessen Umwelt.* OBO 53. Freiburg, Schweiz: Universitätsverlag/ Göttingen: Vandenhoeck & Ruprecht, 1983.

Wise, Michael O. "מי כמוני באלים: A Study of 4Q491c, 4Q471b, 4Q427 7 and 1QH^A 25:35–26:10." *DSD* 7 (2000): 173–219.

———. *The First Messiah: Investigating the Savior before Jesus.* New York: HarperCollins, 1999.

Wiseman, D. J. "Mesopotamian Gardens." *Anatolian Studies* 33 (1983): 137–44.

Wolfson, Elliot R. "*Imago templi* and the Meeting of the Two Seas." *RES* 51 (2007): 121–135.

———. "Seven Mysteries of Knowledge: Qumran E/Sotericism Recovered." Pages 177–213 in *The Idea of Biblical Interpretation: Essays in Honor of James L. Kugel.* Edited by Hindy Najman and Judith H. Newman. SJSJ 83. Leiden: Brill, 2004.

———. "Weeping, Death, and Spiritual Ascent: Jewish Mysticism." Pages 271–303 in *Religion and Emotion.* Edited by John Corrigan.

———. "Sacred Space and Mental Iconography: *Imago Templi* and Contemplation in Rhineland Jewish Pietism." Pages 593–634 in *Ki Baruch Hu: Ancient Near Eastern, biblical, and Judaic studies in honor of Baruch A. Levine.* Edited by Robert Chazan, William W. Hallo, and Lawrence Schiffman. Winona Lake: Eisenbrauns, 1999.

————. *Through a Speculum That Shines: Visions and Imagination in Medieval Jewish Mysticism*. Princeton: Princeton University Press, 1994.

————. "Mysticism and the Poetic-Liturgical Compositions from Qumran: A Response to Bilhah Nitzan." *JQR* 85 (1994): 185–202.

Zaleski, Carol. *Otherworld Journeys: Accounts of Near-Death Experience in Medieval and Modern Times*. New York: Oxford University, 1987.

Zgoll, Annette. "Audienz—Ein Modell zum Verständnis mesopotamischer Handerhebungsrituale: Mit einer Deutung der Novelle vom *Armen Mann von Nippur*." *BaghM* 34 (2003): 181–99.

Zohary, Michael. *Plants of the Bible*. Cambridge: Cambridge University Press, 1982.

Subject Index

Ancient Text Index

Modern Author Index